Tegwen Parry.

Gwynedd, H.

Chapter 11

P. 299

Handbook
            380 - 385.
Sc R
        41 - 46. 55.

Write an essay. by march 11th
An account of any important theme, or
interesting feature of Private Reading.

~~Mary Jod~~

Blodwen

Stella

Bengl

wright Jones

Tegwen

Mary Edward

Yvonne John

~~Nesta~~

LEARNING AND TEACHING

By A. G. Hughes, B.Sc., Ph.D., M.Ed.

EDUCATION AND THE
DEMOCRATIC IDEAL
Nine Talks to Teachers

LEARNING AND TEACHING

An Introduction to Psychology and Education

BY

A. G. HUGHES, B.Sc., Ph.D., M.Ed.

FORMERLY DISTRICT INSPECTOR OF SCHOOLS, LONDON COUNTY
COUNCIL ; SOMETIME LECTURER IN EDUCATION, BOROUGH ROAD
TRAINING COLLEGE AND THE CITY OF LEEDS TRAINING COLLEGE

AND

E. H. HUGHES, B.A., Ph.D.

PART-TIME LECTURER IN EDUCATION, NATIONAL SOCIETY'S
TRAINING COLLEGE OF DOMESTIC SUBJECTS, HAMPSTEAD ;
FORMERLY LECTURER IN EDUCATION, CITY OF LEEDS TRAINING
COLLEGE

LONGMANS, GREEN AND CO.
LONDON   NEW YORK   TORONTO

LONGMANS GREEN AND CO LTD
6 & 7 CLIFFORD STREET LONDON W I

ALSO AT MELBOURNE AND CAPE TOWN

LONGMANS, GREEN AND CO INC
55 FIFTH AVENUE NEW YORK 3

LONGMANS, GREEN AND CO
215 VICTORIA STREET TORONTO I

ORIENT LONGMANS LTD
BOMBAY CALCUTTA MADRAS

First published 1937
Reprinted by Novographic Process February 1938,
October 1938, *September* 1939, *July* 1940,
March 1941, *January* 1942, *June* 1943
October 1944 *and October* 1945
Second edition 1946
New impression 1952
Reprinted 1954

PRINTED IN GREAT BRITAIN AT
THE BOWERING PRESS, PLYMOUTH

PREFACE TO SECOND EDITION

THIS post-war edition is not substantially different from the first edition, for even a great social revolution such as we are now experiencing does not change the fundamental needs and nature of children. It does however necessitate a popular revaluation of the importance of education and a readiness to provide conditions which will make possible the full development of each child in accordance with his " age, ability and aptitude." The Education Act, 1944, is evidence that the public conscience has been awakened, and it has made possible a number of welcome changes in the text of the previous edition. For example, it is no longer necessary to write as if the normal size of a class in school is forty, or of secondary education as if it were a privilege for a favoured few.

The new prospect in education will, it is hoped, remove the reproach that this book is too idealistic to be practical. If this proves to be true the most important change affecting the present edition will not be one of text but of the reader's attitude to many important sections that remain unchanged.

A. G. H.
E. H. H.

ISLEWORTH, 1946.

v

PREFACE

THIS is an introductory text-book in Education. It is designed primarily for Students in Training Colleges who are preparing for an examination in the Principles of Education, but it is hoped that it will also prove useful and interesting to teachers in school who wish to keep in touch with modern developments in educational psychology and methods.

The book is based on experience in teaching Psychology and the Principles of Education in several training colleges over a period of many years, an experience that has been supplemented by educational and psychological research, and by experience in teaching children in many schools of different types. We have attempted to weave into one coherent whole the subject-matter which we have found to be appropriate for a training-college course and which from our wide experience in schools we have also found to be of most value to young teachers. We believe that if psychology is studied in close connexion with the problems that arise in school and classroom it can give teachers a great deal of valuable help. We have therefore developed our subject by considering children and the practical problems they present rather than by discussing the theoretical problems of academic psychology. We have written as simply and directly as possible, but we have tried to avoid the dangers of over-simplification by calling attention to controversial and difficult matters in footnotes.

No study of psychology and education can be real and fruitful unless it is combined with first-hand observation and experimentation. Suggestions for observations and simple experiments have therefore been made throughout the book. Many topics that could not be adequately dealt with owing to lack of space are referred to in the suggestions for discussion and further reading. The book is, in fact, a text-book in the original sense of the term; it provides a text which it is hoped will prove a convenient starting-point for a more exhaustive enquiry into the psychology, principles and methods of education.

We wish to acknowledge our indebtedness to our former training-college students in Leeds, Isleworth and Hampstead, and particularly to the many teachers in London and elsewhere whose work in school and classroom it has been our privilege to observe. Our indebtedness to our colleagues on training-college staffs and in the London inspectorate and to many writers on psychology and education is also very great. We wish particularly to express our gratitude to Professor Cyril Burt, Professor Beatrice Edgell, and Professor Sir T. Percy Nunn for much help and inspiration gained from their teachings, both oral and written.

Finally, we wish to thank Mr. E. H. Betts, B.Sc., and Mr. J. B. Cryer, M.A., for their patient kindness in reading and criticizing the book in its various stages. This acknowledgment does not imply, however, that they necessarily accept all the views we have expressed.

A. G. HUGHES.
E. H. HUGHES.

ISLEWORTH, 1937.

ACKNOWLEDGMENTS

WE wish to acknowledge our indebtedness for many short quotations, the sources of which are given in the text.

In addition, our thanks are due to authors and publishers for kind permission to quote passages of some length from the following books :

The Wainwrights, Edgar Meredith (Grayson & Grayson).
Vision and Design, Roger Fry (Chatto & Windus).
Have You Good Taste?, Margaret H. Bulley (Methuen).
On the Art of Writing, A. T. Quiller-Couch (Camb. Univ. Press).
Reason and Emotion, John Macmurray (Faber & Faber).

A. G. H.
E. H. H.

As an officer of the London County Council I am required to state that the Council is in no way responsible for the views expressed in this book.

A. G. HUGHES.

CONTENTS

"One human teacher who understands the strange mixture of child nature is equal to five millions who think children are simply black, or white or purple."

Jeremy, HUGH WALPOLE.

Chapter I

THE PROBLEM

THIS is a book for teachers and for those about to become teachers. Let us therefore go at once into a classroom, and try to get a general view of our problem.

The room contains a class of, say, thirty pupils. As we enter, we are aware of the class rather than the children, for our first glance reveals not differences but similarities. We see thirty children, all more or less alike : they are, for example, similar in general physical make-up ; they speak the same language ; they make similar movements ; they are probably all wondering who these strange visitors may be. We discern a large common denominator of characteristics, physical and mental.

Our view of the class is made still more definite by our knowledge of school organization and practice. These thirty children have been brought together in a classroom because they possess certain characteristics in common. They are similar in age and in attainments ; they have all had similar training ; they have probably read the same text-books and been imbued with the same ideals. They have been welded into a class:

In schools formerly known as " elementary " schools, the uniformity among members of a class was at one time still further emphasized by calling them a " standard," a term that was originally applied because all the members had reached a certain fairly well-defined standard of attainment.[1]

This view of children as a class was forced upon teachers in elementary schools in the nineteenth century because classes or standards with upwards of 100 on roll were quite common. It is a view that all class teachers, even in

[1] The following are examples of " standards " as defined in the " Revised Code " (1862) :
[1]Continuation of footnote on page 2.

modern times, must sometimes take, and on many occasions it is a perfectly sensible view to take.

But having looked at the large common measure of characteristics among the children in our classroom, let us now take a closer view. We are impressed at once, not so much by the uniformity of general outline as by the infinite variety of detail. The room no longer contains a "class," still less a "standard"; it contains thirty individuals.

In physical appearance no two are exactly alike, and a short time in the classroom is enough to enable us to form a distinctive picture of each individual. These pictures are built up by noticing differences—in general physique, in shape of head, in colour of hair and eyes, and so on. The observation of mere physical differences gives us a picture that will enable us to recognize any member of the class if we meet him in another place.

But while we are forming these first superficial pictures, we become aware of many more subtle differences. The children are not merely statues, each of different shape and coloration; they are living personalities, and each has distinctive qualities that are revealed to us at once by characteristic behaviour such as movement and facial expression.

Continued from page 1]

Standard I.	Reading :	Narrative in monosyllables.
	Writing :	Form on blackboard or slate, from dictation, letters, capital and small, manuscript.
	Arithmetic :	Form on blackboard or slate, from dictation, figures up to 20. Name at sight figures up to 20. Add and subtract figures up to 10, orally, from examples on blackboard.
Standard VI.	Reading :	A short ordinary paragraph in a newspaper or other modern narrative.
	Writing :	Another short ordinary paragraph in a newspaper or other modern narrative, slowly dictated once by a few words at a time.
	Arithmetic :	A sum in practice or bills of parcels.

See *History of Elementary Education*, C. Birchenough, pp. 346-7 (Univ. Tut. Press, 1925).

For example, some children are quiet and placid; others are talkative and lively. The children differ not only physically but also temperamentally. If we stayed longer, we should be able, merely by observation, to get a still more complete picture of each individual. We should feel that we were not only able to recognize individuals, but that we were also beginning to know them.

Our observation of physical and temperamental differences, no matter how detailed it may be, does not, however, give us a complete picture of any individual. We cannot, for example, determine by inspection the pupil who is top of his class, or the pupil who can memorize poetry most quickly, or the one who is worst at arithmetic. But even if we are not teachers, we know from common experience that children differ greatly in such abilities as these. We have here a third main type of individual difference; children differ from one another not only physically and temperamentally but also intellectually.

If we now follow the children into the playing field, we shall be able to complete our picture in still more detail. Under ordinary classroom conditions there is a constraint that tends to emphasize the points of similarity, and to inhibit the differences, especially in temperament. Under the freer conditions out-of-doors the children are, as we say, more natural; they are more likely to reveal their real selves. If we could follow them into their homes, we should get still further insight into their personalities.

It is, of course, possible to create a friendly, happy atmosphere in a classroom so that children behave very naturally. But even so, it is important to remember that a child in school, a member of a class, is often on the surface a very different person from the same child in another environment. This is one reason why teachers find it helpful to observe children outside the classroom—in the playing field and swimming bath, on expeditions, educational visits and school journeys.

As we contemplate the amazing multiplicity of the individual differences that exist among thirty pupils, an important question forces itself upon our attention. Are these differences the result of heredity and therefore inevitable, or are they the result of environment and therefore, in theory at least, avoidable ? It is obvious that no single answer can be given to this question. Red hair and a snub nose are the result of heredity, but poor physique may be the result of bad feeding. Cheerfulness may be a more or less permanent quality, the result of inborn temperament ; or it may be merely a passing phase, the result of anticipating a favourite lesson. Inability to do arithmetic may be due to lack of inherent mental ability, or it may be due to lack of grounding in the essentials. This question and the more difficult one that asks whether heredity or environment is the more important factor in producing differences will occur frequently when we are discussing specific differences in detail. For the present, we merely note that each of the three main types of individual difference may be subdivided into two kinds, those that are inborn and those that are acquired.

Let us now survey classes in different parts of the school. As we do so, we are reminded of still another set of individual differences—those that are the result of differences in age. As children grow older, they develop mentally as well as physically, and in order to adapt ourselves quickly and successfully to children of various ages, it will obviously be an advantage to study the mental differences that develop with increasing age. As a result of ordinary experience we already know in a general way something of these differences. We know, for example, that we must not expect seven-year-olds to be interested in geometrical drawing, or to do long division sums, or to understand Shakespeare. Such knowledge is not, however, sufficiently precise for modern teachers, and we shall in the following pages pay considerable attention to the results obtained by psychological research into the mental development of children year by year. A wise teacher, even in his dealings with a single class, will always take special note of any children who are much below the average age of the class, for otherwise he will almost certainly make unfair judgements of their conduct, ability and attainments.

There still remains one factor to add complexity to our picture of individual differences. Let us go into a school where boys and girls are taught together. Many further questions then arise, and although the man in the street may be ready with confident answers, we shall find that popular opinion is not always a safe guide. For the moment we will note that there are individual differences due to sex, and that in the education of children we must take them into account.

We have now made a rough survey of our problem. We have to educate children who, notwithstanding a certain common basis of characteristics, are nevertheless individual personalities. Each child differs inherently from every other child—physically, temperamentally and intellectually— and these differences are further complicated by differences in training, environment, age and sex.

A clear, vivid realization of the differences among individual children is an essential part of the equipment of any successful educator. We may leave aside for the time being the question whether education should tend to eradicate or to accentuate these differences ; they exist, and if we ignore them, we are bound in our classroom practice to be guilty of much futility. We must approach our task with the certain knowledge that, whatever our ultimate aim may be, no two children are identical in mental make-up any more than they are identical in physical appearance.[1]

It is, of course, necessary, if we are to get any grasp of our problem, to arrive at some knowledge of children in general, to know what is the greatest common measure of their qualities. Ideally, such knowledge should be obtained by the detailed study of a large number of individuals, but this is obviously impracticable within the compass of

---

[1] Beginners are accordingly warned against the common practice of speaking and writing about " *the* child." It is permissible to refer to " *a* child " or to " children," but " *the* child " does not exist, not even the average child.

a single book. We shall therefore devote the next two chapters to a study of " children in general "—their natural endowment and their natural methods of learning. If, however, this study is to be really fruitful, the reader must continually check the statements made, by reference to John and Peter, to Mary and Jane, to the individual members of a class that he knows. Only in this way will he avoid over-emphasizing the similarities in human nature, to the neglect of essential differences. Teachers must never lose sight of the fact that their real work is the education of individual personalities. This is the strongest argument for small classes and it is an argument against the formation of very large schools.

Chapter II

THE NATURAL ENDOWMENT OF CHILDREN

In the preceding chapter we glanced at the complexity of the problems of teaching a class of children and of organizing a school. This survey should have been enough to convince any prospective teacher of the value of a study of psychology, and particularly of the psychology of individual differences. It is true that every one does acquire some knowledge of psychology by ordinary human intercourse, and by the reading of literature.[1] But for teachers, who must be able to adapt themselves rapidly to many different personalities, this is not enough.

We do not, of course, claim that a knowledge of psychology, however profound or extensive, will provide ready-made solutions of all problems, but it will clearly be an advantage to have some fore-knowledge of the potentialities of the children we have to teach.[2]

If we watch a class of three-year-olds in a nursery school, we cannot help being struck by the large amount they have already learnt before coming to school to be taught. We must, however, avoid the error of thinking that all their present accomplishments have been learnt in these three years. They already had a certain equipment when they began their independent existence. They were alive, and seemed consequently to be impelled to a kind of general activity. They did not, like clay, merely receive impressions ; they replied to them. They were ready at birth to make a number of essential movements ; they could,

[1] See, for example, the illustrative extracts quoted on pages 12, 228, 240.
[2] It is interesting to note that, the same argument being true of all people who have to deal with large numbers of their fellows, applied psychology is becoming recognized as an important element in the training not only of teachers, but also of doctors, politicians, preachers, nurses, social workers, salesmen and advertisers.

for example, breathe, blink, suck, cry and kick; they could, by appropriate movements, let their mothers know when they were angry or afraid. We see at once that children do not begin their independent lives " from scratch "; their minds are not, as Locke taught, *tabulae rasae*—clean slates, ready to be written upon. Children, like other animals, bring with them their racial heritage, and psychologists have, in recent years, devoted a great deal of attention to investigating the precise nature of this heritage.

Natural Activity : General and Specific

Creative and Routine Activities.—Observation of children shows that their general activity is of two main kinds; children delight in making new movements, but they also find pleasure in repeating old ones. They seem to be endowed with two very different tendencies—(*a*) to explore the unknown and (*b*) to consolidate the known. At one moment they are experimental and progressive; at another moment they are humdrum and conservative. These two general tendencies are often called respectively the *creative tendency* and the *routine tendency*.

In addition to these two general tendencies to activity, children also inherit definite tendencies to behave in special ways in given circumstances. Even at birth, the life urge, in addition to making children active in a general way, is already prompting them to two special kinds of behaviour, the expression of anger and fear.

Anger.—All children from birth scream and struggle if their bodily movements are seriously restricted. From our knowledge of ourselves we interpret this behaviour as indicating that they are angry. They do not have to learn how to behave angrily any more than they have to learn how to breathe; any restriction of bodily movements acts as an inevitable stimulus for the arousal of angry behaviour.

As children grow older anger is provoked on many other occasions, but all these occasions have this in common: they are times when the children suffer frustration of some kind. Thus they are angry when a pleasant experience is interfered with, when objects are taken away from them, when hunger is not satisfied, when an expected treat is not forthcoming, and when they find themselves unable to carry out their purposes, whether this inability be due to their own incompetence or to interference by another person.

It has been suggested that, in the history of mankind, anger must have been biologically useful, and this perhaps explains why children are born ready to behave in this particular way. Those who were not disposed to react angrily when they were frustrated had a poorer chance of survival than the others, and they were consequently less likely to grow up and propagate their kind. Thus, by a process that is called natural selection, the tendency to react angrily in certain circumstances has in course of time become established in the human race. All children are now endowed with it at birth.

Fear.—Another important element in the endowment of children is the tendency to escape from danger. The clearest and earliest examples are seen (*a*) when children hear sudden noises and (*b*) when they experience the sensation of falling. They are by nature ready, without any learning, to pay attention to these stimuli, to feel afraid, to cry and to flinch. Other fears that, according to our observations, seem to be inborn are the fear of the unknown and the fear of approaching objects.

As children grow older they may show fear on many other occasions, for example, in the dark, in the presence of animals, on hearing thunder. These fears, however, are not inevitable and universal ; consequently psychologists are not agreed that they are inborn. As we shall see later, children very readily acquire new fears as the result of experience.

In addition to those kinds of behaviour that can be observed in children at birth, there are a number of other specialized forms of behaviour that make their appearance in very early days, and they too seem to be part of a child's racial heritage. It is impossible to give a catalogue of these specialized forms of activity that would command the assent of all psychologists, but the following paragraphs indicate the chief forms (in addition to angry and fearful behaviour) that we have ourselves observed in young children.

Curiosity.—We have observed this type of behaviour in the fifth month of life but some other observers have noticed it earlier. Children first show curiosity in the presence of something unfamiliar but not totally strange, as for example when a familiar object is encountered in a new place or when a favourite object is missed from its accustomed place. Later, in the second year, they show curiosity in the presence of hidden things, as is shown for example by their delight in opening drawers and cupboards, and by their desire to know the contents of parcels.

When very young children are in the situations described above, they attend keenly, their expression shows that they are surprised, puzzled, or curious, and they draw nearer to the object of curiosity. We infer from our own similar experiences that they are wondering, that they are experiencing the emotion that we call " wonder."

The " curiosity " type of behaviour is often contrasted with the " fear " type. One involves approach and investigation ; the other involves withdrawal or, in some circumstances, immobility. The biological value of both types is very clear, and children can often be observed in situations where both impulses are at work, the result being either cautious investigation or reluctant withdrawal.

Disgust.—We have observed this type of behaviour in the first year, on occasions when children encounter new foods. Their dislike appears to be due not only to the taste but also to the feel of the food on their tongues, as is shown for example by their objection to lumpy porridge and to skin on milk. Some observers have noticed that very young children show disgust at the touch of fur and slimy substances. It appears that children are by nature disgusted by certain tastes and smells and by certain touch experiences.

When very young children experience something obnoxious, they attend to it closely, their expression indicates nausea, and they spit out or thrust away the offending substance. We infer that they are experiencing the emotion which we call "disgust." The biological value of this type of behaviour is again clearly evident.

Gregariousness and Wandering.—We have found that children, as early as the first month of life, are uneasy and even distressed if left alone, but that they can often be satisfied by being brought into physical contact with another person, not necessarily the mother. It should be noted that the physical contact referred to does not involve cuddling or stroking ; the close presence of another person is enough. This type of behaviour seems to be sheer gregariousness, and to be similar to the tendency that is observed in animals that live in herds.

We may say then that children are by nature ready to pay attention to the presence of other people and that such presence gives them satisfaction.

In the second year, behaviour of an opposite type makes its appearance ; children then show at times a tendency to wander. They are still gregarious, but this tendency does not dominate their lives so completely as it did in the first year ; they slip out when a door is left open and take great delight in wandering off alone.

Assertion.—From one point of view a great deal of the behaviour of children can be described as assertive. When they are angry, or disgusted, or curious, they are in a sense asserting themselves ; the same is true when they are making things or playing games, and perhaps when they wander off down the road. But all these types of behaviour have their own distinctive characteristics, so the term "assertion" will in this book be used in a more limited sense ; it will be reserved for behaviour in which children make a definite stand for themselves as individual persons. Such assertive behaviour begins as early as the fifth month in the form of playful disobedience ; the child is *asserting his independence*. Before the end of the first year, he calls

attention to his achievements ; he is *asserting his importance*.
By the fourth year, he not only indulges in a large variety
of behaviour asserting both his independence and his
importance, but he also gives orders to other persons, he
threatens them, he corrects them, he points out their shortcomings ; he is *asserting his superiority*.

In all behaviour of this assertive type children show by
their facial expression and by their bodily attitudes that they
are experiencing a pleasurable emotion; we call it " elation."

We see then that children are by nature ready to pay
attention to themselves, and that in appropriate situations
they assert their own independence, importance and
superiority, and that they are elated in so doing.

Submission.—The term " submission " is reserved for
behaviour that is the opposite of " assertion " ; it must not
be confused with fear. As the author of *Earlham*[1] expresses
it : " When one of my uncles came tramping mightily
down the passage . . . I should wish to make myself very
small indeed, to slip round a corner, out of sight, with a
casual air. There is no need to be ashamed of the impulse ;
it is not a weakly unimaginative fear. It is rather the sense
of a great deficiency, a want of presence and weight and
stature, moral rather than physical."

Submissive behaviour is shown as early as the first year
in the form of shyness—a desire to retire, to attract as little
attention as possible. This seems to be an example of a
child *feeling his unimportance* (the opposite of asserting his
importance). About the same time children are very ready
in certain circumstances to accept help and suggestion ;
they begin to *acknowledge their dependence* on people (the
opposite of asserting independence). By the third year
their behaviour in some circumstances indicates that they are
feeling their inferiority (the opposite of asserting superiority).

As we have said before, children are by nature ready
to pay attention to themselves ; we now see that in appropriate situations, so far from asserting their independence,
importance and superiority, they are prone to the opposite

[1] *Earlham*, Percy Lubbock (Cape).

types of behaviour and that instead of feeling elated they feel submissive.

We have already noticed that the two emotions, fear and curiosity, may conflict in a child's mind. The same is true of elation and submissiveness, and much childish behaviour is exaggeratedly assertive in order to cover up feelings of submission.

Construction.—Behaviour involving construction begins at the end of the first year. It appears to arise out of manipulation, i.e. mere handling; a child's first construction is probably an accidental piling-up of things, and this is followed by purposeful building. The simplest construction consists then in *assembling material*. In the second year children are not content merely to pile bricks one on another, they proceed to make things—trains, bridges, signals. Construction is no longer confined to mere assembling; it now necessitates *arranging material*. Here again, the beginning is often accidental; something is created, its resemblance to some real object suggests the name, and the idea of making some definite object dawns. This leads to the need for *selecting material*, an activity that develops in the third and subsequent years. Finally, children begin *shaping material* for special purposes, as when they play with sand or mould plastic materials.

Observation of young children shows that they are by nature ready to pay attention to materials that they can use for constructing things, and that they use such materials in the following ways : manipulating, accidental assembling, purposeful assembling, accidental arranging, purposeful arranging, and shaping.

There is no doubt from their attitude of rapt absorption and from their spontaneous exclamations, " I'm making ! I'm making ! " that this constructional activity gives children intense pleasure. It is regrettable that we have no specific name for this emotion. It must not be confused with elation, for although this doubtless is experienced when successful work is contemplated, yet in the actual process of construction there is no suggestion of self-display ; on the contrary, the whole self seems to be absorbed in the activity and to be suffused with the joy of making.

Collecting.—This type of behaviour makes its appearance comparatively late—in our observations, not until the fourth year. At this age children begin to show what can best be described as a collecting fever. At times the fever seems to abate, and interest in collecting may be dormant for weeks. Suddenly, for some mysterious reason, there is another burst of intense interest[1] during which collections are made for the sheer *joy of collecting*. At this early stage the things collected often have no intrinsic interest or value ; stones, dead leaves, pieces of material—all are grist for the mill.

Crying and Laughing.—These common forms of behaviour are very difficult to describe for they occur in so many different situations. Children cry when they are angry, but they also cry when they are in distress. Some psychologists believe that children are endowed with a tendency to appeal for help ; crying may then be considered as the form of behaviour resulting from a thwarting of the appeal tendency. It begins as a cry of distress, but it may end as a cry of anger.

According to our observations, appreciation of a humorous situation begins early in the second year. From the age of 1, children are amused, and laugh when they notice something unusual in a familiar situation. Surprise seems to be an essential element in all humour. The following are examples of humorous situations in the experience of very young children :

(*a*) Watching a man gradually disappearing from view as he descends some stairs.

(*b*) Seeing two labelled bottles exactly alike standing side by side where previously there had been one bottle only.

(*c*) Hearing a sound repeated in a word, e.g., Hong-Kong.

---

[1] The same is true of other types of natural behaviour mentioned in this chapter, particularly curiosity and constructing. This *periodicity of interest* is one worthy of investigation, for it may be a factor of which even modern educationists do not take sufficient cognizance.

(d) Doing or saying something wrong, e.g., breakfast is called dinner, cake is suggested as a plaything, a chair is placed with its back to the table.

A great deal has been written on the psychology of laughter, but for our immediate purpose it is enough to note that children are by nature ready to attend to, and to laugh at, situations that strike them as being humorous.[1]

Imitation.—A great deal of children's behaviour begins in imitation of other people. This copying of behaviour is of two kinds, impulsive and intentional. When children imitate impulsively, their response appears to come without any effort, and often without any signs of enjoyment in the performance ; it appears to resemble reflex actions such as blinking and sneezing. This type of behaviour is shown as early as the end of the first month, when it takes the form of imitating movements such as putting out a tongue or nodding the head. A little later, singing sounds are imitated in the same automatic way ; it may not be an exact imitation but simply a tendency to sing when other people sing. This soon develops, so that by the fifth month, children are observed making an effort to imitate the exact pitch ; intentional imitation of movements develops a month or two later, so that before the end of the first year children are imitating both movements and sounds, sometimes impulsively, sometimes intentionally. It is interesting to observe that at this early stage impulsive imitation is often more successful than intentional imitation. For example, before children can use language deliberately, they are sometimes able to give a spontaneous, parrot-like but quite recognizable imitation of phrases that they happen to hear.

Another important type of imitation, which appears in the first year, is impulsive imitation of emotional attitudes, to which children seem to be particularly sensitive. Young children smile when their parents smile ; they cry when

[1] For summary reviews of the theories of laughter, see *The Psychology of Laughter and Comedy*, J. Y. T. Greig (Allen & Unwin, 1923) ; *The Springs of Laughter*, C. W. Kimmins (Methuen, 1928).

other children cry. This impulsive imitating of emotion, psychologists call *primitive passive sympathy*.

Children do not imitate all the actions they see, even when these actions lie well within their power. The person making a sound or movement, often called the " imitatee," is important in determining whether young children will imitate or not. They appear at first to be more prone to imitate familiar people than unfamiliar, and among persons equally familiar they tend to imitate children more than adults.

Imitative behaviour does not appear to be as specific or inevitable as most of the forms of natural behaviour we have discussed in previous sections. We know that children are sure to be interested in a sudden noise, that they will flinch and experience a definite emotion ; their imitative behaviour, however, is much less definite. We cannot be sure what particular movements or sounds will provoke them to imitate, and we cannot find any one particular emotion that accompanies the actions. Sometimes the children are obviously elated ; at other times, especially when they are imitating an admired adult, they are to some extent submissive. When they imitate impulsively they often show little or no emotion, and when they indulge in imitative behaviour of the type called sympathy they experience the emotion that is being experienced by the imitatee.

Play.— It is universally acknowledged that children are by nature ready to play, that is, to indulge in spontaneous activity which is pursued and enjoyed for its own sake. It begins in the earliest days in the form of *bodily exercise*— kicking, stretching, touching, grasping hands, looking and gurgling—and develops rapidly into sitting, crawling, shuffling, climbing, grasping objects, making sounds, walking, talking, dancing, walking on knees, walking backwards, walking on tip-toe, going up and down steps, touching head with foot, singing, whispering, repeating, running, jumping, stepping over obstacles, romping, walking with eyes shut, shouting, sliding ; making up songs, rhymes and names, and even a language.

Another development of bodily play is seen in the *use of playthings*. This begins with the use of parts of the body, and goes on to include the use of all available objects of convenient size in the environment, both common objects and orthodox toys. These playthings are used in a large variety of ways, and the following catalogue illustrates how this form of play develops—handling, rustling, passing from hand to hand, banging, stirring, tearing, scratching, hitting, splashing, throwing, building, shaking, balancing, kicking, blowing, pouring, turning, opening, closing, pack ng, fitting, scribbling, catching, riding, spinning, digging, smashing, drawing.

There is no form of natural activity that does not come under the sway of the play impulse. A young child's general activity, whether of the creative or of the routine kind, is largely play. Each of the specific forms of natural activity we have described in previous paragraphs may also be indulged in playfully. In the first year, for example, children assert their independence by being playfully disobedient ; in the second and later years they satisfy in a playful manner other natural impulses, for example :

(*a*) protective and gregarious impulses by playing with toy animals and dolls,

(*b*) curiosity impulse by means of a game in which object after object has to be named in response to an enquiring " Ah ? "

In the fourth year children begin to play even with fear, as we can clearly see when they play hide-and-seek.

Natural impulses that do not normally mature until adolescence are also expressed playfully in infancy. In the third year play with dolls is clearly very similar to maternal behaviour of later years ; such play, like many other forms of play, is in all probability started by imitation, but the motherly solicitude exhibited suggests that the maternal impulse itself has been stirred. It should not, of course, be assumed that this playful mothering has the full emotional significance of real motherhood, and the same reservation is necessary when considering the signs of incipient sexual behaviour, which all infants display.

Another important type of play behaviour is *make-believe*. It begins in the second year, and is seen when children pretend to perform familiar activities, and later when they pretend to be other persons. Make-believe play develops rapidly in the third year : inanimate things are treated as animate, non-human as human ; familiar happenings are dramatized ; stories are invented.

INSTINCTS : ANIMAL AND HUMAN

The reader will have noticed that the inborn types of behaviour to which children are prone by nature are similar in many respects to those that, in the animal world, we call instincts.

Most psychologists do, in fact, use the term " instinct " when they refer to the more definite of those inborn tendencies we have described. Thus, they speak of the parental instinct, and of the instincts of flight, fighting, curiosity, disgust, gregariousness, wandering, self-assertion, submission, construction, collecting and sex. There is, however, one very important difference between the instinctive behaviour of man and that of the lower animals. In animals it is relatively fixed and invariable, but in man it is plastic and varied. For example, birds build their nests by instinct, but the urge to construction in children is much less definite ; even their earliest constructions are not made according to any one pattern. As children grow older, this variety increases enormously for, as we say, they learn by experience. This brings us to another most important part of children's natural heritage, viz. their ability to learn. Compared with young animals, children are extremely helpless because their " instincts " are so imperfect and their other powers are as yet undeveloped. But it is in this very imperfection of instinctive behaviour that the germ of possible development lies. An insect emerges with an equipment more or less ready-made, with fairly fixed forms of behaviour and little possibility of development ; a baby is born with very few fixed forms of behaviour, but with the raw materials of mental equipment and with immense possibilities of learning. We ought, therefore, to look upon the helplessness of a baby, not as a sign of its inferiority, but as a symbol of its potentialities.

The same truth emerges when we consider children's play. The long catalogues we quoted on page 17 are evidence of its infinite variety, and of its developing complexity. Play is the natural method by which very young children learn. If children were born with perfect instincts, with definite tendencies to react to the same stimuli in the same ways, they would have no need to learn, and therefore no need to play. The more perfect the instincts, the less a creature plays, and the fewer are its possibilities for intelligent development. This statement is confirmed by the observation that the more intelligent the creature, the longer is its period of immaturity and playfulness. Children, in their play, experiment along the whole range of instinctive behaviour, they remember their experiences, they develop habits and new muscular skills, and according to the degree of their native intelligence they modify and develop their activities. The play of young children is often thought of as something trivial, but this is certainly a profound mistake. It is probably not too much to claim that " when nature began to select species for their playfulness she had turned a corner in the great experiment of evolution and had embarked on the journey which led to the creation of man."[1]

Psychologists do not all agree with the explanation of play put forward above. Though a great deal of children's play suggests that it is a preparation for the earnest activities of life, it has some features that suggest the need for an additional hypothesis. Most children delight in games of hunting and climbing, activities which were the serious business of life for our ancestors. It certainly appears as if racial experiences have left traces on our minds just as our own individual experiences have. These racial memories

[1] *Instinct, Intelligence and Character*, Godfrey H. Thomson, p. 34.

seem to determine some of the forms of our play activities.

Some psychologists believe that racial memory plays a large part in our lives, and they see its influence not only in play but also in the trend of many human interests. It has been suggested, for example, that children in their development recapitulate the history of the race, and that their early interests develop in close correspondence with the main lines of interest revealed in race development. Thus they are supposed to pass successively through definite stages, e.g. tree-dwellers, cave-dwellers, nomadic hunters, pastoral farmers. This theory is generally referred to as *the culture-epoch theory*. Young children certainly show interests in climbing, in making tents and caves, in hunting, in wandering, and in collecting property. It is very doubtful, however, whether the correspondence with racial development is as close as some enthusiasts have suggested ; in any case, even if such orderly development were according to Nature, it would inevitably be interfered with by the normal experiences of modern children. Though it is necessary to reject the extravagant culture-epoch theory, there is considerable evidence that the underlying *recapitulation theory* has a certain validity, particularly in pre-natal physiological development, and in the emergence of instincts during the first year or two of life.

While accepting the idea of racial memory, we must not lightly jump to the conclusion that all experiences leave traces that are transmitted to successive generations. The children of pianists have to *learn* to play the piano, and the children of mathematicians to solve equations. Despite all the education that is given, who can say that each generation does not have to start from the same position as its predecessors ? The bulk of biological evidence is opposed to the idea that characteristics acquired by one generation can be transmitted by heredity to the next. Some experimenters on rats do claim, however, to have shown that an act of skill learnt by one generation with intense, spontaneous effort is learnt more readily by the next generation. The actual skill may not be transmitted, but its learning is facilitated. Perhaps the truth is that man's racial memories are the result of an extremely slow process of heredity. If this is so, a particular form of experience can produce noticeable results only after it has operated for many generations, and it is probably effective only if it arouses intense interest and effort.

Observation of young children reveals then that they have a rich and varied racial heritage. They are by nature ready to apply their minds, to pay attention, to a wide variety of stimuli, and under the influence of emotion varying in kind and intensity to perform a wide variety of more or less appropriate actions. In addition they are endowed, to a far greater extent than other young creatures, with the ability to learn from experience. Education is the process of directing this ability so that children learn (a) to attend more widely and at the same time with greater discrimination, (b) to control their emotions so that their energies are not dissipated in useless fashion, and (c) to deal economically and successfully in thought and action with a wide variety of situations.

We shall, in the next chapter, consider some of the natural ways in which young children learn. We shall then be in a position to return to the classroom and consider how we as teachers can help children to continue their learning.

OBSERVATIONS

1. Make a list of the instinctive tendencies described in this chapter.

Watch a nursery class for, say, one hour, noting as many examples as you can of the working of each instinct.

Repeat the observations with a class of older children.

Discuss the differences between the results.

2. Make a study of the play of two or three children in a nursery class. Watch your subjects for a definite time each day, writing down as far as possible all they do and say.

3. Make a list of the things played with during a week by a young child at home.

Compare your list with a list of the play material in a nursery classroom

Compare also with the list given in *Play in Childhood*, M. Lowenfeld, pp. 46–47.

4. Write a description of the play activities of children during a recreation period : (a) infants ; (b) juniors ; (c) seniors. Discuss the differences.

NATURAL MODES OF BEHAVIOUR CHARACTERISTIC OF CHILDREN

The following instinctive tendencies and emotions should not be thought of as separate one from another, but rather as specialized manifestations of a child's general life-activity. Behaviour is the expression of one great "tendency," the will-to-live; it is not the sum of a number of separate instincts.

Tendency, i.e. mode of behaviour to which children are prone.	Object or situation to which children are ready to attend.	Emotion which children experience.	Action which children perform.
To avoid danger	Sudden noises; falling	Fear	Withdrawal; flight; immobility
To investigate the unknown	Unfamiliar things; hidden things	Curiosity; wonder	Approach; investigation; exploration
To get rid of obnoxious things	Slimy things; unpleasant tastes and smells	Disgust	Recoil; spitting out
To seek company	Other people	Loneliness which, when relieved, gives place to satisfaction	Movement towards other people
To wander	Places remote from usual surroundings	Wanderlust	Roaming; wandering
To assert themselves	Self	Elation; pride	Various actions designed to assert independence, importance, superiority

To submit themselves	Important people	Submissiveness ; humility	Various actions indicating consciousness of dependence, unimportance, inferiority
To make things	Materials for building and constructing	Joy of making	Assembling, arranging and shaping materials
To collect things	Various	Joy of collecting	Making collections
To laugh	Various	Joy ; humour ; amusement	Smiling ; laughing
To cry	Various	Sorrow	Crying
To protect[1]	Smaller or weaker creatures	Feeling of tenderness	Various actions designed to protect and cherish
To take notice of opposite sex[1]	Persons of opposite sex	Sexual feeling	Various actions indicating interest in sex ; ultimately mating
To overcome frustration	Hindrances to the satisfaction of any of the other tendencies	Anger	Screaming ; struggling ; fighting
To play to imitate	General modes of behaviour that involve all the special modes described above		

[1] The protective (i.e. parental) and sex (i.e. reproductive) tendencies are not present in childhood in a fully developed form. They exert, however, a powerful influence on behaviour and development, even in the earliest years.

5. The hints given above for observing play will suggest many other interesting observations of other types of instinctive behaviour, e.g. the occasions on which children laugh, cry, etc.

6. Observe a class in school as suggested in Chapter I. Note as many differences as you can among its individual members.

REFERENCES FOR READING

(Throughout the book, references under this heading are confined to those contained in the short list of reference books given on p. 437.)

Education : Its Data and First Principles, Sir T. Percy Nunn, chapters VII and XI.

Modern Psychology and Education, Sturt and Oakden, chapters I to VI.

Groundwork of Educational Psychology, J. S. Ross, chapters IV to VI.

Instinct, Intelligence and Character, Godfrey H. Thomson, chapters I to IV.

Your Mind and Mine, R. B. Cattell, chapter IV.

The Process of Learning, C. Bloor, chapter XVII.

ADDITIONAL REFERENCES

Social Psychology, Wm. McDougall (Methuen, Twentieth Edition, 1926).

An Outline of Psychology, Wm. McDougall (Methuen, 1923).

Instinct in Man, J. Drever (Camb. Univ. Press, 1917).

Play in Childhood, M. Lowenfeld (Gollancz, 1935).

The Place of Play in Education, M. J. Reaney (Methuen, 1927).

ESSAYS AND DISCUSSIONS

1. The value of psychology for teachers. (A preliminary discussion would be useful at this stage. Students are advised to keep the topic in mind throughout the course and to consider it again later.)

2. Make two lists of school activities (*a*) predominantly creative, and (*b*) predominantly routine.

Discuss the place of the creative and routine tendencies in school work.

3. Choose one of the natural tendencies described in this chapter. Give an account of the ways in which it operated during your own school education.

4. Think of the teachers who had most influence in your own school-days. Consider in what ways they made use of your natural modes of behaviour.

5. Consider the various forms of activity going on around you. Discuss the statement that " instincts are the prime movers of all human activity."

6. The inheritance of acquired characteristics.

CHAPTER III

PRE-SCHOOL LEARNING

WE have in the previous chapter referred to the fact that psychologists are not agreed upon the question of what instincts children inherit. Children begin to learn so soon that it is very difficult to say exactly what is inherited and what is acquired.

When we speak of children learning, we usually think at once of teachers teaching, and we are apt to overlook the fact that in pre-school years children learn very rapidly without any organized teaching, without time-tables, and without any subdivision of knowledge into subjects. Children are joyously, playfully active, and as a result they develop bodily skill, they amass knowedge, and they learn how to adapt their behaviour to the needs of other people. All three types of learning—the development of *bodily skill*, of *knowledge*, and of *appropriate social behaviour*—go on at the same time. Young children's learning is in a sense whole-sale; there is very little that is piecemeal, at least about their methods of approach. Under the influence of the creative impulse they approach their environment as a vague unanalysed whole, and they begin to explore it in all directions.

In the course of this exploration they are continually embarking on some new project, for example, being a railway-man, giving a tea-party, making a garden. Here again the same principle is seen at work. Children plunge into a complex piece of experience and they learn the detail in their stride. This is a principle of fundamental importance in education:
(1) *Learning in early years proceeds by the analysis of wholes.*[1]

[1] The importance of the "whole" is emphasized by the "Gestalt" psychologists, who have provided valuable experimental evidence that the mind works by analysing wholes and not by building up parts. It is this "whole," "shape," "form" or "Gestalt" that gives the theory its name.

For a brief discussion of the theory see *Educational Psychology*, C. Fox, pp. 15 ff.

For an account of how the theory can be applied to education and child development see *The Growth of Mind*, K. Koffka (Kegan Paul, 1924).

Interest and Learning

Observation of children reveals, however, that though most of their learning is done in their stride, they do occasionally find it necessary to mark time. In carrying out a project they discover the need for some skill or for some knowledge that they lack. They then set to work with redoubled effort. If it is skill they want to acquire, they surprise grown-up people by the determination with which they practise ; if it is knowledge they want, they try the patience of the grown-ups by the persistence with which they ask questions. The fact is that in carrying out their self-chosen projects children are so interested that they will, if necessary, cheerfully perform repetitive work that would otherwise be extremely boring. This intense interest is doubtless the secret of the rapid progress that children make during their first three years. We will therefore enunciate our second principle : (2) *Learning in early years is done under the influence of intense interest.*

Instincts and Interests

As we have already seen, children are born with a few natural ready-made interests, for example, an interest in activity, and an interest in fighting against frustration. Very soon after birth further natural interests seem to emerge, for example, an interest in asserting independence, an interest in making things. The instinctive tendencies with which children are endowed are the primary sources of the intense interest that facilitates their early learning in such a remarkable way. For example, a child sees a parcel ; his curiosity is aroused ; he is interested and starts to explore ; he meets with difficulties ; his fighting instinct is aroused ; he is doubly interested, and during the now urgent process of exploration he learns much new knowledge, improves his manual skill, and perhaps he learns the need for social adaptation. On another occasion he sees a dustman at work ; he desires to emulate him ; the instinct of self-assertion is aroused ; he is interested and wants to live experimentally the life of a dustman ; this is impossible, but the situation is saved by the play-impulse : he becomes a dustman, for make-believe overcomes all obstacles. As the game develops the observer can see one instinctive interest after another being aroused—interest in construction as he improvises his cart, interest in asserting superiority as he gives commands to his horse, curiosity interest as he wonders what will serve as a basket, and so on.

We can now state our third principle : (3) *Instinctive tendencies are the prime sources of the intense interest that facilitates children's learning in early years.*

ACQUIRED INTERESTS

It will be remembered that we distinguished between two kinds of instinctive tendencies, those like imitation and play, which were general, and those like fear and anger, which were more specific. There are many stimuli that will start children imitating or playing, but there are at first very few stimuli that will make children afraid or angry. They quickly learn, however, to feel fear and to experience anger in a large number of new situations. For example, young children show no innate fear of animals. Then one day a barking dog suddenly springs out near a child ; he is naturally frightened by the sudden noise, and probably by the approaching object. After this experience the sight of a dog is enough to arouse fear. The child has learnt a new object of fear ; he has acquired a new interest. Many psychologists believe that most childish fears have been " built in " or learnt in some such way.[1]

---

[1] Unlearned automatic reactions, such as flinching from a sudden noise, are sometimes called " *reflexes.*" Learned automatic reactions, such as flinching from a dog, are then called " conditioned reflexes " ; they have been built into the mind as a result of special conditions.

Pavlov, a Russian physiologist, has investigated the formation of conditioned reflexes in great detail by experiments on dogs. He has found,
[*Continuation of footnote on page* 28.

Let us consider another example of how children acquire new interests on the basis of inherited interests. Young children show instinctive interest in things that move, an interest that is probably due chiefly to curiosity. They are still more interested when they can themselves cause the movement, for such activity gratifies their self-assertive impulse, their love of power. Thus they are interested in water flowing from taps, and in pouring water from one vessel to another. One day a child sees a fountain-pen being filled and then held nib downwards. All his previous experience leads him to expect the ink to run out, so the fountain-pen at once becomes a new object of curiosity. The child has acquired another new interest.

Two very important contrasted types of interest that children acquire in early years are " *loves* " and " *hates*." Psychologists use each of these terms to describe attitudes of widely varying intensity. For example, the " loves" include the intense interest of a child in his mother, and also such milder interests as " love of toys " and " love of pets." The interest in dogs already described would be included in the category of " hates," and the same term is used to express a child's feelings of hostility against a baby brother who robs him of some of his mother's affection. This use of

---

Continued from page 27.]

for example, that it is possible to teach a dog to salivate on seeing a black patch, by the simple process of repeatedly presenting food and a black patch together. After a time the black patch without the food is enough to cause the saliva to flow. More than that, a dark grey patch would not do, even though it was so dark that human beings could not distinguish it from black.

Watson, an American psychologist, has experimented with conditioned reflexes in babies. It appears to be very easy to " build in " such reflexes, but very difficult to eradicate them. Some psychologists claim that all our behaviour is in the last resort composed of conditioned reflexes, and that therefore it is in theory possible to make any baby into any desired kind of man by appropriately conditioning his responses in early childhood. This is the extreme form of what is known as Behaviourism. Conditioned reflexes probably play a more important part in mental life than we usually recognize, but it is difficult to accept all the conclusions of the extreme Behaviourists.

For an amusing description of the possibilities of Applied Behaviourism, see *Brave New World*, Aldous Huxley.

the terms may at first sight appear to be extravagant, but it is noticeable that it accords with the usage of young children themselves. Once the words " love " and " hate " become part of their vocabulary they use them very freely and often with great emotional intensity. If we analyse a love or a hate, we find that it has been formed by the grouping of a number of instinctive interests round one centre. For example, a child's love of his mother is the result of many pleasurable experiences connected with her—the comfort afforded by her mere physical presence, the delight afforded by her acts of affection, and, perhaps most important of all, the intense joy obtained in the process of feeding. Thus many varied instinctive interests become grouped round her ; we say the child has acquired a love of his mother ; psychologists say that he has developed a *sentiment of love* for her. Similarly, psychologists speak of developing *sentiments of hate*. Whereas a love sentiment is an organization of interests all tending to bring a child into closer relations with the centre of interest, a hate sentiment is an organization of interests all tending to make a child avoid the centre of interest. It is important to notice that many of the loves and hates of young children are not firmly settled sentiments, and this is particularly true of what we might call the social sentiments. For example, a child may one moment display a sentiment of love for his playmates, but suddenly the opposite feeling is aroused, the game is broken up and a vigorous quarrel ensues. This brings us to another important illustration of the development of acquired interests in pre-school years, viz., the way in which children learn to be sociable.

It is well known that young children are, as a general rule, determined little egoists. We have noted, however, that they appear to be endowed with a desire for company, and with a tendency to be submissive, and it is from these germs that their sociability develops. The reader will appreciate from what has been said about children's assertiveness and about their " loves " and " hates " that the development of sociability cannot proceed evenly and without setbacks ; sociability is a quality that can only emerge slowly and with difficulty from amid the conflicts of intense love and equally vigorous hate. Beginning in the first year with the formation of a mother-love-sentiment, social life in this year is limited to the family circle. Within this circle people are played with, imitated, greeted with pleasure, and missed in their absence. At this stage children develop sociability more rapidly with adults than with other children. But even with adults, their expressions of sociablity alternate with various types of anti-social behaviour. Under favourable conditions, however, children make considerable progress in the desired direction. In the second year they begin to be friendly with people outside the family and to show pleasure at the presence of strangers, but not until the third or fourth year do they show such an active interest in strangers that they will approach them with questions, requests, confidences or offers of help. One very valuable type of experience for the development of sociability is play with other children. It is here that a child learns to control his feelings of hostility and to co-operate with others. Progress in this sphere of social relations is slow, and no attempts should be made to hasten it unduly. In pre-school years children like playing in the presence of other children, but they do not often form groups for co-operative play. When groups are formed, they are always small, and generally unstable. They tend to break up at frequent intervals, sometimes as the result of a quarrel. It is important to realize, however, that childish quarrels are a natural and necessary phase in social development, and that young children must associate with other children so that they may be weaned from over-dependence on adults.

In the development of sociability another important factor is the child's idea of himself, his *self-regarding sentiment*. As we shall learn more clearly in the next section, early experiences are of great significance in determining whether this sentiment shall be a help or a hindrance to the child when he is learning the hard lessons of social adaptation.

We see then that one of the first effects of learning is to widen the scope of all instinctive tendencies. They are aroused by an ever-increasing number of stimuli, and they are expressed in new and varying ways, so that those which beg'n as specific tend to become general. Furthermore, during the process of learning the number of natural interests is enormously increased by the development of new, acquired interests. This, then, is our fourth principle : (4) *As children learn, their primitive instinctive interests are reinforced by new, acquired interests.*

REPRESSED INTERESTS

It will now be clear that a child's mental life very rapidly becomes complex. He is seldom, if ever, under the sway of one definite clear-cut interest. We noticed in the last chapter that pairs of emotions, like fear and curiosity, elation and submissiveness, come into conflict. All this is now greatly complicated by his new acquired interests, particularly by his sentiments of love and hate, and by the inevitable interference and influence of other people, together with frustration caused by his own inability to comprehend and deal with the world around him. Much primitive instinctive behaviour is unsuitable for civilized family life, and cannot be allowed. Children, therefore, have to learn very early in life that some of their strongest interests cannot be indulged. For example, a child soon learns that he cannot monopolize the affection of his mother, but must give way to other members of the family ; this frustration arouses anger and hostility, but he learns further that expression of this hostility meets with disapproval. To take another example, he learns that his interest in bodily functions cannot, on all occasions, be freely expressed. The result is that many natural interests are, as it were, driven underground. We say that children *repress* them. Repressed interests seem to disappear ; they are no longer manifest. A child appears to give up his hostility to other members of the family, and his interest in bodily functions ; he behaves decently.

B*

Modern psychology has revealed, however, that surface behaviour is no sure index of the real state of mind. It is true that children are not aware of those interests that they have successfully repressed ; such interests never come into consciousness, so we say that they are forgotten. But that does not mean that they have ceased to influence behaviour. The child who was frightened by the barking dog continued to be afraid of dogs long after the actual frightening incident had ceased to be remembered. The fact is that behaviour is the result of the working of the whole mind, and not merely of that part of the mind which at a given moment is conscious.[1] Thus, the behaviour of young children is influenced by interests of which they are totally unaware. This influence is exerted in many different obscure and devious ways. It seems as if strong instinctive interests cannot be dammed back completely any more than a river can : they must find some mode of expression.

One very common way in which a child expresses interest of which he is no longer conscious is in his fantasy-play. It is noticeable that many games are played in which dolls and toy animals receive very severe treatment, and that, when playing " fathers and mothers," children are very fond of inflicting punishment. Many psychologists

[1] The mind is often likened to an iceberg, for as the greater part of a berg is hidden under the water, so the greater part of mind functions below the threshold of consciousness. As Nunn says : " Consciousness marks the growing-point of our higher activities, the edge by which they ' cut into reality.' Behind this point, this edge, there is a vast hormic organisation of which a great part is never represented directly in consciousness, while, of the residue, much that has once been conscious can never normally and in its own character reach the conscious level again. Nevertheless, the movements of consciousness, subserving the organism's perpetual self-assertion, are never wholly explicable apart from this organisation, whose history and constitution they express in an infinite variety of subtle ways." (*Education : Its Data and First Principles*, p. 62.)

Our knowledge of the working of the " unconscious mind," as it is called, owes a great deal to Sigmund Freud, the founder of *Psycho-analysis*. According to his view, this part of our mind consists largely of ideas and desires which we have repressed because of their unsuitability for conscious civilized life. Such ideas and desires sometimes rise into consciousness during dreams, but even then they are generally disguised. Dreams cannot, therefore, be taken at their face value, for their " manifest content " is very

[*Continuation of footnote on page* 33.

believe that children are, in these ways, expressing guilt and hostility, the real origin of which they have forgotten. In this form of play they also find compensation for their physical deficiencies. There is no doubt that play is an important safety-valve for repressed interest, and that one of its most important functions is in affording harmless expression to emotions that would otherwise tend to find expression in undesirable ways. For example, repressed hostility to parents, unexpressed in play, might tend to find expression in the bullying of other children or in cruelty to defenceless animals.

Similarly in fantasy-play children provide themselves with interim explanations of phenomena that would otherwise baffle them. A four-year-old child wonders what it is that moves the sun and he asks for an explanation; an adult answers as well as he can, but no scientific explanation is of any real help to the young enquirer; he therefore " forgets " the unsatisfactory adult answer and his own question. But his mind continues to work at the problem and suddenly one day he exclaims, " The sun is a bird, it's got wings." In this way his fantasy enables him to keep alive his interest in the movement of the sun.

Fantasy is only one way in which repressed interests

Continued from page 32.]

different from their " latent content." As men have recognized from ancient times, a dream must be interpreted before its real significance can be appreciated.

Psycho-analysis has been the subject of a great deal of criticism, and two of Freud's own disciples, Adler and Jung, have founded independent schools of psychology.

Adler considers that the sexual aspect of our instinctive equipment is of less importance than the self-assertive aspect, and the central idea of his psychology is man's love of power. Adler's system is usually referred to as *Individual Psychology*, though, of course, this title is often used, and legitimately so, of other forms of psychology.

Jung attaches great importance to the hereditary nature of the " unconscious mind." He thinks of " the unconscious " as the source of man's highest aspirations and of his noblest inspirations, a view which has long been held by many artists and poets. For example, D. H. Lawrence urges us to discover, if we can, " the true unconscious, where our life bubbles up in us, prior to any mentality. The first bubbling life in us, which is innocent of any mental alteration, this is the unconscious. . . . It is the spontaneous origin from which it behoves us to live." (*Psycho-analysis and the Unconscious.*)

find expression. Sometimes, after the repression of an interest in a forbidden or in an incomprehensible subject, the interest is diverted to another subject, similar psychologically but socially more acceptable. For example, most three-year-olds are curious about the origin of babies, but even when sensible adults answer their questions straightforwardly, many children find difficulty in understanding and accepting the answers. In time they " forget " these answers and repress this interest. Many psychologists, however, believe that young children's persistent questions about how things are made have their genesis in such a repressed interest. Thus the curiosity about the origin of babies may find a useful outlet by being diverted to the origin of non-living things. The child is not aware that the apparently new interest he is showing has any connexion with the previous interest, for this has been repressed and forgotten. This process by which a child unconsciously transfers interest from one subject where expression is forbidden to another similar subject where expression is permitted is called *sublimation*.

Another way in which repressed interests influence behaviour may be illustrated by the following example. As a result of unwise treatment, a child's natural interests in biological problems become associated with strong feelings of guilt. Let us suppose that little opportunity for fantasy-play is given ; some sublimation probably takes place, but again let us suppose that no encouragement is given to the child's incessant questions about non-personal things. What can happen ? The guilt element in the curiosity will predominate and anxiety will develop ; instead of the child continuing to develop a natural, eager, enquiring, happy personality, he will tend to acquire many of the characteristics of the " difficult " child—lack of concentration, apathy, anxiety, stupidity, laziness and naughtiness. Baffled in his efforts to use his mental and physical energy in creative ways he generally fritters it away, though he may occasionally find an outlet in the form of uncontrolled outbursts of destructiveness.

We have chosen interest in personal biological problems as our example because it provides a clear illustration, but we do not suggest that all difficulties among children spring from repression of this type of interest. It should be remembered that children are endowed with a variety of natural interests and that strong ones such as the interest in avoiding danger and in acquiring power must also be considered, if anything like a complete picture is to be obtained.

We have been able to give only a few random examples of the way in which strong instinctive interests are repressed, and of how these forgotten interests continue to influence behaviour and subsequent learning. They are, however, probably sufficient to give the reader some appreciation of the emotional complexity of the minds of young children and of the importance of our fifth principle : (5) *The learning of young children involves the repression of interests, which are then forgotten. Such interests nevertheless continue to exert strong influences on subsequent behaviour and learning.*

INTELLIGENCE AND LEARNING

In our account of pre-school learning we have found it necessary to say a great deal about emotion. This is because the emotional side of life in early childhood is relatively stronger than the intellectual. Most of the instincts with their emotional accompaniments are clearly discernible in the first few weeks of life, but intelligence, although it is an inborn capacity, is not nearly so evident. One reason is that very young children have so little skill, so little bodily control, that it is very difficult to understand what is going on in their minds. Again, the higher forms of thinking necessitate language, and until a child learns at least to understand speech he lacks the essential tools of reasoning. It has been found, for example, that in pre-speaking days children solve practical problems as animals do—by actual and continued trial and error.

Recent research suggests that psychologists have in the

past under-estimated the extent to which young children make use of intelligence. At first the intelligence is rudimentary, but such observations as the following indicate that it is a factor by no means negligible in early learning.

As early as the fourth month, some children show that they are aware of small differences in familiar things. For example, a change in position of a pendant light-switch over a cot evokes surprise and causes a child to move his head from side to side. The child behaves as if he is aware that there is a difference between " the switch as it is " and " the switch as it was." He has had two sets of experiences, but he arrives at a third piece of knowledge—the knowledge of the difference. This is an act of intelligence, and psychologists describe it by saying that the child has educed a relation, in this case a relation of difference.[1]

Another example of the early use of intelligence is the following. A child of five months is holding a tempting morsel in his right hand ; his hand is then grasped by a person standing behind him ; the child transfers the food to his left hand and thence to his mouth.

A study of the development of curiosity in early years confirms the view that children do think and reason at a

---

[1] C. Spearman has suggested that the ability to educe relations and correlates constitutes the essence of intelligence, which he calls " g." The following examples from an intelligence test will help to explain the processes :

Underline the right word—

big	small	SAME	OPPOSITE
wide	broad	SAME	OPPOSITE

These examples require the eduction of the relations of oppositeness or identity.

Sometimes when a relation has been educed, it had to be used in conjunction with a third item, as in analogies :

heat is to sun as sharpness is to . . .

This example requires the eduction of the relation between heat and sun (a relation of attribution). Then something has to be found of which sharpness is an attribute, e.g. knife. This latter process is called the *eduction of a correlate*.

All acts of intelligence can be analysed in the last resort into these two processes, eduction of relations and eduction of correlates. See *The Nature of Intelligence and the Principles of Cognition*, C. Spearman (Macmillan, 1927).

much earlier age than was formerly believed. As a result of experience, they notice similarities and make generalizations. Then occurs some new event that does not accord with one of these generalizations ; the disparity is noticed and a question is asked. For example, a three-year-old notices that carts have wheels ; he is interested in the use of wheels on his own toys ; he makes a working hypothesis as to why carts have wheels. Then one day he sees a low-flying aeroplane—" Why do aeroplanes have wheels ? They don't want them up there," he says. A four-year-old having as a result of much play with water made for himself a generalization about water flowing, sees some cooling bacon fat on a dish—" Why don't gravy roll about like water ? " he asks.

It will be noticed that in all the above illustrations the intelligent behaviour of young children was provoked by a problem, and that the problem was one which interested the child. In fact, it would not be an over-statement to say that without interest there would be no problem. Another significant fact about children's problems is that they often arise out of immediate practical activities, or they relate to subjects with which children have become intimately familiar as a result of many practical activities in the past.

We can now state our sixth principle : (6) *Young children use intelligence when learning, and this intelligence is evoked by interesting problems connected with their practical activities*.

CONCLUSION

A study of pre-school learning contains many valuable suggestions for those who teach in schools. The most important is that, when learning is actuated by strong interest on the part of the learner, very little teaching is needed. The more we study children in pre-school years, the more we discover of their capacity for spontaneous learning. The result is that many skilled actions, as for example, walking, which were formerly taught deliberately and often with much trouble, are now left for the child to learn by himself. Of course, a great deal depends on providing the right environment, on giving the right kind of help when it is asked for, and particularly on maintaining a happy, encouraging attitude to children in their struggles. But all this is very different from the conventional idea of teaching as an activity synonymous with the giving of information. It suggests that the main function of a modern teacher is to make spontaneous learning possible. Perhaps the best measure of the success of a school is given by the ratio of the amount of learning done to the amount of teaching given. Many of the suggestions in succeeding chapters of this book will be made with this idea in mind.

Another important corollary follows. The more spontaneous the learning in a classroom, the fewer are the possibilities of making mistakes in the technique of teaching. For this reason gifted teachers are often justifiably impatient of the type of detailed suggestions about the giving of lessons which loomed so large in the " method " books of last century. It is, however, not easy to inspire thirty individuals to learn spontaneously under ordinary classroom conditions, and there is a danger that young teachers may treat technical advice with undeserved contempt. Attention to " old-fashioned " technique may be very desirable in the early days of a teacher's career, for it is only the genius or the expert who can afford to be unorthodox in his methods. We shall therefore incorporate in succeeding chapters some apparently trivial, but nevertheless important, details relating to the technique of teaching.

As we have seen, the learning process involves the whole body and mind of the learner. In order to get a clear view, however, it is necessary to study various aspects of learning one by one. When children learn, they attend and observe, they form habits and images, they remember, think and imagine. These aspects of learning form the subjects of five separate chapters. When studying them, however, the reader must continually remind himself that these aspects of a single activity are isolated merely for convenience of exposition.

Children cannot, for example, observe without thinking, they cannot think without remembering, and so on.

The same warning is necessary when studying the five chapters that deal with the main trends of learning—the development of intellect, character, sociability, skill and taste. Just as the process of learning is a single indivisible whole, so the results of learning constitute a whole; intellect, character, sociability, skill and taste are all inter-dependent. Particular pieces of learning may be predominantly intellectual or emotional or muscular; they may arise from the teaching of separate subjects such as mathematics, music and physical training. But in the last resort they all affect the whole personality.

OBSERVATIONS

In order to appreciate the vast amount of learning accomplished in early childhood, it is desirable to observe some very young children either at home or in a nursery school. The following are some suggestions which may prove interesting to those who have opportunities for observing a young child :

(a) Try to determine the extent of his vocabulary.

(b) Make a list of the skilled movements he has learnt, e.g. using a spoon, doing up buttons.

(c) Make a list of the questions he asks.

(d) Note his social behaviour in different circumstances, e.g. with his mother and with strangers, with older and with younger children.

(e) Make a list of a day's activities, distinguishing between creative and routine activities.

(f) Make a list of the chief interests displayed in a day. Consider in each instance what instinctive tendencies are the sources of the interest.

(g) Make a list of actions and remarks which apparently involve the use of intelligence.

REFERENCES FOR READING

Education, Sir T. Percy Nunn, chapters XII to XIV.
Modern Psychology and Education, Sturt and Oakden, chapters VIII and IX.
The Process of Learning, C. Bloor, chapter IV.

ADDITIONAL REFERENCES

The Psychology of Infancy, V. Hazlitt (Methuen, 1933).
Psychological Care of Infant and Child, J. B. Watson (Allen & Unwin, 1928).
The Mental Growth of the Pre-school Child, A. Gesell (Macmillan, 1926).
Social and Emotional Development of the Pre-school Child, K. M. B. Bridges (Kegan Paul, 1931).
Intellectual Development in Young Children, Susan Isaacs (Routledge, 1930).
Social Development in Young Children, Susan Isaacs (Routledge, 1933).

ESSAYS AND DISCUSSIONS

1. Give an account of some important characteristics of natural learning in pre-school years.

2. Show how teachers in school may profit from a study of pre-school learning.

3. The value of fantasy-play in childhood.

4. Discuss the statement that, in school, teachers are prone to teach too much and children are apt to learn too little.

CHAPTER IV

INDIVIDUAL DIFFERENCES

WE reviewed in chapter I the three main kinds of difference —physical, temperamental and intellectual—that are observable among children in a class. We noted that some of these differences were the result of heredity, and that some were caused by experience. Our study of pre-school learning has indicated that inborn mental qualities may be profoundly influenced by early acquired interests, both conscious and unconscious. In fact, it is now generally acknowledged that no period of life is so potent in producing individual differences, both of character and intellect, as the first five years. On the other hand, we have probably a great deal yet to learn about methods of educating children in later years. This is perhaps particularly true of the period of adolescence, and many educationists now believe that it is possible to do a great deal to re-educate young people during these impressionable years which in many ways resemble the years of early childhood.[1]

TEMPERAMENTAL DIFFERENCES

Temperamental differences among children are observable on the first day of life. It is possible, for example, to distinguish the placid babies from the lively ones, and continued observation shows that such a difference persists in later years. Similar differences have been noticed between children of the same family even prenatally. It is

[1] There are extreme forms of maladjustment that are not susceptible to any methods that even skilled teachers can devise. They are analogous to bodily disease that will not yield to diet, but that needs surgical treatment. One kind of treatment for extreme cases is *psycho-analysis*, but teachers are advised to look upon such treatment as being of the nature of " surgery " rather than of " nurture." As such, it is outside their province.

clear therefore that, however profoundly temperament and character may be influenced by early experiences, there is an innate basis of temperament. The modern theory is that this inborn temperament depends largely on the functioning of certain ductless glands, for example, the thyroid gland, the adrenal glands, the pituitary and sex glands.[1] These glands secrete fluids which the blood absorbs; and chemical substances, called hormones, in these fluids exercise an important influence on bodily growth, on physical appearance, and on temperament. In fact, attempts have been made to work out connexions between physique and temperament, and it appears that there is some basis for the popular view that fat people tend to be easy-going and placid, whereas lean people are more likely to be active and worrying.

> " Let me have men about me that are fat ;
> Sleek-headed men and such as sleep o' nights.
> Yond Cassius has a lean and hungry look ;
> He thinks too much ; such men are dangerous."
> —*Julius Cæsar*, I. ii, 191.

It is always tempting, when studying human nature, to be led away by facile generalizations, and it is particularly dangerous to draw conclusions about children's temperament from their personal appearance, for their physical type may ultimately be very different from what it appears to be in childhood.

Galen's classification of temperament.—It is interesting to note that the traditional classification of temperament (suggested by Galen, A.D. 130) is based on a physiological theory. Thus the *sanguine* person was supposed to be well supplied with blood. This, it was said, made him fickle and changeable ; it caused him to flit joyfully like a butterfly from one project to another. The *choleric* person was said to have excess of bile, and this was believed to be the reason why he was headstrong, determined, and easily provoked to anger. For the *melancholic* person, a fluid called black bile

[1] See *Hygiene and Health Education*, M. B. Davies, chapter XV (Longmans, 1932).

was invented, and this was supposed to make him prone to sorrow and depression. The *phlegmatic* person suffered from excess of phlegm, and as a result was placid, slow to move and not easily aroused by emotion. The fact that these terms have survived and are still found useful is some evidence that, despite the erroneous physiological explanations, the classification itself has some validity.

Many other attempts have been made to classify temperaments. The usual plan is to describe two opposite types such as *stable-minded* and *unstable-minded*, *explosive* and *obstructed*, *impulsive* and *deliberate*, *extravert* and *introvert*. This method has a definite advantage, for most people do not belong clearly to any one type. However, by using a two-fold classification, each person can be rated according to his position between two extremes. In any class of children, it is, for example, possible to find extraverts and introverts, and between these extremes the remainder can be graded according to their degree of extraversion or introversion.

Extraversion and introversion.—The extravert is the talkative, cheerful, self-assured, sociable child who openly and readily, and in a sense aggressively, expresses his emotions. When angry he will smack or fight, but the introvert may remain quiet or merely fling himself about. The extravert looks for approval and demands attention, whereas the introvert waits until he and his achievements are noticed. The extravert is ready to assert his superiority in situations where the introvert will be content merely to maintain his independence, and this often by subtle and indirect methods. The extravert rejects criticism firmly, whereas the introvert would rather take care to avoid it.[1] Such differences may be observed between children during the first five years, and they are sometimes very clearly marked even between children of the same family. The characteristic temperamental attitude permeates all their activities, and it is most easily seen in their spontaneous play.

[1] In later life the extravert becomes the man of action and of quick decisions, while the introvert is the thinker or the dreamer who tends to be oblivious of his environment and often of the passage of time.

It is important to note that both introverts and extraverts have made valuable contributions to life, and that there is no question of superiority but only of difference. Neither introversion nor extraversion, however, is socially desirable when it is extreme, and an understanding teacher can do much to help both types of children. It is hardly necessary to say that such methods as ridiculing the introvert to bring him out of himself, or harshly repressing the extravert to keep him in his place, are bad. When considering treatment, it is necessary to start from the position that a pupil's temperament is, if not fixed by heredity, at least largely determined on a fixed innate basis during the first five years. We should therefore not aim at moulding a person after our own image, for that is impossible even if it were desirable. The most we can do is to help each individual to make the best of his own personality. It is particularly necessary to be tolerant of children whose temperament is very different from our own, and to encourage such a spirit of toleration among our pupils. We can also vary our procedure so that all children get a chance of making a contribution in their own way, taking care if we are extraverts to avoid excessive use of oral lessons and questioning, and being on our guard if we are introverts against an irrational and exaggerated belief in the virtues of private study. We can by kindly encouragement and by the wise use of group work help the introverts to widen their social circle ; we can encourage them to take an increasing share in dramatic and oral work. We can tactfully teach the extraverts to have consideration for others, and by introducing them to interesting projects we can teach them the need for persistence. It is probable that among children the moderate extraverts generally get more than their share of attention and praise. They are socially pleasant, they speak up, they are quick to answer, they take the lead in oral lessons. The quiet child who surprises us by his good performance at the term examination has probably been under-valued during the term because we have failed to appreciate his good but unobtrusive qualities,

Perseveration.—Another way of dividing children into temperamental groups is by classifying them as high and low perseverators. Perseveration is looked upon sometimes as a kind of lag in nerve processes, and sometimes as mental inertia which makes a person continue an activity when all real need for continuing it has passed. Since the effect of perseveration is to give a certain stability to behaviour, and since the effect of a strong will is similar, it has been difficult to get a clear conception of perseveration as distinct from will.

Attempts have been made to measure perseveration by means of tests, the nature of which will be best appreciated if the reader applies the following experiment to a number of subjects :

The inverted S *test.*—The subjects must be urged to work hard all the time and to make well-shaped letters.

(*a*) Write S S S S as fast as possible for 30 seconds and then pause for a minute or two.

(*b*) Write Ƨ Ƨ Ƨ Ƨ as fast as possible for 30 seconds and then pause again.

(*c*) Repeat (*a*) and (*b*), making two minutes' work in all.

(*d*) Write S Ƨ S Ƨ S Ƨ as fast as possible for two minutes. (Care must be taken to see that subjects do not falsify the results by writing their letters from right to left in (*b*) or by doing all the letters of one kind and then filling in the gaps in (*d*).)

The perseveration score is found by subtracting the total number of letters written in the second two minutes from the total number of letters written in the first two minutes. It is obvious that the number difference will be greater for those people in whom the nervous lag or the mental inertia is greater, that is, for the high perseverators.

The perseveration that is measured by tests of this kind is motor, but experimental work suggests that people who show high perseveration in motor tests tend to show it also in ideas, sensations, emotions and strivings, that is, throughout their mental life. Perseveration of the nonmotor type has been investigated largely by means of questionnaires. The following questions, based on those asked originally by Lankes, a pioneer in this work, are likely to be answered affirmatively by high perseverators :

1. When you have heard a tune does it tend to recur again and again to your mind ?

2. When you have travelled by boat or train do you experience the sensations of travelling after the journey is over ?

3. If something upsets you early in the day does it put you in a bad mood for the rest of the day ?

4. Do you sometimes carry out a task and then realize that you have forgotten why you started it ?

5. When you are occupied do you become oblivious of what is going on around you ?[1]

Reliable answers to questions of this type cannot, of course, be obtained from children, but teachers will find it interesting to observe temperamental differences of this kind among children in their classes. A knowledge that people differ by nature in the ease with which they can take up new work, or a change of work, and that these differences are not necessarily the outcome of differences in intelligence, should prevent us from making hasty generalizations about the children we teach.

Tests of temperament.—A good deal of research has been done, and is still being done, on temperament. Reference has already been made to tests of perseveration and to questionnaires. Some tests of temperament are based on word-association. For example, in the Pressey Cross-Out Test, the subject is presented with lists of words. In one list he has to cross out words that strike him as having unpleasant associations ; in other lists he crosses out words that denote something to be ashamed of, or afraid of. The total number of words crossed out gives some indication of the subject's readiness to experience emotions, and the actual words he crosses out indicate whether, temperamentally, he is a usual or an unusual person.

[1] See *Temperament Tests II.*, R. B. Cattell, Brit. Jnl. Psych., Vol. XXIV, pp. 20–49.

Quite a different type of test is the Downey Will-Temperament Test, which is based on the theory that temperament is revealed in every movement. Hand-writing movements are the ones chosen for the tests, and the traits investigated are speed and ease of reaction, aggressive qualities, and persistence. These are shown by the subject's ability to vary his writing according to directions, by his ability to carry on in spite of interference, and by the care he takes when asked to imitate a given specimen of handwriting.[1]

Many of the modern investigations into temperament are based on observation rather than on direct experiment. The observing may be carried on either during an interview or over a longer period of time, but in either case the observations should be made by a group of people and they must be made according to some standardized procedure. For example, a list must first be made of the traits to be observed and each trait must be carefully described. Burt, who has done much to develop a well-standardized technique for such interviewing, makes up his list in the following way. He starts each list with all the fundamental emotions, such as fear, aggression and curiosity ; he then adds all the commoner interests, sentiments, complexes and social habits acquired by persons of the age and type he is examin-ing.[2] If he is investigating the temperament of delinquent children, the second part of the list includes such traits as passion for clothes or adventure, whereas if he is preparing to give vocational guidance it includes such traits as industry and initiative.

The list having been made, the traits when observed must be assessed according to some definite plan. For this purpose a rating scale is used. For each quality the subject is given a numerical mark ranging from 5 to 1 according to the strength of the quality, or a literal mark, A, B, C, D or E. A means much above the average ; B, slightly above

---

[1] See *The Will-Temperament and its Testing*, June Downey (New York, 1923).
[2] *The Young Delinquent*, C. Burt, p. 415 (Univ. Lond. Press, 1925).

average ; C, average ; D, slightly below average ; E, much below average.[1]

Finally, the situation in which the person is judged must be arranged. Questions must be prepared beforehand. These, of course, will vary according to the ultimate purpose of the interview. Burt uses questions such as the following when he is investigating temperament in order to help delinquent children :

Does your brother tease you very much ?

Does your mother often scold you ?

When he is giving vocational guidance, he uses questions such as :

What are your hobbies ?

What games do you usually play ?

Burt suggests also that performance tests (see pp. 56–58) provide a standardized situation. While a child is doing the test the observer can notice such points as the speed of his movements, his reaction to success or failure, and the presence or absence of self-criticism. Burt further suggests that situations where children can behave naturally, and special occasions such as a tea-party or a visit to the Zoo, will throw a good deal of light on temperamental differences.

Temperament in the classroom.—There are at present no actual tests of temperament that are of practical use to teachers in school. A study of the work that is being done is, however, of value in suggesting to teachers possible differences between their pupils, and situations in which these differences will be revealed. For example, the way in which children move can be observed in drill and games ; the way in which they make movements with tools can be observed in handwriting and craft lessons. In handwork lessons we can easily see how our pupils react to success and failure ; we can notice whether they have initiative or

[1] R. B. Cattell, in his book, *A Guide to Mental Testing* (Univ. of London Press, 1935), recommends as being more easily and fairly applied a scale of three degrees in which B is the average. Outstandingly strong cases can be marked A + and outstandingly weak ones C —. No other plus or minus sign should be allowed.

whether they need to be set to work. In the playground we can study our pupils in a situation that is more natural than the classroom, and on occasions like school concerts we can see how our pupils react to unusual conditions. All these observations will help us to understand the different temperaments of individual children.

Temperament is a very convenient term to use when we wish to refer to all those mental qualities other than the purely intellectual, but it is obviously a term that is used loosely and one that, in the present state of knowledge, it is difficult to define. It refers to a very complex set of qualities, and it is impossible to describe any child's temperament adequately in a short verbal formula. The above classifications and descriptions should therefore not be looked upon as pigeon-holes into which individuals must be fitted, but rather as suggestions of the types of difference that can be recognized. The following are some questions that should be borne in mind when the temperament of a pupil is being considered :

(*a*) Does he express his emotions readily ?.
(*b*) Is he predominantly aggressive or submissive ?
(*c*) Is he actively sociable or does he wait for others to make advances ?
(*d*) Is he sociable with all or only with intimates ?
(*e*) Is he impulsive or cautious ?
(*f*) Is he self-assured or apprehensive ?
(*g*) Is he changeable or persistent in his interests ?
(*h*) Is he stable or variable ?

In the past both psychologists and teachers have paid far more attention to intellectual differences than to temperamental differences. This is not surprising, for intellectual differences cannot be ignored since they affect directly the output of work of all kinds. Furthermore, intellectual differences are to a large extent quantitative and have attracted attention just because they are measurable. On the other hand, the more subtle, the more qualitative differences of temperament can escape attention and in teaching it is possible to ride rough-shod over them. It is not suggested that teachers ought to make a detailed psychological study of each pupil's temperament ; it is rather a question of developing sensitivity to each different personality in the class. In a word, we must treat each pupil as a person, and respect his personality.

INTELLECTUAL DIFFERENCES

A few minutes' mere observation of a class is enough to give us a picture full of detail so far as physical differences are concerned. If we deliver a short lecture to the class we may be able to add to our picture a few details of some of the more obvious temperamental differences. If we *teach* the class for a few minutes many of the intellectual differences are revealed. Some pupils have remembered more of previous lessons than others, and although everyone has had a large common fund of general experience, some have learnt much more from it than others ; some are intelligent and are consequently able to grasp an argument readily, while others are, as we say, " slow-witted." Teachers have, of course, always known these facts, but their full significance was not realized until psychologists began systematically to measure the intellectual differences between one child and another.

Intellectual differences are not observable at birth, for until children begin to learn we have no means of estimating their ability to do so. Ability to learn can only be measured by its results. Many attempts have, however, been made to measure it by other methods. Some investigators have tried, for example, to find a correspondence between intelligence and the size and shape of the skull. Others have had a profound belief in facial expression as an index of intelligence. But when these methods have been subjected to the test of careful scientific investigation, they have all been found to be so unreliable as to be useless. All modern methods of measuring intellectual differences are *ad hoc* methods. If we want to measure a child's ability to remember we do not look for a memory " bump " but we give the child something to memorize and then measure the result. If we want to measure his ability to reason, we give him a set of problems to solve, and so on.

So far, although we have used the word " measure," we have said nothing about the unit of measurement. It is easy to see that by giving two children the same test, we could find out who was the abler at the time the test was given. If, however, one child was ten and the other fourteen, the result would be of little value, and even if both children were the same age we should still not know in any precise way the extent of any difference that the test revealed. Just as the same bowl of water may appear warm or cold to your hand according to whether your hand is at a lower or a higher temperature than the water, so a child may appear dull or bright according to the degree of intelligence of the child with whom he is compared. It is necessary to have some standard of reference.

This standard is obtained by finding the average performances of large groups of children of given ages. Thus, for example, Gesell has, by means of a large number of detailed observations, compiled " norms " of development for children aged 4, 6, 9, 12, 18, 24, 36, 48 and 60 months.[1] By observing the behaviour of an individual child over a wide range—motor characteristics, language, adaptive behaviour, personal social behaviour—and then comparing it, item by item, with what most children can do according to Gesell's norms, it is possible, even during the first year, not only to say whether a child is above or below normal in learning capacity, but also to estimate the actual extent of his capacity above or below the normal. The following are isolated examples of adaptive behaviour intended merely to indicate the type of development that is observable during early years. They are quite inadequate by themselves for purposes of diagnosis at this early stage but they serve to emphasize an important fact that is often over-

[1] For details see *The Mental Growth of the Pre-school Child*, A. Gesell (Macmillan, 1926).

looked, viz. that definite development in learning capacity can be distinguished in early months.[1]

Normal development of adaptive behaviour in early months (from Gesell) :

Four months : notices large objects ; may notice spoon on table.

Six months : notices small objects on table ; picks up objects from table ; bangs spoons.

Nine months : manipulates spoon and saucer ; looks for fallen object ; reaches with marked persistence.

Twelve months : places cube in cup or corner ; recovers cube concealed by a cup ; retains cube in either hand and takes a third.

Eighteenth months : accepts fourth cube and retains three ; builds blocks in tower imitatively.

Two years : builds block tower of three or more ; folds paper once imitatively.

Three years : builds block tower of four or more ; combines two parts of severed picture.

Binet tests.—The first standard scale for measuring learning capacity was devised by a French psychologist, Binet (1857–1911). His object was to detect children who were mentally defective, and he started by trying to find a number of ordinary everyday acts that were characteristic of each age. That is to say, he aimed at finding what was the normal attainment of 3-year-olds, 4-year-olds, and so on. Each test was given orally and individually to a large number of children of all ages. The percentage of children in each age group giving correct answers was then found. Many tests had to be rejected, some because the differences from year to year were too small, others because the differences were abrupt or irregular. For each test that appeared to be satisfactory, Binet found the age at which from 60 to 70 per cent. of the children passed, and he then allotted it to that

[1] For a description of more recent developmental tests, see *Testing Children's Development from Birth to School Age*, Charlotte Buehler and Hildegard Hetzer (Allen & Unwin, 1935).

age. In this way, he made a series of about five tests for each year from 3 to 14. These tests have been translated and adapted by Terman for use in America and by Burt for use in England.[1] The following are examples from Burt's version :

Age 3. Understanding simple commands.
  1. Show me your nose.
  2. Show me your eyes.
  3. Show me your mouth.

Evaluation.—All should be correctly performed ; but free encouragement may first be given.

Naming simple objects.

Materials—A penny, a closed knife, and a common kind of key. What is that ? (showing each object successively).

Evaluation.—All three must be named, but slight errors such as " money," " pennies " for " a penny " are allowable.

Each test must always be given in exactly the prescribed form, and the answers must be evaluated according to detailed instructions which have been compiled on the basis of thousands of answers that children have given. Equally important is the need for the tester to be on good terms with the child he is testing ; he must adapt his procedure so as to get the maximum effort from each individual. In order to obtain reliable results, it is necessary for all persons who administer the Binet tests to be specially trained.

[1] The full scale can be found in the following books : Burt's Revision : *Mental and Scholastic Tests*, C. Burt (King, 1921) ; *Mental Tests*, P. B. Ballard (Univ. Lond. Press, 1920) ; Terman's Revision : *The Measurement of Intelligence*, L. Terman (Harrap, 1919).

The Binet tests are sometimes criticized on the ground that they involve to a considerable extent other factors than the general factor that Spearman calls " g." See *A Guide to Mental Testing*, R. B. Cattell (Univ. Lond. Press, 1936). The answer is that the Binet tests are useful to teachers for that very reason ; while they may not give a scientific measurement of the abstract intelligence factor called " g," they do give a reliable measurement of a child's ability to profit by school education, an ability that is compounded of temperamental factors and of intellectual factors such as memory and verbal aptitude as well as of the general factor " g." On this point, see *The Health of the School Child* (H.M.S.O., 1936), pp. 124–126.

If, by using Binet's scale, a child aged 5 is found to be 4 on the scale, it means that he has developed only as far as most 4-year-olds. We therefore say that he has a *mental age* of 4. Such measurements are usually expressed as a single percentage ratio : $\dfrac{\text{Mental age}}{\text{Chronological age}} \times 100$. This is called the mental ratio or intelligence quotient (I.Q.). Thus, the I.Q. of the dull child mentioned above is 80.

Group tests of intelligence.—As we have said, the administration of the Binet tests needs a trained specialist. Moreover, the tests can be given to only one child at a time, and the testing of a single child takes from 30 to 60 minutes. Such tests are not therefore of great practical value to teachers. Psychologists have, however, devised written tests which, like ordinary examinations, can be given to groups of children. These group tests are standardized in the usual way. They are given to large unselected groups and the average mark for each year of age is found. If these data are plotted on a graph, then the mental age corresponding to any given score can be read off. The tests are easy to administer, though great care must be taken to follow the directions in every detail. Such group tests can be used in schools and they give teachers interesting and helpful information about the intelligence of individual pupils.[1] It may be objected that the use of such tests is unnecessary because teachers already know, as a result of their daily contact with pupils, how intelligent or unintelligent they are. To a large extent this is true, and it is important to note that the ultimate criterion of the validity of intelligence tests is the extent to which they agree with the judgment of teachers who know their pupils well.[2] But

[1] For examples of group tests of intelligence the reader is referred to the many standardized tests now published. See, for example, *Group Tests of Intelligence*, P. B. Ballard (Univ. Lond. Press, 1922) (an interesting book which contains a variety of tests) ; *Cattell Group Intelligence Scale*, R. B. Cattell (Harrap, 1930).

[2] The extent of this agreement is measured by the *coefficient of correlation*. For example, let us suppose that a class of children is ranked in order of merit for intelligence by a teacher, and also by an intelligence test, and that the following results are obtained :

	Teacher's Estimated Order.	Intelligence Test Order.	Difference in Rank (d)
A.B. . .	1	1	0
C.D. . .	2	3	+ 1
E.F. . .	3	5	+ 2
G.H. . .	4	2	— 2
I.J. . .	5	4	— 1
K.L. . .	6	10	+ 4
M.N. . .	7	6	— 1
O.P. . .	8	9	+ 1
Q.R. . .	9	7	— 2
S.T. . .	10	8	— 2

The coefficient of correlation (r) may be obtained by using the following formula :

$$r = 1 - \frac{\Sigma(d^2)}{\frac{n(n^2 - 1)}{6}}$$

d is the difference in rank for each pupil ; n is the number of pupils).

In the example above

$$\Sigma d^2 = 0 + 1 + 4 + 4 + 1 + 16 + 1 + 1 + 4 + 4$$
$$= 36,$$
$$n = 10,$$
$$\therefore r = 1 - \frac{36}{\frac{10 \times 99}{6}}$$
$$= 1 - \frac{36}{165}$$
$$= 1 - .22$$
$$= .78$$

If the agreement were perfect, the two lists would be identical. Thus, Σd^2 being 0, r would be 1.

Similarly, if one list were the exact reverse of the other, Σd^2 would be 330, and r would be — 1.

If there were no correspondence between the lists, Σd^2 would be halfway between 0 and 330, i.e. 165, and r would be 0.

It will be seen that the coefficient of correlation can vary from + 1 (perfect correspondence) to — 1 (perfect non-correspondence), and that if there is no correspondence, the coefficient is zero. In actual practice, the correspondence between teachers' estimates and intelligence tests is good enough to give a correlation coefficient of about 0.7.

For other methods, see *How to Calculate Correlations*, Godfrey Thomson (Harrap, 1924).

[*Continuation of footnote on page* 56

C

the judgment of teachers is relative ; we can arrange our pupils in an order of merit for intelligence, but we cannot, without measuring their intelligence, assign I.Q.'s to them. A standardized intelligence test not only gives us an order of merit indicating that one pupil is more intelligent than another, but it also gives us a measurement of the extent of this difference so that we can, if necessary, compare the intelligence of pupils who are in different classes or in different schools. An intelligence test sometimes gives surprising results. A pupil may appear dull in class and yet do well in the test ; he is probably an intelligent pupil who for some reason is apathetic to school work, and has consequently concealed from us the fact that he has ability. Finally, an intelligence test has the further advantage of giving us information about our pupils in a very short time. It is not too much to say that by using a group intelligence test a teacher can obtain in an hour more knowledge of the intelligence of the individuals of his class than he could by ordinary methods during a term.

Performance tests of intelligence.—These tests are intended particularly for those people who for one reason or another suffer from a language handicap—very young children, deaf people, feeble-minded people, people like canal-boat children and immigrants, who have had unusual school careers. None of these can be satisfactorily tested by any tests that are mainly verbal. Slum children, too, are relatively handicapped in tests that consist exclusively of verbal problems, for their vocabularies, both spoken and written, are smaller than the vocabularies of children in more favourable circumstances. Their restricted vocabularies, it should be noted, are not necessarily the result of low intelligence ;

Continued from page 55.]

There are many purposes for which teachers in school can use the method of correlation. The following are suggestions :

(*a*) Correspondence between the orders of merit of a class on promotion from the infant school, and a year later.

(*b*) Correspondence between the orders of merit in different subjects.

(*c*) Correspondence between the orders of merit for oral and written composition.

they are, to some extent at least, a result of lack of normal experience with words. When testing the intelligence of such children, it is therefore desirable to supplement verbal tests by tests in which words are not needed, that is, by performance tests.

In these tests words have been largely replaced by concrete material. Although the problem is presented in concrete form, it is a problem that calls for reasoning and judging just as the verbal problems do ; a child's success depends on the efficiency of his thinking and not on the dexterity of his movements. For example, in the Healy Picture Completion Test I, the child is presented with a large picture mounted on wood, in which ten holes have been cut, thereby removing essential objects from the picture. The child is then given fifty smaller pictures, each one of which would fill any of the holes. The problem is to choose for each hole the small picture that makes the best sense. To do this satisfactorily, the child must study the picture, judge what the people are doing, think what is the missing object and choose the appropriate little picture to complete the sense.

The cube construction test is another type of performance test. The materials for this are three wooden blocks to serve as models, and three sets of one-inch cubes with which to make these models. Two of the models are painted on some of the sides and one is quite plain. The cubes are all painted on some sides and plain on others. The problem is to duplicate each model in turn with the allotted cubes, getting painted sides where they should be painted and plain sides where they should be plain. Since the plain model, a two-inch cube, has to be constructed with eight cubes all painted on three sides, it will be seen that this test cannot be accomplished successfully without forethought. If a subject set out to solve the problem by repeated trial he would not score highly, since there is a time limit for the work and the assessment depends on the number of moves taken.

A third type of performance test is the scale of mazes

devised by Porteus. These range in difficulty from a simple diamond-shaped path for age 3 to a complicated square maze for age 14. In the first one the child simply has to trace with a pencil the way round the path, but in the later ones he has to find the way through the maze without crossing lines and without going down any blocked paths.

In verbal tests a child must be given a large number of questions and he cannot be assessed on any one ; similarly in performance tests he is given a group of tests and then his average score is calculated. There are many types of performance tests, but they all have this in common : they test the subject's ability to choose material that satisfies given conditions, and to perceive relations between different parts of the presented material.[1]

Although, as we have said, performance tests were primarily designed for people suffering from a language handicap, they have since been found useful in other ways. For example, they act as a check when testing those people who, instead of suffering from a language handicap, have special linguistic facility, and so may be rated too high on tests that are predominantly verbal. They act as a " shock absorber " for nervous people who would be unable to do themselves justice at first in a verbal test, either oral or written. They are used when studying people as a pre- liminary to vocational guidance, for some work needs ability that is practical rather than verbal ; and, as we have seen, they provide situations in which people reveal many of their temperamental characteristics.

Intelligence quotients.—It has been found that a child's mental ratio or intelligence quotient is generally constant. This means that if children are dull or bright in early years, they will in normal circumstances be equally dull or bright as they grow up. A boy of 5 with a mental age of 4 will, when he is 10, have a mental age of 8 ; during childhood his mental age will always be about 80 per cent. of his chronological age.

[1] For a fuller account of these tests, see *Performance Tests of Intelligence*, Frances Gaw (Industrial Fatigue Research Board, Report No. 31).

There are some exceptional children whose mental ratios are not constant, whether they be measured by intelligence tests or whether their intelligence be assessed by teachers on the basis of their all-round performance in school work. A child who through some serious illness has been deprived of the usual activity in the first few years of life may appear at first, even when tested on the Binet scale, to be duller than he really is. It seems probable that children of this type account for many of those who are classed by teachers as " late developers."[1]

Another important fact about intelligence is that it develops fairly steadily until the age of about 14–15. The rate of development then slackens and, so far as intelligence tests show, intelligence ceases to develop after the age of about 16. That is to say, the intelligence of children develops in very much the same way as their height. Thus, a boy with an I.Q. of 80 will never reach a mental age of more than about 13. An interesting and important corollary is that a bright child born of rather dull parents will actually be more intelligent than his parents by the time he reaches adolescence ; when this happens, it may make the child's social development very difficult.

The fact that intelligence ceases to develop in late adolescence does not mean that a grown-up person of wide experience and knowledge is no more effective in meeting

[1] Late development is a subject on which we have at present little or no precise information. It is clearly a matter that is in need of careful investigation, especially as the type of secondary education may be fixed for many children by their school record up to the age of 11.

In addition to the type of late developer mentioned above, there are certainly some children who, if tested by intelligence tests, would always reveal themselves as being intelligent, but who nevertheless fail to make satisfactory progress in school subjects during the early years of their school life. The causes are probably various, e.g. abnormal temperamental characteristics, such as extreme timidity, irrational dislike of teachers or school, deep-seated emotional conflicts, lack of grounding in the fundamental subjects of reading and number. These handicaps may later be overcome, and the child then appears to be a late developer. The " cure " may be the result of the cumulative influence of school, or it may be caused by some lucky chance—a beneficial change of atmosphere on transfer from primary to secondary school, a change of teacher, or the introduction of a new, attractive subject.

the problems of life and business than when he was a callow youth of 16. Our ability to solve a problem depends not only on our native intelligence but also on our familiarity with the data involved, and perhaps also on the feeling of confidence that comes from familiarity with the particular type of problem. That is why intelligence testers are careful to select as subject-matter for their tests only that knowledge which is likely to be common to all, and why they also recommend that testees should be made familiar with the types of tests before the actual intelligence test is given. Intelligence tests are, however, so constructed that when children have become familiar with them through one or two trials, no further coaching is of any help.[1] An adult is no better at solving the problems of an intelligence test than he was when he was 16. But the problems of life are more varied and complicated, and it seems likely that our ability to solve them grows for some years after adolescence. This is not due to any increase in our intelligence, in our sheer ability to think, but rather to an increase in our knowledge and experience. In other words, although intelligence may not develop after adolescence, there is no such limit to the development of intellect, and a developed intellect increases the effective use which we can make of our native intelligence.[2]

The distribution of intelligence.—Now let us consider a large group of children who are not specially selected in any way,

[1] Any serious attempt to coach children to do intelligence tests is a waste of time. Professionally it is worse than that, for it is an attempt to defeat the object of the test.

[2] While intelligence is the capacity for making new adaptations, intellect is more ; it includes intelligence and well-organised knowledge. An intelligent person, by neglecting to use his intelligence in acquiring and organizing knowledge, remains a person of poor intellect. An unintelligent person, by memorizing knowledge, may become relatively learned, but he can never become a person of good intellect.

"This is the explanation of the vast importance of the comparatively small differences of native intelligence displayed by children. The small superiority of the more intelligent child may, by cultivation and the development of intellect, become the vast superiority of the man of great intellect to the ordinary man." (*An Outline of Psychology*, Wm. McDougall, p. 379, Methuen, 1923.)

for example, a primary school of 500, in a district where the social status of the parents is neither exceptionally high nor exceptionally low. If the mental ratios of all the children were obtained, it would be found that they ranged from below 70 to over 130, and that there were no abrupt breaks or gaps between dull and average children or between average and bright children. There would probably be some children at every point on the scale of mental ratios from 70 to 130+. There would, however, be large numbers clustered about the 100 point and very few at the extremes. If we tested a very large random sample of the whole school population we should get a result similar to that shown in Fig. 1.[1]

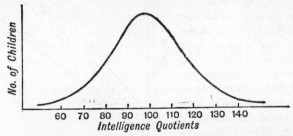

FIG. 1.—Distribution of intelligences.

The facts discovered by surveys of the intelligence of school children are of great significance for teachers. They should prevent us from thinking of children as falling into a small number of well-defined and distinct categories,— mentally defective, dull and backward, average, bright. For administrative purposes it is necessary to use such labels, but for teaching purposes it is necessary to remember that

[1] This curve is the same as we get if we perform an experiment in which the laws of chance operate, e.g.:

Toss four coins, say 100 times, and plot the number of occasions on which the following combinations are obtained: all tails; 1 head, 3 tails; 2 heads, 2 tails; 3 heads, 1 tail; all heads.

The curve is called the *Curve of Normal Distribution*.

It has been found that similar results are obtained if we plot curves for physical traits, e.g. height.

there is no sharp dividing line between one category and another. The pupils at the bottom of a " backward " class are hardly distinguishable from the best pupils in the school for mentally defectives, and the pupils at the top of a " backward " class are practically the equal of the least able pupils in ordinary classes. The need for individual methods should now be obvious.

When considering individual methods it is useful to distinguish between *individual teaching* and *individual work*. Individual teaching is particularly necessary for the mentally defective and dull at one end of the scale, but the bright children at the other end, who can to some extent teach themselves, are in particular need of individual work. A corollary of particular interest to administrators is that there can be no justification for abrupt differences in the size of classes as we proceed from one category to another. For

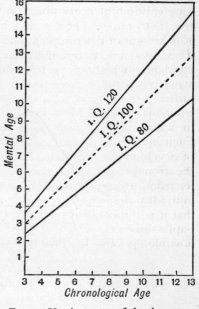

FIG. 2—Varying rates of development.

example, if classes of twenty are reasonable in schools for mentally defective children, it follows that classes of forty or even thirty dull children in other types of schools are indefensible.

Another important point which emerges from the results of intelligence testing is that individual differences become more difficult to cope with as children grow older. Consider the development of intelligence in two children whose I.Q.'s are respectively 80 and 120. Since the I.Q.'s are constant the disparity in mental years increases each year. Beginning with a difference of 1.2 years at age 3, it is 2 years at age 5, 4 years at age 10, and 5.2 years at age 13 (see Fig. 2).

In the infant school these two children could be catered for satisfactorily ; they could if necessary be taught by individual methods in the same class. At the end of the primary school course the situation is more difficult, as the gap between them has widened to four mental years. From the point of view of intelligence alone, one pupil should still be working with pupils of 8 or 9, although he is 11. This, however, is unsatisfactory, for although he is still a child in intelligence he is probably in the pre-adolescent stage physically, termperamentally and socially. The only satisfactory solution is to arrange that while one pupil has a bookish type of education the other is educated by methods in which the approach is more predominantly concrete. Each needs a curriculum specially devised to suit his stage of development considered as a whole. We have here one of the strongest reasons for choosing the age of 11 or 12 for transfer from primary to secondary schools ; it is the age at which individual differences in mental ages have become so wide that it is difficult, on the intellectual side, to educate all the pupils satisfactorily in one small school. The following are possible dividing lines for the various types of education :

I.Q.	Type of Education	Percentage in the Population.
50 and below	Ineducable idiots ; occupation centres.	0.2
50–70	Mentally-defective pupils ; special schools.	2
70–85	Dull and backward pupils ; special secondary-school education.	10
85–115	Normal pupils ; secondary-school education.	76
115–130	Bright pupils ; grammar or technical secondary-school education.	10
130–150	Very bright pupils ; grammar secondary-school education.	2
150 and above	Exceptional pupils ; grammar secondary-school education, ultimately university honours.	0.2

C*

The dividing lines are not more than very rough guides, for even when considering the most suitable type of intellectual education for a pupil, factors other than level of intelligence as measured by tests must be taken into account, for example, the pupil's character and ambitions, the nature of his home and the attitude of his parents. So long as some courses of secondary education are shorter than others, some parents will choose the short courses because of pressing economic needs.

It is important to draw a clear distinction between types of secondary education and types of secondary school. A number of different types of secondary education are necessary, but it does not follow that each needs a separate type of school. Many educationists are opposed to the policy of segregating children in different schools according to the degree of their intelligence, and they would prefer to have all children over 11 educated together in " omnibus " secondary schools, often referred to as multilateral schools. From the point of view of the social development of individuals, and particularly of social solidarity, there is much to be said for this plan. It would still be necessary, in order to give each child a suitable intellectual education, to organize children in different groups within the school according to their ability, for children at widely different levels of intelligence not only need to go at different rates, but as we shall see later, they also need to travel by different routes. They would, however, all participate in a common social life. If the present system of different types of schools for children over 11 persists it will be most important to ensure that all are given equality of status, which means equality in amenities, size of classes, allowances for books and apparatus, and scales of salaries. It also involves the closest possible contact between one type of school and another, so that all pupils participate to some extent in a common social life ; e.g. leagues for games, district sports competitions, musical and dramatic festivals must be organized to include each type of school. There must also be free interchange of pupils who are found to be in the wrong schools ; and even when all this has been done much patient work and a radical change in social outlook will be required before each type enjoys equal prestige in the eyes of parents.

It is necessary to recognize individual differences in intellectual ability and to provide for them, but in doing so, we should beware lest we perpetuate an educational system in which we emphasize undesirable social differences that ought to be eliminated for the benefit both of individuals and of the community.

Another important question that arises from the suggested grouping of children according to intellectual ability is the percentage of pupils for whom the different types of secondary education should be provided. This is obviously bound up with the question of the secondary-school curricula. In the opinion of many educationists, at least 25 per cent. should receive a grammar-school education, and consequential drastic changes should be made in the grammar-school curriculum. Such a change, it is argued, would be beneficial not only to the more able pupils who were hitherto educated in senior and central schools, but also to many of the pupils already in grammar schools, for whom the customary academic course never has been really suitable. It is generally agreed that there ought also to be a large increase in the provision of the type of education now called " junior technical." Hitherto little or no such provision has been made in many areas, and even in progressive areas it has been carefully limited to meet the estimated needs of industry. Experience has shown that junior-technical curricula make a very strong appeal to natural interests, and they may well be the best means of providing a liberal education for many pupils irrespective of the type of career which they may eventually choose. It appears therefore that what is usually called " modern-school " education may come to be reserved for those who fail to be selected for education of the grammar-school or technical-school types. It will be most regrettable if these pupils are segregated in so-called modern schools, for such schools could not hope to enjoy equal prestige with the others. One solution of this difficulty would be to organize secondary education in large multilateral schools catering for all kinds and levels of ability. A compromise would be to organize two types of secondary school, one providing bookish curricula of various types, and the other more practical curricula of which the junior-technical type would be one. The first might be called " grammar secondary schools " and the second " modern secondary schools," reserving the term " technical " for post-secondary-school work. It is in fact no more appropriate as a description of a practical type of secondary education than the term " professional " for an academic type. The antithesis between professional and technical education, and between cultural and vocational education at the secondary-school level is a false one, and the sooner it disappears the better.

Special aptitudes.—It must not be assumed that differences in intelligence are the only type of intellectual difference found among school children. It is true that they must always loom large in a teacher's view of his class, if only because intelligence enters into all forms of mental activity. Intelligent children are, *on an average*, superior to unintelligent children not only in solving problems, but also in memorizing, in drawing, in handwork ; they make better prefects and they are more skilful at games. Exceptions to this general rule have probably already occurred to the mind of the reader—a dull boy who is good at handwork, a clever girl who is " no good at games." These exceptions remind us that defects in intelligence may be offset to some extent by merits of other kinds, and conversely that high intelligence may be offset by special defects. They remind us that, useful as intelligence tests may be, they measure only one aspect of a child's personality. Qualities such as a stable temperament or exceptional muscular skill are valuable assets, and they are not always accompanied by high intelligence.

Recent research has revealed that, in addition to intelligence which is a general factor pervading all activities, there are other factors which are operative only in special activities.[1] Agreement has not yet been reached as to what special aptitudes there are, and still less as to their exact nature. It is, however, generally agreed that children may differ in respect of the following :

(a) Memory.
(b) Verbal or linguistic aptitude.
(c) Mechanical aptitude.
(d) Arithmetical aptitude.
(e) Geometrical aptitude.
(f) Manual aptitude.
(g) Musical aptitude.
(h) Drawing aptitude.

Two children may be equally intelligent, but one may excel in English and not in arithmetic, while the other excels in arithmetic and not in English. On the two-factor theory this difference may be explained by assuming that although both children are equally endowed with the general factor, intelligence, they are not equally endowed with the special factors ; one has more aptitude for language, but the other has more aptitude for arithmetic. This is probably true, but it is almost certainly not the whole explanation. Experience in educating children who suffer from special forms of backwardness suggests that many of them are backward not so much on account of inherent lack of special aptitude, but rather on account of emotional disturbance. There is no doubt, for example, that many children are backward in arithmetic because they have lost confidence in their ability, and it is suggested that premature forcing is a very common cause. Conversely, special ability is often due to intense interest aroused by a stimulating teacher.

As a consequence of all the differences so far described— differences of temperament, intelligence, interests, special aptitudes—children in a class differ widely in attainments.

---

[1] This theory, which has been formulated by Spearman, and is supported by a great deal of experimental evidence, is generally known as the *Two-Factor Theory*. See *The Abilities of Man*, C. Spearman (Macmillan, 1927).

These differences in attainments and the methods of measuring them will be dealt with in chapter XIX.

Differences between the Sexes

The most important fact discovered by psychologists about sex differences is that they are, generally speaking, much smaller than is popularly believed. Compared with the individual differences that psychological tests have shown to exist within one sex, they are very small indeed, especially on the intellectual side.

Boys and girls differ slightly in their rates of development, both physical and mental; they seem, as Burt says, to play " a sort of statistical leap-frog, now one up, now the other, throughout their whole school course."[1] Thus, for example, between the ages of 11 and 14, girls are, on an average, slightly taller and heavier than boys, but from 15 onwards the boys outstrip the girls. Similarly, between the ages of 11 and 14, girls remember better than boys but the difference does not persist. Differences in the rates of development are very slight and of little significance to teachers ; many of them are probably connected with the fact that the age of puberty is earlier for girls than for boys.

As judged by intelligence tests, boys and girls are, on an average, equal. The range of ability is, however, greater among boys than among girls, so that there are more outstanding boys at both ends of the scale of intelligence. The fact that there have been more men of genius than women does not mean that men are generally more intelligent than women ; it is probably to a large extent the result of this difference in variability. The influence of tradition must also be remembered, for the recent " emancipation " of women has shown that many popular beliefs about differences between the sexes need modifying.

The greatest differences are in respect of such physical characteristics as height, weight and strength. On the mental side women are more acute than men in sensory

[1] *Mental and Scholastic Tests*, p. 193 (King, 1921).

discrimination, but as we pass from such simple mental processes to the complex process of reasoning the differences tend to decrease until, as we have said, they disappear.[1]

From the point of view of teaching the most important differences are differences in temperament, special aptitudes and interests. The non-aggressive emotions, tenderness, submissiveness and fear, are more pronounced in girls ; the aggressive emotions, domination, assertiveness and anger, are more pronounced in boys. This is probably one reason why boys are involved in street accidents and in delinquencies more often than girls. It is not, however, the only reason, for account must be taken of the fact that owing to domestic duties girls are not in the streets as much as boys.

Girls are superior to boys in linguistic ability ; they read more and write more. Boys are superior to girls in mathematical and mechanical ability. Girls are more skilful than boys in making movements that require independent finger control, but boys excel in movements requiring strength and speed of movement. Little is known as to how far such differences in aptitudes and interests are inborn, and how far they are acquired as a result of differences in the traditional games and occupations of boys and girls. In his researches with the Binet tests, Burt found a singular parallel between tests which are easier for girls and those which are easier for children of a better social class. He comments as follows : " Sheltered, supervised, detained at home, girls, like children of the better classes, incline to sedentary lives and engage in literary pursuits ; and, like those children, they consequently excel in linguistic work and conversational activities. Boys, like children of both sexes in the slums, have more to do with practical, perceptual, out-of-door pursuits. They are sent to shops with money. They are allowed to play and wander in the streets. They are encouraged to handle tools—to construct toys for amusement and articles for use. No wonder that—like the

[1] *The Mental Differences between the Sexes*, C. Burt and R. C. Moore, Jnl. Exper. Pedagogy, Vol. I, p. 384.

poorer child, whose lot in life for the present restricts him, and for the future destines him, to menial tasks and manual labour—boys grow more ready with hand and eye than with tongue or pen."[1] On the other hand, many sex differences in aptitude and interest make their appearance very early in childhood and they seem to persist even where both sexes have similar opportunities for practice. It therefore appears that they at least have their origin in some inborn differences between the sexes. They may ultimately be found to rest on subtle temperamental differences that still remain to be elucidated.

INDIVIDUAL DIFFERENCES AND VOCATIONAL GUIDANCE

Individual differences are important not only while children are at school but also when they leave school and seek employment. If they are to go on developing harmoniously, their occupation, like their school work, must suit them physically, intellectually and temperamentally. They should then be able to work with satisfaction to themselves and to their employers. A person in an unsuitable employment finds this difficult, if not impossible, and he is likely to become not only a bad worker but also a weak citizen. For the benefit of society and for the well-being of the individual, it is important that a right choice of employment should be made.

Just as " difficult " school children forced us to reconsider our methods of education, so " difficult " employees are forcing us to reconsider our methods of choosing occupations. All children will benefit by the knowledge gained from a study of particular individuals, for as such knowledge spreads it will make observation more pertinent and advice more reliable.

Any attempt to guide people into suitable occupations must be based on a knowledge both of the work and of the people. A great deal of information about occupations has already been collected by social workers and industrial

[1] *Mental and Scholastic Tests*, p. 196.

psychologists. Available jobs have been noted and information has been collected as to the amount of training necessary and the wages offered. The occupations of adults have been classified and the average intelligence of people in each class has been estimated. The results of this survey are given in the following table, which should be compared with the table given on page 63 :

Intelligence Quotient.	Vocational Category.
Over 150	*Highest professional*, e.g. lawyer, physician, university teacher, architect.
130–150	*Lower professional*, e.g. teacher, secretary, surveyor, engineer.
115–130	*Clerical and highly skilled*, e.g. book-keeper, electrician, compositor, hospital nurse.
100–115	*Skilled*, e.g. tailor, cabinet-maker, bus-driver, routine typist.
85–100	*Semi-skilled*, e.g. barber, laundry worker, domestic servant, miner.
70–85	*Unskilled*, e.g. packer, labeller, farmhand, sweep.

This collecting of information is being supplemented by a more intensive study of individual occupations to discover what are the particular mental and physical qualities and abilities that each demands. For example, some occupations make most demand on a good verbal memory and others on creative imagination. Some need initiative, but for others conscientiousness is more important. Some call mainly for manual dexterity and others for mechanical aptitude. Even among occupations grouped as manual, success may depend on such different qualities as speed of movement, precision of movement, or strength of movement. By studying workers who are outstandingly successful, or unsuccessful, in particular occupations, by subjecting them to various tests, and by rating them for temperamental qualities, psychologists can decide what are the essentials for success in that occupation. They build up a kind of pattern of the successful teacher, the successful salesman, and so on.[1]

With this knowledge behind him the vocational psychologist must then study the individual, with a view to finding work that fits him, and it must be remembered that the work must satisfy not only his present powers but also his future needs. Here again the procedure is usually collecting of information supplemented by more intensive study, this time of the individual. Information must be collected as to the wishes of the parents and of the child ; as to the possibility of money being spent on the training or the necessity for immediate earning. Sometimes school records can furnish additional information. The usefulness of such records varies very much. Where the teacher or head teacher is interested in finding suitable work for his pupils he will gradually build up for himself a technique to guide his observations. If in addition to this he is acquainted with the modern study of individual differences, and with some of the means used to assess such differences, he will know more precisely what observations to make and what terminology to use for expressing them. Records compiled in this way can be very valuable indeed. It is not suggested that teachers should take over the specialized work of vocational guidance, but that they should hand over to an expert such information as they themselves have found useful in educating the children. Such information will include particulars about the children on the following points :

1. General intelligence, as measured by standardized tests of intelligence.

2. Educational attainments, as measured by standardized tests of attainments (see chapter XIX).

3. Special interests, as shown, for example, by choice of books, hobbies and subjects for composition.

4. Special abilities, as shown by any particularly good work, or by any part taken in general school activities.

[1] For examples of such occupational patterns, or profiles, see *Your Mind and Mine*, R. B. Cattell, p. 291.

5. Temperamental and moral qualities, as shown in a variety of situations.

5. Medical history, with a list of any defects, and with remarks as to suitability or unsuitability for particular types of occupation. In practice it has been found that remarks as to unsuitability, *contra-indications* as they are called, are most useful.

Furnished with such a record the vocational psychologist knows what specialized tests of aptitudes and abilities it will be necessary to administer. We can look upon vocational guidance as a gradual narrowing down of the field of choice. For example, the level of occupation, i.e. professional, skilled, etc., will be determined by the level of the individual's intelligence. If he is too intelligent for his work he is likely to be dissatisfied, and if he is not intelligent enough he is likely to be worried. In neither case will he do good work. The particular trade or type of work, e.g. mechanic, carpenter, clerk, etc., will be determined by special interests and aptitudes, and finally the particular variety of that work will be determined by a consideration of temperamental qualities. For example, of those who are fitted for clerical work some may prefer to work alone and others may need the company of their fellows. Of the girls who are fitted for domestic service some may prefer to work in a small household, and others, who are more sociable, may get on better in an institution.

The work of vocational guidance is still in its infancy, but although much remains to be done much has already been achieved. The value of the guidance that has already been given can be seen from the results of an experiment carried out with one hundred school-leavers in London in 1923. These children were studied and advice as to occupation was given. After two years a " follow-up " enquiry was made and particulars were obtained concerning eighty-two of the children. It was found that forty-nine of them were in work similar to that advised, and thirty-three, for one reason or another, were in dissimilar work. There were thus two convenient groups for comparison. Of the forty-nine who had followed the advice, forty-one were satisfied with work, pay and prospects, seven were satisfied with the work but not with the pay or prospects, and only one was really dissatisfied with the work. Of the other thirty-three, thirteen were satisfied with work, pay and prospects, six with the work but not with the pay and prospects, and fourteen were really dissatisfied with the work. An enquiry into the amount of changing of occupation in each group showed that there had been more changing, and so presumably more dissatisfaction, in the group that did not follow the advice given. It is remarkable that of those who followed successfully the advice given, fifteen had received advice contrary to their own suggestions. Results such as these certainly show that a start has been made in the right direction and promise well for future developments.

Conclusion

We have in this chapter reviewed a large variety of individual differences and for convenience we have referred to them in three separate categories—physical, temperamental, intellectual.

It will be evident, however, that all the differences are interrelated. Temperamental differences seem to be actually correlated with physical differences, and even the differences revealed by intelligence tests are not independent of temperamental factors. Further, it seems certain that observable differences in special subjects such as music and manual work are due in no small measure to the influence of physical and temperamental factors. Once again we as teachers are confronted with the need for considering the whole personalities of our pupils. In order to understand them it may be necessary to concentrate first on one aspect, then on another, now to apply an intelligence test, then to observe the influence of temperament, at one time to consider such physical conditions as nutrition and sleep, at another time to think of special abilities in isolated subjects. But as we do so we must beware of allowing our view to be obscured by specious labels—dull, lazy, backward, phlegmatic, I.Q. 90. No child can be adequately described in a word, still less by a numerical mental ratio. In the end we must always come back to the whole child and as we do so we shall always feel that, however defective some individuals may be in certain directions, nevertheless all have some promising possibilities.

OBSERVATIONS AND EXPERIMENTS

1. Using the questions on page 49, study the temperament of a few individual children who clearly belong to different types.

Make notes of each child's behaviour and write short descriptions of the temperaments as you observe them.

2. Observe the testing of some children by someone qualified to administer the Binet tests.

As you do so, notice that temperamental differences are also revealed as the testing proceeds.

3. Administer a group test of intelligence to a class and arrange the children in order of merit according to the results of the test.

Ask their teacher to arrange the children in order of merit according to his estimate of their intelligence.

Using the method described on page 55, find the coefficient of correlation between the two orders.

Discuss with the class teacher any individuals whose test performance is very different from his expectation.

4. Try to discover the special interests and special abilities of some children who apparently have only a low degree of intelligence.

(For further suggestions, see footnotes on pages 55, 58, 60.)

REFERENCES FOR READING

Education, Sir T. Percy Nunn, chapters IX and XIII.
Groundwork of Educational Psychology, J. S. Ross, chapters XIII and XIV.
Educational Psychology, C. Fox, chapter XI.
Instinct, Intelligence and Character, Godfrey H. Thomson, chapters XVII, XVIII, XX, XXI, XXII.
Psychology and Practical Life, Collins and Drever, chapters II, IV, V, VII.
Your Mind and Mine, R. B. Cattell, chapters II, III, XI.
The Process of Learning, C. Bloor, chapters XI, XVII.

ADDITIONAL REFERENCES

Mental Tests, P. B. Ballard (Univ. Lond. Press, 1920).
Talents and Temperaments, Angus Macrae (Nisbet, 1932).
Occupational Misfits, S. Bevington (Allen & Unwin, 1933).
Methods of Choosing a Career, F. M. Earle (Harrap, 1931.)

ESSAYS AND DISCUSSIONS

1. Examine some questions from group intelligence tests. Discuss how far they test intelligence as distinct from knowledge.

(For explanation of what constitutes the essence of intelligence, see footnote on page 36.)

2. The relative values of individual and group tests of intelliegnce.

(Consider: age of testees; different temperaments; ease of administration; understanding of questions.)

3. The present state of tests of temperament.

4. Tests of special aptitudes.

5. Non-verbal tests of intelligence.

6. The effects of temperament, intelligence, special interests, and special aptitudes on school progress.

7. The choice of age 11 as the dividing line between primary and secondary education.

8. The organization of secondary education, i.e. of the education of pupils over the age of 11.

(Consider: separate schools of different types as at present, or large multilateral schools.)

9. Co-education.

(Read: *Differentiation of the Curriculum for Boys and Girls respectively in Secondary Schools*, H.M.S.O.)

10. The teacher's part in vocational guidance.

CHAPTER V

THE DEVELOPMENT OF HABITS

IN chapter II we considered those types of behaviour that are the result of inborn tendencies ; such are generally called instinctive. In chapter III we saw that on the basis of instinctive activity a young child quickly learns new forms of behaviour. He learns to dress himself, to say nursery rhymes, to wash his hands before meals. Such behaviour is the result of acquired tendencies and is called habitual ; the actions themselves are called habits. In the course of time our habits become so fixed that habitual behaviour seems almost as natural to us as instinctive behaviour. As we say, " Habit is second nature."

TYPES OF HABIT

When we review our habits we find examples over the whole range of our behaviour, but they can nevertheless be placed into fairly well-marked classes. There are *habits of movement* such as writing, knitting or swimming. These are really skilled actions and will be considered in more detail in chapter XII, " The Development of Muscular Skill." Then there are *verbal habits*, such as our habit of saying " Twenty-four " when we are asked " What are six fours ? " These verbal habits will be studied in chapter IX, when we are dealing with memorizing. A third class of habit comprises *social habits*, such as courtesy and neatness ; these will be met with again in chapter XIII, " The Development of Taste." Fourthly, there are *moral habits*, such as truthfulness and diligence ; this type must be considered in chapter XI, " The Development of Character." Finally, there are our *habitual ways of thinking and believing* which we shall deal with in chapter X,

" Thinking." In all these different kinds of habit there is yet sufficient similarity to warrant a study of habit in general before we meet particular types in their own sphere.

How Habits are Formed

Repetition is the basis of all habit-forming. We act in the same way again and again until behaviour of this kind becomes easy and can be accomplished with very little, or even with no, conscious direction. Mere repetition is not, however, enough to ensure the efficient formation of habits. For rapid and permanent learning the repetition must be of such a nature that it affords the learner feelings of satisfaction. Sometimes the mere knowledge that progress is being made is enough to ensure satisfaction ; but, especially with young children, this intrinsic satisfaction sometimes needs to be reinforced, for example by adult praise, or by the feelings of superiority aroused in competition. On the negative side, the repetition must not arouse any spirit of resistance. No lasting effect in the desired direction is produced if repetition is forced upon unwilling learners. On the contrary, much harm may be done, for a definite resistance to learning may be set up.

The behaviour that ultimately becomes habitual may be prompted by a conscious desire to imitate, as when we deliberately set out to copy the movements of another person. It may, on the other hand, be the result of more or less unwitting response to suggestions received from people in our environment, as when we drop into the mannerisms of people around us, become courteous as a result of living among courteous people, or develop a habit of tidiness as a result of growing up in tidy surroundings. Many people feel that this suggestive influence is more fruitful of good results than direct instruction. This is certainly true when we are trying to inculcate such general habits as diligence and courtesy, but when the habit is of a more specific kind, such as an act of skill, conscious imitation of a teacher will probably give the better result. There is, however, one advantage that spontaneous unwitting imitation always has over deliberate imitation that is done to order—it cannot arouse feelings of resistance. On the contrary, being of an instinctive nature, it is always accompanied by feelings of satisfaction. Herein lies one of the chief reasons why the natural learning of young children at play is so effective. For example, children readily acquire an undesirable accent from a playmate and yet they may make a very poor response to direct speech training. The different result is, to some extent at least, due to a difference in teaching method. The playmate does not set out to instruct, and consequently he arouses no unpleasant feelings of inferiority. If we add to this the fact that the play is enjoyed we see that the conditions for learning are ideal. The learner responds instinctively and without any feelings of compulsion or shame. Direct teaching, on the other hand, is always in danger of becoming unwanted exhortation or even unpalatable admonition. It follows, therefore, that the mark of a good teacher of habit is the skill he displays in avoiding such danger.

It is obvious that the best teacher will be one who can ensure that all repetition is accompanied by satisfaction. To do this he must secure the goodwill of the learner and maintain it by every possible means. He must be careful to avoid arousing the antagonism of the learner by too much insistence on the learner's shortcomings, or his own perfection. Encouragement rather than criticism should be the rule and where criticism is necessary it should be kindly and not destructive. Above all, the repetition must make an appeal to the learner's instinctive interests, a point to which we shall return in subsequent pages.

The good teacher of habits is also one who studies children so that he knows which habits a child is ready for. Complicated habits of movement like those involved in ordinary writing are unsuitable for most 3-year-olds, and adult standards of behaviour such as " Ladies First " are unsuitable for a young child to whom differences of sex among his playmates mean very little.

Where a habit is to be formed deliberately there is great value in a good send-off. It is worth while, for example, to give a class notice when the formation of some new habit is to be tackled and to choose for its introduction some opportune occasion, if possible, an impressive one,—the beginning of a new term, the first day with new books. The occasion should be chosen when there is a reasonable chance of a long run of practice without any likelihood of the need for exceptions. It is obviously bad policy, for example, to start training a class in a habit of regular attendance during a spell of bad weather. When habits are being formed one short period of slackness may undo the effects of many weeks of patient training.

The Treatment of Undesirable Habits

In contrast to the problem of forming good habits there is the problem of eradicating bad ones. Such habits are of two kinds :

(a) Those that are the result of weakness of some kind in previous training, such as bad writing habits.

(b) Those so-called " nervous " habits such as nail-biting that are the outward sign of emotional unrest. These latter are hardly habits in the true sense of the word, since, although they are repeated continually, they were not necessarily acquired by repetition.

With undesirable habits of the first kind the general principle is to concentrate as far as possible on forming new habits so that the old ones will disappear for lack of exercise. It is often better, for example, to try to teach a bad writer a totally new style, than to try to improve his old style. A teacher confronted with a class that has been allowed to develop a habit of standing up and waving hands when a question is asked, should institute a new way of indicating readiness to answer, e.g. folding arms. Alternatively he should concentrate on receiving answers only from children who are seated, rather than on admonishing those who are standing. The general principles of habit-forming apply with particular force in all this remedial work, and particular attention should be paid to the rule that no exceptions be allowed until the new habit has become well established.

The treatment of "nervous" habits is more difficult. It is not merely a question of replacing a bad habit by a good one, but of removing what is probably a deep-seated emotional cause. Our guiding principle must be the avoidance of conflict. Any frontal attack, such as punishing a girl who bites her nails, is likely to do more harm than good, for it will merely aggravate the existing trouble by accentuating the girl's feelings of hostility, guilt and shame. Even should the habit disappear as a result of punishment, its place will most likely be taken by some other "nervous" habit. The trouble can only be solved by apparently neglecting the bad habit, and by doing everything possible to increase the child's confidence and self-respect. It is fairly safe to assume that one object, perhaps unconscious, of the bad habit is to attract attention. Therefore, with a nail-biter it might be helpful to show solicitude for the girl's appearance, and unobtrusively to let her see how nails are usually cared for.

The Value of Habit

The ability to form habits is a very necessary condition for any development in behaviour. Those creatures whose behaviour is from birth stereotyped and fixed form no new habits ; they exhibit no power of adapting themselves to new conditions. It is obvious, too, that when certain forms of behaviour become easy, when we are able to perform them with little or no attention or effort, much time and energy will be saved—time and energy that can be given to initiating and practising new forms of behaviour. For example, when writing becomes habitual we can use it as a tool and give our whole attention to what we are doing with the tool. Young children, however, need to attend to the writing itself, and so long as they are at this stage they cannot use it successfully as a means of expression. Some habits are a necessary foundation for further progress. A child must walk before he can run ; he must know his tables in order to make fresh advances in arithmetic.

Habits also save a good deal of worry and rebellion. The student who has formed a habit of sitting down to work at a particular time will find that there is little need to make a conscious effort to start work and, as a rule, little tendency to rebel against the need for work. The child who has been successfully trained to put away his toys, does so as a matter of course without argument or persuasion, and without any feelings of being hardly treated. The shy child who has learnt an habitual formula for delivering verbal messages or for making enquiries will gain much confidence from knowing just what to do in a situation which, to him, is always complicated by emotional difficulties.

The formation of desirable habits is one of the best ways of controlling instinctive behaviour that would be socially undesirable. The instinctive impulse to seize food can be controlled by a habit of waiting to be served, by a habit of offering food to other people (a form of adult behaviour that makes a strong appeal to children), and even by the rapidly disappearing habit of grace before meals. Many people nowadays are beginning to think that in our desire to avoid the evils of repression we have underestimated the valuable stabilizing influence of habit in all matters of work and social behaviour. It is possible that many of our adolescents would find life less bewildering if they had a larger equipment of established habits of decent social behaviour.

Dangers of Habit

As we have said, a habit once established is carried on with the minimum of attention. Herein lies its danger. It may persist when its usefulness is over, and in this way it may prevent us from acquiring new and more valuable habits. People who have always acted in a particular way, and thought along particular lines, are in danger of becoming "old fogeys," unable to adapt themselves to changing conditions. It is good for us sometimes to direct our attention deliberately to our actions and beliefs and to decide whether they now have any real value or whether they have merely acquired a spurious value through long acquaintance. A habit sometimes prevents progress because it has been acquired in too narrow a way. An example will probably make this clear. A child had formed the desirable habit of going to sleep every day after his dinner. Since the habit had been established without conflict the child was able to enjoy every day a calm refreshing sleep. Unfortunately, however, the habit was the narrow one of sleep-in-the-perambulator and not the more general one of sleep-any-where, so that when the child was too big to lie comfortably in the pram the whole sleep habit collapsed and had to be relearnt in other situations. If a habit is to operate in more than one situation it must be practised in more than one situation. Habits that have been acquired in a narrow fashion are often used in a blind unreasoning way. The following is an example from school work. Children who have arrived at the "borrowing" stage in subtraction are often taught to say "add ten." Practice is given until the whole process becomes habitual. But it is not uncommon to find children repeating this formula quite mechanically in any subtraction sum, even where there is no need for the adding, and so getting an unmanageable answer. Here the practice has evidently been too narrow in scope. Obviously, at first, it must consist of examples which all demand the operation of the new habit. At this stage the habit is likely to be the narrow one of always adding. Later, however, the examples should be varied, some needing the adding and some not. Thus the children will learn to use the new habit reasonably, not unintelligently. This is a most important principle in education, and a clear realization of its value will help to prevent us, on the one hand, from underestimating the value of habit, and, on the other hand, from trusting in the power of habit too implicitly.

OBSERVATIONS AND EXPERIMENTS

1. Choose some desirable habit which you wish to form for yourself. Draw up a scheme for self-training in the light of principles enunciated in this chapter, and put it into practice.

2. From direct observation of a class make lists of (a) good and bad social habits, (b) individual " nervous " habits.

3. Observe a lesson devoted to the formation of some kind of habit, e.g. handwriting, speech training.

Make a list of points of procedure that are in accordance with the principles of efficient habit-forming.

REFERENCES FOR READING

Modern Psychology and Education, Sturt and Oakden, chapter XVI.
Educational Psychology, C. Fox, chapter V.

ADDITIONAL REFERENCES

Talks to Teachers, William James, chapter VIII (Longmans, 1920).
Principles of Psychology, William James, chapter IV (Macmillan, 1890).
Mental Training and Efficiency, F. H. Hayward, chapter IV (Sidgwick & Jackson, 1921).

ESSAYS AND DISCUSSIONS

1. Make a list of social habits in which a class of given age ought to be trained.

Discuss the practical measures of training.

2. Make a list of bad habits commonly met with in classrooms.

Discuss practical measures of dealing with them.

3. Discuss Rousseau's dictum that we ought to " form a habit of forming no habits."

Chapter VI

THE DEVELOPMENT OF INTELLECT

IF we consider a child about to leave school and then think of what he was like ten or twelve years earlier, the most obvious change, apart from a change in physical size and prowess, is a great increase in knowledge. The school leaver knows more than he did ; his intellect has developed. We are so accustomed to this fact that it has become common-place, and it is not until we ask how this knowledge has been acquired that we begin to realize what a wonderful and complicated process it is.

It is difficult, if not impossible, to imagine what a child's first knowledge of the world is like. James has suggested that, at birth, the world must appear to be " a big, blooming, buzzing confusion." In using the word " confusion," he was perhaps crediting the infant with an adult mental attitude, but in any case a baby's first knowledge of his environment must be very vague and lacking in detail compared with the knowledge that he soon acquires. Impressions pour in through all his sense organs, and these impressions form the basis of all his knowledge. How is it possible for an infant to create orderly knowledge from what appears to us to be a " buzzing confusion " of sense impressions ?

He is able to begin to acquire knowledge because, being alive, he has an urge to be generally active.[1] Then, as we have learnt, he begins at birth to select parts of his environment and to neglect the rest. He attends to certain objects

---

[1] This urge is a fundamental property of life, and various writers have suggested different names for it, e.g. *élan vital* (Bergson), *horme* (Nunn), *libido* (Freud). It is seen in operation as the driving force not only behind conscious activities but also behind activities of which we are not normally aware, such as breathing, heart pumping and digestion. See *Education*, chapter III, " The Will to Live," Nunn.

and situations because he is endowed with appetites and instincts ; when he does so, we may imagine that the remainder of his environment is, for the time being, a vague, undifferentiated background. This power of attending is clearly very valuable for the acquisition of knowledge and it will be discussed in more detail in chapter VII.

The next steps in the development of knowledge are made possible because every experience leaves behind some trace on his mind. For example, having once attended to his mother at feeding time, the next experience of feeding is different ; it is influenced by the impression of his previous experience, which, in some mysterious way we do not understand, his mind has retained. This " retentivity " is obviously at the root of all learning, and it is important to note that a child retains many impressions, although he may not be aware that he has done so. This explains why in modern methods of teaching so much emphasis is placed on giving children experiences without necessarily expecting all the details of these experiences to be remembered (see pp. 336–7). We cannot say we have remembered until we have recalled the impression of a past experience, that is to say, until we are aware that we have retained it. This topic, *remembering*, we shall discuss in chapter IX.[1] Meanwhile we may note that the effects of sense impressions vary according to a child's mental attitude, although it seems probable that no sense impression is totally without influence.

Let us now return to the young child and follow his progress in acquiring knowledge. It will be clear that very early in life he begins to know his mother. His instincts impel him to attend to her in many situations, and his mind retains impressions of these interesting experiences. In a similar way he acquires knowledge of many interesting things in his environment. These items of knowledge do

---

[1] The ability to retain " the past," whether with or without awareness, is often called " *mneme*." The reader will appreciate that instinctive behaviour can be thought of as an example of " mnemic " activity ; we do not remember the experiences of our ancestors but nevertheless our minds bear the impressions of such experiences. See *Education*, chapter IV, " The Living Past," Nunn.

not, however, grow in isolation. For example, a child knows his mother in a number of situations, the most important of which is, for him, the feeding situation. He attends to her and to the act of feeding together, and as a result, he links together in his mind the impressions left by the two experiences—presence of mother and taking of food. Psychologists say that the two sets of impressions or ideas have cohered or become associated. By this process, *association*, knowledge becomes knit together in an organized whole so that, as McDougall has suggested, it may be compared to a " bush woven over by a multitude of spider's threads, stretching from leaf to leaf ; each leaf being directly connected with many others by these threads."[1] For teachers, there are two important facts about the process of association. First, items of knowledge cohere only when we have attended to them together ; or, in other words, when they have some common interest or meaning for us. Second, the strength of the associative links depends on the keenness with which we attended to the original experiences. These facts explain why the early knowledge gained by young children is relatively well organized. It is gained by intensely interesting experience, and this experience is of such a broad, general kind that each item of knowledge is firmly associated with many other items. The psychology of association is clearly of great importance to teachers and it will be necessary to refer to it again when discussing remembering (pp. 139–147), thinking (p. 157), and also when reviewing the general art of teaching (pp. 335–339).

So far, in our account of the development of intellect, we have emphasized three aspects of the process :

(*a*) *Selecting* : the knowledge acquired is largely determined by a child's instinctive interests.

(*b*) *Retaining* : a child retains impressions of his experiences, the strength of each impression depending on the intensity of his interest.

(*c*) *Associating* : a child links together those impressions

[1] *Outline of Psychology*, p. 396 (Methuen, 1923).

D

left by experiences that have a common interest for him.

Thus our account has dealt with the selection, increase and organization of knowledge. Simultaneously the child has been developing in another way. His knowledge has not merely increased, but it has become more detailed and precise. " The advance of intellect," as McDougall says, " is from knowledge of a few objects of a very highly general type, towards knowledge of the multitude of concrete individual objects and their peculiar qualities and relations."[1] As we have said (p. 25) children learn by analysing wholes. This brings us to a fourth aspect of the process of developing knowledge :

(d) *Discovering details :* a child, under the influence of interest, discovers the qualities and relations of objects in the situations to which he attends.

One of the earliest types of relation to be discovered is the relation of difference. Thus a child learns to discriminate between an apple that can be eaten and a ball that cannot, between his mother who feeds him and a stranger who frightens him. He learns to discriminate between objects,—their size, shape, position and qualities. Modern educators rightly lay stress on the importance of giving young children adequate practice in sense discrimination as a basis for the subsequent development of intellect, and as Montessori has shown, the sense of touch and the muscular sense are important as well as the senses of sight and hearing.

Important as actual sense experience is, the development of knowledge would be very slow if a child were restricted to experience of this type. He would, for example, be unable to compare and contrast a ball and an apple unless they were actually present to the senses at the same time. Under such limitations the range of detailed knowledge of the kind we have been describing would be very narrow indeed. Fortunately a child's mental activity is not limited in this way, for he is able to supplement sense experience in two ways, and thus accelerate the development of his knowledge.

[1] *Outline of Psychology,* p. 382 (Methuen, 1923).

Very early in life he is able to experience things " in his mind " even though the actual things are not present to his senses. Having experienced an apple, he is able, if it should be taken away, to see it with " the mind's eye," and in a similar way, to smell it, touch it, grasp it, and taste it. We say he is able to form *mental images* of the apple. It is believed that images first arise in a child's mind when some unexpected delay happens in the course of a familiar cycle of interesting events. For example, a child hears his mother preparing food, he hears her approaching footsteps ; then, contrary to the usual routine, she stops outside. In such a situation the child probably " sees " his food mentally. He has formed a mental image and in so doing he has made an important intellectual advance, for in future his behaviour will be influenced not only by physical experiences but also by mental images. As his experience widens, his available stock of images increases. He is able to compare one image with another, and one image with a sense experience, and so the development of his detailed knowledge is accelerated. The role of images in the development of knowledge in school will be discussed in chapter VIII.

The second way of accelerating the development of knowledge is by means of language. A child has a natural urge to communicate his feelings, knowledge, and wishes to others, and it is this urge that gives rise to language, a fact that can be illustrated from the development both of child and race. At first an infant communicates by means of gestures and vocal sounds, and later he supplements these methods by scribbling and drawing. In these activities we have the begginings of language and, it will be noted, both spoken and written language develop from a collection of natural signs to a system of artificial signs. Further, it is interesting to note that at first a child combines gesture and sound ; his first cries of discomfort and his early babblings of satisfaction are accompanied by movements of his whole body, and he only learns gradually to subordinate bodily gesture to vocal sound. A similar sequence is observable in the history of the race, and language to-day still retains some marks of its early origins. There are, for example, African languages in which the spoken words are unintelligible unless they are accompanied by bodily gestures ; for these people conversation in the dark is impossible. In more highly developed languages the connexion of word sounds and gestures is less obvious but it is nevertheless discernible. The words " yes " and " no " (and the corresponding words in many other languages) are perhaps a relic of the bodily gestures associated respectively with the acceptance and intake of food and with its refusal and expulsion. Such words have been called " sound metaphors " ; their sound conveys a suggestion of their meaning which originally was conveyed largely by means of bodily gestures.

Many of the sounds made by animals and infants are emotional in origin, and some words, like " pooh-pooh," appear to have arisen from such sounds. Here again we have words that tend when spoken to suggest their own meaning. The sound of the word " growl," for example, is reminiscent of the sounds made by animals to express the emotional state associated with " growling," and the same " gr " sound is present in other words, like "grumble," " groan," " grouse," that have in some degree a kindred meaning. A third type of word is the onomatopœic word, like " bow-wow " and " splash " ; such words have developed from the vocal sounds originally made in imitation of the sounds associated with the object or action named.

The connexion between the sounds of words and the mental stages and bodily actions to which they refer is doubtless one reason why children learn to speak so quickly ;[1] a child is not aware of this connexion, but in

[1] Early childhood appears to be a particularly good time in which to learn spoken language.

Cf. J. W. Tomb : " It is a common experience . . . in Bengal . . . to hear English children of three or four years old who have been born in the country conversing freely at different times with their parents in English, with their *ayahs* (nurses) in Bengali, with the garden-coolies in Santali, and

some intuitive way he feels that the word is appropriate and consequently he is quick to make the necessary associations. An infant makes many associations between objects, actions and words before he is able to speak the words himself. That is to say, he understands more words than he uses, just as, later in life, his reading vocabulary is more extensive than his speech vocabulary. The learning, which is based on imitation, is further facilitated in several ways. A child uses words to express his urgent wants and when a wrong word fails to produce the desired result he learns by the mistake without any direct teaching. He also learns by having mistakes pointed out to him. His desire for, and pleasure in, successful communication are, however, so intense that many parents and teachers prefer to trust largely to natural learning and to reduce direct teaching to a minimum. As Hazlitt has pointed out, there is a danger of making a child confused and he then " begins to associate disagreeable experiences with his efforts at talking and these in their turn inhibit future efforts."[2] Another fact, of great importance to teachers, is that children do not develop speech facility only by using words to express needs and to communicate experiences, but also by incessantly repeating words and phrases for the sheer pleasure of saying them.

Psychologists have made many studies of the order in which different parts of speech enter into the vacabularies of young children. There is, of course, much overlapping, but broadly speaking the successive peaks in acquisition

with the house-servants in Hindustani, while their parents have learnt with the aid of a *munshi* (teacher) and much laborious effort just sufficient Hindustani to comprehend what the house-servants are saying . . . and to issue simple orders." Tomb concludes that " children must possess a capacity, not based on ' intelligence,' of intuitively placing the correct meanings on spoken sounds, a capacity which they retain up to a certain age, but, in the majority of instances, lose altogether as they approach adult life." (*On the Intuitive Capacity of Children to Understand Spoken Language*, Brit. Jnl. Psych., Vol. XVI, pp. 53-55.)

Hazlitt also calls attention to the extraordinary rate of progress in the acquisition of language that is possible in favourable circumstances. " Many intelligent children of 3 in fortunate environments have larger vocabularies than uneducated adults of average intelligence." (*The Psychology of Infancy*, V. Hazlitt, p. 60 (Methuen, 1933).)

[2] *Op. cit.* p. 60.

are as follows : interjections, nouns, verbs, adverbs, adjectives, prepositions.[1] Another important way of considering a child's language development is in terms of sentence construction. His first sentences are single words helped out by gesture and circumstance, but by two years of age most children can combine words to form sentences though, compared with adult speech, their sentences show certain infantile characteristics.[2] From this stage, vocabulary increases rapidly, words become more meaningful and sentence formation more complicated.

The next major advance is learning to read and write. These operations are to-day generally taught together, the tendency being to postpone formal instruction for most children until the age of five or later. There are several reasons for this postponement. First, it gives children time to acquire the essential foundation for learning to read, viz. a good speaking vocabulary. Second, it gives time for natural physical development, thus avoiding eyestrain and the strain imposed by the premature training of small finger muscles. Furthermore the processes of learning to read and write can be completed more rapidly at the later age, and there is thus less danger of children being bored, and a good chance of their developing a desirable emotional attitude to the subjects from the beginning. Another important feature of modern methods is that children begin to learn reading by being introduced to interesting sentences ; analysis into words comes later, and into letters and sound-elements still later. Thus reading is learnt as talking is learnt and as all real knowledge of any kind is learnt,—by a meaningful " whole " method.[3] But, just as children delight in sheer repetition when learning to talk, to walk or to do anything else, so they delight in sheer phonic drill when learning to read, and most teachers provide opportunities for this kind of work at some stage.

[1] See V. Hazlitt, op. cit., p. 55.
[2] For details, see The Development of Sentence Structure in Childhood, W. Boyd, Brit. Jnl. Psych., Vol. XVII, pp. 181-191.
[3] See The Sentence Method of Teaching and Reading, J. H. Jagger (Grant, 1929).

Having traced in general terms how children develop a knowledge of words, let us enquire how this acquisition accelerates the development of their knowledge of the world around them. It is obvious that language enables children to profit by direct instruction, by the study of books and by asking questions ; these topics will be discussed in chapter XVIII, " The Art of Teaching," and chapter XIX, " Questioning." Language also enables children to continue the acquisition of knowledge from their own experience. The learning of names at once increases their interest in discriminating ; the two processes, the discovery of differences and the acquisition of words with which to describe these differences, are mutually helpful. All men are no longer " dad-dads " when words like " uncle " and " grand-dad " are known ; all books are no longer merely " books " when a child has acquired such words as " volume," " pamphlet," " novel," and " textbook." In short, increase in vocabulary is one method of increasing a child's ability to observe (see chapter VII). The wider and richer the vocabulary, the more a child is able to appreciate literature of all kinds, the more he is able to appreciate the fine discriminations made by former generations who, in McDougall's words, " have given conventional or traditional permanence to the discriminated classes and objects by labelling or naming them." By means of language a child " is led and aided to repeat these discriminations ; is led to split up the flux of sense-impressions, which is the world as presented to its senses, along the traditional lines, to discriminate those kinds of objects which the experience of mankind has found to be of greatest practical importance."[1]

Language further helps a child to notice similarities in the things around him and thus to form general notions. He is enabled not only to differentiate animals called "dogs" from animals called " cats," and animals called " terriers " from animals called " collies," but since so many animals are called " dogs," he begins to discover the essential

[1] *Outline of Psychology*, p. 384 (Methuen, 1923).

attributes of dogs. Thus, he is enabled to think of " dogs " in general without reference to images of such dogs. We say he has formed a general notion, a pattern, or a concept of dogs ; he has acquired a general idea of " dogginess." This concept, which works largely below the threshold of consciousness, influences his behaviour in the presence of dogs and it influences all his thinking about dogs. Conversely the concept itself is continually being modified and enriched by further relevant experiences. In a similar way children develop, with the aid of language, concepts of many kinds. The reader will now find it interesting and profitable to try to work out how he himself has developed some of his important concepts. We will take as a further example the development of a number concept.

The first definite step towards acquiring a concept of " two " is taken when, about the age of 2, a child's attention is arrested by noticing two identical things, e.g. cigarette packets, in close proximity. Previously he has noticed one on many occasions, but the sight of two is a new and fascinating experience. He is told, " *Two* packets," and from this time he takes a keen interest in finding two identical things,—two knives, two plates, two shoes. The next step is the recognition of two similar but not identical things, e.g. two spoons (a teaspoon and a tablespoon), two hats (a lady's and a man's). Next comes the stage when he recognizes two dissimilar objects as " two," e.g. a knife and fork, a pen and pencil. Thus, helped by repetitions of the number series, the notion of " two-ness " gradually emerges ; all associations with material things drop away and a child begins to use the word " two " or perhaps the symbol 2 in its general sense. His notion of " two " is further enriched by subsequent arithmetical experience when he learns that 2 is $6 - 4$, $\frac{1}{2} \times 4$, $\frac{1}{4}$ of 8, and so on.

The above illustration shows clearly how all symbols,— words, number symbols, mathematical symbols, maps, diagrams—can become part of our mental stock-in-trade. They should be introduced at an opportune moment when they will be appreciated as an expression in shorthand form of the results of experience, and then their meaning should be enriched by use in many different situations. Their full significance is not appreciated in a single lesson, still less as the result of a single telling ; as Thomson says of words, they need to ripen to maturity in the mind.[1] Any attempt to force the pace by presenting symbols without an adequate background of experience merely results in loading the mind with useless lumber. For a time symbols acquired in this way can be manipulated with apparent success ; words that have been memorized but are only half-understood can be used in parrot-like fashion. Sooner or later, however, progress is arrested, for there is a limit to the amount of verbal knowledge that a child will memorize. There is, however, no limit to the amount of real knowledge that a child will acquire through experience if he has the necessary language. Experience and language must therefore advance together, each reinforcing the other. If acquired in this way, words, as we have seen, help to make children obser-vant ; they help children to form mental images and general concepts. The function of language does not, however, end there, for, as we shall learn later, children are able with the help of words and other symbols to recombine images and to use concepts they have obtained as a result of actual sense impressions.[2] They can, for example, imagine what life is like in other lands and what life was like in bygone

[1] *Instinct, Intelligence and Character*, p. 115.

[2] It is interesting to note, as Nunn points out, that as children grow older and their intellects develop, their general knowledge becomes differentiated along three distinct but related lines—the practical, the æsthetic and the ethical. In this chapter we have emphasized the development of practical knowledge, the kind of truth that helps children to gain a useful intellectual control over their environment. This environment is both material and social, and in view of its importance, we shall consider the development of practical social knowledge more particularly in a separate chapter (XVI, " The Development of Sociability "). We shall also give special considera-tion to æsthetic and ethical knowledge (chapter XIII, " The Development of Taste," and chapter XI, " The Development of Character "). But, as the emphasis changes from one chapter to another, it is important to remember that all knowledge has a common origin,—the impulse to gain an intellectual control of the world. In all our separate discussions we are dealing with a single topic, " The Development of Personality." See *Education*, pp. 220-224, Nunn.

D*

times ; they can create, in imagination, knowledge that is outside the bounds of probability. They can think out solutions to problems without having to experience the actual situations ; given certain data they can deduce new knowledge from them.

Thinking and imagining are obviously most valuable means of developing intellect and their place in school work will be discussed in chapter X.

OBSERVATIONS AND EXPERIMENTS

1. Observe how the development of children's intellects is reflected in their compositions and drawings.

(For this purpose, Burt's median samples for each mental age will be found very useful. See *Mental and Scholastic Tests*, pp. 395-398, " Compositions on School " : pp. 383-394, " Drawings of a Man.")

2. Record " snapshots " of a child's speech at intervals of, say, three months between the ages of 2 and 7.

Use these records to investigate the child's development in extent of vocabulary, use of different parts of speech, sentence construction.

(A speech " snapshot " is a verbatim record of everything the child says during, say, ten minutes. All the snapshots should be made, as far as possible, under similar conditions.)

3. Record sentences uttered spontaneously by children of different ages. Trace the development of sentence construction with age. Notice factors influencing development, e.g. intelligence, social status.

4. Investigate, by tactful questioning of individuals, the range of experience of children in a slum school at different ages.

(Before beginning, it is necessary to make a list of suitable questions, e.g. Have you seen the sea ? Where ? Have you ever been in a train ? tram ? bus ?)

5. Make another investigation similar to the previous one, but concentrate on extent of general knowledge.

6. Give the following Binet tests to children of appropriate mental ages. Record the answers and observe how they indicate development of intellect.

Year 5. Giving definitions. (Most children at this age define in terms of use.)
Say : You have seen a chair. You know what a chair is.
Tell me, what is a chair ?
And so on with these words : horse, fork, doll, pencil, table.

Year 8. Giving definitions. (Most children at this age define in terms superior to use.)
Say : What is a shop ?
And so on with these words : tiger, football, soldier.

Year 12. *Giving definitions of abstract words.*
Say : What is pity ? What do we mean by pity ?
And so on with these words : revenge, charity, envy, justice.
[For details of satisfactory and unsatisfactory answers at each stage,
see *The Measurement of Intelligence*, L. M. Terman (Harrap, 1919).]

7. Give the following Binet tests, and record the answers :
Year 7. *Giving differences between two things.*
Say : You know what a butterfly is. You know what a fly is. They
   are not the same, are they ? In what way are they not the same ?
And so on with the following : stone and egg ; wood and glass.
Year 8. *Giving similarities ; two things.*
Say : I am going to name two things which are alike in some way, and
   I want you to tell me in what way they are alike. Wood and coal :
   in what way are they alike ? And so on with the following : an apple
   and an orange ; brass and silver ; a ship and a motor car.
Year 12. *Giving similarities ; three things.*
Procedure : As for Year 8, with the following groups of words : rose,
   potato, tree ; snake, cow, sparrow ; penny, piece of wire, knife-
   blade ; wool, cotton, leather ; book, teacher, newspaper.
[For a discussion of the reasons why children find it easier to give differences than similarities, see *The Psychology of Infancy*, V. Hazlitt, pp. 99–103
(Methuen, 1933).]

8. Investigate how children of different ages describe pictures. Use one
picture and say : Look at this picture and tell me all about it.
   For a similar Binet test, see Terman, *op. cit.*
   Binet distinguishes the following stages of development :
Year 3.   Enumeration of objects.
Year 7.   Enumeration and description.
Year 12. Interpretation.

9. Investigate how children's power of comprehension develops. This
can be done conveniently by giving the following Binet tests. The ages
given are the mental ages at which each type of test can be passed :
Year 4.   What must you do when you are sleepy ?
   What ought you to do when you are cold ?
   What ought you to do when you are hungry ?
Year 6.   What ought you to do if it is raining when you start to school ?
   What ought you to do if you find that your house is on fire ?
   What ought you to do if you are going somewhere and miss your bus ?
Year 8.   What ought you to do when you have broken something which
   belongs to someone else ?
   What ought you to do when you notice on your way to school that you
   are in danger of being late ? What ought you to do if a playmate
   hits you without meaning to do it ?
Year 10. What ought you to say when someone asks your opinion
   about a person you don't know very well ?
   What ought you to do before beginning something very important ?
   Why should we judge a person more by his actions than by his words ?

REFERENCES FOR READING

Handbook of Suggestions for Teachers, New Edition, 1937, chapter XI.
Education, Sir T. Percy Nunn, chapter XIV.
Modern Psychology and Education, Sturt and Oakden, chapters X, XIV.
Groundwork of Educational Psychology, J. S. Ross, chapter III.
Instinct, Intelligence and Character, Godfrey H. Thomson, chapters XII, XIII.
Experimental Education, R. R. Rusk, chapters V, VI, and pp. 129-132.
The Process of Learning, C. Bloor, chapters VI, VII.

ADDITIONAL REFERENCES

Outline of Psychology, Wm. McDougall, chapters VIII, XV (Methuen, 1923).
The Nature of " Intelligence " and the Principles of Cognition, C. Spearman, chapters XV, XVI (Macmillan, 1923).
Mental Life, B. Edgell, chapters VI, VII (Methuen, 1926).
Aspects of Child Life and Education, G. Stanley Hall, " The Contents of Children's Minds " (Ginn, 1912).

ESSAYS AND DISCUSSIONS

1. Mention six important concepts that influence your work as a teacher. Choose one and outline its development in your own mind.

2. How would you help children to develop the following concepts ? area ; climate ; pressure ; parliament ; honesty.

3. The sentence method and the phonic method of teaching children to read.

4. Methods of developing children's vocabulary.

5. The values and limitations of sense-training.

CHAPTER VII

ATTENDING AND OBSERVING

A TEACHER is teaching only when the children are learning and in order to learn children must attend. A good teacher, therefore, must know not merely the subject-matter he has to teach but also how to present it in such a way that the children will attend to it. When children attend they adopt a mental attitude of alertness; they listen, watch, think, ask questions. This attitude is accompanied by certain unmistakable bodily signs; alertness is expressed both in general posture and in facial expression; concentration is shown by an absence of fidgetiness, and, in fact, of any activity that would distract. It has been observed that when people are attending very intently, even their breathing is shallow, a fact that is reflected in the common phrase, " breathless attention." There are, however, individual differences in the bodily accompaniments of attention, and wise teachers will recognize this fact by allowing individuals to depart in minor ways from conventional postures when a class is showing rapt attention. It should be noted, however, that something can be done to help children to attend by training them in habits of suitable bodily posture. It is, for example, sometimes advisable to start work with young children by very brief exhortations to sit up and look ; with older children, the habit of sitting up when an oral lesson is about to begin should be established and such exhortations should no longer be necessary. There are other occasions when it may be advisable to rely on the intrinsic interest of the lesson to catch and hold children's attention ; on these occasions, the lesson is started and the right bodily postures follow as a matter of course.

In chapter II we learned that all children are born ready to pay attention. They are instinctively interested in, and therefore ready to attend to, such stimuli as sudden noises, a frustration of their movements, or a sensation of falling. We also learned that during the first year of life many other natural interests make their appearance, for example, interests in hidden things, in strange things, in building materials, and so on. When children are a year old they are therefore ready by nature to attend to a large variety of stimuli. All these natural interests were, in the history of the race, biologically useful, for they made children attend to those objects in their environment that really mattered to them in their struggle for survival. But life in a civilized community of to-day is more than a mere fight for survival and it demands our attention to objects that matter for other reasons than their mere survival value. Furthermore, many of those objects of attention that once had a survival value are now relatively unimportant.

We see, therefore, that we do not need to teach children to attend, for they can already attend by nature, and a wise teacher will, in the course of his daily work, exploit this natural tendency to the full. However, some of the things, like arithmetic and sewing, to which we want children to attend are not so naturally interesting as some primitive occupations, such as climbing and chasing. Herein lies a problem—how can we help children in school to attend to the more or less sophisticated activities that are necessary for modern life, and how can we help them to control their impulses to attend to the more attractive primitive activities that were necessities of life for their forbears?

As we have implied above, there is an intimate connexion between attending and being interested. We can look upon each of our interests as a permanent readiness to attend to particular stimuli, and it is important to remember that even when we are not attending to one of those stimuli our interest in it still exists. Against this theory it may be objected that we often have to attend to a subject in which we are not interested. This is true, but if we enquire further into our behaviour, we find that our motive for attending is still interest. We are not interested in the subject itself, but we have some other interest which can only be satisfied if we attend to this subject. The relation here between interest and attention is indirect but none the less real. Thus we attend to a distasteful examination subject because we are interested in the examination result. Our real direct interest is an instinctive interest—fear of public opinion, fear of economic distress, an interest in surpassing our fellows, an interest in fighting difficulties. This is the answer to our problem of how to help children to attend in school to those topics that are, either absolutely or relatively, not intrinsically interesting. We must put such topics into a setting that will arouse instinctive interest. Thus, for example, a boy interested in making a model will attend keenly to the necessary mathematical problems—the same problems which in a conventional textbook have most likely bored him. The same immediate result might have been obtained by a very different method. The boy might have been given the textbook problems with a threat of punishment if they were not done. In this case he would attend, but instead of the motive being the positive instinctive interest in construction, it would be the negative instinctive interest in avoiding pain. The ultimate results would obviously be very different. The boy who pays attention in order to avoid punishment is likely to look upon mathematics as a possible cause of trouble, and is on the way to acquiring a real distaste for mathematics. On the other hand, the boy who pays attention because he wants to make his model, looks upon mathematics as a source of satisfaction, and is on the way to acquiring a new interest in addition to his primitive interest in construction—an interest in mathematics itself.

When, therefore, we appeal to instinctive interests in order to help children to pay attention to subjects that are not in themselves interesting it is desirable to avoid negative instinctive interests such as those arising from fear, and to use positive ones such as interests in construction, curiosity, or self-assertion. Then not only shall we help children to attend to what is relatively uninteresting, but we shall also encourage the development of new interests. Thus we shall extend the range of things to which children are ready to pay attention.

It is sometimes objected that if we give children interesting work, or if we present work so as to arouse interest, we are depriving them of valuable training, the discipline of hard work and the discipline of having to attend to what is not interesting. Consider first the question of working hard. If it were really true that children did not work hard when they were interested this would be a very serious objection, but a moment's reflection will assure us that this is not so. The child who tries and tries again is the one who is interested in what he is doing ; the child who quickly gives up is the one who is not interested in his work. By giving children interesting work we are making it possible for them to work hard at their work instead of working hard at keeping their minds off other more interesting matters. In interesting work the effort goes into the work ; in uninteresting work the effort goes largely into the attending. It is as well here to remind ourselves that children are not interested in work that is too easy. In fact, the challenge conveyed by confronting them with something difficult is often a good method of inciting them to attend. The second objection to interesting work was that the children were missing the excellent disciplinary value of having to attend to something that made no appeal to them. If this were true the objection would be a serious one, but the fact is that we cannot entirely cut out all uninteresting work. Even the most interesting job has its moments of drudgery. We may enjoy making a dress, but thoroughly detest the stage of putting on the fasteners. Our keenness to finish the dress will help us to attack this dull job wholeheartedly so that we shall be getting practice in a very useful habit, the habit of attacking our work, whatever it may be, with vigour. We see here one of the dangers of not presenting work to children in an interesting way. They are liable to develop a habit of attacking their work in a lifeless, spiritless way and of never expecting that the work will eventually become interesting.

Reasons for Attending

In many books on psychology statements will be found to the effect that there are different kinds of attention. Attention is, for example, sometimes classified as volitional and non-volitional, the distinction being whether the attention is sustained by an act of will or not. Other psychologists distinguish between voluntary, non-voluntary and involuntary attention. Voluntary attention corresponds to volitional attention, that is to say, it is sustained by an act of will.[1] Non-voluntary and involuntary attention are sub-divisions of non-volitional attention. Both types are sustained by direct instinctive interest, but an act of involuntary attention is characterized by the fact that it is in opposition to the person's dominant interest of the moment. For example, the attention we give to a fascinating novel is non-voluntary. If, while we are reading, a door slams, our attention is diverted from the reading and given to the noise. The latter kind of attention is called involuntary.

Beginners are advised, however, to avoid as far as possible speaking or writing of attention as if it were an entity in itself. It is much clearer to think of children attending than to think of acts of attention that children perform. If we do this the above classifications are seen to be nothing more than statements of the various reasons why children attend, and there is no reason to speak of different kinds of attention. This is, for teachers, a much more profitable way of looking at the subject and it will prevent us from ever making absurd references to children "using this or that kind of attention." When, in any given situation, we consider why children are attending the following questions will be helpful :

1. Are the children attending because they have a direct natural interest in the subject ?—

   E.g. young children engrossed in making a self-chosen model.

[1] It will be seen that a psychologist uses the word voluntary in a special sense as being equivalent to volitional. It must not be confused with the everyday use of the word.

2. Are they attending because they have an indirect natural interest in the subject ?—

   E.g. children working hard at arithmetic for competitive purposes.

3. Are they attending because they have a direct acquired interest in the subject ?—

   E.g. children working hard at arithmetic for the sheer joy of the work.

4. Are they attending because they have an indirect acquired interest in the subject ?—

   E.g. children working hard at arithmetic because their self-respect compels them.

In many situations it will be found that a child is attending for more than one of the above reaasons. For instance, when a child is engaged in making an interesting model in any form of craft lesson, he attends to the work because of his direct natural interest in construction ; because of his indirect natural interest in self-assertion ; because of his direct acquired interest in the particular craft which has resulted from previous experience of it, and because of his indirect acquired interest in himself as a person who produces good work.

DIVISION OF ATTENTION

The following experiment will help us to give an answer to the question " Can we attend to two things at once ? "

1st minute : Write the alphabet backwards from z to a as many times as you can. Count the number of letters you have written.

2nd minute : Count 1, 4, 7, continuing to add 3 each time. Write down the number you reach.

3rd minute : Rest.

4th minute : Write the alphabet backwards and count in threes at the same time. Keep both activities going. Do not switch from one to the other. Write down the last figure you say and count the letters you have written.

Compare the amount achieved in the last minute period with the results of the first and second periods.

Most people after this bewildering experience need no statistical evidence that they cannot attend to two things at once even for a minute. However, it is worth while looking at the results to see what they show. If we could really attend to two things at once for a minute we should expect to see as much work done in the fourth minute as in the first two minutes together. If we have attended to both activities together at any time during the fourth minute we should expect the work done to be more than half the work done in the first two minutes. Most people find they accomplish less than half. That is to say, they have actually lost time by trying to attend to two things at once.

When people are apparently successful in attending to two things at once their success can be explained in one of the following ways :

1. They have combined the two things so as to make them one. It has been shown by experiment that we can attend to five or six separate dots on a card provided they are near enough together to be seen all at once. They then constitute for us one group of irregularly arranged dots. Five or six appears to be the limit for adults if the arrangement is irregular. If, however, the dots are arranged in a pattern, as on playing cards, the group can be much larger. Similar results are found with the number of auditory stimuli that we can apprehend at one time.

2. They are attending first to one thing then to the other with great rapidity. People differ very much in their ability to do this. Some people seem naturally to attend with great concentration, becoming absorbed in what they are doing, and oblivious of all that is going on around them. The range of their attention, at any one moment, is therefore small. Many great men of science belong to this type. Other people seem able to attend to many things in quick succession. They can attend over a wide range, a very useful accomplishment for mothers, teachers and business

men. Such differences, which seem to be more a matter of temperament than of intelligence, are noticeable even in children of school age, and form a strong argument for some measure of individual work. It is obvious, too, that when choice of occupation is being considered these differences are very important. Some occupations call for intensive attending, others for distributed.

3. They may be doing two things at once but they are not attending to them both. One of their activities has become automatic, and so can be carried on without any attention. We can *do* a great many things at once if all or all but one, are automatic ; but we cannot attend to two or more separate things at once. It is important to remember that activities that are automatic for us are no: necessarily automatic for children. For example, when we express our ideas in writing we can let the writing take care of itself and attend to the ideas. Young children cannot do this. With them both the writing and the ideas must be attended to. If they try to do both at once one or both will suffer in the process. Teachers will get some idea of the demands such work makes upon children if they will try to write an essay in copper-plate handwriting, or, assuming that they are not expert typists, if they will try to compose directly when using a typewriter. They will find that the level of their composition, and perhaps of their spelling, is decidedly lower than usual.

CONTINUITY OF ATTENTION

How long can we continue attending to the same object ? We often say we have concentrated our attention on a particular problem for an hour or two. A little reflection, however, will show us that the object of our attention was by no means the same throughout. We attended now to one aspect of our problem, now to another. We attended to the statement, to the given data, to possible solutions, to the conclusions we reached ; we had been attending not to the same object but to a constantly changing one.

The fact that we cannot attend to a simple object for any length of time without a break can be easily demonstrated in the following ways :

(*a*) Listen to a watch ticking in a quiet room. Place the watch so that the sound is just perceptible. (If necessary, wrap the watch in a cloth to deaden the sound.)

The sound apparently fades away at intervals. This phenomenon is of course due to the fact that we are not attending continuously.

(*b*) Concentrate your gaze on the accompanying figure.

The apparent changes from a convex to a concave solid are due to fluctuations of attention.

Experimenters have found that we cannot attend to simple objects like those used in the above experiments for

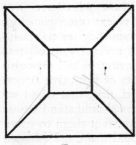

FIG. 3.

more than 5 or 6 seconds at a time. At the end of this short period we cease attending to the simple object and we attend to some competing stimulus.

If we want children to attend to a subject we must arrange that the subject does change : we must suggest new points of view ; we must introduce an illustration ; we must vary the form of activity. Oral lessons, for example, must be broken up into short periods during which children listen, look at pictures, write notes, read books, ask questions.

Even with a changing object our attention is not continuous. If we are engaged on a problem for an hour or two there are moments when we attend to the room in which we are working, to the thought of what we will do when the problem is finished, or to the recollection of some interesting news we have recently heard. These interruptions are only temporary because our interest in the problem is so great that we return to it again. If we come to a standstill with our problem, if we find that we can develop it no further, it is likely that one of these so-called interruptions will become a more lasting object of our attention. It will be seen then that the length of time for which, with minor fluctuations, we can attend to a particular object will depend on how long we can continue to get new views, new ideas. This depends very largely on our previous knowledge about the object. We are not surprised to learn, therefore, that children need more frequent change of occupation than adults.

Young children are interested in activity and in concrete objects rather than in ideas, and so they attend more readily when there is something to see, hear, taste, touch or smell. When they do try to attend to the ideas of other people as expressed in words they find it necessary to reinforce the listening by looking at or touching the speaker. Very young children give only fleeting attention to voices heard on a gramophone or wireless, and those who have progressed sufficiently to listen so such voices often get close to the instrument and gaze at it. When they try to attend to their own ideas they often find it necessary to express them aloud in words, a form of behaviour which has also been observed among even the adults of primitive tribes. The practical application of this fact is, first, that when we want children to attend to our ideas we should stand where they can see us, and, second, when we want them to listen to us for any length of time we should make use of such concrete aids as gestures, illustrations, models and blackboard summaries.

THE EFFECT OF DISTRACTIONS

During oral lessons it is sometimes necessary to recall the attention of individuals who are attending to distracting stimuli, for example, to a fly on the window-pane or to their own day-dreams. This recalling should be done unobtrusively and if possible without breaking the continuity of the instruction ; a look or a question is often enough. Nothing is more likely to make children inattentive than teaching punctuated at frequent intervals by petty admonitions. Other distracting influences are one's own sensations. Thus a person in ill-health, or a person placed in an uncomfortable position will find it difficult to attend to anything else. The same is true to some extent when the position is luxuriously comfortable.

Children are more likely to be affected by distractions than adults are, but there are wide individual differences among both adults and children. Some people, not necessarily those who generally find it difficult to concentrate, are seriously handicapped by any kind of noise. Carlyle, working in his sound-proof room, is a good example. Other people, however, seem actually to benefit by a moderate amount of distraction. They make a great effort to compensate for the distraction and as a result they concentrate even more effectively than they otherwise would have done. It is probable, however, that prolonged work under such conditions will cause strain and irritation. Loud, intermittent noises appear to be the most distracting; low steady noise, on the other hand, may become part of the background of work and cause little, if any, trouble to the worker.[1]

Teachers vary considerably in their reactions to noise made by children in the classroom. Some are unperturbed by it while others are irritated. The criterion we ought to adopt is a simple one ; is the noise preventing the pupils from attending to the work in hand or is it the natural and inevitable result of useful activity ?

ATTRACTING ATTENTION

When we accuse a child of being inattentive we mean that he is not attending to our lesson ; we do not mean that he is not attending to anything. The fact is, that during his waking life, a child is always attending to something, but, as we have learnt, he cannot attend to two things at

---

[1] See pamphlet, *Noise and School Buildings*, issued by the Anti-Noise League, 66 Victoria St., London, S.W.1.
See also *The Problem of Noise*, F. C. Bartlett (Camb. Univ. Press, 1934)

once. When a child attends to one thing it follows that he must be inattentive to many other things.

In school we often want children to stop attending to one thing and to begin attending to something else. We want them to stop talking among themselves, or to stop doing practical work and listen to a general order. In everyday language, we say we want to " attract their attention." If we give our order without warning, some children will not be able to attend to it because they will still be attending to the task in hand. We therefore ring a bell, rap on the desk, or even shout, so making use of the children's inborn readiness to attend to loud noises. Then we make some such remark as " Stop work, and listen to me." After this preparation the children are ready to attend to the order. Inexperienced teachers are often inclined to neglect this important step of attracting children's attention. They then find it necessary to resort to the expedient of repeating their orders, maybe several times. The result is that children soon develop the undesirable habit of not attending to any order the first time it is given.

It should be noticed that bell-ringing and desk-rapping are used simply as methods of attracting attention. The children attend to the teacher as the maker of the noise, but unless he goes on to arouse deeper interests they will quickly return to their former occupation or to something else that to them seems worth while.

Sometimes we want to make sure that children attend to a particular impression such as a heading on a blackboard, an important word in a sentence, or an important fact in a lecture. Here we make use of the fact that children are naturally interested in something different, in something that contrasts with their own previous experience or something that contrasts with the background on which it is placed. Such contrasts can be obtained in many ways—by the use of coloured chalks, underlining, italics, gestures or spoken emphasis. It should be noted that emphasis in speech can be obtained in a variety of ways, by speaking loudly, emphatically, solemnly, slowly, softly and so on.

It is interesting in connexion with methods of attracting attention to study popular adevertisements with a view to deciding why they are so effective in compelling us to attend to them.

OBSERVING

We have seen that attending depends on interest. A good observer, however, needs more than an interest in his subject. A boy and his mother may both be intensely interested in a new locomotive, but the probability is that the boy will observe much more about it than his mother does. Where she sees just a locomotive, he sees a locomotive of a particular class. He quickly observes the special features of this class, for he has, as it were, a ready-made plan to direct his observing. As compared with his mother he observes essentials in a systematic way. Again, where his mother sees a certain number of wheels, which she probably has to count, he sees a pattern of wheels and knows how many there are without counting. The boy attends to the engine in a more effective way than his mother because his previous knowledge helps him to observe groups of related facts instead of isolated ones. Not only is the mother observing these isolated facts unsystematically, but she is also trying to memorize them. The boy, however, is merely recognizing parts ; he is not memorizing them. In this recognition he is greatly helped by the fact that he knows the names for the parts. One word is enough to label the part for him while his mother has first to find the words to describe the parts and then to rely on this more or less " wordy " description.[1]

The boy does not even need to get a clear and complete view of each part before he recognizes it. He would say, for instance, that he saw the steam dome, whereas actually he inferred that it was there from the small part of it that

[1] See *Educational Psychology*, C. Fox, pp. 56–74. Fox describes some interesting experiments the results of which emphasize the importance for accurate observation of well-assimilated knowledge both of subject-matter and of terminology.

he saw. The amount that we can observe seems to depend largely on the meaning we can read into our impressions;[1] extent of knowledge is more important than acuity of vision. We observe what we know. The Red Indian in his native woods observes much more than the white man does, not because his eyesight is better, but because his relevant knowledge is greater. This principle has many applications in school work. Children are unobservant more often because they lack knowledge than because their eyesight is defective. They fail to notice the large variety of wild flowers in our hedgerows because they know neither the flowers nor their names ; they do not observe exactly how the craft teacher holds his tools until they have had some instruction in tool manipulation ; inexperienced users of a microscope often have to be shown a picture of what they ought to see before they can actually see it.

The ability to read meaning into an experience occasionally leads us into error. When we " see " a human figure where there is really only a coat hanging on the door, we are interpreting wrongly. We are suffering from an illusion. In certain emotional states we are very prone to suffer from illusions. When we are afraid we are often uncritical and ready to jump to conclusions. When we are anxiously waiting for a friend we see him many times before he actually arrives. When we are anxious not to observe a certain fact we are very likely to overlook it. As the proverb says, " None so blind as those who won't see." Trained observers are aware of these dangers. They therefore try to separate observed facts from inferred facts, and they are constantly on guard lest their fondness for their own theories should lead them to ignore facts that do not agree with those theories.

Much of the unreliability of evidence is due to similar causes. Some witnesses are untrustworthy, not because

---

[1] In all our seeing, hearing, tasting, etc., there is a good deal of interpreting. Psychologists recognize this fact by applying the word " sensation " to the mere result of stimulating a sense organ, and by using another word, " perception " for what we should ordinarily call seeing, hearing, etc.

they are deliberately untruthful or because they cannot see and hear well, but because they cannot distinguish between the facts that they observe and the inferences that they draw from them. Some again fail to give true evidence because they are unaware of the effects of their prejudices. Prejudice may make them observe some things while remaining blind to others, and it may then colour the interpretation of the facts they do observe. As we might expect, little children are often very unreliable in giving evidence, and teachers should be aware of this so that, on the one hand, they make discriminating use of children's evidence, and, on the other hand, they do not hastily accuse a child of being untruthful.

Applying the above considerations to school work, it follows that if we want to train children to be good observers we must pay attention to the following principles :

1. *Good observing is facilitated by the efficient use of sense organs.*

As we have seen, the possession of good sense organs will not of itself make a child a good observer. It is obvious, however, that defective sense organs may be a severe handicap. It is important, therefore, to take care that children who suffer from defective hearing or vision sit in the front of the class, and that children for whom spectacles have been prescribed wear them regularly.

The fact that we must have sense organs of some kind in order to observe has led some teachers to suggest that practice in using sense organs would be valuable as a means of training good observers. As far as we know, sensory acuity depends more on endowment than on training and cannot be improved to any marked extent by practice. Even if such an improvement could be effected it would not necessarily bring with it an improvement in observing. When we observe, we see with our " mind's eye " as well as with our bodily eye, and provided that the bodily eye is reasonably efficient, we shall be more successful if we seek improvement along mental rather than along physical lines.

2. *Good observing depends upon interests.*

We have seen that observing depends to some extent on interests. People whose interests are very narrow may be good observers but only in a very limited field, so limited in fact that for ordinary practical purposes we call them unobservant. We are all familiar with stories of learned men who are oblivious of changes in their environment, even such sudden changes as oncoming traffic or holes in the pavement. If we want to make our pupils good observers in a wide field we must help them to develop wide and varied interests in people as well as in things, interest in art as well as in science, interest in other countries as well as their own, interests in the future as well as in the past and the present.

It might be objected that, even so, observing will be limited and children will still fail to observe many things in their environment. Would it not be better to try to develop in them an interest in observing itself, so that they would become generally observant, and go about ready and eager to observe anything and everything, from the number of newsagents' shops in a particular street to the types and colours of motor-cars waiting outside the station? Expressed in this way, the suggestion is seen to be unworkable. We cannot observe everything. We must select. If we observe those things in which we are interested the selection is systematic and orderly; we observe only those things that have meaning and value for us. If, however, we observe for the sake of observing the selection is haphazard or, as often happens, it is governed merely by the strength of the stimulus we receive; consequently we observe many things that are meaningless and of little or no value to us.

When children are observing the results of experiments in science it is very important that they should select the relevant points and neglect all others. They will do this if they are interested in these points, and that is why science teachers should take particular care that pupils understand the purpose of experiments before they are performed.

Teachers should, of course, be careful not to tell pupils beforehand the result of an experiment. Children do not in this case need to know precisely what to look for, but they do need to know the type of thing to look for so that they look intelligently and do not merely stare.

The same principle applies to the conduct of educational visits. If properly organized, these visits are not occasions for mere indiscriminate sight-seeing ; the children have a grasp of the main purposes of the visit before they start and as a result they select the things relevant to this purpose. They observe intelligently. The child who observes things in which he is interested may be compared to a magnet that gathers iron filings to itself, but neglects non-magnetic material. The child who observes anything and everything is like the vacuum cleaner that collects all particles regardless of their nature. The analogy can safely be taken a little further. The magnet, having collected the filings, magnetizes them and holds them ; the vacuum cleaner exerts no power on the dust that it collects and easily lets it slip away again. So with the child. He assimilates those facts that are important to him ; they become part of him and he can usually reproduce them when required. He can, however, do nothing with unrelated facts collected indiscriminately ; they are like lumber, unorganized and difficult to find when wanted.

3. *Good observing depends upon knowledge.*

As we have seen, knowledge is another aid to observing. Knowledge of the type of thing to look for is generally helpful ; sometimes knowledge of precisely what to expect is necessary. In addition to these types of knowledge we also need knowledge of words. The knowledge of the necessary vocabulary enables children to express what they observe, to describe it accurately, and consequently to remember it easily. Children who know the technical names for the parts of flowers will be better observers of a new flower than those who lack this knowledge.

The close connexion between language and observing

is recognized in the teaching of English. Exercises in careful observing form the basis of very useful lessons, for they force children to search for the exact words to describe what they observe and thus to become conscious of many fine distinctions of meaning among words in common use. It is, for example, a fascinating exercise to listen to the sounds made by water moving in various ways and then to find words to describe the sounds observed.

If knowledge is to make children observant, it must not be the conventional knowledge that is learnt by heart from text-books; it must be knowledge that has direct points of contact with the children's environment. Children who learn history exclusively from conventional text-books are likely to be less observant of the historical significance of things around them than children whose history lessons are supplemented by educational visits. Children who learn academic science in laboratories will be less observant of the scientific phenomena in their ordinary surroundings than children whose science lessons are closely connected with everyday life.

4. *Good observing depends upon a respect for accuracy.*

It is a good plan to require children to give an account of what they have observed, for it is an effective way of developing in them a habit of observing carefully. The reports are also helpful because they enable teachers to check the accuracy of children's observations, to correct any misapprehensions, and to call attention to any important facts that have been overlooked. In this way children will gradually learn that accuracy is important, and they may in time develop something of the attitude of the man of science who preserves an open mind about the facts he observes and who is aware of the danger of being swayed by prejudice.

LISTENING

The term " observing " is usually applied to seeing and looking. Exactly the same principles operate when knowledge is gained through any of the other senses. A child who uses his eyes well is called a good observer ; a child who uses his ears well is called a good listener, and so on. In order to develop good listeners we must apply the same principles that we laid down for training good observers. It should be noted that training in listening is no less important than training in observing, and school life provides many opportunities. Children should be trained to listen to orders, to questions, to short lectures. A very useful exercise for training children to listen is dictation, and it should be noted that the reproduction may be either oral or written. Sentences, couplets, verses should be dictated as wholes, and as children grow older and more proficient the exercises should be made more difficult so that a real effort to remember is required. If teachers want to train children to listen, they should be careful to develop a habit of speaking no more loudly than is necessary for children to hear. We do not turn a limelight on everything we wish children to observe ; we ought not to shout everything to which we wish children to listen.

Wireless lessons provide excellent training in listening, and the conduct of such lessons provides a clear illustration of the application of the four principles we have suggested for training in observing.

Wireless lessons.—Good reception is clearly the first essential. The children should be comfortably seated in a quiet room free from distractions, for it is clear that distractions are more harmful to listeners than to observers. Generally speaking children should be allowed to concentrate on the single act of listening. The writing of notes on the blackboard should be reduced to a minimum and as a rule the writing of notes by the children should not be encouraged. There are, however, individual differences, and some older pupils find note-making an aid to concentration.

Some wireless lecturers are very clever at creating a natural atmosphere ; they talk so intimately to their unseen audiences that each pupil feels that he is being addressed personally. Nevertheless, pupils listening to wireless lessons are bound to miss the stimulus of the teacher's presence ; they miss the variety of gesture and facial expression that ordinarily helps to keep them attending. Intrinsic interest and relevant knowledge are therefore particularly important in this type of lesson and some special preparation is generally desirable. Unless the pupils come with at least a background of appropriate ideas, the wireless lecturer has little hope of holding their attention for the twenty minutes that is the usual length of wireless lessons. From the point of view of interest, the lecturer has one valuable asset ; being a specialist or a person with intimate first-hand knowledge of his subject he is usually able to present striking facts that of themselves arrest and hold the children's attention. The wireless lesson should never aim at giving an ordinary lesson that could be given by a teacher who has studied books ; it should provide something that teachers cannot give.

Our fourth principle—respect for accuracy—is also important. The lesson should be followed by some work designed to test its effects and to remove misapprehensions. There need be no fear that such " following-up " will kill enthusiasm ; on the contrary, experience shows that pupils rapidly improve in their powers of listening if the results are regularly tested, and that they experience pleasure as a result of this increased power.

CONCLUSION

It is commonly asserted that some particular subject or type of training is valuable for developing " attention," " concentration " or " observation." It is interesting to note that there is no abstract noun corresponding to " listening," and consequently we are forced to write, talk and think not of training the faculty that enables children to listen but of training *children*. We are not tempted to think of " listening " as a faculty that exists by itself. We can train listeners but not listening. Despite the common use of abstract nouns the same is psychologically true of " attention," " concentration " and " observation." They are not faculties that can be trained. As we have seen, the factor that determines in any given situation whether children attend, concentrate or observe is not their possession of well-trained faculties but the whole situation—the habits, ideals, interest and previous knowledge of the children on the one hand, the nature of the subject-matter on the other hand.

It cannot be too often reiterated that teachers have to deal with children and not with psychologists' abstractions. In order to keep this fact clearly in mind, beginners are advised to avoid as far as possible the use of such words as " attention," " observation " and " concentration."[1] The words " attending," " obeserving " and " concentrating " are safer, for they at least remind us that we are dealing with living beings. The best plan of all, however, is to use the common nouns, " observers " or " listeners," or alternatively to use adjectives and to speak of " attentive " or " observant " children. The more we keep " children " in the forefront of our psychological discussions, the less likely we shall be to indulge in foolish talk or futile practice.[2]

OBSERVATIONS AND EXPERIMENTS

1. For an experiment on division of attention, see page 104.
2. For experiments on fluctuation of attention, see page 106.
3. Observe a class of young children doing practical work under free conditions.

Notice individual differences in attending as shown in (a) length of time

---

[1] As we shall see in subsequent chapters, the same advice applies to such words as " association," " imagination " and " memory."

[2] The danger of using abstract nouns is well described by Quiller-Couch : ". . . push your suspicions out among the whole cloudy host of abstract terms. ' How excellent a thing is sleep,' sighed Sancho Panza ; ' it wraps a man round like a cloak '—an excellent example, by the way, of how to say a thing concretely : a Jargoneer would have said that ' among the beneficial qualities of sleep its capacity for withdrawing the human consciousness from the contemplation of immediate circumstances may perhaps be accounted not the least remarkable.' How vile a thing—shall we say ?— is the abstract noun ! It wraps a man's thoughts round like cotton wool." *On the Art of Writing*, p. 79 (Camb. Univ. Press, 1917).

E

devoted to one occupation, (*b*) number of objects attended to in a given period, say 15 minutes, (*c*) readiness to be distracted.

4. Make a list of the subjects to which you attend most easily. Compare your list with a friend's list and try to account for the differences.

5. Examine children's accounts of an educational visit.

Analyse the accounts to show (*a*) facts that were noticed by all the children, (*b*) facts noticed only by certain individuals. Try to account for the common interests and the individual differences.

6. Observe a wireless lesson.

Notice : (*a*) preparation ; (*b*) fluctuations in attention due to (i) environment, (ii) subject-matter, (iii) lecturer's style ; (*c*) subsequent work.

7. Observe a class at work during a session.

Note the methods used (*a*) to attract attention, (*b*) to hold attention. Note also distracting influences.

8. Practise compiling and writing blackboard summaries designed to attract and hold attention. Get your effects by good arrangement, careful and restrained selection, bold headings, underlining, use of coloured chalks.

9. Teachers in charge of practical classes need to be observant. A knowledge of important points to be kept under observation will be a great help. Make a list of such points for one of the following : (*a*) science room, (*b*) craft room, (*c*) domestic subjects room.

10. Observe a child who is exceptionally " inattentive " in school. Note the things to which he attends.

11. For further experiments on attention see *An Introduction to Experimental Psychology*, C. W. Valentine (Univ. Tut. Press, 1913).

REFERENCES FOR READING

Modern Psychology and Education, Sturt and Oakden, chapter XI.
Groundwork of Educational Psychology, J. S. Ross, chapter X.
Experimental Education, R. R. Rusk, chapter IV.
Educational Psychology, C. Fox, chapter III.
A Primer of Teaching Practice, Green and Birchenough, chapter VI.
Instinct, Intelligence and Character, Godfrey H. Thomson, chapter XV.
Psychology and Practical Life, Collins and Drever, chapter IX.

ADDITIONAL REFERENCES

Outline of Psychology, Wm. McDougall, chapter IX (Methuen, 1923)
Herbartian Psychology, J. Adams, chapter VI (Heath, n.d.).
The Psychology of Study, C. A. Mace, chapter II (Methuen, 1932).

ESSAYS AND DISCUSSIONS

1. Discuss educational visits from the point of view of observing.

(*Consider :* (*a*) preparation ; (*b*) the visit ; (*c*) subsequent work.)

2. Discuss the effect of making an effort to attend on (*a*) output of work, (*b*) development of character.

3. Discuss methods of training children to be attentive.

(*Consider :* habit, interest and knowledge.)

4. It is often said that " Nature Study trains the powers of observation." Criticize this statement.

CHAPTER VIII

IMAGING

MENTAL images are reproductions of sense experiences. They differ from these sense experiences, or percepts, in being less vivid and striking, in being less stable, and in being detached from the world around us. People vary very much in the vividness of their imagery, and the same person varies from time to time according to his interest in the original experience and according to his state of health. Feverish patients and highly nervous people do sometimes have such vivid imagery that they find it difficult to distinguish between images and percepts, but we regard their conditional as pathological ; we say they are suffering from hallucinations.

Kinds of Images.—Try to get images of the following kinds :

1. Visual, e.g., Your bedroom, a friend, a motor-car.
2. Auditory, e.g., A tune, the shriek of an engine, the barking of a dog.
3. Kinæsthetic (or motor), e.g., Writing your name, striking a ball, carrying a heavy weight.
4. Tactile (or cutaneous), e.g., The feel of velvet, the irritation of rough wool, the feel of sand between your toes.
5. Gustatory, e.g., The taste of vinegar, of porridge, of oranges.
6. Olfactory, e.g., The smell of hay, of paint, of roses.
7. Organic, e.g., Toothache, thirst, drowsiness.

Investigation has shown that most people are able, if necessary, to get all kinds of imagery, just as most people can experience all kinds of sensations. When, however, their spontaneous imagery is investigated they appear to show a preference for one kind or another, but as a rule not such a strong preference for one kind of imagery as to exclude all other kinds. Those who show a strong preference for visual images are generally called visiles. Similarly, we speak of audiles, motiles and tactiles. A teacher who has some predominant preference for one kind of imagery is very apt to attach too much value to teaching methods in which his favourite type of image is used. In considering the use of imagery in school, it is therefore very important to bear in mind that in this, as in all mental processes, there are individual differences among the children we teach.

Many visual, auditory and kinæsthetic images are images of words rather than of objects. These verbal images are more common in adults than in children. Many people who at first think they use little or no imagery find, on introspecting, that they use a good deal of verbal imagery.

The use of imagery.—Most people can improve their imagery by practice, and this is certainly worth doing. Teachers should not only train pupils, in appropriate circumstances, to form relevant images, but they should also seek by practice to develop their own powers of imagery. If a teacher has a clear visual image of the scene or process he is describing, he will tend to use vivid, colourful words that attract and interest the children ; he will tend to use concrete terms that children understand, and which in their turn arouse images in the children's minds.[1] Similarly when reading descriptive literature to a class it is helpful to form mental images, and to look upon the reading as a process of presenting a cinematograph picture.

We often use imagery when we try to *remember* some-

[1] It is interesting to note, as Thomson points out, that vividness of speech and comprehension can be improved if we let our minds dwell on the original picture which words convey, e.g. *consideration*, a consulting of the stars ; *companions*, people who break bread together.

"There is no great fear," Thomson says, "that an over-cultivation of such imagery would lead to a narrowness of usage—not many are so able to see the pictures their words paint as to be hindered in their thought. Most of us only too soon come to use the words as counters without concrete imagery, a tendency which brings to some the power of generalizing and abstract thinking, but which brings to a greater number only verbosity and parrot-pattering fluency." (*Instinct, Intelligence and Character*, p. 91.)

thing. We ask ourselves, " Did I or did I not post that letter ?" Then perhaps we get a visual image of the red pillar box, or an auditory image of the letter falling into the box, or a motor image of reaching up to the slot, and we remember we did post the letter. If we try to remember the date of an event in history, we may get a visual image of the history chart we used at school or an auditory image of some one saying the date. The fact that imagery is an aid to remembering is one of the reasons why in teaching we should present knowledge through as many senses as possible. In teaching spelling, for example, we spell the word aloud, write it on the blackboard, and require the children to write it themselves either on paper or in the air. When children are engaged in studying a book, we encourage them to write notes[1] and we reinforce the study by oral work of some kind.

When we reproduce past experiences by forming images we are said to be *imaging*. Sometimes, however, we select and combine our images in accordance with a purpose. We are then said to be *imagining*.[2] We are not merely reproducing the past, but we are creating something new.

For example, we may want our pupils to imagine what an Amazon forest is like. We should, of course, first show them a picture, but the children must do a great deal of mental work before they have really imagined what the forest is like. Much of this mental work they do spontaneously as they look at the picture, but in some directions we can usefully help them by comparing the scenes in the picture with the images, not necessarily visual ones only, that they are able to form of trees, woods, overgrown

[1] Adult students differ in their views as to what kind of note is most helpful. Strong visualizers generally prefer notes in diagrammatic form ; they prefer, for example, a genealogical table to a descriptive paragraph.

[2] Some psychologists use the terms " reproductive imagination " and " creative imagination." By " reproductive imagination " they mean the use of imagery in remembering, and by " creative imagination " they mean the use of imagery in order to create something new. In this book we use the terms " imaging " and " remembering " when the activity is mainly reproductive, and the term " imagining " when the activity is mainly creative.

places, twining creepers, hot steamy air, dim light, shafts of sunlight, brightly coloured birds and large insects. Their imaginative understanding of the forest can be still further enriched by reading a graphic account of a journey through an Amazon forest. The children then add to the images suggested by the picture, kinæsthetic images of cutting, struggling and stamping, tactile images of smooth stems and prickly leaves, and organic images of feelings of drowsiness and fatigue. In this way we make it possible for the children to imagine, with some degree of truth, places they have never seen. It is more difficult to help children to imagine events and scenes in ages long ago, but the same principles apply. The successful teacher of history is one who is able to help children vividly to recreate the past.

The vividness of the visual imagery of young children is shown by the remarkable pictures they draw, and many modern teachers use this imagery as a basis for the teaching of drawing. Many psychologists would claim that the visual images of young children are generally pictures possessing real artistic quality. Similar work has also been done in the teaching of composition by getting children to describe their mental pictures.[1]

Imagery is also an aid to the appreciation of literature. If we can call up our own past experience in the form of images, we are able to enter into the feelings of the writer, to enjoy his apt choice of words and to understand his allusions. Experiment has shown, however, that if appreciation is to be real, imagery must come spontaneously. Any laboured attempt to seek or construct an image during the reading detracts from the enjoyment of the passage and destroys its unity. The image can arise spontaneously only if it is the result of past experience. If, therefore, we wish our pupils to enjoy a poem we must first satisfy ourselves that they have the right background of experience, or if necessary, arrange that they get it some time before the poem is read. The time of the reading is not the moment for providing the necessary background. This does not

[1] See *The Child Vision*, Dorothy T. Owen (Longmans, 1920).

mean that the literature that children study should be limited to that which deals directly with their own lives, but that it should have points of contact with their own experience so as to enable them to enter into the new experience imaginatively.

When the poem has been read only once the images may be very vague, even though the children have enjoyed the reading. Here a few questions from the teacher, such as " What can you see ? ", " What did you hear ? ", " Are there any colours in your picture ? " will help the children to develop their images, and make them ready to hear the poem again. On the other hand, questions about the meanings of words may do very little to develop imagery and if used to excess they may spoil the reading which, instead of being an opportunity for lively imagination, becomes merely an occasion for an exercise in vocabulary.

Images are often suggested too by the sounds of the words and the rhythm of the verse. In fact, it is actually possible for children to enjoy and to some extent appreciate a poem without understanding the words at all. If the reading is not good, the proper sounds will not be heard and rhythm will be spoilt, and the children's imagery will be the poorer. Practice in reading the poem or passage is therefore a much more important part of a teacher's preparation for a literature lesson than searching for meanings of words in a dictionary.

Thinking or problem-solving is another mental process in which we use imagery. For example, Betts,[1] in his investigations into imagery, gave his subjects the following problem and found that they all used imagery :

" A squirrel is clinging to one side of a tree, and a man is standing opposite on the other side of the tree. The man walks round the tree, but the squirrel also moves round the tree, so as to keep just out of the man's sight. They continue this movement until each has gone entirely around the tree. Has the man gone round the squirrel

[1] *The Distribution and Function of Mental Imagery*, G. H. Betts (Teachers' College, Columbia University, 1909).

" (a) in the sense of having been in front, behind and on both sides of him ?

" (b) in the sense of having been east, west, north and south of him ? "

Many people find that the most useful kind of imagery in a problem of this kind is diagrammatic rather than pictorial, a representation of relations between objects rather than of the objects themselves. Such an image contains no unnecessary details and helps one to focus attention on the important points. Children are helped to form images of this kind by actually making plans and diagrams as well as pictures.

There is a tendency for the use of imagery, especially pictorial imagery, to decrease with age. Children's thinking is carried on very largely by a succession of pictorial images. Without these images there would be no thinking. Images, however, give rise to ideas, and adult thinking is more a succession of ideas in which images may at times play a very small part. In fact some psychologists consider that it is possible to think without having any images at all. Much of the imaging reported by adults seems merely to accompany the thinking without necessarily helping it. At times imagery may actually hinder thinking. For instance, imagery that is irrelevant to the purpose in mind, or that is unnecessarily detailed, clouds the issue instead of clearing it. There are, however, some problems where the actual percept would facilitate thinking, especially for children, and it is in solving problems of this kind that imagery is certainly useful.[1]

Investigation into the images that children use shows that these images are largely the result of out-of-school

[1] Cf. Kelvin who is reported to have said that he could not understand a theory unless he could make a model of it. On the other hand, when Galton enquired into the imagery of Fellows of the Royal Society he found that they relied more on abstract thinking than on visual imagery. It seems probable that much advanced modern thinking in science is independent of imagery. It is important for teachers to remember, however, that children's thinking, even in science and mathematics, often needs the support of concrete imagery.

experiences ; that is, experiences in which the children were intensely interested, and in which all their senses and a good deal of active movement played a part. Children form images as a result of doing things, not merely by hearing about them. This is one of the strongest arguments in favour of practical work, of " learning by doing." As methods of learning in school approach more nearly to methods of learning out of school we shall find that our pupils are not merely memorizing useful facts, but are developing images and ideas that will help them to understand a problem and to criticize a solution. A little practical work in measuring pints and quarts will do more to improve a child's ability to solve problems about pints and quarts than much repetition of the fact that two pints make one quart. Practical work—whether in the form of practical arithmetic, practical geography, school journeys, or educational visits—consumes time, but if the work is wisely chosen the time spent may be an excellent investment.

OBSERVATIONS AND EXPERIMENTS

1. Read some short passages of descriptive literature and observe the images that arise in your mind. Consider how far they enhance or hinder your appreciation of the passages.
2. When walking in unfamiliar country with the aid of a map try to picture the scenery before you actually see it.
3. Investigate what use you make of images when you remember (a) dates in history, (b) the route to the station, (c) the positions of places on maps, (d) the spelling of difficult words, (e) tables in arithmetic, (f) geometrical constructions, (g) the chemical composition of water.
Compare your results with those obtained by other people.

REFERENCES FOR READING

Modern Psychology and Education, Sturt and Oakden, chapter XIII.
Educational Psychology, C. Fox, chapter IV.
Instinct, Intelligence and Character, Godfrey H. Thomson, chapters IX and X.
Experimental Education, R. R. Rusk, chapter VIII.
The Process of Learning, C. Bloor, chapter VIII.

ADDITIONAL REFERENCES

See footnotes on pages 124, 125.

E*

ESSAYS AND DISCUSSIONS

1. Choose a subject of the curriculum in which you are specially interested. Discuss the use of imagery in connexion with its study.

2. Discuss from the point of view of teaching (a) the advantages, and (b) the dangers of a strong tendency to use visual images.

3. What is a mental image ?
Enumerate the possible kinds of mental images. Choose the three kinds that are of most value in school and illustrate how they can be profitably used.

CHAPTER IX

REMEMBERING AND FORGETTING

WHEN we say a child has a good memory we may be thinking of the ease with which he learns, the length of time for which he remembers, or the facility with which he recalls something that he has learnt. It is convenient to treat the subject of remembering under these headings, that is, learning, retaining and recalling.

LEARNING

When we speak of learning we may mean learning the actual words of a passage by heart, or we may mean getting the grasp of the meaning of the passage without necessarily retaining the original words. When it is necessary to make a distinction we may conveniently call the first kind, memorizing or learning by heart, and the second kind, studying. In actual practice the two kinds of learning are not mutually exclusive, for, as we shall see, careful study facilitates learning by heart, and, conversely, a limited amount of well-chosen learning by heart helps to give point and definiteness to study that otherwise might produce vague and unsatisfactory results. It is, for example, very desirable to memorize tables and formulæ in mathematics, a framework of dates in history, a minimum of essential facts in geography, and a selection of striking passages in literature. When studying an important passage from a textbook pupils should make a framework of headings that they can remember; these headings will then act as cues to help in recalling both the general meaning and the details of the passage.

The most important condition for successful learning is that our pupils shall be actively desirous of learning. They must attend whole-heartedly to the work and not be content with mere mechanical repetition. Repetition is usually necessary, but it is not enough by itself. There must also be an effort to learn.

Experiment 1.—The effect of effort on learning by heart.

Get some one who is not doing the experiment to prepare two lists of thirty words, the lists to be as far as possible equal in difficulty, having regard to the length and unusualness of the words.

(*a*) Take one of the lists and read it through once, making no effort to memorize the words. At the end of the first reading make a mark on paper to record one repetition. Then read the list again in the same way and continue, keeping a record of the number of repetitions, until you feel you know the list.

(*b*) Learn the other list, keeping a record as before, but this time make an effort to learn.

Compare the number of repetitions necessary for each list. If many people are doing the experiment some should choose one list for effortless repetition and some should choose the other list. This method minimizes the chance of results being influenced by a difference in the difficulty of the lists.

Most people who do this experiment find it impossible to keep the first set of repetitions quite effortless ; they begin to wonder how much they know, and then they find themselves making an effort to recall. This does not, however, invalidate the experiment if they remember that they are comparing the effect of great effort with the effect of little effort, not with the effect of no effort at all.

The above experiment shows conclusively that we learn much more quickly when we really try to learn. We see, therefore, how important it is that our pupils should learn with the intent to learn, that they should feel that their learning is worth while. The intent to learn comes normally as a result of interest in the matter to be learnt. It is a commonplace that a boy will learn easily such facts as batting averages and speed records, even though he finds difficulty in learning arithmetical tables and historical dates. We say he has a good memory for the one kind of fact, and a poor memory for the other. We all find such differences in ourselves, a good memory for tunes, a poor memory for faces ; and they are all largely attributable to differences in interest, differences that influence our attending to the facts, and that cause us to welcome some and merely tolerate others.

When the material itself does not provoke the necessary effort, teachers must find other means of doing so.[1] One fruitful plan is to set a certain amount of learning to be done in a given time. The time limit acts as an incentive and provokes the necessary effort.

The second important condition is that our pupils should try to understand, to see meaning in, the material to be learnt.

Experiment 2.—*The effect of meaning on learning.*

(*a*) Read carefully the following list of nonsense syllables once only. When you have finished cover the syllables and write down all that you remember.[2]

MUB POV RIN TAD WUF GAK PED BOF DIB YOD HIK MEL HOR DUP FEG BAM.

(*b*) Repeat with the following words :

GAS LIP BUD RAN FIN WED TOP SUN CAB NOR PEG HUM MAN LET DIN JOT.

[1] In this connexion read again the section on " Interest and Attention," pp. 99–102.

[2] In the foregoing experiments two different methods for measuring the effectiveness of the learning have been used. In Experiment 1 the lists were repeated until known and the number of necessary repetitions was taken as a measure of the effectiveness of each method of learning. In Experiment 2, each set of words was repeated once only, and the amount remembered after one repetition served as a measure of efficacy. In each of these experiments the testing was done *immediately* after the learning. To make the investigation into remembering more complete, the material is often re-tested after an interval, for ability to remember well when tested immediately is not necessarily combined with ability to remember after an interval. When we are re-testing after an interval we may either record how much we remember or, if the material were repeated until known on the first occasion, we may re-learn it and then use the number of repetitions necessary for re-learning as a measure of the effectiveness of the original learning. All these methods are used in experimental work on memory.

(*c*) Repeat with the following words :
BOYS SNOW FUN NOISE PELT ICE POND SLIDE LAUGH SKATE SLIP PUSH CRACK HOLE PULL RUN.

(*d*) Repeat with the following words :
TWO GIRLS RAN OFF DOWN THE ROAD WITH THEIR DOG AND SAW OUR BIG TOM CAT.

Compare the results. Most people find that the number of syllables remembered increases as the material becomes more meaningful ; as a rule they have no difficulty in recalling all the sixteen words of the sentence, but they find it impossible to remember all the separate nonsense syllables. Furthermore, success in remembering a particular nonsense syllable is often due to the fact that it suggests a particular word and so acquires a meaning. It is interesting here to turn to the Binet tests, based as they were on observations of actual performances. Some of these tests are tests of immediate memory, two kinds of material being used, viz. digits and sentences (see experiments I.A., I.B. and I.C., pp. 151–2). The table below shows how much children of different ages can remember immediately after one presentation.

Mental Age	No. of Syllables.	No. of Digits.
3	6 to 7	3
4	12 to 13	4
5	—	—
6	16 to 18	—
7	—	5
10	20 to 22	6
14	—	7

In school we must not, however, lightly take it for granted that material which is meaningful for us is also meaningful for our pupils. They may be merely repeating more or less meaningless sounds, and then the learning by heart will be a slow process. Before setting children to memorize it is therefore an economy of time to help them to study the material. Prose or verse should first be read as effectively as possible and then, if necessary, the children's appreciation should be further deepened by class discussion ; it may sometimes be desirable to show illustrations,[1] to suggest the making of mental images, to elucidate the meaning of unfamiliar words or phrases. Before tables or formulæ in mathematics are memorized, they should be " discovered," built up, and used to solve examples. Intelligent preparation designed to make the material more meaningful will do much to reduce the labour of learning by heart.[2]

In the previous experiment some learners reproduce the sentence incorrectly because they attend mainly to the meaning and do not attend to the individual words. When reading for information this is generally all that is necessary. Children, however, read impulsively and they need to be trained to study carefully. While attempts to memorize the actual words of textbooks are to be deprecated, children need to be taught that study often involves more than a cursory, casual reading.

In all learning it is useful to pause for a moment or two after the learning before taking up some other occupation. The learning process seems to go on after we have ceased our repetitions, and if we immediately attend to something else we interfere with this part of the learning process. This important fact can be demonstrated by the following experiment :

Experiment 3.—The effect of a pause after learning.

The material used may be lists of nonsense syllables or

[1] For a useful experiment on the value of a map in studying, see *An Introduction to Experimental Psychology*, C. W. Valentine, p. 37 (Univ. Tut. Press).

[2] For similar reasons students are well advised to read semi-popular books by the great masters of their subjects in order to get a grasp of the subject as a whole. For example : *Introduction to Mathematics*, A. N. Whitehead (Williams & Norgate, 1919) ; *Arm-chair Science*, Ray Lankester (Methuen, 1919–20). A study of the former book would tend to obviate meaningless symbol-juggling ; a study of the latter would light up obscure details of anatomical and other scientific studies.

words to be learnt by heart, or passages of which the meaning is to be remembered. Nonsense syllables are the most convenient, as it is easy to get lists of equal difficulty. In the previous experiments, as our aim has been largely to illustrate a truth rather than to make measurements, we have ignored the possible effects of fatigue and practice. In this experiment we may adopt a device that is sometimes used to cancel out these effects. That is, instead of learning only two lists, one followed by a pause and one followed immediately by other work, we learn four or even six lists. After list 1, 3 and 5 pass on immediately to the reading of a book for two minutes before testing, but after lists 2, 4 and 6 rest for two minutes. The results of lists 1, 3 and 5 are combined and the results of 2, 4, 6.

So far, we have three conditions that are important in all learning, no matter whether we are learning by heart or studying to acquire meaning. We come now to some other devices that are especially useful when learning by heart.

Spread the repetitions.—Experiment has shown that it is more profitable when memorizing poetry, for example, to make two repetitions on each of six consecutive days than to make twelve repetitions on one day. When the repetitions are spread, provided they are not spread over too long a period, we get the benefit of the pauses between the learnings. Furthermore, each day we arrest the process of forgetting that has set in since the previous day, and since the poem is " in our minds " for several days, we increase the chances of new associations being formed between it and the ordinary happenings of everyday life. We decrease the possibility of being bored with the learning, for we come fresh to the task each day, ready to concentrate attention on it. Thus we have the benefit of six initial repetitions instead of one.

Learn as wholes.—It is better to learn a poem by reading it straight through than by learning it a line, or two lines, at a time. Beginners are often unwilling to follow this advice because the " whole " method seems to them a hopeless one. They do not see how they are progressing, and they miss the encouragement that comes with the knowledge that another section has been mastered. It must be admitted that the available experimental evidence on the effectiveness of the " whole " method is conflicting; the balance of evidence, however, favours it. There are, moreover, several reasons why, on theoretical grounds, we should expect the " whole " method to be superior to a " part " method. As we have seen, meaning is a great aid to memorizing, and the repetition of a whole poem is generally more meaningful than the repetition of a part. Again, if we consider learning by heart as the forming of associations between words, it is obvious that when we read the poem straight through we associate each word with the one that should follow it ; we associate the end of one line with the beginning of the next, and not with the beginning of the same line, or of a preceding one. If we learn by sections, say of four lines, we are more likely to connect the end of line 4 with the beginning of line 1 than to connect it with the beginning of line 5. Such wrong practice brings unfortunate results ; we find ourselves reciting the same lines over and over again, unable to progress to the next section.

We must not, however, ignore the fact that the " whole " method is sometimes discouraging, and that occasionally some lines of a poem present special difficulty. A slight modification of the whole method is therefore often desirable. If the poem is very long, it should be broken into suitable smaller "wholes"; if any part gives special difficulty, that part should be repeated more often than the rest of the poem. But whatever adaptations are made, the first few repetitions and the last few should always be repetitions of the whole poem.

The advantage of the " whole " method of learning is seen especially when a poem is re-learnt after an interval. A child may have apparently forgotten a poem, but a very few repetitions are sufficient to re-establish it. Experiment has shown that the re-learning of poems that were originally learnt by a " whole " method needs fewer repetitions than the re-learning of poems learnt on a " part " method.

Systematize the facts to be learnt.—This is merely an application of the fundamental principle that we should try to see meaning in the material we are learning and to relate one fact with another. Those facts that belong together are learnt together. In many modern vocabulary books the words are grouped round a central theme ; in many spelling books words are grouped as examples of some special rule, or as exceptions to it. When children are being trained to study, they should be taught how to make systematic notes under suitable headings ; if the textbook is a good one, this is not difficult, for a careful author systematizes his knowledge before he attempts to write his chapters and paragraphs.

It is easy to convince oneself of the value of systematizing by the following experiment :

Experiment 4.—The value of systematizing.

Find a number of people who do not know the Morse code. Arrange them in two groups, putting good, average and indifferent learners into each group, so as to make the groups as even as possible. Set one group to learn the Morse signs, working straight through the alphabet from A to Z. For the other group, rearrange the letters, putting similar ones together, e.g. those that are all dots, those that are all dashes, those with a dot or two dots in the middle, those with a dash or two dashes in the middle, and so on.

Make use of rhythm where possible.—Before the value of meaning was appreciated, rhythm was the great aid to learning by heart ; tables, letters, grammatical rules were chanted to the prescribed rhythm, a rhythm that was so compelling that the significance of the actual words was often not appreciated. In the swing of the pendulum against such unintelligent repetition we have sometimes gone too far and neglected to use rhythm where it would be useful. There is still a place in school for the rhythmical chanting of tables and for the learning of important facts arranged in attractive rhythmical form. Rhythm is one means of binding words or sounds together so that when we learn, say, four words connected by rhythm we are learning one unit, a set of four words, not four units each consisting of one word. If a list of nine separate digits is read to a group of adults many of them will find difficulty in reproducing those nine digits correctly ; but, if they are arranged by rhythm into three threes, very few of the adults will experience any difficulty in repeating them. In this connexion it is interesting to notice that many un-skilled mental testers invalidate those Binet tests that test immediate memory. They read the digits with a rhythm and with modulation of voice instead of in a regular mono-tone, and so they give a test that is very much easier than the one that Binet standardized.

RETAINING

At the beginning of this chapter we decided to consider remembering under the headings of learning, retaining and recalling. So far, we have dealt with the conditions that are favourable to learning, but we have been unable to ignore questions of retention and recall, for we have had to use ability to recall as a measure of the efficiency of learning, and it is obvious that facts can only be recalled because, in some way, they have been retained. We do not know how facts are retained and at present our knowledge about a person's ability to retain is very slight. We notice that some people seem able to retain facts for a very long time and that others appear to forget them very quickly. Such differences used to be attributed to differences in native retentiveness, but we are beginning to realize that these ob-served facts may be interpreted in another way. They may be due to differences in power to recall rather than to differ-ences in power to retain. One fact is becoming very clear, we certainly do retain much more than we can recall. The work of psycho-analysts has shown us that experiences that we cannot recall for ourselves may yet persist and influence our present behaviour, and may even be recalled to mind if we can find the right cues. Further evidence is found in experimental work on re-learning. Having learnt a poem,

we may, after an interval, be quite unable to recall it. Then
we re-learn the poem, but we re-learn it much more easily
than we learned it originally. Although we could recall
nothing, we have yet retained something. Furthermore, we
are all familiar with the fact of reminiscence. A name that we
cannot recall may suddenly come to mind when we are not
trying to recall it. Ballard investigated this phenomenon,
and found that if he set children to learn a poem and tested
them immediately and again at intervals, they could often
reproduce more after two or three days than they could
immediately after the learning. In the interval they regained
some parts and lost others. At first they regained more than
they lost and not until after two or three days did the amount
lost outweigh the amount regained.[1] We have already seen
that we can improve our methods of learning. Now comes
the question, " Can we improve our retentiveness ? " The
usual answer to this question has been, " No." Retentiveness was believed to be a purely physiological matter,
conditioned by the quality of our brain material, which
was incapable of improvement. Experimental work by
McDougall has suggested, however, that we can improve
our retentiveness. He gave subjects practice both in learning and in re-learning. They learned a set of syllables one
day and re-learned it the next day. This was continued for
three months. At the end of this time all the subjects had
improved both in learning and in re-learning. This result,
as it stands, gives no indication of improved power to retain.
It could be easily accounted for by better methods of learning that would affect both the original learning and the
re-learning. But some of the subjects had improved decidedly more in re-learning than in learning. This fact
cannot be accounted for by improved methods of learning
and does suggest that some improvement in retaining had
been effected.

As a matter of fact, many of our ideas about remembering
are undergoing some change. In years gone by it was

[1] *Reminiscence and Obliviscence*, P. B. Ballard (Brit. Jnl. Psych. Mon.
Supp., 1913).

usual to emphasize the close connexion between learning and habit forming. Bergson, however, pointed out that, although much of our learning is of this kind, yet some of it bears no resemblance to habit forming. We may learn a list of nonsense syllables by saying them over and over again, and we say we remember them as a result of this repetition. But we may also remember the occasion on which we started learning, the room in which we worked, the people who worked with us, an interruption that happened during the learning ; and these memories are not the results of repetition and have no affinity with habits. Such memories Bergson called true memories. They are often accompanied by imagery and are related to a definite time and place, quite unlike our habit memories. We see therefore that when we recall we may either follow a well-worn track, as happens when we recite a poem that has been previously learnt by heart, or we may adventure into our past and recall experiences that have occurred on one occasion only. It is, of course, possible that these two types of " memory " are not different in kind ; the " pure memory " may be looked upon as an example of learning by an experience that is so full of meaning and interest for us that a single presentation is enough. In this connexion, it is interesting to note that Mason contends that a single reading of a passage of literary merit is enough to enable children to learn its meaning (see p. 383).

RECALLING

We have seen that ability to recall depends to some extent on the way in which the learning was done. If our pupils learn with a will, if they understand and use what they are learning, if they spread the repetitions, then there is a reasonable chance that they will retain what they learn and be able to reproduce it when required. Having learnt a poem, they only need an appropriate cue and the poem comes to mind ; having learnt the 6-times table, they recall " 18 " immediately they hear " six-threes." On the other hand, we all know that even though facts are learnt and retained, recall is by no means always certain. Sometimes we have to prompt our pupils, to try first one cue and then another, before they are able to recall the wanted fact.

Sometimes it is desirable to prepare a special cue beforehand, as when we tie a knot in our handkerchief to remind ourselves to post a letter. We attend to the knot and the letter together so that they become associated. When, later, we see the knot we remember the associated letter. Mnemonics help us in the same way. They are simple cues, well within our comprehension, to help us to remember facts that for us are not entirely rational. It follows therefore that if we are tempted to teach our pupils a large number of mnemonics we ought to ask ourselves whether or not we are trying to teach too many meaningless facts. The value of a mnemonic is well illustrated by the following example. Suppose we want to make sure that we can reproduce, when required, the names of the planets in the order of their distance from the sun. If our knowledge of astronomy were sufficient, we might get a visual image of a chart or we might reason out the order from other known facts. Failing these sensible clues, we have to hang our list on to such a simple peg as the following sentence : " Men very easily make all jugs serve useful necessary purposes." It will be seen that the initial letters are sufficient to remind us of the list we need, namely, Mercury, Venus, Earth, Mars, Asteroids, Jupiter, Saturn, Uranus, Neptune, Pluto. In this example we associate the sentence with the names of the planets ; the sentence is for us a simple cue.

In all these examples the cues help us to recall because we have taken care to associate each cue with the one fact or experience we wish to remember and not with any other. But in everyday life the associations between our ideas and experiences are by no means so simple. As we have seen, our items of knowledge are connected by a network of associations. For instance, the word " dog " may suggest to us a particular dog we know, or it may suggest " cat," or " bark," or " faithfulness " or many other words.

Why then at any given moment does one link work rather than another ? What determines in any given situation which of the many associated ideas in our minds shall come into consciousness ? These questions can best be answered by a simple experiment :

Experiment on free recall.—Take a sheet of paper and put down the numbers 1 to 20. Against No. 1 write any word, say " town." You will then notice that other words come to your mind in rapid succession. Write these words down quickly, allowing your mind to work as freely as possible. Be careful not to reject any word that occurs to you, however inconsequent it may appear. Stop when you have written twenty words. Now examine your words and see if you can suggest any reason why each of these particular words came to your mind.

You may find it helpful to consider the following lists made by training-college students on May 13th, 1935, just after the Jubilee celebrations. The given word was " carriage."

List 1.—Carriage, king, procession, Horse-guards, jubilee, decorations, morning, dawn, heat, brilliance, soldiers, horse, saddles, leather, soap, water, polish, floor, hearthstoning, housewifery.

List 2.—Carriage, physical training, pumps, laces, petticoats, laundry, steam, engines, steel, earth, sea, ships, funnels, sea-gulls, air, fire, smoke, flames, flood-lighting, jubilee, crowds.

Both lists contain references to the Jubilee celebrations that had taken place recently. We can often trace the recalled word to some recent experience. Links that have been recently made are very likely to operate again. Recency, then, is one of the factors that determine which particular idea will be recalled by a given word at a given time.

Sometimes an idea has been so recently in mind that for all practical purposes we should say we are still thinking of it. For example, the unusual response, " physical training " in the second list could be explained in this way. Just before the experiment the student in question had been discussing a teacher of physical training. " Carriage " then suggested to her not a vehicle but bodily carriage.

In both lists we can find pairs of words that are frequently used together, e.g., steam and engines, earth and sea, sea and ships, ships and funnels, soap and water. In these examples the strength of the link depends not on the fact that it was made recently but that it has been made frequently. It has been strengthened by repetition, just as the links between the words in a poem or in a multiplication table are strengthened by repetition. Frequency, then, is one of the factors that influence recall.

Both lists contain words that are connected with house-craft, e.g., polish, floor, hearthstoning, housewifery in List 1, and laces, petticoats, laundry in List 2. The students who made the lists were studying housecraft and their replies were influenced by their permanent interest in this subject. It is unlikely that they were actually thinking about house-craft when the experiment started, but their interest makes them always ready to think about it. A permanent interest is, then, another factor that influences recall.

Sometimes words come to mind that cannot be explained in any of these ways. The link has been formed neither recently nor frequently. It has been made potentially active neither by the ideas in our mind at the moment nor by our permanent interests. Its potency is due to the fact that, when the link was originally made, we were stirred by a strong emotion such as curiosity, fear, suspense, or pride. For instance, if at any time we have seen people rescued from a burning house, the link " fire—rescue " is just as likely to operate for us as the link " fire—place." We have here an example of what Bergson would call " true memory " as opposed to " habit memory."

If a number of people perform the above experiment, starting all together, there will be a good deal of variety in the time taken to complete the twenty words. The rate of work is influenced partly by temperamental, and partly by intellectual, factors. Some people are quicker " off the mark " than others ; after receiving a stimulus they give the response quickly. We say they have a short re-action time. Teachers should be aware of these individual differences in reaction times, so that they may guard against unwise impatience with children who react slowly. It is not, of course, suggested that all slowness is tempera-mental. Experiment has shown that slowness in thinking is a characteristic of low intelligence. There are thus two kinds of slowness,—(a) intellectual slowness or slowness in thinking, and (b) temperamental slowness or slowness in making a physical response. When setting intelligence tests, it is therefore necessary to frame questions that call for thinking and not merely for a quick automatic response ; otherwise, the test will be a test of temperament rather than of intelligence.

If we examine again the lists on page 141, we see that the words fall into groups relating to separate topics. If there were very little grouping, that is, if the topic changed with nearly every word, it would take longer to get the required number of words. It has been found that a tendency to expand a topic is characteristic of the more intelligent children. The backward ones, as Burt[1] says, " exhaust an idea in barely naming it." Binet included a free recall test among his tests of intelligence. Normal 11-year-old children, having been started off with the words " box, coat, tree, cart " can say sixty words in 3 minutes. It is found that those children who pass the test easily give relatively large groups of words that are related. In discussing this test, Burt suggests that a study of the actual words given by the children is worth while, since it throws light on their intelligence and on their interests. Unusual words, abstract words and logical con-nexions between words, indicate a good intelligence. A large number of repetitions, on the other hand, suggests " the mental stereotypy of the deficient." The topics mentioned give us some idea of the child's interests and show us which subjects he is ready to attend to. Occasionally we notice that a child hesitates at some point during his recital

[1] *Mental and Scholastic Tests*, C. Burt, p. 60.

of the words ; this probably indicates that the topic called to mind is one to which he is unwilling to give expression.

The actual time taken to find a word is of great interest to a psychologist. He can measure it to a thousandth of a second by using a Hipp's chronoscope. His procedure is slightly different from the one we have been considering. Instead of presenting one word and asking the subject to supply a chain of words, he presents words one at a time and asks for one response to each given word. If the measured times for one person are examined it will be found that most of them are fairly similar ; they approximate to the person's usual reaction time for that kind of work. There may, however, be some abnormally quick responses and some abnormally slow ones. These are interesting because they throw light on the mental content of the person being tested. He may have a special reason for wanting to show no hesitation and so responds with unusual alacrity. On the other hand, the response that comes first to mind may be one that he is consciously or unconsciously unwilling to give, and so he loses time in searching for a suitable word. Sometimes the given word arouses no response at all ; such a degree of inhibition suggests that some deep-lying emotional complex has been tapped. The word-association method has been extensively used by psycho-analysts to explore the mental content, especially at unconscious levels, of their patients. It has also been used for the detection of crime, and possibly it will in time be more widely used for this purpose. If a suitable list of stimulus words be given, it is almost impossible for any person to conceal guilty knowledge. He would give himself away, if not by his words, at least by his reaction times. Obviously this is a method to be used only by psychological experts.

So far we have been considering what happens when we are required to make no effort to control the ideas that come to mind. In everyday life, we do occasionally let our minds " wander " in this way, but when we are trying to remember something, or trying to solve a problem, or trying to invent a new piece of apparatus, we tend to recall only those ideas that are relevant to our purpose. The recall, in that case, is not as free as in the foregoing experiment ; it is controlled by purpose. The influence of a directing purpose can be easily demonstrated by the following simple experiment :

Experiment on controlled recall.[1]—In the following list there are ten words. Put a sheet of paper over the list until you have read all the instructions. When you are ready move the paper so as to expose the first word. Read it and write down the word that first comes into your mind as in the " free-recall " experiment. Do not try to think of any particular word ; just let your mind work. After you have written down the word note whether you had imagery of any kind and whether this imagery was useful to you or not. Then expose the next word and deal with it in the same way. Continue in this way until you have completed the list. You will find it convenient to arrange your work as follows :

Stimulus Word.	Response.	Imagery.
1. boat . .		
2. daisy . .		
3. wool . .		
4. bicycle . .		
5. piano . .		
6. tree . .		
7. man . .		
8. ink . . .		
9. sword . .		
10. fire . .		

[1] The process here referred to as " controlled recall " is usually referred to as " controlled association." Similarly, in the previous experiment, the process used is generally termed " free association." All recall depends upon association, but it seems clearer, since the associations we use when we remember have been already forged by past experiences, to use our nomenclature. When we hear the word " fire " we do not *then* associate the ideas of " fire " and " engines " ; we recall the word " engine " because the two ideas are already associated in our minds. The reader will see that in " controlled recall " also, the associations, generally speaking, already exist. If a new association is formed, it is the result of thinking rather than of remembering. As the term " rational memory " implies, there is no clear-cut division between thinking and remembering. As Burt says, " In memory the association between the facts is not itself made conscious or explicit ; in reasoning, the child not only associates two things, but also clearly perceives the relation between them." (*The Primary School*, p. 265 (H.M.S.O., 1931).)

Repeat the procedure with the following list, but this time, instead of giving any word that comes to mind, you must *give a part* of the object named. For example, if the stimulus word were " knife," a suitable response would be " handle." Be sure you know exactly what you have to do before you start.

GIVE A PART.

Stimulus Word.	Response.	Imagery.
1. chair . .		
2. bicycle . .		
3. song . .		
4. tree . .		
5. sword . .		
6. house . .		
7. piano . .		
8. street . .		
9. blouse . .		
10. daisy . .		

Repeat the procedure again with the following list. This time you have a different task. You must give the class to which the object belongs. For example, if the stimulus word were " herring," a suitable response would be " fish."

GIVE THE CLASS.

Stimulus Word.	Response.	Imagery.
1. man . .		
2. blouse . .		
3. daisy . .		
4. table . .		
5. sword . .		
6. linen . .		
7. song . .		
8. bicycle . .		
9. boat . .		
10. tree . .		

You have probably noticed that some words occur in two lists and some in all three lists. Now examine your responses to these words and notice the influence of your purpose, i.e., to find a part, or to find the class, in determining the response. You will probably find that you have given a different response to the same word each time it occurred, usually without any recall of the previous response. You probably also found that there was no need to keep reminding yourself what your purpose was. Some subjects, once they start, do not think explicitly of their purpose again throughout the list. Others think of it if they happen to think of an unsuitable response first. It seems as if our purpose gives us a certain mental " set " or bias so that we are not merely helped to reject unsuitable words if they do recur, but we are actually prevented from recalling them at all.

Purpose is probably the most important of all the factors that influence recall, just as intent to learn was the most important factor in learning. We can see by referring to the experiment again that it was more powerful than recency, for under the influence of a purpose quite a different response was given from the one that had been given a few moments before. We can also see that it is stronger than frequency, for under the influence of a purpose the response to " man " is a word such as " human-being " instead of the usual response " woman." When there is no definite purpose, then such factors as recency and frequency become important ; but when there is a clear purpose, as when we are trying to remember all the facts that bear on a problem, then recency and frequency are seen to be relatively unimportant.

We can now summarize the factors that influence recall :

1. Purpose.
2. Permanent interest.
3. Strong emotion accompanying the original experience.
4. Recency.
5. Frequency.

FORGETTING

We have seen that we retain much more than we can usually recall, and that facts that elude us one moment slip into our minds at another ; there appears to be some ground for presuming that no experience is ever entirely forgotten. It is probably more correct, therefore, to look upon forgetting, not as a failure to retain, but as inability to recall. This description of forgetting covers both the kinds with which we are now familiar : the " passive " forgetting that takes place with the lapse of time when the original learning is incomplete, or when the original experience is relatively insignificant ; and the " active " forgetting that is the result of a wish, conscious or unconscious, to banish from our minds ideas that may cause painful feelings.

Our ability to forget, or as we have described it, our inability to recall, must be looked upon, not as a misfortune but as a merciful dispensation. If we can preserve our mental equilibrium by forgetting unpleasant experiences, for the time being at least, we benefit by the forgetting. Again, when we forget unimportant or irrelevant details we are so much the more able to concentrate on facts that are important. If every thought brought back with it all the ideas that are associated with it, we should be overwhelmed with material and unable to make any good use of it. For clear thinking it is probably just as important to " forget " irrelevant details as to remember relevant ones.

Let us consider first " active " forgetting, the repression of memories that would either be unpleasant in themselves or that might act as cues to recall other unpleasant experiences. We are all familiar with forgetting of this kind. We forget to post a letter that will commit us to some undesired social activity, or, feeling that we have been overcharged for some services rendered, we send a cheque but forget to sign it. Sometimes a more permanent inability to remember is traced to a similar repression, as when a dislike of one's own name is found to be the cause of an inability to remember names in general.[1] As teachers we want our pupils not only to learn well but also to recall successfully. If the learning is done under pleasant conditions, inspired by interest, accompanied by satisfaction at overcoming difficulties and by the joy of achievement, recall is very likely. If, on the other hand, the learning is distasteful because of boredom, lack of achievement, or even actual punishment, recall is by no means so likely. This statement is apparently contradicted by the fact that people can learn poetry as a punishment and remember it for life. A fuller invesitgation into the circumstances, however, usually shows that, unwillingly as the learner may have started, he yet found some measure of satisfaction in the learning. It sometimes happens that in our desire to give a child the joy of achievement we actually give him a feeling of despair or irritation. For instance, a child asks a question and we turn his question back again and set him to find the answer. This treatment is stimulating if used with discretion, but it is often exasperating, and has the added disadvantage that it may leave the learner uncertain of the correct answer. Facts learnt under such circumstances are often forgotten.

Let us consider next the forgetting that is due to the lapse of time. As we have already seen, an experience that was tremendously significant for us is relatively unaffected by the passage of time, but material that we have learnt by repetition—dates, tables, poetry—seems to fade from our minds. Experiment has shown, that apart from the gains due to reminiscence, the rate of forgetting of such material is most rapid soon after the learning, and that it then gradually slows down. By suitably spaced revisions, however, we can keep pace with this forgetting. Since the forgetting is rapid at first, we should start revising soon after the learning and then revise at intervals. The intervals between revisions can safely be made longer and longer, since the rate of forgetting is slowing down. This fact is of practical

[1] For further examples of this kind of forgetting, see *The Psychopathology of Everyday Life*, Sigmund Freud (Fisher Unwin, 1914).

importance to teachers, for it reminds us that neither haphazard revision done merely to fill in occasional periods nor a single burst of concentrated revision at the end of term is as valuable or economical as systematic revision at properly spaced intervals.

CONCLUSION

It will now be useful to gather together the main points discussed in this chapter. We have seen first of all that remembering depends more on a pupil's desire to learn, on the way in which he receives new knowledge and associates it with what he already knows, and on the extent to which he uses it, than on the degree of retentiveness with which he is endowed. We have also seen that his retentiveness can perhaps be improved by practice. Everything indicates then that for all practical purposes we can help our pupils to improve their memories, since we can certainly influence their attitude towards learning, and we can teach them during the learning to establish cues that will help them to recall facts when they want them. These considerations also suggest that adults should learn and remember as well as, or perhaps better than, children. Adults can attend more effectively and they have a better organized body of knowledge into which to fit new facts. They are therefore able to grasp new knowledge more easily than children can, and to recall it more readily when wanted. In fact, recent experiment has suggested that ability to learn, provided the material is meaningful, probably increases as long as general mental activity remains unimpaired. When the material to be learnt is nonsense material, the superiority of adults is not so marked, for then their greater and better organized knowledge is not so valuable.

The popular belief that children remember better than adults is without foundation. Children appear to have exceptional memories, but our estimates are probably unreliable for two reasons. First, we tend to notice the way they remember exceptional happenings only ; second, we notice their power of remembering because it is relatively so much better than their ability to think and reason. We also tend to think of childhood as the best time for learning because in old age the experiences of childhood are recalled even when the experiences of yesterday are forgotten. One reason for this is that experiences of childhood are often more vivid than those of later life, and another reason is that many of these early experiences have been thought about again and again. That which is learnt first has the best chance of being used most.

OBSERVATIONS AND EXPERIMENTS

1. Experiments on Immediate Memory.
Give the following Binet tests (Terman Revision) to children of appropriate ages :

A. *Digits.*

Say the following digits distinctly, on a monotone and without any rhythm at the rate of one per second. Do not repeat the series. Say to the child, " Listen and say these numbers after me."

		For use after failure with first set.	
Year 3.	6-4-1	3-5-2	8-3-7
Year 4.	4-7-3-9	2-8-5-4	7-2-6-1
Year 7.	3-1-7-5-9	4-2-3-8-5	9-8-1-7-6
Year 10.	3-7-4-8-5-9	5-2-1-7-4-6	
Year 14.	2-1-8-3-4-3-9	9-7-2-8-4-7-5	

The child passes if he gets one series quite correct.

B. *Syllables.*

Say the following sentences distinctly but naturally.
Say to the child, " Listen and say this after me."

Year 3 (a) I have a little dog.
   (b) The dog runs after the cat.
   (c) In summer the sun is hot.
Year 4 (a) The boy's name is John. He is a very good boy.
   (b) When the train passes you will hear the whistle blow.
   (c) We are going to have a good time in the country.
Year 6 (a) We are having a fine time. We found a little mouse in the trap.
   (b) Robert had a fine time on his holiday. He went fishing every day.
   (c) We will go out for a long walk. Please give me my pretty straw hat.

F

Year 10 (a) The apple tree makes a cool pleasant shade on the ground where the children are playing.

(b) It is nearly half-past one o'clock; the house is very quiet and the cat has gone to sleep.

(c) In summer the days are very warm and fine; in winter it snows and I am cold.

If the child succeeds with sentence (a), sentences (b) and (c) need not be used.

The child passes if he gets one sentence quite correct or, after year 3, if he gets two sentences with not more than one mistake in each.

Consider the bearing of these results on dictation lessons.

C. *Facts.*

Hand the child a copy of the following passage, clearly printed or typed, and say, " Read this aloud as carefully as you can." After the reading, remove the passage and say, " Now tell me all you read." If the child fails through trying to give the exact words say, " In your own words."

Year 10. Manchester, September 5th.—A fire last night burned three houses near the centre of the city. It took some time to put it out. The loss was five thousand pounds, and seventeen families lost their homes. In saving a girl who was asleep in bed a fireman was burned on the hands.

The maximum number of items is 21. The child passes if he scores 8, having read the passage in not more than 35 seconds with not more than two mistakes.

Consider the bearing of these results on private study lessons.

2. Experiments on memorizing poetry.

A. (a) Teach a class a short poem. Give a short appreciation lesson (10 minutes) prior to the learning and then let the class learn the poem for 10 minutes.

(b) Take a similar short poem with the same class. Let them learn the poem unaided for 20 minutes. The experimenter also should learn this poem.

(c) Test the amount of learning in each case by getting the children to write out as much as they can remember immediately afterwards.

Compare the results of the two methods. Compare also the amount learnt by the adult experimenter with the amount learnt by the best pupils.

B. Devise an experiment to test the relative effectiveness of learning (a) by parts, (b) by wholes.

3. Make a collection of all the methods you see employed by experienced teachers to help children to memorize multiplication tables.

4. Keep a record of your own failures to recall during a period of, say, three months. Try to account for these failures.

REFERENCES FOR READING

Modern Psychology and Education, Sturt and Oakden, chapter XII.
Groundwork of Educational Psychology, J. S. Ross, chapter XI.
Educational Psychology, C. Fox, chapter VI.
Instinct, Intelligence and Character, Godfrey H. Thomson, chapter XXIV.

Experimental Education, R. R. Rusk, chapters VII, XIII.
The Process of Learning, C. Bloor, chapter IX.
Psychology and Practical Life, Collins and Drever, chapter VI.

ADDITIONAL REFERENCES

Directing Mental Energy, F. Aveling (Univ. Lond. Press, 1927).
An Outline of Psychology, Wm. McDougall, pp. 293–311 (Methuen, 1923).
The Economy and Training of Memory, H. J. Watt (Arnold, 1911).
Remembering and Forgetting, T. H. Pear (Methuen, 1922).
The Psychology of Study, C. A. Mace (Methuen, 1932).
The Art of Study, T. H. Pear (Kegan Paul, 1930).
Remembering, F. C. Bartlett (Camb. Univ. Press, 1932).

ESSAYS AND DISCUSSIONS

1. Useful and useless learning by heart in school.
2. Discuss the following :
(a) " Childhood is the golden age of memory."
(b) " It is more important to know where to find information than to
    have it actually in mind at the moment."
3. Ways and means of helping children to improve their ability (a) to
memorize, (b) to study.
4. The value of forgetting.

CHAPTER X

THINKING AND IMAGINING

IN previous chapters we have considered several aspects of the process of learning,—attending, imaging, habit-forming and remembering. We have seen that each of these aspects involves all the others. Our minds work as a whole. For example, the more we know about a subject the more easily we attend to new aspects of that subject and the more readily we remember new facts connected with it.

In this chapter we shall concentrate on another aspect of learning, the process in which we use results of past experiences to meet a new situation, to solve a problem. This kind of mental activity is usually called thinking.[1]

As teachers we are concerned not merely with imparting knowledge but with training our pupils to think for themselves, that is, to use the knowledge they have, in order to arrive at further knowledge. As we saw in chapter IV their ability to think depends to some extent on inborn intellectual, and perhaps temperamental, qualities. Some children are by nature more likely to be good thinkers than others, but all children can by wise training be helped to develop their thinking powers fully, and to direct their thinking to worthy ends.

Before we can help children to think we must analyse the process of thinking to see in what it consists. A very simple way of doing this is to watch yourself solving a clue in a cross-word puzzle. You may, or you may not, reach a successful conclusion, but while you are trying to reach one you are thinking. You will probably begin by repeating the clue to yourself once or twice, perhaps aloud, certainly rather deliberately. Then you will dwell on each item,

---

[1] As Spearman has shown, all real thinking depends on the ability to educe relations and correlates. See footnote, p. 36.

noticing what ideas each one brings to mind. You look for relations of likeness, difference and cause among the different sets of ideas. Perhaps you perceive a relation, but you are not necessarily satisfied with the solution it suggests. The word you have found may not fit the given space or may not contain a required letter. If you are a cross-word expert you will sometimes reject solutions that are otherwise satisfactory because they do not show that particular neatness that you expect in these puzzles ; the solution fits but it does not fit " with a click " and so you reject it. You continue to search. You repeat the given clue and examine it carefully to see if there is any point you have overlooked ; you dwell on each item again ; you examine the ideas that come to mind and eventually there is a " flash " and you see the solution.

THE ART OF THINKING

After the above exercise in introspection you will be ready to identify the following stages in the thinking process :

(i) Appreciation of a problem to be solved.
(ii) Collection of adequate relevant data.
(iii) Arriving at a conclusion.
(iv) Testing the conclusion.

It will be convenient to consider each step separately to see how we can help our pupils in their thinking.

(i) *Appreciation of a problem to be solved.*—The problems that we appreciate best are the ones that occur directly to us, not the ones that are propounded to us by other people. Our own problems arise out of our own activity, and they seem worth while. So it is with children. As we have seen in chapter III, the first problems that they solve are practical ones, concerned with concrete material ; they are not affairs of words and abstract ideas. For example, imagine a child playing with taps in the bathroom, watching the water flow and stop. After a time comes the question,

" How does the water come ? " This is a real problem ; it arouses his curiosity. He may need some help before he solves his problem, but he has certainly appreciated it and begun to think about it. When children do not think about the problems we set them, we must not hastily infer that they are unable to think. Failure may be due, not to their inability, but to our unwise choice of problem. Our problem may make no appeal to their interests ; it may not seem worth while to them. We have already pointed out in chapter VIII how important practical activity is for the development of images and ideas. We now see that it is also important as a source of problems that children really appreciate, as a means of stimulating children to think. It is interesting to notice here that a problem that is appreciated in one setting may not be appreciated in another. For example, the writers recorded some of the problems about taps and pipes, propounded spontaneously and followed up eagerly by a young boy during his active play. One day, when he was sitting quietly by the fire in a room where there were no taps, his own questions were put to him again. In this setting the problems aroused no interest. With a little urging some half-hearted but incorrect replies were obtained. The next day in the bathroom the same questions were again put to him. This time they were welcomed and activity followed. Taps were turned, pipes examined, and eventually correct answers were given. In the presence of the actual object the question meant something to the child, and started him thinking.

As children grow older they are not so dependent on the presence of concrete objects. Words become more meaningful and situations can be imagined. If, however, we ask our pupils questions in words that are unfamiliar to them, and if we suggest problems that deal with data outside their experience, we must not be surprised if they are unable to solve the problems. Most teachers have had practical experience of the importance of wording and subject-matter. They have seen, for example, a look of puzzled incomprehension change to one of confident understanding when unfamiliar francs were replaced by well-known pence in a problem in arithmetic.

(ii) *Collection of relevant data.*—Having appreciated and grasped the problem we now begin to collect facts that may eventually help us to produce a solution. We may first collect those facts that we already know.[1] If we have no very definite line of investigation to follow we may just wait and see what ideas are suggested by the problem. As we know, the suggestions will not be quite free and random. They will be controlled by our purpose. The more completely we appreciate the purpose the more effective will it be in giving our minds that " mental set " (p. 147) that predisposes us to remember relevant facts and not to remember irrelevant facts. Sometimes, instead of remembering, we have to acquire data by reading, by asking questions and by making observations. Here again our purpose determines which facts we notice and consider worthy of remembering. We can help our pupils in this stage of their thinking, first, by making sure that they do grasp the problem, and second, by putting them in the way of remembering and finding the necessary data. That is, we can arrange for appropriate revision, and we can suggest books to read and observations to make. We can take appropriate steps to help children to memorize the necessary facts. In the reaction against an excessive amount of rote work in favour of more rational learning it has sometimes been forgotten that remembered facts are the very stuff with which we think. Children can no more think without facts than the Israelites could make bricks without straw.

If children are left entirely alone with their problems they often waste a good deal of time, and what is more serious, they forget their purpose, or lose heart owing to long-deferred success. We are more likely to make them in-

[1] There is often confusion about the relation of memory to intelligence. A good memory is no guarantee of good intelligence. We sometimes find even mentally defective children who remember well. On the other hand, a good memory is a great aid to thinking, since it supplies material. The ability to use the material creatively, to think about it, depends on intelligence.

dependent thinkers by ensuring that their early efforts meet with some success, than by leaving them to their own resources.

This stage in the thinking process may be very short, as, for instance, when children are solving a problem in arithmetic, or it may be spread over hours, days or weeks, as, for example, when children are engaged in such a project as finding out how a fountain pen works. It is good for children to have some problems that they cannot solve in a few moments, and herein lies one of the chief values of the project method in teaching, and of the device that many teachers use, of closing a lesson by propounding a question to be solved at some future date. When children live with a problem, they become aware of the way in which evidence accumulates, and they have time to perceive relations between one item of knowledge and another. There are times, too, before the solution is reached when the thinker is not consciously occupied with the problem ; times when he is attending to something else or is apparently doing nothing. Such times must not be looked upon as interruptions in the thinking process ; they are often essential to it. They are incubation periods that make possible the germination of a new thought. Graham Wallas[1] has shown how important these periods are for any real creative work, and has warned us that superficiality is often the result when facts are acquired hastily and used immediately. The students who produce original answers to examination questions are, as a rule, those who have had time to live with their problems and to let the collected data lie fallow, not those who have hastily collected facts the previous night. It is important to remember, however, that these times of apparent inactivity lead to positive results only when they follow a preparatory stage of effortful attention to the problem. In the early stages of approaching the problem they are worse than useless. As Graham Wallas says : " There are thousands of idle ' geniuses ' who require to learn that without a degree of industry in Preparation and Verification, of which

[1] *The Art of Thought*, Graham Wallas (Jonathan Cape, 1926).

many of them have no conception, no great intellectual work can be done, and that the habit of procrastination may be even more disastrous to a professional thinker than it is to a man of business."[1]

Just as people may fall into bad habits that will hinder thinking, so too they may form good habits that will facilitate thinking. Teachers will find it useful to train their pupils in habits of systematic procedure. In problems of a scientific nature, where observations have to be made, systematic procedure in planning observations and in recording facts will promote thoroughness in the collecting of data. Furthermore, orderly arrangement of the data when collected will facilitate that comparison of one item with another that eventually leads to a " flash " of insight, and the formulation of a theory.

(iii) *Arriving at a conclusion.*—Sometimes we arrive at a conclusion by well-defined stages, by considering an accumulation of well-arranged evidence and by the gradual elimination of possibilities. Suppose, for example, we want to discover what conditions are necessary for seed germination. We arrange experiments with seeds, excluding, one at a time, such factors as water, air, light and warmth. If our preparations have been careful, if our observations are systematic and if our patience is sufficient, we shall in time be able to draw a conclusion. At other times we do not see each step of the way ; we jump to conclusions. Our procedure is imaginative rather than logical. This is what in everyday life we sometimes call guessing. A good guess is not a wild random shot. It is the outcome of knowledge gained by previous concentration on the problem. On the other hand, it cannot be compared with the steady following of a trail. It would be better described as an intelligent adventure. Whenever we arrive at a new conclusion our thinking has to some extent been of this adventurous, imaginative kind. Even the systematic elimination of possibilities that seems to be so essentially a matter of careful and ordered procedure could not have been carried out

[1] *Op. cit.*, p. 88.

successfully unless the posibilities had been first discovered, or shall we say imagined.

When we teach inductively, when we aim at the discovery of facts by our pupils rather than at the imparting of facts to them, we are expecting them to form their own conclusions. Suppose we want them to discover that the sum of the angles in a triangle is always 180°. We state the problem clearly without giving any hint of the answer. We then proceed to collect data ; we measure the angles in a great many triangles of varying shapes and sizes. We record the sum for each triangle and some of our pupils notice a similarity about the totals ; they are all round about 180°. One makes the suggestion, " Perhaps the total will always be 180°". We now have a hypothesis to test. It is in this stage of thinking, the framing of hypotheses, in imaginative thinking as we have called it, that we shall notice the greatest differences among individual children. They will not all be able to make suggestions, and we should probably only muddle the less intelligent ones if we tried to make them discover solutions. In academic problems they will have to use the hypotheses suggested by other people. Having grasped the purpose of the work, and having collected relevant data, they are the more ready to find the hypothesis reasonable when it is suggested, and to use it successfully if it is found satisfactory. We, ourselves, do not often formulate hypotheses of great importance or originality. Like the children we have been discussing, we remember and use the discoveries of other people. For instance, we wonder why one child is having difficulty with reading. Scientific investigation into " reading " difficulties has shown that the causes are many—physical defects, intellectual deficiencies, emotional disturbances, unsuitable teaching methods, and absence from school at a critical period. Knowing the usual causes, we can, when we have collected the necessary data, make suggestions as to the probable cause of backwardness in a particular child.

The fact that many children do not readily frame hypotheses about the kind of data we present to them in school and the fact that the hypotheses when framed are often wrong have sometimes led people to suppose that children are unable to reason. We read sweeping statements to the effect that children do not reason before the age of 12 or 13. General experience with pre-school children makes us feel that there is something wrong about such statements. Our suspicions are shown to be well founded when we consider the results of scientific observation and experiment. It appears that young children are capable not only of forming hypotheses, or arriving at thoughtful conclusions, but of performing any kind of reasoning of which an adult is capable. Children differ from adults not in the kind of reasoning they can do, but in the range and complexity of subjects about which they can reason. In this connexion it is interesting to compare questions set for various ages in Binet tests. The problems are all similar in type but the situations show a steady development from those that the children will certainly have experienced to those that they will most probably have to imagine.

Age 4.   What must you do when you are sleepy?

Age 6.   What ought you to do if it is raining when you start to school?

Age 8.   What ought you to do if you broke something that belonged to some one else?

Age 10. What ought you to say if some one asks your opinion about a person you don't know very well?

A similar development is shown in Burt's Reasoning Tests.[1]

Age 7.   Kate is cleverer than May.
         May is cleverer than Jane.
         Who is the cleverest, Jane, Kate, or May?

Age 9.   Three boys are sitting in a row.
         Harry is to the left of Willie.
         George is to the left of Harry.
         Which boy is in the middle?

[1] *Mental and Scholastic Tests*, C. Burt, p. 239 (King, 1921).

Age 12. I started from the church and walked 100 yards.
I turned to the right and walked 50 yards.
I turned to the right again and walked 100 yards.
How far am I from the church ?

As children's interests widen, their range of subjects will
also widen. As their ability to attend to ideas expressed in
words develops and as their span of apprehension increases,
the complexity of subjects about which they can reason
will also increase. It is probable that children's inability,
before the mental age of 10, to detect the absurdities used
by Binet, is due to an inability to hold the different parts of
the statement together in mind. Burt, as a result of his
investigations into the reasoning powers of school children, concludes, " All the elementary mechanisms essential
to formal reasoning are present before the child leaves the
infants' department . . . if not before."[1] Isaacs, after her
experience with children at the Malting House School,
Cambridge, comes to a similar conclusion about children's
thinking : " . . . development goes on not by the sudden
appearance from time to time of entirely new abilities. It
shows itself rather in a progressive increase in the child's
power to handle issues that are relatively remote from
immediate experience, less concrete and more general in
character, more complex in type, needing a wider background of knowledge."[2]

When we watch children we see that their opinions are
often formed under the sway of emotion. They exaggerate
or belittle the importance of data according to its effect on
themselves and according to their own predilections. If
on one or two occasions their games have been prevented
by rain, then " It always rains on games afternoons." If a
child whom they dislike knocks them down in the playground, then the blow was intentional. We, too, are often

[1] *The Development of Reasoning in School Children*, C. Burt, Jnl. Expl.
Ped., Vol. V.
[2] *The Children we Teach*, S. Isaacs, p. 144 (Univ. Lond. Press, 1932).
See also *Intellectual Development in Young Children*, by the same author
(Routledge, 1930).

like children in the way we reach our conclusions. We may decide that a scheme of reorganization is bad because it means that we shall be displaced from our present comfortable school, or, on the other hand, that it is good, because it will provide an opportunity for a much deserved transfer. We arrive at conclusions that accord with our accepted beliefs, with our moods and with our wishes, conscious and unconscious. It is probably impossible for us to rid ourselves of all prejudice but, by being aware of it, we may at least escape some of its undesirable effects.[1]

(iv) *Testing the results of thinking.*—We see then that it is very necessary to test the results of our thinking. They must fulfil given conditions and they must not contradict well-established truths. This is a stage of thinking that children find irksome. Having arrived at a conclusion they want to accept it. We have to train them to proceed with caution. Sometimes we shall do this best by letting them act upon their conclusions until they are brought up against a difficulty and see for themselves that something must be wrong. At other times we shall immediately bring forward some contradictory fact that they have overlooked, or of which they were ignorant. Whatever we do, we must proceed tactfully and with no suggestion of adult infallibility, or we may, in our desire to train them to think cautiously and correctly, undermine their faith in their own ability to think.

With young children, then, we shall start our training in testing conclusions, by encouraging them to suspend judgment and check data from which conclusions were drawn. We can also encourage them to be precise in the use of language, and we can occasionally demand from them definitions of the terms they use. With the adolescents we can give a more systematic training in the art of reasoning and of testing conclusions, for they have usually begun to take an interest in the process of reasoning as well as in the results obtained by it. They can examine their own general statements and see upon what individual experiences these state-

[1] See *Prejudice and Impartiality*, G. C. Field (Methuen, 1932).

ments were based. Thus they will arrive at a knowledge of the process of induction. They can examine the use made of general statements and the conclusions drawn from them, and so arrive at a knowledge of the process of deduction. A knowledge of logical forms, though not essential for correct thinking, is very valuable for teachers, for it should help to make them sensitive to fallacies in arguments.[1]

The habit of testing conclusions is of general importance throughout life. A good citizen has to learn that other people's conclusions need to be tested before they are accepted, and he must realize how skilfully appeals to emotion may be masquerading as appeals to reason. He must realize too that he himself often argues illogically, and may be predisposed to accept statements that appear in print and statements made by people whom he regards in any way as his superiors.[2]

FANTASY AND IMAGINATION

In our analysis of the process of thinking we have found that much of our thinking is conscious, purposeful, and logical. We grasp a problem, concentrate on it, collect evidence and draw conclusions. We found, however, that there are times when we can hardly be said to " draw " the conclusions ; we arrive at them, they occur to us, sometimes when we are not consciously occupied with the problem. The thinking has been going on at subconscious levels. When the problem is one that is very important to us, or one that calls for originality, some of the thinking is likely to be of the subconscious kind. People have even been known to solve their problems during sleep. It is said that the inventor of sewing machines dreamed the solution to his

---

[1] For the many sources of error in reasoning students should consult a text-book in elementary logic. See also *Exercises in Thinking and Expressing*, J. W. Marriott (Harrap, 1923) ; *Clear Thinking*, R. W. Jepson (Longmans, 1936).

[2] See *Education for Citizenship in Secondary Schools* (Ox. Univ. Press, 1936), chapter XV, " Clear Thinking," G. C. Field ; chapter XVI, " Accurate Thinking," R. H. Thouless.

problem of modifying an ordinary sewing needle to fit the conditions imposed by his machine. After much unsuccessful experimentation, he dreamed one night that he was being threatened by savages who were brandishing spears, and strange to say, a thread of sinew ran through the blade of each spear. Here in the image of the spear was the much-sought clue : put the eye of the machine needle in the point instead of at the other end. It should be noted, however, that the subconscious activity was only a part of the whole process of solving the problem. Without previous concentration the inventor would probably not have had so apt a dream, neither would he have grasped so surely the meaning of the image. The success was not so much a matter of chance as it appeared to be.

Recent investigations with very young children have shown that much of their thinking is carried on at subconscious levels by means of images, and when they tell us fanciful stories or produce imaginative pictures they are often giving expression to solutions or partial solutions to some of their problems.[1] Consider, for instance, the example quoted on page 33. The child suddenly says, " The sun is a bird, it's got wings." This is more than the fanciful remark it appears to be. The child had been puzzled by the apparent movement of the sun. He had questioned adults, but owing to his lack of knowledge their explanations were meaningless to him. He then continued working at the problem in his own more circuitous way. Probably the moving sun suggested images of other moving objects until in the image of a bird he found a satisfactory solution. If the child's drawings had been examined at this stage, they too would probably have revealed something of his preoccupation with this problem of the moving sun.

We have in the past been inclined to look upon day-dreaming and the play of fancy as idle pastimes, undisciplined and serving no useful purpose. Since they were carried on largely by means of images, we were ready to concede that

[1] See *Imagination in Early Childhood*, Ruth Griffiths (Kegan Paul, 1935).

such idle indulgence in imagery might, with training, develop into the disciplined and constructive use of imagery that we call imagination. We now know that fancy, or fantasy, is also a primitive method of solving problems that will, with wider experience and more organized knowledge, lead on to the disciplined activity that we call thinking. Thinking and imagining are closely related. We can, in fact, draw no hard and fast line between them. Both involve the eduction of correlates and both are controlled by a purpose. The activity that we call thinking is illuminated by imagination, and the activity that we call imagining is guided by ideas. They merge one into the other. The most creative forms of thinking, as we have seen, involve most imagining and the highest forms of imagining involve most thinking. Both are necessary for the complete solution of a problem, and neither can come to perfection without the other. Any difference there may be between thinking and imagining perhaps lies in the purpose of the activity rather than in the activity itself. When we think, our purpose is to arrive at a conclusion that we consider true and safe to act upon. When we imagine, our purpose is to arrive at an artistic creation. We speak of a literary or musical masterpiece as a work of imagination, and we speak of a good logical argument as a triumph of thought.

Since the results of imagining are not necessarily true, some people have been impressed with its possible dangers. They realize that the power to select and combine images so as to form new images is a useful one, but they contend that the images so formed should be in accordance with the real world as we know it. A playful and fantastic use of imagery, they say, should be discouraged, since it tends to confuse children and to hinder them in the process of adjusting themselves to the real world. It may lead them to accept unreal solutions to their problems instead of encouraging them to face the world as it is. One of the best-known educators to hold such a view is Montessori, and in consequence of this view she would banish fairy stories from the curriculum for young children. However, the very antiquity of our fairy stories would lead most of us to suspect that they have served a useful purpose in the past, and make us hesitate to deny our children this part of their literary heritage.

Observation of children who have plenty of scope for free, practical activity makes us doubt whether normal children do experience serious confusion. Most of them, by their conversation, make it quite clear that they do distinguish between their real and imaginary worlds. The few who are unable to do so are usually those who have retreated into the imaginary world as a relief from an unattractive real world. To deny them fairy stories would not cure the trouble ; it would merely suppress a symptom. On the positive side there is much to be said for an occasional excursion into an imaginary world such as is provided by fairy tales. Children project themselves into the stories they hear ; they enjoy their temporary power and secure a harmless discharge for feelings that would cause conflict in a real world. The temporary relaxation is valuable, just as any other form of play is valuable. As an habitual method of solving problems, we should condemn day-dreaming, just as we should condemn a life of continuous physical play for our growing boys and girls. Children progress not by stifling their fancies but by turning their fancies to some useful purpose. They must, however, keep their ability to play with fancy, for, in mental life as well as in physical, " all work and no play makes Jack a dull boy."

As we have already suggested, practical activity is usually a sufficient corrective for the dangers that may lie in fantasy. When a real object has to be made, children must recognize the limitations imposed by their purpose and by their materials. But practical work not only acts as a check on unbridled fancy, it also provides opportunities for positive training in imagining. Past experience, very often in the form of images, must be drawn upon, and these images, if they are to be useful, must be clear and accurate. Some attempt must also be made to imagine the new object before work is started, and to foresee the results of various lines of activity. It is interesting here to notice that practical work is often actually inspired by some flight of fancy. For example, children like to dramatize stories they hear, or activities they observe. Properties of some kind are often necessary for this dramatization, and articles such as old wooden boxes are pressed into service. Adaptations often have to be made. Perhaps the box would be improved by paint or wheels, or perhaps it needs to be cut away in places, and so the children are launched on a really practical project. Imagination then may be not the substitute for action but the inspiration of action.

Ability to imagine depends on the power to image and the power to use these images constructively. Any attempt to encourage children to imagine must work along these lines. We have already said in chapter VIII that the images children use arise from their practical experience. We must arrange that this experience is reasonably wide and varied, and we must give children opportunities for recalling their experiences accurately. But this is not enough. We must provide experiences that call for imaginative understanding or appreciation. We must tell them stories of all kinds and let them see beautiful pictures and hear beautiful music. We must also give them opportunities for expressing the results of their imaginings in writing, drawing, handwork, dancing and music.

As we have already implied, we shall find great differences among the children we teach in their power to imagine, since this power is closely linked up with their degree of general intelligence. As Burt says : " For the most part the inventive genius, the creative writer, seem simply to be persons of high general intelligence who apply their general intelligence in their own particular sphere ; and what determines that sphere is chiefly the interest, the education, or, it may be, the predominant type of mental imagery of each man, rather than any unanalysable gift of fancy or imagination." Burt also tells us, however, that there is some evidence for a small specific factor in imagination that is independent of intelligence and is probably connected with originality of mind.[1]

TESTS OF IMAGINATION

A good deal of experimental work has been done on imagination in children. Some of the tests used aim at finding out how the children work up material that is presented to them. One test that has been used for this purpose is the Rorschach Ink-Blot Test. The material consists of a standardized series of large ink blots, and the children are asked to say what they look like. No limit is set as to the number of suggestions they make. Tests of testimony are also used. In these a story is read to children, or a picture is shown to them, and after an interval they reproduce what they have heard or seen. When imagination is being investigated, the most interesting parts of the responses are the departures from, and elaborations of, the original material. Other tests aim mainly at testing the children's ability to finish " in imagination " incomplete drawings and to fill in omissions in passages of print. Both of these exercises demand an imaginative construction of the whole, given some of the parts. An interesting series of questions was used by Spielman and Gaw in an experiment in vocational guidance that was carried out in 1926 under the direction of Dr. Cyril Burt.[2] It is obvious that some occupations involve designing, planning and foreseeing possibilities, all of them creative activities. In one test the children were asked to design a new pillar box different from those in use now and to make explanatory notes as to the purpose of the alterations. In another they were shown a maze drawn on paper. The method of construction was explained to them and they were then asked to construct a maze on a given piece of paper, making the path from the gate to the centre as complicated as possible. As we have seen, the power to imagine finds different outlets with dif-

---

[1] *The Measurement of Mental Capacities*, C. Burt (Oliver & Boyd, 1927).
[2] *A Study in Vocational Guidance*, Industrial Research Board (H.M.S.O., 1926).

ferent people, so other tests, linguistic rather than executive, were also given. For instance, the children were asked to write down as many different predictions as possible in answer to the question, " What might happen if every one could walk and swim at the rate of 100 miles an hour ? " These experiments were followed up by a questionnaire, containing among others the following questions :

1. Have you ever written any stories out of school ? About how many have you written out of school during the last year ?

2 Do you ever paint or draw out of school ? Do you like copying pictures or do you prefer making up new ones ?

3. Have you ever imagined a room just as you would like it best ? What was it like ?

4. Do you often try to invent things ? Describe the most important thing you have ever invented.

The questionnaire is interesting to teachers, for although few of them have time to experiment directly many will find in the questions asked suggestions for making incidental observations.

OBSERVATIONS AND EXPERIMENTS

1. Give Burt's Reasoning Tests to selected children of appropriate ages. [See *Mental and Scholastic Tests*, C. Burt, pp. 239–242 (King, 1921), or *Handbook of Tests*, C. Burt, pp. 91–94 (King, 1923).]

2. Keep a record of mistakes in reasoning made by children of various ages.

3. Give a " predictions " test to a class of secondary-school children. For example, What might happen if no one grew taller than 3 feet? or, What might happen if no one could speak ? Give the children 10 minutes in which to write down as many different answers as they can. Allow 4 marks as the maximum for each answer, 2 for practicability and 2 for difference from other suggestions offered. Compare the results with the children's achievements in imaginative drawing and composition.

4. Take a small group of children who have failed to solve a problem in arithmetic. Try to find the cause of the failure. Consider previous knowledge, language, emotional attitude and interest.

5. Observe a nature study lesson, a needlework or woodwork lesson, a music lesson and a physical training lesson. What problems, if any, did the children have to solve ?

REFERENCES FOR READING

Modern Psychology and Education, Sturt and Oakden, chapters XIII, XIV and XV.
Groundwork of Educational Psychology, J. S. Ross, chapter XII.
Interest, Intelligence and Character, Godfrey H. Thomson, chapter XXV.
Experimental Education, R. R. Rusk, chapters VIII, IX.
The Process of Learning, C. Bloor, chapter X.

ADDITIONAL REFERENCES

The Art of Thought, Graham Wallas (Cape, 1926).
The Art of Thinking, Ernest Dimnet (Cape, 1929).
How we Think, John Dewey (Heath, 1910).
How Children Learn, F. N. Freeman, chapter XI (Harrap, 1919).
The Mind and its Education, G. H. Betts, chapters IX and XII (Appleton, 1916).
Mental Training and Efficiency, F. H. Hayward, chapter IX (Sidgwick & Jackson, 1921).

ESSAYS AND DISCUSSIONS

1. Routine as an aid and as an enemy to thinking.
2. Inductive and deductive methods of teaching.
3. Choose a subject of the curriculum in which you are specially interested. Discuss how in teaching it you can give children scope for (*a*) thinking, (*b*) imagining.
4. The value to a teacher of a lively imagination.
5. The educational value of practical subjects, with special reference to thinking and imagining.
6. Discuss " Lack of imagination is at the root of all the cruelties and all the selfishness in the world."
7. Sources of error in thinking. (Consider : lack of knowledge, prejudice, impatience, laziness.)

Chapter XI

THE DEVELOPMENT OF CHARACTER

We speak of characters as being good or bad, strong or weak, and we think of the ideal character as one which is both strong and good. We say a person has a fine character if we know that in any circumstances he can be depended upon not only to choose the path that he believes to be morally right, but also to persist in it at all costs.

Stages of Character Development

We do not expect a young child to have a finely developed character; his behaviour, as we learned in chapter II, is determined largely by his instinctive impulses, and there is at first no question of right or wrong about his actions. He is neither moral nor immoral; he is a creature of impulse. Very soon, however, he learns that some actions have painful effects; the floor is hard and fire burns, so he begins to control his natural impulses. His character development has begun. He has reached a first and lowly stage of moral control—*the prudential stage* in which control is exercised through fear of physical consequences. The next stage is reached when he differentiates in his environment between things and people. He then finds that some actions are followed by adult approval which is pleasurable, while others are followed by results of an opposite nature. His actions begin to be further controlled by adult authority. He has now reached what is called *the authoritarian stage*. As his social circle widens, he becomes conscious of himself as a member of a group, and he finds that his actions must be controlled in accordance with public opinion if he is to retain the pleasure that he finds in group membership. This is *the social stage*, and it is the highest stage of moral control that some people reach. Their impulses are controlled externally—by prudence, by authority and by the force of public opinion. Such people are not fully developed; they have not completed the process of growing-up. The highest stage is not reached until a person is able to exercise a personal control over his impulses. That is to say, his conduct is regulated by an ideal which he has set up for himself. Confronted with the need for making a decision as to a particular line of conduct, he has still to weigh the physical consequences of his proposed action, to consider authority as embodied in regulation and law, to estimate the probable direction of public opinion. None of these, however, is the final arbiter; a person who has reached the highest stage of moral control—*the personal stage*—will in the last resort be guided by an internal force, the force exerted by his ideal self. His line of action will be that which is in harmony with the type of man he has set up as his standard, and if necessary he will flout public opinion, ignore authority, and disregard all consequences. Fortunately, the number of occasions on which such a drastic line of action becomes necessary is, in modern civilized life, very small. Men of character do, however, occasionally find it necessary to act in defiance of public opinion.

So far as pupils in schools are concerned, the attainment of this highest stage of moral control must remain an ideal to be striven for rather than a goal to be reached, and the lower the school-leaving age the more our pupils will fall short of this ideal. The school community should, however, be " an *idealized* epitome or model of the world,"[1] so that, if pupils must leave at an age when they can only have reached the stage of social control, they have at least had some practical experience of conduct controlled by a worthy type of public opinion, and this experience will, we hope, have some permanent influence on the ideal self which will later regulate their conduct.[2] There is, however, no

[1] *Janus and Vesta*, B. Branford, p. 145 (Chatto & Windus, 1916).
[2] Compare what is said about the influence of " school tone " on p. 194.

stronger argument for the raising of the school-leaving age than the fact that character at the age of 14 or 15 must be immature. Under present conditions promising development is arrested and much of the excellent work of schools in helping pupils to form good and strong characters is undone.

Consider now some practical lessons to be learnt from our knowledge of the psychological development of character. In the first place, character is a result of growth and not a product of moulding. As in other kinds of learning, we must be content to help pupils to pass successfully from one stage to another. It is doing more harm than good to try to force the pace, and in no department of school life are we more strongly tempted to indulge in premature forcing than in the realm of moral training. We are beginning to learn to accept and take pleasure in the crude but sincere work of young children in art and craft ; we are beginning to find out what can reasonably be expected from them in intellectual spheres. Childlike conduct, however, is inconvenient to us adults, and we tend therefore to denounce it on moral grounds. We pride ourselves that we are moulding character, but we are more probably warping it. Paradoxically, the more we try to force the pace, the more likely we are to arrest development. This is because, in our hurry to get results, we over-emphasize the importance of authority.

We must now sound a warning note about psychological stages of development. The labels we have used indicate a hierarchy of types of moral control, but it should not be assumed that the higher types are completely absent at any given age. One of the most important results of modern research into child development is the discovery that from a very early age all mental abilities are present, at least in embryo form. Thus when we say that nursery-school children are in the " prudential " stage, we mean that the type of control which has most influence on them is the steady inexorable control of the physical environment, but we must not assume that the other types are totally without meaning for them. Bearing this in mind, we can make the following suggestions :

(a) It is important to let nursery- and infant-school children experience the results of unwise actions so far as this can be done without causing them serious bodily harm.

(b) At the infant- and junior-school stage, children need the support and help of adult authority.

(c) At the senior-school stage, the authoritarian attitude should have given place to a system of social control.

(d) Before a pupil leaves school, he should have had some experience of personal responsibility for his own conduct.

We see therefore that the development of character is a process of learning, a process during which primitive instinctive impulses are gradually brought under control. The conduct of a young child, being at the mercy of a number of very different instincts, is variable ; the conduct of a person of character is steady and reliable. Let us consider how the change is effected.

The first step towards control is taken when a child is faced by a complex situation. For example, seeing a bright object high up on a shelf, he is at first impelled by curiosity to reach for it. But climbing experiences have taught him that he may fall and hurt himself, so his behaviour is checked by feelings of fear. The two conflicting emotions blend, and the object no longer blindly attracts him ; it fascinates him. His conduct has lost some of its impulsiveness.[1] This type of behaviour, particularly characteristic of the prudential stage, leads through repetition to the formation of some simple habits. The child has now taken a second step towards controlled behaviour, for impulsive instinctive action begins to be replaced by habitual controlled action.

[1] It is interesting to consider the complex emotions that result from the blending of various simple emotions, e.g., disgust and anger produce scorn ; if assertion is added the scorn changes to contempt ; disgust and fear produce loathing ; wonder and submission give rise to admiration.

Conversely, complex emotions, such as envy, jealousy, gratitude, may be resolved into their components.

The learning of habits is continued during the authoritarian and social stages, when a child is greatly helped by adult and social control. He learns, for example, to ask for permission before he plays with his brother's toy. Such early habits are at first specific, but in time they become more general. The habit of asking permission to use one particular toy is extended to the general habit of asking permission before a child plays with anything that does not belong to him. The formation of useful specific habits and the gradual generalizing of such habits is one of the important functions of infant and junior schools. The outward result of this learning is that children become orderly persons.

A third way in which instinctive behaviour is controlled is by the development of new, acquired interests. As we saw in chapter III (pp. 28–31), these interests are usually called sentiments and they are of two main kinds, loves and hates. Children learn, for example, to love their school. They then try to make their behaviour conform to the ideal behaviour for which their school stands, and it follows as a direct result of this sentiment (or ideal) that their conduct both in and out of school is more controlled than it otherwise would be. The self-control that results from the adoption of a high ideal is clearly of a higher type than the control that results from habit. We must be careful, however, not to underestimate the value of habit, for in remaining true to their sentiments, in living up to their ideals, children are greatly helped if in earlier years they have developed a good foundation of useful habits.

The development of character is largely a question of the growth of worthy sentiments, of lofty ideals. At first, children will tend to form sentiments for particular persons and things within their own experience, sentiments such as love of parents, respect for teachers, admiration of older pupils, love of home, love of school. Later, the range of sentiments will increase in many ways. In one direction it will widen to include a love of their own town and native country ; in another direction it will extend to include heroes both of history and of fiction. A further widening of the circle of sentiments occurs when children acquire interests not only in particular persons, but also in persons of an admired type. Admiration of Richard I, Nelson and other heroes gives rise to an admiration of men of courage in general. Finally, children may acquire interests in the abstract qualities characteristic of their heroes ; they develop moral sentiments like love of truth, admiration of courage, hatred of cowardice.

It is much easier to form sentiments for intimate than for remote persons and things, for particular people than for people in general, for concrete objects than for abstract ideas. These principles can be illustrated by considering the growth of sentiment such as patriotism. It must begin at home with the child's parents ; then it is widened to include playmates and other homes, teachers and schools, the district and the people who live in it, and so on until the sentiment includes town, county and country. Concepts like town and nation are difficult for children to grasp, and so the growth of sentiments must be helped by forms of concrete symbolism, mayors and their impressive robes of office, flags and the Crown. Finally, the sentiment of patriotism should be widened to include humanity in general, and for this purpose sentiments of respect for other nations must also be cultivated. Genuine international feeling can only be developed by a patient and gradual widening of healthy sentiments the roots of which are at home.

In the formation of sentiments the influence of the gregarious or herd instinct plays a very important part. Individuals separated from the physical presence of their fellows experience loneliness and so they seek company. In a similar way we tend to feel outside the group unless we are in harmony with the feelings and the ideas of the people among whom we live. This is the psychological basis for the irresistible, silent influence wielded by a school on its members. Many sentiments are therefore formed in the social stage just as many habits are formed in the prudential and authoritarian stages.

The personal stage is marked by a still further unification

in the interests of an individual. In early infancy he gradually becomes conscious of himself as an individual, and as
he grows up his ideas of himself undergo many changes.
He tends to identify himself first with one type of hero and
then with another. Gradually, however, as a result of his
varied experience and of the habits and sentiments he has
acquired, he forms a more or less settled idea of the person
he conceives himself to be. He sets up an ideal person as
his pattern or, as the psychologist says, he forms a self-
regarding sentiment. The effect of this is to bind together
all the other sentiments he has formed. Thus the self-
regarding sentiment becomes the keystone of his character.
All his conduct is regulated, consciously or unconsciously,
by it. He has become a man of character. When faced
with the need for a moral decision, he brings his self-
regarding sentiment into action, or, as we say, he exerts his
will. He is under the influence of the ideal self he has
built up as his pattern, and his conduct is determined in
conformity with it. It is this sentiment, this conscience,
this ideal,—the name is unimportant—which gives stability
to his conduct.

Applying this theory to school life, we see that character-
development means that, as children pass through school,
they pass through a stage in which they are kept in order
to a stage in which they discipline themselves. A study of
order and discipline will therefore help us to recapitulate
in a practical way the psychological theories of character-
development that we have so far outlined in this chapter.

Order and Discipline

If we want to get clear ideas of the significance of the
term " discipline," there is nothing more helpful than to
note its close etymological affinity with the word " disciple,"
and also the important distinction in meaning between the
terms " discipline " and " order." A disciplined class is a
class of disciples ; a disciplined pupil is a learner. It is
clear at once that an orderly class is not necessarily well

disciplined, for pupils may be sitting still and yet they may be learning nothing; they may be the slaves of a tyrant and not the disciples of a master. Nevertheless, a disciplined class is usually an orderly class, for some orderliness is a necessary condition if thirty pupils in one room are to learn effectively. Or, looking at the situation from another angle, some degree of orderliness is an inevitable state of affairs when thirty individuals have settled down to work in a classroom. The kind of order will vary from one lesson to another according to the kind of learning in progress. Sometimes the necessary order will involve silence, as, for example, when pupils are composing; sometimes it will involve stillness, as, for example, during a lecture; at other times it will involve noise and movement, as, for example, when craftwork is in progress. It is important for beginners in the art of teaching to decide on the degree and kind of orderliness that they deem to be reasonable and necessary in each type of circumstance, and then to be resolute in maintaining it. If common sense be used in deciding upon a reasonable kind of orderliness, beginners are advised then to be as strict as possible. It is easier to give " a little more rope " to a well-ordered class than it is to " rope in " a class which has become disorderly. It is common knowledge that children prefer order to disorder, and that they are happier with teachers who can control the class than with those who cannot. One important reason is that a strict teacher, by maintaining order, makes it possible for children to do the best work of which they are capable, and in this way he enables them to experience a very satisfying joy of achievement. It is probable that lazy children sometimes find mental relief when, as a result of the influence of a strict and respected teacher, they complete a good piece of work. It is not, of course, suggested that a teacher should be harsh or unsympathetic; on the contrary, as we said previously (p. 50), he should always be careful to respect the personalities of his pupils. But the kindest form of control is that which is firm and steady. Children need the same qualities in their social environment as they find in their physical environment. As they walk about the classroom, they know that they cannot throw themselves on the floor with impunity, but they also know that there is no likelihood of a board giving way beneath them or springing up capriciously to hit them. The physical environment controls them rigorously, but it does not enslave them; it forms a settled framework in which they can for the most part live safely and confidently, but it is a framework in which they also have freedom to live adventurously and even dangerously. They need a similarly settled framework of social control. It must be control that supports them and gives them confidence in themselves, but it must not bear so hard on them that they lose the desire for adventurous living, both mental and physical.

In considering this question of social control in school, it is most important to remember that all children in pre-school years have been subjected to control, some of it probably of an unwise character. But even if we assume that their upbringing has been as perfect as possible, we cannot escape the fact that social control in early years produces a very definite mark on children's minds, a mark that we cannot ignore. It is very difficult to understand the inner workings of the mind of a very young child, and psychologists are not agreed on the various theories which have been advanced in explanation of children's social behaviour. But the fact remains that the behaviour of young children suggests that they are subject to severe mental conflicts—love conflicts with hate, fear with curiosity, destructive impulses with social ideals. The result is that children have vague feelings of guilt and sub-conscious dreads of punishment. If this picture be true, it will be seen that kindly external control is for children a psychological need. It helps them to live up to their ideals, it lessens the force of mental conflicts, it gives them the comforting experience that adults can control them without hurting them—in a word, it relieves mental tension. This is another reason why children prefer order to disorder.

As Dr. Susan Isaacs suggests, a little child cannot make use of an absolute " freedom " ; it is necessary, to quote her words, " that his parents and educators should represent to him a stable and ordered world of values, closely related to his real abilities at any given age, and based upon an understanding of his psychological needs, but yet firm and unwavering in themselves. . . . If this real external control is mild and tempered, although firm and secure, it enables the child to master his destructive impulses and learn to adapt his wishes to the real world. If he neither finds fulfilment of his phantastic dreads in the outer world, nor is left at their mercy in his inner world by having no external support, but is slowly educated by a tempered, real control, mild and understanding and appropriate to each situation as it arises, he is led forward on the path of real achievement."[1]

THE ART OF KEEPING ORDER

It is often said that order in a classroom depends largely on the " personality of the teacher." It is certainly true that some persons seem to incite a class to be disorderly while others never know what it is to have an unruly class. Most beginners have some difficulties, and the easy power of control of most experienced teachers is an acquired accomplishment rather than a natural endowment. It is doubtful whether the art of keeping order can be taught by instructions, but it can certainly be learnt by experience. The following hints, however, may help some beginners to short-circuit the learning process :

Routine.—It is not easy for a fallible human being to maintain the steadiness of mild control that is so desirable for training children. One important aid, however, is classroom routine. We have already noted (p. 8) that children are endowed with a routine tendency. One consequence is that they readily fall into a settled way of doing things that have to be done repeatedly, and in fact they like

[1] See *The Psychological Aspects of Child Development*, Susan Isaacs, pp. 39–40 (Evans, 1935).

a certain measure of routine. Teachers can therefore save themselves much trouble and their pupils some irritation by instituting fixed ways of doing the trivial tasks of the daily round. The distribution and collection of books and material, the opening of windows, the drawing of margins, the order of assembling and dismissing—all matters such as these should be done according to a fixed routine without a word from the teacher. The most orderly classroom is generally one in which the fewest orders are given. When taking over a new class, it is well to bear in mind that children are sticklers for routine, and it is therefore necessary to be patient and tactful in introducing alterations to existing routine. In many good schools the head teacher arranges that some matters shall be subject to a school routine, and in this way unnecessary and irritating changes are avoided as pupils pass from one class to another. With older children it is often a good plan to discuss proposed changes in routine before putting them into operation. Once a good system is working, a great deal of time and energy is saved and much friction avoided. Furthermore, new pupils can be absorbed without fuss or trouble, for they learn the accepted routines by silent imitation instead of by wordy instruction.

Appear confident.—A teacher's authority in a classroom is not merely his personal authority, which may of itself be puny and ineffective. A teacher is a symbol of a whole hierarchy of authorities, and children are ready to acknowledge this, though they are not fully conscious of it. On the other hand, they are quick to detect the slightest sign of embarrassment or indecision and to take advantage of it. Some things are bound to go wrong, and it is well therefore to expect such happenings and not to appear surprised at or worried by them. Some mischances are bound to appeal to children's crude sense of humour; it is well to be prepared for this and to join confidently in the fun. A teacher who can laugh with his class is not likely to find himself in the awkward position of being laughed at. It is, of course, desirable to reduce mischances to a minimum, and thorough preparation is one important means of increasing confidence in front of a class. This applies to the subject-matter of lessons, to the organization of work, to the distribution of books and materials and to the preparation of apparatus.

Be sincere.—Children are quick to appreciate a teacher who is sincerely interested in them and their work. Such a teacher during oral lessons sees the individuals before him rather than the class. Each pupil therefore finds himself frequently under his teacher's eye, and there is little or no occasion for interrupting the work by petty admonitions. A teacher who is interested in each individual will not talk at one section of desks, nor will he as a rule stand so near his class that he cannot see individuals at the sides. Beginners may find it helpful to adopt mechanical rules on these matters—for example, to stand so many yards from the front line of desks, to avoid turning completely away from the class when writing on the blackboard, and so on. It must be emphasized, however, that there is little real virtue in such rules and that in modern teaching they must often be broken. The fundamental rule is to behave in the classroom so that no one feels he is being neglected.

Give children scope for activity.—It is probably true to say that most of the difficulties in maintaining classroom order arise because we are trying to make children conform to an unnatural standard of silence and inactivity. There must be oral class-teaching in school and children must be trained to listen. In many classrooms, however, training in listening is negatived by excess of oral teaching that bores the pupils and forces them to adopt the defence of daydreaming or petty misdemeanours. It is a very good rule to punctuate all oral lessons with short periods of activity—children can, for example, write notes, draw sketches, act scenes, write answers to questions. Less talking and more activity—this is perhaps the most helpful advice for any teacher who finds it difficult to keep order. In a classroom where children are happily active, it is seldom necessary to give an order beginning with " Don't."

G

See that every order is obeyed.—The fewer the orders, the easier it is to put this precept into practice. We have already suggested some means of reducing the number of orders—a reasonably tolerant attitude towards noise and movement, a recognized routine for recurring details, the use of " the teacher's eye," the provision of opportunities for activity. When it is necessary to give an order in words, the attention of the class should be secured before the actual order is given, for children engrossed in an interesting task can be literally deaf to a teacher's voice (see p. 110). If all these conditions are fulfilled, an order given to the whole class should be obeyed promptly by every pupil, and no exception should be tolerated. If disobedience is general, as sometimes happens in an unruly class, the whole class should be told to return to the " as-you-were position," and the order should be repeated firmly. Correlative to the orders that a teacher gives are the promises or threats that he makes, and he cannot expect his orders to be obeyed if his promises or threats are not fulfilled. Children are very quick to learn whether a teacher means what he says, and his authority is seriously undermined if he indulges in threats that he does not or cannot carry out. Warnings are sometimes necessary, and promises of reward are sometimes useful, but it is necessary to be cautious lest the future becomes over-heavily mortgaged.

An order should not be addressed to a class unless it refers to the class as a whole. It is, for example, irritating to children who are working to be continually interrupted by admonitions addressed vaguely to no one in particular. Individual delinquents should be dealt with individually, and for this purpose a look or a gesture is often enough.

Make a judicious use of praise.—A cheerful teacher who is able to appreciate sincerity in children's work and who is not dismayed by its natural crudity is less likely to have trouble in keeping order than a complaining teacher who is anxious to see children achieving adult standards prematurely. Indiscriminate praise is futile, but in many schools there is room for a large increase in the use made of praise and a corresponding decrease in the use made of blame and fault-finding. In marking the composition of young children, for example, it might be worth while to concentrate on praising its merits; in any case the marking of errors should always be done in a spirit of optimistic helpfulness and not of pessimistic complaining. The same principle applies to questions of conduct.

Institute a team system.—Opinions may differ as to the desirability of dividing a class into teams with a system of marks for meritorious work and conduct. Ideally, such a system should be unnecessary with older children, and when used for younger children, there is little chance of developing a real team spirit in which individual members co-operate for the good of the team. There is no doubt, however, that young teachers with large classes find some such system a very great help. Even if we admit that in essence it is a system of individual rewards and punishments, there can be little objection to it, for the rewards are small and the punishments are mild. Moreover, as skill in class management is acquired the system can and should play a decreasing part in the life of the class.

Punishment.—This is a subject that often arouses strong feelings when it is debated. But, whatever our personal views may be, we must admit that punishment has some place in the maintenance of classroom order and that all teachers use it in some form. The punishment may consist merely of a mild expression of displeasure; it may be an angry exclamation; it may take the form of deprivation of marks or privileges; in the last resort, it may be corporal punishment. But, whatever form it may take, it should always aim at making a pupil a better member of the school or classroom society, and thus ultimately a better member of the larger societies that he will join in adult life. Punishment should in fact be looked upon as a reaction of society, designed to preserve its own well-being. If this principle, that punishment is a social matter, be observed, it will prevent us from using punishment in unworthy ways. We should not use it, for example, as a form of retribution for what we conceive to be an affront to our personal dignity. Neither should we punish children, even by the mild expression of displeasure, for failings that are the result of poor natural endowment ; the remedy for such failings must be sought in a reorganization of the school community so that even its least gifted members can make some contribution to its welfare. On the positive side, punishment should be recognized by the pupils as a whole as being both just and necessary. It should help the offender to control his anti-social impulses, and this is only possible if he feels that the general sense of the community is on the side of authority. This remedial aspect of punishment is so important that teachers ought to watch carefully the effects of the punishments they inflict ; if the same pupils are being punished term after term, it is a sign that the punishment is failing in its main objective and that some more effective remedy needs to be found. It is, indeed, doubtful whether punishment alone is ever really efficacious, and a wise teacher will discreetly follow up a punishment by unobtrusive influences designed to help the offender to choose and follow the right path.

While the main intention of punishment should be remedial, it may also have two secondary effects. It may act as a deterrent, and it may be looked upon by children as a form of retribution. As we have seen, children are very severe in their dealings with offences committed by playmates, and many psychologists believe that this severity is one of the effects of their own feelings of guilt. Many parents have noticed what a calming influence punishment may have on children, and it may well be that this is due to the fact that children feel that the punishment has expiated the offence ; having made the necessary retribution, their minds are at rest. In this connexion, it should be noted that anger is to children a very human quality, and one that they understand. This remark should not, however, be interpreted as an excuse for a continual display of anger in the classroom ; it is merely intended to suggest that on appropriate, rare occasions anger may be a healthy form of expression to use against young offenders, and it may suit children better than a display of pious grief. As in all dealings with children, we ought, however, when meting out punishment, to bear in mind the fact of individual differences. There are some nervous, sensitive children for whom a look of reproach is as severe a punishment as an angry reprimand would be for others.

The same general principles apply to corporal as to other forms of punishment, but if angry words ought to be rare, corporal punishment ought to be still rarer. Its use should always be recognized as a sign of failure, though it is not suggested that under present conditions such failure could always be avoided. Corporal punishment is often, however, an easy way out of immediate difficulty, and one that beginners especially should for that reason avoid. There is also another insidious danger in the use of corporal punishment, and it lies in the fact that some of us find a special pleasure in inflicting pain. Many readers will probably deny that this is true of themselves, but the tendency is so widespread that it behoves us all to be careful ; we may find many worthy reasons why corporal punishment is good, but the real source of our fervent advocacy may be a sadistic tendency.[1] It is very easy to develop a habit of using corporal punishment in the early months of a teaching career instead of struggling to overcome difficulties by more desirable though more troublesome methods. That is why some education authorities and many wise head teachers do not allow assistant teachers to administer corporal punishment during their first year of service. This may appear to be a hard rule, but there is no doubt that it is a wise one. It need hardly be added that regulations regarding corporal punishment should always be scrupulously observed, for they are made in the interests both of teachers and pupils. An irregular angry blow may cause serious

[1] Conversely, some persons find pleasure in submitting to the infliction of pain. This is called masochism. These two tendencies—masochism and sadism—may have an important bearing on the attitude of individual teachers and pupils to the question of corporal punishment.

physical harm, and teachers will be· well-advised to adopt for themselves the army rule that even the slightest touch constitutes an assault and is forbidden. On the rare occasions when corporal punishment is deemed necessary, and it should be reserved for serious offences, it should be adminstered in an approved way. There are now many schools where corporal punishment is no longer necessary, and we as educationists should certainly work towards the ideal of its complete banishment from our schools. As Nunn says, " The conviction, once so deeply rooted in the teaching profession, that punishment and the fear of punishment are the natural foundations of school government, is gradually being recognized as merely a barbarous superstition."[1] The abolition of all corporal punishment cannot be achieved by a word of command from those in authority over class teachers. It is an ideal the realization of which depends on many factors, and some of them are not within the direct control of schools. We need, for example, far more wisdom in the early upbringing of children, together with housing conditions that will give children a chance of a healthy, active life. In school we need smaller classes, particularly for infants and juniors, so that children may be increasingly taught by methods that appeal to their natural interests.

DISCIPLINE

In our discussion of the art of keeping order, we have hinted several times that the best kind of order is that which is a natural outgrowth of happy activity in the classroom. Some reformers have boldly taken up the position that this is the only kind of order that is worth having. True to their principles, they have allowed their classes to start in a state of chaos, and not until the pupils themselves felt the need of order was the question discussed. The class then made rules and order was established, not so much by the will of the teacher as by the will of the class itself. It will,

[1] *Education ; Its Data and First Principles*, p. 232.

however, be agreed that though such experiments are valuable we cannot as a general rule afford to neglect the influences of tradition ; we cannot afford to allow each set of pupils to start from " scratch." Having developed a school tone, we cannot break it up and start afresh at the beginning of each school year. And, as we have seen, we are strengthened in this position by the findings of modern psychologists who have shown that young children need the support and help of adult authority. It is of first-rate importance, however, that in all our plans for keeping order we should bear in mind the desirability of helping children to keep themselves in order. This is the underlying principle of many experiments in " self-government." Young children, as we have seen, cannot be expected to govern one another wisely, but they can be given little individual responsibilities in matters appertaining to school equipment and material. In the infant and junior stage a scheme of monitors to look after things such as books, pencils, windows, doors, can be worked successfully and with profit. In the senior stage a system of prefects with limited responsibilities for the conduct of their fellows is a natural development. Many teachers of older children will find it possible to go further and try the experiment of converting the class into a miniature parliament responsible for framing rules of conduct, and at times into a miniature law-court for the trial of offenders. At all stages of school life it may be necessary to impose order upon pupils, but such order should never be an end in itself ; it should be a stepping-stone to something higher. This brings us to the subject of discipline.

It is regrettable that the word " discipline " is often used as if it were a synonym for " order," and it will help to clarify our thinking if we use it in a more limited sense. Discipline, we suggest, is a term that should be reserved to describe a state of mind ; order, on the other hand, is merely a state of affairs. Order is of two kinds, somewhat similar in outward appearance but radically different in origin. It may be a state of affairs imposed on unwilling pupils by external authority, or it may be a state of affairs resulting naturally from the fact that pupils have willingly submitted themselves to certain good influences. This willing submission to outside influence is the very essence of discipline. When a teacher is able to keep a class in order, we usually call him a good disciplinarian, but the term " disciplinarian " ought to mean much more than that. A disciplinarian is a person who can help pupils to submit themselves willingly to disciplinary influences; he is a person who has the art of making disciples. Bertrand Russell's description of the modern parent expresses admirably the qualities of a real disciplinarian: " He wants his children to be as unconstrained in his presence as in his absence; he wants them to feel pleasure when they see him coming; he does not want a fictitious Sabbath calm while he is watching, succeeded by pandemonium as soon as he turns his back."[1]

It is clear then that discipline is a state of mind, the acquirement of which needs the active co-operation of the pupil himself. True discipline is always in the last resort self-discipline. It is equally important, however, to remember that there can be no discipline without disciplinary influences. When we talk of " free discipline " we do not mean that children are left free to do what they like. As a matter of fact, this is impossible, for if all external constraint could be removed, children would still be at the mercy of their own conflicting impulses. Free discipline, as far as the term has any meaning, implies that the children submit themselves freely or willingly; it therefore means nothing more than the term " discipline " as we have defined it. Schools that work on " free-discipline lines " are schools in which little importance is attached to order imposed by any authority other than the child himself. They are aiming, as all good schools aim, at promoting real discipline, but they differ from ordinary schools in that they leave children at all times as much as possible to their own devices. Many modern psychologists believe there is a danger that such methods may put too great a strain on young children.

[1] *On Education*, p. 141 (Allen & Unwin, 1926).

On the other hand, it is probable that those advocates of " free discipline " who make a success of it exercise far more control over their pupils than they are aware of.

DISCIPLINARY INFLUENCES

We must now consider briefly the disciplinary influences to which we want our pupils willingly to submit themselves. The first influence and the most powerful is that of the community—school or class. As we have said (p. 177), the herd instinct makes children very susceptible to the force of public opinion, and if the tone of a school is good a pupil is at once under a desirable disciplinary influence, for he is a very exceptional child who does not willingly submit himself to the influence of what is done or not done by his fellows. It is impossible to describe in detail what constitutes a good tone, for it is a very complex subtle affair to which many personalities have made a contribution, and the tone of each school has its own individual characteristics. Broadly speaking, however, the tone of a school should be such that pupils feel they are living in a society where hard work, beautiful things, adventurous thinking, muscular skill, good fellowship, moral virtues, strenuous games are all valued not only by teachers but by the school as a whole.

Next to the influence of the school tone comes the influence of individual members of staff, an influence that is, of course, already partly reflected in the school tone. We have referred to the question of personality when discussing the keeping of order. All that need be added here is that the possession of a strong personality may enable a teacher to keep order without effort, but it does not necessarily make him a good disciplinarian. A strong personality, unless accompanied by an alert, well-stored mind, and by a real sympathy with children and a keen interest in their development, may actually prevent children from becoming disciplined in the best sense of the word.

A third disciplinary influence is that afforded by school studies, for these should lead a pupil to appreciate human abilities vastly superior to his own, superior even to those of his teachers. As a child becomes disciplined, he submits himself to the influence of master thinkers, writers, artists and craftsmen. He is filled with the desire to follow in the steps of one or more of these masters, and, as Nunn says, " his position is that of an apprentice striving to learn the trick of the master hand."

It will now be clear that disciplinary influences are not mere negative forces of restraint ; their main function is directive and inspirational, and the restraint they exert is of the nature of a by-product. Under good disciplinary influences a pupil has scope to make mistakes but he also has successes that spur him on to fresh efforts. Gradually he learns the great lesson of self-control—control of his intellect, his emotional impulses and his muscles. He has become a willing, eager disciple of some of the great personalities of the past, and in his efforts he is helped and supported by the good influences of his school and teachers. The result is that his whole self, mind and body, becomes more shapely ; he is on the way to becoming a disciplined person capable of independent thought and action, an acceptable and helpful member of society and a very different person from one who needs to be kept in order by a so-called " good disciplinarian."

CONCLUSION

We have seen that a person of character is one whose life is regulated by a worthy ideal. Our task in school is to help each pupil to form such an ideal for himself, and this is exactly what we have described in other words as helping him to become a disciplined person. In chapter IV we described some of the individual differences that we find among children. It is clear that, given equality of educational opportunity, differences in intelligence determine to a large extent subsequent differences in intellectual attainment. Similarly, differences in temperament show themselves in characters of various types. This is another reason why it is wrong to set out with the idea of moulding character according to one set pattern. It is probably true to say, however, that experience has more effect on the development of character than it has on the development of intellect. It is impossible to help an inherently dull child to grow into a clever scholar, but it is possible to help almost any child to develop a character that is at least worthy. In fact, one of the most encouraging features in experiments in the education of adolescents is the capacity for social and moral development that is shown in school activities by many pupils whose intellectual attainments are meagre.

We must not, however, fall into the error of thinking that moral development and intellectual development proceed in watertight compartments. Success in intellectual studies is necessary in school for the development of self-respect, without which little progress in character development can be made, and it follows therefore that the provision of a suitable curriculum for dull children is an urgent necessity. Again, it is in their intellectual studies that children meet a wide variety of personal ideals from which they can choose according to the needs of their particular temperaments. Many of the moral sentiments, respect for thoroughness, truth, tidiness, are also taught incidentally in the course of ordinary lessons. The same is true of another important group of sentiments—love of home, town and country.

It is probable that children's ideals are formed and their characters developed much more surely and healthily by the all-round normal life of an active school than by any direct moral lessons. Stories of the lives of great men and women of all types, and an appreciation of their work obtained in the ordinary lessons of the usual school curriculum are much more likely to inspire children than lessons specially designed for that purpose. The team spirit is developed by participation in group work, social functions and team games rather than by lectures on the subject. In a word, children's characters are developed by experience. In the sphere of morals the general principle holds that children learn by doing more than by listening. This does not mean that a word of direct moral instruction is always out of place. A wise teacher will seize many little opportunities for a word in season, particularly with older pupils. But the word will arise directly out of some actual incident, and the point will not be laboured. As a rule, it will be designed to help pupils to make more general some ideal that they have acquired in one or more specific settings. When a general ideal has been formed, it will affect children's behaviour at all relevant points, and lessen the need of further specific training.

A very suitable occasion for bringing together similar lessons learnt in a variety of separate settings is the school assembly. Generally speaking, this will be done by a short address during the customary service. Occasionally a special service may be held in which hymns, prayers, reading, music and address are all chosen with a view to focusing attention on one important theme.[1] The school assembly should never be allowed to become a perfunctory ceremony; still less should it be made the occasion for giving out trivial routine notices or for making petty complaints about breaches of school rules. It should be a function, religious in the best sense, where each pupil is helped to see the unity underlying all the diverse activities of school life, and where he is helped to combine many subsidiary sentiments into one master sentiment, a lofty sentiment of self-regard.

REFERENCES FOR READING

Handbook of Suggestions, New edition, 1937. (See *Index* : Character training.)
Education, Sir T. Percy Nunn, pp. 198–201, 229–233.
Modern Psychology and Education, Sturt and Oakden, chapters VIII, IX, XVII.
Instinct, Intelligence and Character, Godfrey H. Thomson, chapters XXII, XXIII.

---

[1] This important idea has been developed by Dr. F. H. Hayward, who suggests that such services should be called " Celebrations." Most schools already hold annual celebrations on Empire or Commonwealth Day, and on Armistice Day. Hayward suggests that there should be five annual celebrations in every school—Home, Town, Country, Empire, League of Nations. For examples of celebration services, see *Books of School Celebrations*, F. H. Hayward.

Your Mind and Mine, R. B. Cattell, chapter IX.
Modern Education, T. Raymont, chapter X.
The Process of Learning, C. Bloor, chapters XIII, XIV, XV.

ADDITIONAL REFERENCES

The Approach to Teaching, H. Ward and F. Roscoe, chapter V (Bell, 1928).
An Outline of Psychology, Wm. McDougall, chapter XVII (Methuen, 1923).
The Making of Character, J. MacCunn (Camb. Univ. Press, 1908).
The Dawn of Character, E. E. R. Mumford (Longmans, 1925).
The Foundations of Character, A. F. Shand (Macmillan), 1914).
Principles and Methods of Moral Training, Welton and Blandford (Univ. Tut. Press, 1909).

ESSAYS AND DISCUSSIONS

1. Discuss the following :
   (a) The prefect system.
   (b) The " house " system.
   (c) Competition and co-operation in the classroom.
   (d) Self-government.
   (e) Direct moral instruction.
   (f) School rules, written and unwritten.
   (g) Means of developing healthy self-respect among pupils.
2. It is often said that punishment should be made " to fit the crime." A similar principle underlies the theory that punishment should be a " natural consequence " of the offence.

   Montessori, for example, isolates children who interfere with the work of others.

   Discuss the principle in relation to some common delinquencies that have to be dealt with in school.
3. Discuss the following :

   " Physical punishment I believe to be never right. In mild forms it does little harm, though no good ; in severe forms I am convinced that it generates cruelty and brutality . . . it accustoms boys to the idea that it may be right and proper to inflict physical pain for the purpose of maintaining authority—a peculiarly dangerous lesson." Bertrand Russell in his book, *On Education*, p. 141 (Allen & Unwin, 1926).
4. One of the most urgent needs in the world at large is a healthy attitude towards authority, neither timid or obsequious on the one hand, nor defiant or rebellious on the other.

   How can schools help to lay the foundation of such an attitude ?
5. Discuss the following quotations in which a clear distinction is drawn between " order " and " discipline " :

   " School order consists in the maintenance of the conditions necessary if school life is to fulfil its purpose."

   " Discipline consists in the submission of one's impulses and powers to a regulation which imposes form upon their chaos, and brings efficiency and economy where there would otherwise be ineffectiveness and waste." Sir T. P. Nunn in his book, *Education: Its Data and First Principles*, pp. 198-9.
6. What can schools do to train will-power ?

   (" ' The Will ' is character in action," W. McDougall, *An Outline of Psychology*, p. 442.)

CHAPTER XII

THE DEVELOPMENT OF MUSCULAR SKILL

LET us think of some of the movements we make in the course of a day. We wake up, blink and stretch our limbs ; we get out of bed ; we sneeze ; we dip our hands into hot water and if it is uncomfortably hot we snatch them away ; we dress, run downstairs, use knives and forks, write letters, do sewing or woodwork, play games. Some of these movements, such as blinking and sneezing, we could do perfectly at birth. We call them reflex movements. They have not involved any learning, for the ability to do them formed part of our natural endowment. Contrasted with these movements are others, such as those used when dressing or writing, that we have had to learn. Some of them we learned at home in pre-school years, but many of them we learned at school under the guidance of teachers. Two important questions arise—(a) How do children learn to make skilled movements ? (b) What can teachers do to facilitate this learning ?

We noted in chapter II that children were born with a tendency to be generally active and with some specific tendencies to act in special ways in certain circumstances. These instinctive reactions form the basis of all the skilled movements that we have learnt. Some of our simple movements, such as stretching and snatching our hands from hot water, are still largely instinctive, but, unlike reflex movements, they have become somewhat more skilled as a result of our experience. The wonder of the process of acquiring skill is, however, most clearly appreciated when we reflect on a more complicated action such as writing. We adults can now write with the minimum of attention and with very little fatigue. But it was not always so. Watch a young child trying to write his name. He is working hard with his mind and body ; gripping his pencil tightly, he makes each stroke with painful effort ; he puts out his tongue, twists his body, and obviously gets tired by his exertions. The adult's performance is very different. He holds his pencil lightly, and with a continuous, easy, flowing movement he signs his name ; there is no suggestion of hard labour. Compared with the child's clumsy movements, the adult's skilled movements look neater, smoother and easier. These are the essentials of a skilled action as contrasted with a clumsy one, and we will now consider each in turn.

The neatness of skilled movement.—This characteristic neatness appears, first, because the skilled person makes no unsuccessful movements, and second, because he makes no unnecessary movements. Economy of movement is a sure index of real skill. A young child learning to use a pencil or a pair of scissors moves parts of the body that are not directly concerned with the action he is trying to perform. It seems as if the effort is so great that it must spread to all parts of the body. That is why an unskilled worker needs so much more elbow room than a skilled worker. From one point of view we can think of the process of acquiring skill as the gradual elimination of unsuccessful and unnecessary movements.

The smoothness of skilled movement.—If we compare an expert knitter with a child learning to knit we see that the expert makes one continuous movement whereas the child makes at least four separate movements for each stitch. This example illustrates another important stage in the development of skill ; not only are useless movements eliminated, but also the useful ones are combined to form a single movement. This is generally described by saying that the various component parts of the movement are co-ordinated. Co-ordination is largely a question of using the right amount of force at the right time. The unskilled worker exerts too much force and applies the force unevenly, whereas the skilled worker uses just as much force as is necessary and keeps the balance, as it were, between the various parts of the movement. A girl who is learning to use a treadle machine often finds that one foot is too strong for the other, and consequently she produces a series of jerky movements instead of a continuous, steady, up-and-down movement. We see then that as skill is acquired useless movements are dropped, separate movements become combined, and force is controlled.

The ease of skilled movement.—This characteristic is partly the result of the gradual simplification of movement that we have considered above. The more skilful the movement, the less work is done and the easier the action appears. But ease of movement is also connected with mental attitude. As skill is acquired, the learner needs to attend less closely to what he is doing. His action becomes automatic and he is able to attend to the result rather than to the action. He has the air of easy mastery.

MOTION STUDY

Modern methods of motion study have shown that even experienced workers often make many unnecessary and unrhythmical movements. Some of the unnecessary movements are caused by bad placing of the apparatus used and would therefore be obvious to any critical but unprejudiced onlooker. In one factory the output of work was increased by 266 per cent. when the parts to be assembled were arranged in a definite and convenient order. Other unnecessary and unrhythmical movements were not so obvious and needed a more detailed study of the workers' procedure before they were detected. Gilbreth, one of the pioneers of scientific motion study, devised for this purpose the chronocyclographic method. He attached a lamp to a convenient part of the worker's body or of his tool and photographed it in motion. By suitable devices he was able to measure both the time and scope of the movement and to determine the various directions taken. Eventually a wire model of the movement was made and this was then studied at leisure and from all angles. It was particularly instructive to compare the models for skilled and unskilled workers performing the same operation, for they showed that skilled workers made fewer movements and that these movements were also more rhythmical.

How Skill is Acquired

There is only one fundamental method by which skill is acquired, viz. the method of trial and success. It consists in repetition carried on by a learner who is eager to succeed. Given this condition, the learning proceeds according to a simple psychological law. This law states that when an action is performed it tends to be stamped in if it is accompanied by pleasure, but it tends to be stamped out if it is accompanied by pain. Now, if the learner is eager, success brings pleasure, but failure brings pain. Thus, there is a tendency for successful actions to be repeated and for unsuccessful ones to drop out. In its simplest form, learning by trial and success calls for no enforced attention to the activities of other people, it demands little or no power of reflecting on past experiences, and it can be carried on quite well without the use of words. It is therefore a method that is particularly suitable for very young children. In school, however, much can be done to increase the proportion of successful actions, and in this way the learning process can be accelerated. We will now consider some important ways in which teachers can help and encourage children to acquire skill.

Interest.—As we have reiterated several times in this book, the first essential in learning is that pupils should want to learn. The keener they are, the more intense is the pleasure that accompanies success, and consequently the more effective is the learning. It is, of course, possible to provide extraneous rewards and punishments—good and bad marks, prizes and penalties. It is possible to use the stimulus of competition in many ways, some less undesirable than others. But the teacher who is teaching skill should aim at inspiring his pupils with higher motives, for most children are ready to be spontaneously interested in acquiring skill. As we have seen, they are by nature active creatures and they have an instinctive urge to make things. The acquisition of skill in these pleasurable forms of behaviour produces still further accessions of pleasure, for it helps to satisfy children's love of power. But the influence of skill on personality may go deeper than the mere satisfaction of primitive instincts. As children acquire skill in movement and mastery over the materials they are using, their energy, instead of being absorbed in the bare essentials of the activity, is released in increasing measure and becomes available for other purposes. This surplus energy may, of course, be frittered away in daydreaming, but under suitable conditions it may be used for the creation of grace and beauty. The dance, instead of being merely a collection of accurate steps, becomes a graceful performance ; the exercise book, no longer necessitating laborious care, affords scope for beauty of arrangement and perhaps for restrained embellishment. Any form of practical work in which skill has been acquired becomes a vehicle for the expression of beauty ; it provides scope for the highest type of self-expression.[1]

Much can be done to increase interest by taking children to art galleries and museums, to exhibitions of school craftwork, to expert demonstrations. The attention of children can be drawn to beautiful common objects and an occasional reminder be given that these things have been produced by skilled craftsmen. Cinematograph films of beautiful skilled movements by expert athletes and craftsmen also play a part in inspiring modern children to develop their own powers. Coming to more specific problems, the interest of children in making a model, in mixing a pudding,

---

[1] It is interesting to note that the operation of this fundamental principle of education, like that of others described in this book, can be seen clearly in the history of the race. The weapons and cooking utensils of early man were plain and unadorned, but as skill was acquired they became more than merely useful ; they became beautiful. This theory of beauty in craftwork is often attributed to William Morris ; it is eloquently described by Nunn in his book, *Education : Its Data and First Principles*, p. 91.

in painting a picture can often be intensified by showing them worthy examples before they begin. It is a good plan for teachers to have a piece of their own work in progress in the craftroom ; if possible, work that is far in advance of their pupils' ability.

Teaching by demonstration.—All the suggestions in the preceding paragraph were given, not in order to encourage children to imitate, but in order to fill them with a desire to acquire skill for themselves. It is important to note, however, that watching skilled movement is not without influence on the acquirement of skill, for, as we learned in chapter II, children cannot help imitating. Even if they do not imitate deliberately, they will do so unwittingly, and this impulsive automatic imitation, as we suggested on page 15, may often be very successful—sometimes more successful than imitation that is intentional. But if we watch children, we find that as their intellectual powers develop, as they become capable of more sustained attention, they are not content to try more or less blindly until they succeed. They want to be shown how to make the movement so that they may know the right way to proceed. Thus they acquire the form of the movement by deliberately imitating other people, and as a result they accelerate the learning process. The method of trial and success is still necessary, for it is only in this way that they can acquire facility in executing the movement the general form of which they have grasped.

Demonstration is an important method of teaching skilled movements. During the demonstration, the pupils attend to the exact way in which the movement is produced, they probably imagine themselves performing the movement, and later they set to work to imitate the action as closely as possible. Most apparently simple operations are actually complex ; they contain more than one simple manipulation. When teaching a new operation, a teacher should therefore first analyse it so that he can demonstrate it clearly and definitely step by step. Each separate manipulation should be performed so that it stands clearly defined. When learning to knit, for example, the pupil must first imitate the holding of the needles and of the wool and then each step of the process. The importance of combining the separate movements into one whole should, however, be kept in mind from the start. Before children begin to learn the details of any manipulation, it is therefore desirable that they should have become familiar with the sight of a skilled worker performing the whole operation. In the final manipulation all the separate movements that have been demonstrated must be fused into a harmonious whole ; they must, as Alexander says, be performed " all-together-one-after-the-other."[1]

Demonstration as a teaching method is sometimes condemned on the ground that it does not afford the pupils sufficient scope for initiative. Critics contend that it offers too few opportunities for thinking and that it produces clever but limited performers instead of educated workers. The advocates of demonstration reply that without demonstration pupils waste time because they adopt unsatisfactory methods that have subsequently to be unlearnt, and they also miss the incentive that is supplied by a good model. Both statements are half-truths.

The critics of demonstration need to be reminded that present-day hand-tool operations have survived the test of time ; both the tools and the methods of manipulating them have developed as a result of the critical experience of generations of skilled craftsmen.[2] The methods and tools used by Cellini in the sixteenth century for making a bowl are still used by craftsmen in the twentieth century. When teaching children a new manipulation, such as the use of a tool, it is obviously desirable to teach from the beginning the method of holding and of use that experts agree is the best. It is necessary to show children how to hold a sewing needle and how to use a plane, care being taken, of course, to allow minor deviations that individuals may find necessary

---

[1] See The Use of the Self, F. Matthias Alexander (Methuen, 1931).

[2] Although this is true of craftsmen using hand-tools it is not necessarily true of routine workers. Some of their methods, as we saw in the section on motion study, may be very extravagant both of time and effort.

on account of special physical idiosyncracies. Another reason for teaching the correct movement from the beginning is that movements once learnt are relatively permanent ; they are not so easily forgotten, for example, as poetry or prose that has been memorized. Generally speaking, movements are learnt for the purpose of achieving some end that is keenly desired. If, therefore, children acquire a wrong or faulty habit of movement, it is very difficult to alter it, for the habit of " end-getting " continually leads them to relapse into the old movement. In spite of all remedial teaching, they find it impossible to concentrate on the " means-whereby."[1]

Although demonstration is a useful and necessary method of teaching, there is always a danger of using it to excess. When, for example, children are making something that necessitates the use of skilled movements already acquired, little demonstration or instruction should be given ; we should then leave as much as possible to the initiative of the pupils themselves. Girls who have learnt how to chop suet and to mix ingredients can quite well use these skills in making a pudding without further demonstration of them. Boys who have acquired the necessary manual skill should be encouraged to design their own models and to plan their own work. Some help will often be necessary, but it should, as far as possible, be sought by the pupils and not forced upon them gratuitously before they have had a chance to think for themselves.

We may sum up the present discussion by stating the general principle that new movements should generally be introduced by demonstration and practised under supervision, but that finally the pupils should be left as free as possible to use their acquired powers to carry out plans on their own initiative.

This principle provides an answer to the vexed question of the teacher's function when children are engaged in creative work of an artistic nature. It is clearly an occasion when children should be left as free as possible. A child is

[1] See *The Use of the Self*, F. Matthias Alexander, p. 62 (Methuen, 1931).

not, however, necessarily free if he is merely left alone with tools and materials. Freedom is limited by a lack of technical skill no less than by an interfering teacher. If we give an infant some wood, nails and the necessary tools, he is not free to make a box, however intensely he desires to do so. If, on the other hand, we give him some wax or clay he may well be left alone ; he has enough mastery over his fingers and the clay to be free to satisfy his creative impulses. The same is true of very young children when they are painting pictures and patterns ; they are skilled enough to be free. If a child is engrossed in painting a picture, no outsider can possibly help by thrusting upon him unwanted advice. The child's vision is his own unique possession, and any set form of skilled movement demonstrated by a teacher is likely to warp his expression rather than make it more perfect. This does not mean that no teaching of technique is ever necessary. Technique must be taught in connexion with all skilled manipulations, but the occasion must be wisely chosen. The moment when a child is absorbed in creative work that is giving him intense satisfaction is obviously not an occasion for attempting to teach him technique. On the other hand, if a boy wants to construct something in wood or metal, the necessary technique of construction must often be taught before he can begin, and such teaching is a help and not a hindrance to his creative powers.

When helping children to acquire skill, three factors must be considered, viz., emotion, technique and thought. The emotional factor is fundamental, for unless children feel an urge towards expression, little progress is possible. This urge may vary in intensity from mere willingness to enthusiastic desire. If intense emotion is aroused the pupils will think ; if, in addition, they have the requisite degree of technical skill, beauty will appear. One of the most difficult problems in teaching is to see that, from the earliest stages, emotion and technique, desire and ability, keep step in development. At first, the urge to expression tends to out-race the power to perform ; later, unless we are careful, we find ourselves teaching technique that is out of step with our pupils' creative impulses. It is this pre-mature teaching of technique, the development of skill for which children feel no need and see no use, that tends to bring direct teaching of manipulations into disrepute. It cannot be too strongly emphasized, however, that direct teaching is necessary, and that, generally speaking, children need to practise a graded course of technical exercises. We cannot afford to neglect the large body of traditional know-ledge built up by generations of skilled artists and craftsmen.

Teaching by verbal instruction.—It is sometimes possible to teach a movement by describing it in words instead of by demonstrating it. This method of teaching skill can only be successful if the learner has had sufficient experience to enable him to form clear mental images of the movements described. Even if diagrams are given the movements are often still difficult to image. This is probably why few women ever learn to use the accessories to a sewing machine, in spite of the detailed directions given in the book of instructions. The difficulty of imaging can, however, be lessened by providing clear simple diagrams showing the movement at successive stages.

In spite of all difficulties, we must not ignore intsruction as a teaching method, especially when we remember that as educators we are concerned with after-school development as well as with present proficiency. At first, oral instruction and description should accompany demonstration. Our language is not rich in words to describe muscular sensa-tions, and many teachers find themselves distressingly in-articulate when they attempt such description. They would therefore do well to practise not only the demonstration of their art but also the verbal description of it. These de-scriptions, if accurate and simple, will do something to help children to follow written instructions when they are older.

The description of processes can be facilitated by teaching and using appropriate technical terms. It is, for example, both clearer and shorter in woodwork, to refer to " the panel " and " the stile " of a door rather than to " the flat piece " and " the piece that goes up and down." Similarly

in weaving " the warp " is preferable to " the long cottons."
Pupils should also be encouraged occasionally to describe
their own activities either orally or in writing and should
be given help in acquiring the necessary vocabulary. People
who have good visual imagery will naturally find this easier
than those who rely more on kinæsthetic imagery. This
suggests yet another value in the exercise. It should help
the teacher to know more about each individual's method
of learning so that he may adjust his teaching accordingly.
Some children, the visiles, learn more by the " look " of the
movement ; others, the motiles, learn more by the " feel."
Some motiles actually need at times to be put through a
movement to get the " feel " of it before they can perform it.

The value of reflection.—The learning process can also be
shortened by reflection, for by this means it is possible to
influence the acquisition of both form and facility. A person
of experience does not start from " scratch " in learning a
new movement. He examines the whole situation ; he sees
that some movements will be useful and others valueless.
If the movement involves the use of a tool, he knows
within limits what can be done with that tool. In this way
he " tries " the movement mentally so that when he starts,
his attack is purposeful and guided by his reflections instead
of being fumbling and chancy. We can see the two kinds
of behaviour illustrated very clearly if we compare an animal and a human being each tackling a puzzle box. The
animal runs about and perhaps by chance comes upon the
opening to the box ; the man examines the box in likely
places and so narrows down the field of his activities.
Learning by reflection is obviously a method for a person
of experience, one who is widening his skill rather than
one who is starting to acquire a particular skilled movement.
It is nevertheless a method that we should occasionally use
with our older pupils if they are to get the full educational
benefit from the work they do.

Most people are agreed, too, that we should reflect after
the movement has been made and not during the process.

While we are making the movement we should attend to the result we want to achieve, but afterwards it is often useful to go over the movement again in imagination to see why it was particularly successful or where it fell short of our intentions. If, as the result of our movement, we produce a concrete object, the criticism can be directed first of all to the finished product and then back to the process. Of course, we must use discretion in requiring our pupils to do this, for we do not want to make them unduly introspective or self-critical.

To sum up, the fundamental method of acquiring skill is the method of trial and success. The amount of repetition may be lessened, however, if pupils see the action performed by a skilled worker, if they are able to benefit by directions, and if they can reflect upon their perform-ances and be consciously guided by their mistakes and successes.

Rhythm.—We have already said that, as skill is acquired, separate movements become smoothly combined. It is in attaining this smoothness, the result of controlling both speed and force, that rhythm is useful. The most obvious rhythm to use is the rhythm that we hear in music. Most of us have noticed how the separate steps of a dance become grouped and fused as soon as we perform them to music. Many teachers of typewriting find that their pupils tap regularly and evenly if they work to the sound of a gramo-phone. This use of music reminds us that many of our skilled workers in the past worked to the sound of music, the music of their own voices, and the children who learned from them would from the very beginning learn to work rhythmically. In many skilled actions, such as writing, sewing, and drawing, school methods have neglected rhythm, with the result that our productions are jerkily irregular and lacking in beauty. Modern methods of teaching handwriting are designed to recapture this rhythm in movement. Exercises are designed to give the children practice in making rhythmical movements so that they may feel and enjoy the rhythm and eventually form a habit of rhythmical movement. A reform of this kind is needed in sewing. Very few of the children in our schools sew with a free and rhythmical action. Most of them are guided entirely by the sight of what they are doing and not at all by the feel of the movement. The trend in favour of large decorative stitches, instead of fine sewing for young children, is a reform in the right direction, but much still remains to be done. We still tend to over emphasize in early stages the practising of single stitches, whereas, if we concentrated on the movement rather than on the product, many early exercises would be devoted to the rhythmical making of a succession of stitches. The immediate results would be less perfect, but in the long run the acquisition of the desired skill would be more rapid and efficient.

We need also to pay attention to tools and materials. We sometimes see children struggling with a needle which is so large that they cannot hold it properly ; with wool which is too thick for the needle so that it will not slip through the material easily ; with material which is so tough and resistant that a continuous rhythmical action with the needle is impossible. Unsuitability of tools is one of the greatest hindrances to skilled rhythmical action. The tool must not be so small that actions become cramped, nor so large that a good grasp is difficult, nor so heavy that a controlled movement becomes impossible.

We have to remember that our bodies are also, in a sense, tools. Unlike ordinary tools they are continually developing. The young child's body is an unsuitable tool for some activities, and any attempt to force these activities before the tool is ready will lead to badly co-ordinated, unrhythmical movement. Many teachers nowadays recognize this fact, and there is a general tendency to postpone such activities as writing and needlework until the children are ready to tackle them successfully.

The value of confidence.—Confidence in ability to succeed is essential when any skill is to be acquired. Without this confidence movements are hesitating and indecisive, and there is little urge to practise in the face of difficulties.

Some people are temperamentally more ready than others to have confidence in themselves, but even such people, especially if they are young, are likely to lose that confidence if they do not at an early stage meet with a certain measure of success. This is yet another reason why work that is much too difficult for the learner should not be attempted. When children are working through a graded course of practical work, each advance brings them to a new difficulty when fine production cannot be expected. It is therefore a good plan occasionally to set simple exercises to advanced pupils and to expect a high standard of execution. This type of work provides a very useful mental tonic.

Sometimes confidence is lost, not because the work is too difficult, but because the relation between teacher and pupil is not an easy one. The teacher perhaps is over-anxious and fussy. Perhaps he is afraid to let his pupils make a mistake, or fears that they are going to hurt themselves with a dangerous tool.[1] Of course, we cannot allow children to risk life or limb, but there are other ways of protecting them than by continually saying, " Be careful." The children should be taught first of all how to hold and carry all tools safely, and this proper use should be insisted on. Experienced teachers do not allow pupils to run in practical workrooms, and do not allow any articles to be left lying on the floor where people have to walk. If such simple safety rules are made and kept, and if classes are small enough to ensure effective supervision, it should be possible to achieve that calmness of manner which is essential for teachers of skilled movements.

Some teachers undermine the confidence of their pupils by the way in which they criticize the work that is being

---

[1] Some people may object that it is unwise to allow children to use a dangerous tool. There are at least two good answers to this objection. First, it is hardly possible to avoid using dangerous tools ; even such common articles as scissors and pen-nibs are extremely dangerous if wrongly manipulated. Second, it is good for children to experience the sense of power that they get from the correct and successful use of a tool, especially a so-called dangerous one. This experience is especially valuable for those children who are generally timid.

done. They pay too much attention to what is wrong and too little to what is right. Where it is necessary to point out mistakes the correction should be made without any suggestion of blame or fault-finding. The learner must be stimulated but not harassed. The teacher is a trainer, not merely an assessor.

Fluctuations in progress.—Training in any act of skill needs great patience, for progress is by no means steady. We often find that our pupils mark time or even go back temporarily. Sometimes the fluctuations are very slight, in which case they may be looked upon as accidental and likely to right themselves. A distraction, such as a prospective school concert, or an anticipated visit to the dentist, may cause a temporary deterioration in skill in any form of practical work. Sometimes the arrest of progress is more lasting and it then becomes necessary for the teacher to seek for the reason.

The teacher who finds his class at a standstill should first ask himself if boredom is the cause. The cure for boredom is change of some kind ; change in the materials used, change in the groups for working, or a change of occupation altogether. The incentive supplied by an examination or by a competition will often overcome boredom, but this kind of incentive should be sparingly used. If the work is to be educational, the incentive should come mainly from the work itself.

Another possible cause of arrested progress is fatigue. If the fatigued worker is really skilled the loss of skill may be merely temporary, but if the worker is a learner the situation is more serious. He is still in the position of forming a habit and if he continues to practise when he is fatigued, he practises movements that are undesirable and often difficult to eradicate. He does not merely lose his skill for the time being, but he forms habits that will prevent him from acquiring skill in the future. For this reason teachers should see that the practice period is not too long, especially when new movements are being learnt. Ideally, a practice period should be of such a length that the pupils are fresh and enthusiastic at the end of it, and in any case it should not be so long that they are either bored or fatigued.

Although fatigue is a common cause of the development of bad habits it is not the only cause. Where the supervision of practice is not efficient, and where the stimulus of a good example is lacking, bad habits of work will often arise without the worker being aware of them. For this reason it is important that teachers of practical subjects should watch their pupils when they are actually at work; they should notice how tools are being manipulated, and not rest content with merely assessing the value of the results achieved.

A temporary arrest of progress often takes place even when all the conditions of learning appear to be satisfactory. Many investigators have called attention to the existence of what are described as plateaux in the learning curve, and until recently such plateaux have generally been considered as necessary phases in the process of learning a skilled movement. This is now considered doubtful. However, from the point of view of practical teachers, periods of apparent stagnation do occur, and it is often difficult to explain them away as being due to boredom, fatigue, or the development of bad habits. A possible explanation is that some change is taking place in the way in which the action is being performed, perhaps a different grouping of the separate movements, or a different emphasis on one part of the movement, with the result that, for the time being, the movement is less efficiently performed. Once the worker has become used to this new method of work, progress is again made. It is important that teachers should recognize the possibility that periods of marking time may be necessary for purposes of consolidation; they should be ready at such times to reassure and encourage their pupils; they should be on their guard against accentuating the difficulty by unnecessary worry.

TEACHERS OF SKILLED MOVEMENTS

It is often remarked that good executants—expert athletes, craftsmen, gymnasts—are not always good teachers. It may be helpful, therefore, to review briefly some of the special qualities that a teacher of skilled movements should possess. He must be able not only to demonstrate a complete act of skill but also to analyse his movements and, if necessary, break them up or slow them down so that his pupils may observe them in detail. This is not easy, for attending to the production of a movement and decreasing the natural speed at which it is usually made often spoil its perfection. Many of the movements taught in school are, however, relatively simple, and most teachers could, with practice, give satisfactory slow-motion demonstrations of them. With some of the more complicated movements needed in industry the objection may be more serious, and for this reason the use of slow-motion pictures and of stereoscopic models may be desirable.

The teacher of skill should be able to make his pupils' observations more discriminating by directing their attention to the parts of the body involved, and by describing both the appearance and the feel of the movement. Very few learners of golf would notice of their own accord how important the left arm is in making a correct swing. This explicit knowledge of the way in which a movement is produced is again very useful to the teacher when he is supervising the practical work of a learner. He knows what to look for and how to set about correcting wrong movements. The teacher, unlike the learner, must be able to attend to the process as well as to the product. In the past we have probably erred as teachers in concentrating our attention too exclusively on the result. We have seen the need for simplification, but we have sought it by analysing the product instead of the movement ; we have seen the need of correcting errors, but we have tended to indulge in futile grumblings at defects in the product instead of helping our pupils to correct the mistakes in movements that produced these defects. In short, we have approached our task from the wrong end.

The Teaching of Handwriting

Handwriting is a form of skill in which most teachers are actively interested, and it may therefore be useful to recapitulate the principles of learning and teaching skill by a review of methods of teaching this universal craft.

The first essentials are to help children to gain mastery over the tool and to help them to control the scribblings in which they all delight. For the first purpose, children are given such interesting preparatory exercises as the filling-in of shapes made with Montessori insets, and they are given plenty of opportunity for free imaginative drawing. For the second purpose, writing patterns involving the essential movements required for writing are being increasingly used. All this preparatory work, it should be noted, is done with large soft pencils or crayons—tools that young children can hold without strain. All the movements required are large, free and rhythmical ; they are not cramped by narrow guiding lines. With work of this character, there is less likelihood of children adopting harmful postures than there would be if they were engaged in making small, careful, cramped movements. The large pencil also helps them to adopt good methods of holding. Both posture and manipulation of tool are, however, matters on which children require expert and tactful guidance from teachers.

The next step is to give children the " feel " of the correct movements. This is done by some method of tracing over a good copy. One time-honoured device is to require children to write over the copy with a dry pen ; in the Montessori method, children trace sand-paper letters with the forefinger ; in one modern method, children use tracing paper.[1] This recognition of the value of making the correct rhythmical movement from the start has been responsible for the abolition of the slow copying of strokes and pot-hooks as an introduction to writing. Some reformers, for example in the Decroly School, have reacted

[1] See *Writing and Writing Patterns*, Marion Richardson (University of London Press, 1935).

very strongly against the " pot-hook " method, and their pupils begin by " writing " whole sentences ; the teachers rely on the children's intense interest in writing to bring order out of chaos. Other reformers, as for example Marion Richardson, recognize the value of analysis but instead of analysing writing into elements they analyse the essential movements made in writing, and require their pupils to practise these simple movements. This emphasis on fairly quick rhythmical movements appears to be psychologically sound, but it is obviously opposed to the printscript method of writing. From the point of view of ultimate skill in handwriting it seems very doubtful if children ought to begin by learning unjoined print-script. Advocates of this style generally argue that it helps children to learn to read and that it produces neat results. The answer to these arguments may be that we have been over-anxious to get " results " in reading and writing at a prematurely early age. When we understand more about the education of young children and when infant-school classes are of a more reasonable size, it may be found unnecessary to teach children such a disjointed method of writing as print-script. There is always a general tendency to make the introduction to formal handwriting much later than formerly. It is undesirable to prescribe any definite age at which children should write, for they differ widely in their abilities and interests. The ideal plan would be to continue the informal preparatory exercises and to wait until each child, like those described by Montessori, bursts spontaneously into writing. The advantages of postponing formal writing are many. Children come to the work with relatively controlled muscles, and they consequently make fewer initial mistakes. This early success encourages them, gives them confidence, and makes their learning rapid. There is also less temptation to require children to write slowly ; a reasonable speed and a rhythmical action can be practised from the beginning. The handwriting of children taught in this way is more likely to be beautiful and it is less likely to deteriorate than the careful laboured writing that has been painfully built up by drill at a premature age.

CONCLUSION

In the past a great deal of attention has been given in school to methods of imparting knowledge, but very little consideration has been given to methods of developing skilled movements. This is largely due to the fact that school education has been predominantly bookish. We are now beginning to appreciate that education should concern itself with the whole child. As Jacks has well said, " The human body is naturally *skill-hungry*, and until that hunger is satisfied it will be ill at ease, craving for something it has not got and seeking its satsifactions in external excitements which exhaust its vitality and diminish its capacity for joy. Short of skill, the perfect health even of the body is impossible."[1] As this truth is realized activities such as physical training, dancing, games, speech training, craftwork, will be given a much more important place in the curricula of schools than they have had in the past. If well taught they can make a very important contribution towards the development of a well-balanced personality ; it is therefore hardly possible to overestimate the urgency of improving our methods of teaching skill. The importance of skill in industry has, not unnaturally, already received much attention, and there is no doubt that by utilizing the results of the research of industrial psychologists we shall in the future be able to make important advances in our methods of helping children to acquire skill in all the movements they make in different forms of practical work. In proportion as we are successful, our pupils will find scope in practical work, not merely for accuracy and efficiency, but also for the highest form of self-expression, the creation of beauty.

---

[1] *The Education of the Whole Man*, L. P. Jacks, p. 166 (Univ. Lond. Press, 1931).
The importance of muscular skill for promoting mental and physical health has been impressively demonstrated by F. M. Alexander. See his books, *The Use of the Self* and *Constructive Conscious Control* (Methuen).

H

OBSERVATIONS

1. Make a list of the tools used by children in various school subjects. Observe children using these tools and make suggestions for the treatment of any incorrect or inexpert use you notice.

2. Collect specimens of children's handwriting at different ages. Examine them for signs of developing physical skill.

3. Examine a practical workroom and decide whether furniture and tools are so placed as to facilitate smooth and efficient working.
Make suggestions for improvement and justify them.

4. Learn to use a new tool, e.g., typewriter, or accessory to sewing machine. Keep a record of your own progress, noting methods of learning, output and accuracy of work, feelings of confidence, etc.

REFERENCES FOR READING

Handbook of Suggestions, New edition, 1937, chapters V, VII, VIII, IX, X.
Experimental Education, R. R. Rusk, pp. 214-20 (Longmans, 1921).

ADDITIONAL REFERENCES

How Children Learn, F. N. Freeman, chapter VIII (Harrap, 1919).
Skill in Work and Play, T. H. Pear (Methuen, 1924).
The Psychology of Skill, W. F. Book (University of Montana).
Applied Motion Study, F. B., and L. M. Gilbreth (Routledge, 1917).
Manual Skill, J. W. Cox (Camb. Univ. Press, 1934).
Handwork as an Educational Medium, P. B. Ballard (Geo. Allen, 1910).

ESSAYS AND DISCUSSIONS

1. In the *Concise Oxford Dictionary*, "skill" is defined as follows : "Expertness, practised ability, facility in doing something, dexterity, tact."
Show that each of the above shades of meaning is important to the teacher of skill.

2. The word "skill" is derived from an Old Norse word "skil," meaning "discernment."
Bearing this fact in mind, discuss the limited value of imitation as a means of teaching skill.

3. Choose an activity that necessitates skilled movement, and discuss in the light of the principles enunciated in this chapter the part that a teacher could usefully play in helping children to learn it.
[Consider, e.g., a ball game, a dance, typewriting, a specific exercise in physical training, handwriting, a particular operation in some form of handwork, playing a musical instrument.]

4. The use of dangerous tools in school.

5. The study of skill in factories as a means of improving the teaching of skilled movements in school.

6. Education should aim at developing "a sound mind in a sound body." (Cf. Discussion No. 11, p. 255.)

Chapter XIII

THE DEVELOPMENT OF TASTE

We propose in this chapter to consider taste in the sense in which it is defined in the *Concise Oxford Dictionary*, viz.,

> "faculty for discerning and enjoying beauty or other excellence especially in art and literature; disposition or execution of work of art, choice of language, conduct, etc., dictated by or seen in the light of this faculty."

It will be clear that the chapter is not to be confined to a discussion of æsthetics, though it cannot omit reference to this difficult subject. It will refer to " other excellence " in art and literature as well as to beauty, and it will be concerned not only with art but also with those questions of conduct known as good manners, together with such *et cetera* as tidiness, orderly arrangement and disposition of pictures and classroom furniture. From the point of view of practical teachers there is much to be said for using the word " taste " in this wide sense, for the plan will enable us to discuss together many important aspects of school life without being unduly delayed by philosophical controversies as to whether they can all be rightly considered as examples of " the beautiful."

Taste is obviously a matter of " feeling " rather than of " thinking," and it is not surprising therefore to find that it makes its appearance early in the lives of children. Nevertheless, although we have more or less detailed records of many aspects of child development—social, emotional, intellectual, physical—very little systematic observation of the development of taste in young children seems to have been made. It is well known that infants are attracted by brightness, and it has also been observed that as early as the seventh month of life children show marked colour preferences. Speaking generally, they are more attracted by " warm " colours such as red and yellow than by " cold " colours such as green and blue. They take delight in listening to singing and to tunes played on musical instruments. They have a strong interest in rhythm which is shown in many ways—they love to listen to rhythmic rhymes and very early they take a delight in being rocked rhythmically to and fro. As soon as they have acquired the necessary muscular control, they also enjoy making rhythmic movement themselves. Much of their spontaneous expression— in speech, writing and drawing—has very pleasant artistic qualities. From the age of 2, children give evidence of finding pleasure in the beauties of nature—in things seen in the sky, in trees and flowers, and in the songs of birds. On the negative side, young children are repelled by fear of loud sudden noises, and by disgust when certain obnoxious tastes, smells and touch sensations are experienced. In this respect taste is similar to all other aspects of personality ; it develops on a complex basis of instinctive pleasure and unpleasure.

Children are very sensitive to facial expressions, and by the age of 4 most of them understand the meanings of the words " pretty " and " ugly " as applied to faces ; they can distinguish between drawings of ugly and pretty faces. (See Binet tests for age 4.) Young children make frequent use of such opposites as " nice " and " nasty," " lovely " and " horrid." Their interest in matters of taste seems to develop earlier than their interest in reasoning or in morals, and for this reason many teachers try to inculcate desirable habits by appealing to children's sense of taste rather than to their sense of moral right and wrong, or to their understanding of logical reasons. It is often more effective to suggest that some anti-social behaviour is " ugly " or " horrid " than to try to convince a child that it is morally wrong or to explain to him reasons why he should not indulge in it.

The above description of the excellences of taste in young children will probably sound untrue to many adults.

This is because we tend to concentrate our attention on those elements of childish behaviour that offend our adult notions of propriety and consequently to overlook the fundamentally good standards of æsthetic taste that young children do possess. We object, for example, to the noise that children make, to the untidiness of their play-rooms and to their dirty hands and faces. These are, according to our definition, matters of taste, but they are obviously matters of social rather than of æsthetic training; they belong to the sphere of good manners rather than to that of æsthetic sensitivity.

It must also be remembered that the taste we have been considering is that of young children below the age of 5. It is very noticeable, at least under present conditions, that the artistic quality of children's expressional work tends to decrease as the children grow older. It has also been found by experiment that there is a decline in æsthetic appreciation between the ages of 7 and 14.[1] This falling-off in the power to create and enjoy beauty is probably due to several causes. It is certainly due partly to the fact that most children grow up in an ugly environment and among people who take little, if any, interest in beauty. Another possible contributory factor is that they may receive bad artistic training in school, especially in literature, composition and drawing lessons. This point of view is strongly suggested by Roger Fry, who points out the perturbing facts that " the average child has extraordinary inventiveness in design and the average adult none whatever " and that " in between these

[1] See *Art and Counterfeit*, Margaret H. Bulley (Methuen, 1925); *Have You Good Taste?*, Margaret H. Bulley (Methuen, 1933); *An Enquiry as to the Aesthetic Judgments of Children*, Margaret H. Bulley, Brit. Jnl. Educ. Psych., Vol. IV, pp. 162–82, 1934.

In her experiments, Miss Bulley used the method of " paired comparisons." In one experiment she used four pairs of pictures; in another, pairs of photographs of common things such as chairs, coffee-pots, wineglasses, embroidery. Each pair contained a good and a bad example as judged independently by each member of a team of competent artists and art critics. The subjects were required to choose the better in each pair. The percentage of correct choices was taken as a measure of the subject's æsthetic sensitivity.

two states there occurs the process known as art teaching."[1]
It is only fair to add that in between there also occurs the
process of growing-up, and that in this process the average
child must outgrow to some extent his life of fantasy and
imagination, and his artistic vision must be somewhat
clouded by the practical needs of life. It is interesting to
note, however, that in her experiments Miss Bulley found
at least one school where the pupils did not appear to suffer
the usual decline in taste ; it was a school in which the art
instruction was particularly enlightened, and the result at
least suggests that schools are not altogether blameless in
this matter. We shall discuss the practical details of æsthetic
education later in this chapter, but meanwhile it is necessary
to enquire into the nature of æsthetic appreciation.

THE NATURE OF ÆSTHETIC APPRECIATION

This has long been the subject of controversy, and it is
difficult to set out any simple body of generally-accepted
truth. This fact in itself probably indicates that appreciation of beauty is a complex mental process, and we should
therefore beware of accepting as the whole truth one simple
theory, no matter how plausible it sounds. In this, as in
other psychological problems, each theorist is very apt to
concentrate on that aspect of the truth that appeals to his
particular temperament. There is no doubt that, even if
there are universal canons of beauty, popular taste is also
influenced by a large number of other factors—personal
factors such as individual peculiarities of experience, temperament and habit, social factors such as local custom and
contemporary fashion.

The subject has been approached experimentally by
asking persons to state the reasons why certain works of art
give them pleasure. On the basis of the reasons given it is
found that people can be classified in four types according
to the attitude they usually display. The commonest is *the
associative type*. Such people enjoy a work of art because of

---

[1] *Transformations*, Roger Fry, p. 46 (Chatto & Windus), 1926.

the pleasant associations that it arouses. Thus they may like a picture or a tune because it reminds them of happy moments in their childhood, of an enjoyable holiday or of some proud occasion in their lives. A second type is called *the physiological or subjective type*. It is so-called because the reasons given are couched in physiological or emotional terms. The work of art affects them physiologically with a consequent effect upon their moods or feelings ; thus, for example, they enjoy a picture because, as they say, it makes them feel gay or cheerful. A third type is called *the character type*. When they enjoy a work of art it is because they recognize in it some personal experience that they can share ; they attribute some character to it. Thus, for example, they speak of cottages in a picture *sleeping* in the valley ; a drawing may appeal to them because, as they say, the lines seem to be alive. The fourth and the rarest type is *the objective type*. Such people approach a work of art critically, and they appraise it in intellectual rather than in emotional terms. They like a picture because of its composition or they refer to such qualities as the balance of light and shade and the harmony of colours.

It should be noted that none of these reasons is a sure indication of genuine æsthetic appreciation. This is obvious when we reflect that they are types of reasons that might lead us to take pleasure in things that have no artistic merits ; they might, for example, all be given as reasons for liking a pleasant holiday-snapshot, or a pretty illustration on the cover of a popular magazine. As a matter of fact, the four types have been revealed when people have given reasons for preferring one colour to another,[1] and it can hardly be maintained that a single colour can be a work of art ; a colour can be agreeable but not beautiful.

Many people like works of art because they excite their

---

[1] See *The Psychology of Beauty*, C. Valentine, pp. 27-31 (Jack, 1919) :
Association type : colours liked because they suggest health, sunshine, etc.
Subjective type : colours liked because they stimulate, soothe, etc.
Character type : colours liked because they are jovial, fearless, etc.
Objective type : colours liked because they are pure, saturated, etc.

admiration. Many call attention to the wonderful detail, to the marvellous skill of the artist; and when looking at a picture their highest praise may even be that it is "almost as good as a photograph." Closely akin to this type of pleasure is that which arises from a realization that an object is perfectly adapted for its purpose. But again it must be objected that, although some works of art may reveal wonderful technical skill or a high degree of technical efficiency, the same qualities may often be found in things quite outside the realm of art; a realistic advertisement poster or a stream-lined steam engine may excite our admiration, but it does not follow that either is necessarily beautiful. Another objection to "fitness for purpose" as a criterion of beauty is that the beauty of an object may be quite irrelevant to any function that the object serves; we have only to think, for example, of the beautiful patterns that decorate many of the things we use in everyday life.

It is very doubtful whether statistical methods applied to a large unselected group of people can give us any reliable idea of the nature of æsthetic appreciation. Even if most people were capable of appreciating beauty, they would probably be quite incapable of giving an adequate description of their æsthetic experiences, especially as they are untrained in introspection and inexperienced in describing mental states. It may therefore be more profitable to consider the descriptions given by a selected group of persons who are particularly sensitive to beauty. We append four such descriptions, dealing with three very different forms of art:

Appreciation of the beauty of music.

"A tingle in your chest, and an ache where the music is going to rush into you.

"Nor even mad on the choruses, though they could give you a shock, with proud electricity all over. It was more the blending of the singing and the whole band. An orchestra, properly.

"When a player called Gyp or another called Solomon,

when they stood right up with their trumpets to start 'Let the Bright Seraphim in Burning Row,' straight off at the first few notes, long before the singing began, you got right into wide-open heaven. Archangels a-plenty, out of the end part of the Bible, and Thrones and Dominations and Powers, and a shudder and a stirring in all the blazing, glittering tribe of them. All a-weaving in and weaving out, wheeling together and manœuvring and making skating-figures in the air. Like pigeons in the sun, but a lot more glorious.

. . . . . .

" A pattern wove into you. . . .

" Only, archangels and pigeons are only an illustration of what nobody could explain. Not dreams nor pictures really, but a new way of feeling, and of belonging to the proper pattern and design that you knew had always been there waiting to be hatched out, waiting to open out like the trick flowers they sell in the street to be put in a glass of water.

" Belonging to you for good, and making you belong to them. Starting up inside, when you least expected. Nobody can rob you of that, anyway, however they shut you up inside walls. Seizing you unexpected, like a fit of sneezing. Shivers all up and down your spine, and floods of light right all over through you. Silvery and steely and bronze-metal notes, all chasing warm and cold into glittering rivers and waterfalls.

" No use. If you don't know, you won't know, that's all about it."

The Wainwrights, Edgar Meredith, pp. 69–71 (Grayson & Grayson).

Appreciation of the beauty of a bowl (from the potter's point of view).

" Everything that went to the making of our bowl, ideas of holding, spilling, pouring, steadiness, ideas of depth, width, curves, met, fused and became one in the

H*

heat of our creative energy. Everything discordant, disordered, melted away, until something deep down in us, love of order, balance, unlaboured movement, sighed contentedly, satisfied. It is almost as if the bowl had made itself in answer to this love, this compulsion. It is true that from time to time we stopped, cocked our heads on one side and criticised our handiwork. We added a deliberate touch here, another there. But in the main the heart made the bowl with the help of the head."

Have You Good Taste?, Margaret H. Bulley, p. 4 (Methuen).

Appreciation of the beauty of a bowl (from the contemplator's point of view).

"Suppose, for example, that we are looking at a Sung bowl ; we apprehend gradually the shape of the outside contour, the perfect sequence of the curves, and the subtle modifications of a certain type of curve which it shows ; we also feel the relation of the concave curves to the outside contour ; we realise that the precise thickness of the walls is consistent with the particular kind of matter of which it is made, its appearance, of density and resistance ; and finally we recognise, perhaps, how satisfactory for the display of all these plastic qualities are the colour and the dull lustre of the glaze. Now while we are thus occupied there comes to us, I think, a feeling of purpose ; we feel that all these sensually logical conformities are the outcome of a particular feeling, or of what, for the want of a better word, we call an idea ; and we may even say that the pot is the expression of an idea in the artist's mind. . . . But in all this no element of curiosity, no reference to actual life, comes in."

Vision and Design, Roger Fry, pp. 32-3 (Chatto & Windus, 1920).

Appreciation of the beauty of architecture.

"The beauty of an edifice consists in an exact proportion of the parts within themselves and of each part with the whole : for a fine building ought to appear as an entire and perfect body wherein every member agrees with its fellow and each so well with the whole that it may seem absolutely necessary to the being of the same."

Palladio (1750)—quoted by Burt in *How the Mind Works*, p. 300 (Allen & Unwin, 1933). Burt adds that Palladio's precepts might apply to every work of art.

The above quotations emphasize the complexity of our subject. If we consider what constitutes beauty, we are told that it " consists in an exact proportion of the parts within themselves and of each part with the whole," and the idea is reinforced by the use of such words as blending, weaving and fusing, pattern, design, order and balance. There is a subtle kind of perfection about a work of art and this is perhaps its essence ; it is a whole, a unity—and as we contemplate it we feel the harmony of the relations between part and part, and between parts and the whole. This special kind of feeling indicates to us that we are experiencing beauty. It is an experience, however, that baffles description even by a novelist—" If you don't know, you won't know, that's all about it." It is now generally agreed that æsthetic experience is in its essence the same no matter what form of beauty is being contemplated. " Whenever we say that a work of art is beautiful—we imply by that statement that it is of such a kind as to produce in us a certain positive response, and that if we compare in our minds responses experienced in turn in face of different works of art of the most diverse kinds—as, for instance, architectural, pictorial, musical or literary—we recognize that our state of mind in each case has been of a similar kind.[1] It is the specifically æsthetic state of mind."[2]

[1] *Transformations*, Roger Fry, p. 1 (Chatto & Windus, 1926).
[2] There is little agreement among experts who have tried to analyse this state of mind. Burt suggests that there are four stages in the perception of beauty. (1) A mass of conscious and unconscious associations are brought to bear and a meaning is imparted. (2) This meaning is seized in a state of mild emotion and we respond to the emotional experience of the artist embodied in his work. (3) The emotion communicated is a human emotion and the work of art seems dimly to suggest a personality behind. (4) The emotional experience expresses itself through the form imposed upon the
[Continuation of footnote on page 226.

It should now be clear that the types of reasons given by ordinary persons when they are asked why a work of art appeals to them are often nothing more than accompaniments or at the most contributory factors to the true æsthetic experience. As such, they ought not to be emphasized in school lest pupils come to attach undue importance to them. It is justifiable to ask such questions for experimental purposes, but it is very doubtful if they enhance appreciation. It is, for example, very doubtful if any good purpose is served by asking children why they like a poem, a picture, or piece of music. The roots of æsthetic appreciation are in the unconscious mind, and children are bound to be less articulate about the appeal of beauty than they are about the more superficial appeals that a work of art may have.

With young children it is equally futile to try to explain to them why they should like any given work of art. The only positive result is the acquisition of meaningless verbal formulæ, which too often are subsequently used in order to gain adult approbation.[1] Negatively, children may react against the instruction and acquire a distaste for the whole subject. Thus premature verbal teaching is apt to produce either insincere prigs or blatant philistines.

A corollary of this principle of avoiding explanations is the principle that the first impression of a work of art has a special significance, and no distractions of any kind should be allowed to intervene. A new picture should be hung for a time in a special place, a new pot exhibited in

---

Continued from page 225]
sensuous material, through rhythm, through pattern, through a system of relations that unifies the whole.

This pattern or design we grasp intuitively. We thus enter into the imaginative emotional experience of the artist; we recreate it, as Croce says. See *How the Mind Works*, C. Burt, pp. 309–10 (Allen & Unwin, 1933).

[1] cf. the following quotation : " More than most peoples, we English are apt to let our visual sensibility be dominated by words. . . . The English tend to see things through their names. They are apt, that is to say, to put things like ' church ' and ' cottage ' into the category of the beautiful, and things like ' bungalow ' and ' pylon ' into the category of the ugly, irrespective of their actual appearance. It may be the same building, whether it be called ' cottage ' or ' bungalow,' but the attitude to the thing is determined by the association of the name applied." (*The Times*, January 8th, 1936.)

a place of honour. If a new poem is to be introduced, verbal difficulties should be removed days or even weeks beforehand ; in Hayward's phraseology, all metaphors must be pioneered. Then, when the first impression of the poem is given by as good a reading as possible, there are no technical difficulties to interfere with the child's enjoyment.

In matters of taste, as in all other aspects of education, children learn by experience, and the first duty of teachers is to help them to acquire this experience. This can be done in two ways—by arranging a beautiful environment that children can contemplate, and by giving them opportunities for creating simple forms of beauty for themselves.[1] In these ways children can be given standards of taste and beauty that they will tend to apply for themselves. It may be that in later adolescence, when there is apparently keener interest in art and an increased sensitivity to beauty, children who have received this type of training would benefit by some direct instruction in the underlying principles of the arts in which they are most keenly interested, but such instruction should be given only by expert specialists.

At the same time it is important that all teachers should have some appreciation of the fundamental principles of beauty and some realization of the nature of genuine æsthetic experience. We cannot tell our pupils what beauty is, but we can show them examples of it. We must, therefore, at least know how to avoid the grosser kinds of bad taste. In connexion with problems of taste in the classroom it is helpful to ask oneself two types of question—the first

---

[1] " Complete detachment from the content, from a bias of any kind, . . . is scarcely possible to simple human nature ; and we ought not from the point of view of a theoretical prejudice to despise the attitude in which æsthetic appreciation is intermingled with that of the subject treated. Although the little child practically never displays unmixed æsthetic feeling, yet it exists within him, and with more mature growth and appropriate, careful guidance, his pleasure in pictures, dances, songs and stories will increasingly develop into the capacity of enjoying the purely æsthetic qualities which are offered in these forms. We must, however, be careful not to allow a false æsthetic feeling to drag even the little child away from his interest in the subject-matter and thrust upon him purely æsthetic enjoyment and judgment." (*Psychology of Early Childhood*, W. Stern, p. 329 (Allen & Unwin, 1924).)

relating to the object or arrangement under consideration, the second relating to one's own feelings in regard to it. The following are suggestions :

A. Relating to the object.

1. Is the object a satisfactory whole ? Or has it some discordant and incongruous elements ?

An untidy classroom obviously does not satisfy this criterion. Many other examples can readily be thought of— a woodwork model decorated by machine-made ornament glued to its surface, a badly balanced vase, a child's picture composed partly of ruled lines, a leather bag decorated by a coloured picture.

The last example illustrates the fact that each kind of material has its own possibilities and limitations. If these are ignored, incongruity appears ; the object is less beautiful than it might be. For example, a wooden mantelpiece is much more beautiful if it reveals the nature and the natural beauties of wood than if it is painted to look like marble. Much of the best modern work is beautiful because its creators have frankly recognized this principle. Buildings made of concrete are plain, not because decoration in itself is artistically wrong, but because concrete is an unsuitable material in which to create elaborate ornament.

If the object is one that has a practical use, its function is clearly part of the whole and nothing in its design should interfere with this function. The top of a writing table, for example, should not be decorated with carving however beautiful the design of the pattern may be in itself. Similar considerations would lead us to reject " arty " camouflage, which is often used to disguise the appearance of common objects ; a telephone set, for example, should be well designed as a telephone set and not dressed up to look like an ornament.

In the constitution of " wholeness " the proportion of part to part, and part to whole is a very important factor ; it is a fundamental element in design. A box or a piece of furniture may be beautiful by reason of its proportions apart from any question of decoration ; it may, in fact, be perfectly plain. A clock case may be ugly because it is out of proportion with the clock face ; instead of appearing as a pleasing and suitable support for the clock, it looks like an incongruous piece of furniture into which a clock has been put.

The strong influence that proportion exerts on our mental attitude has been demonstrated by experiments with such simple shapes as oblongs. It is found that the most pleasing oblong is one the proportions of which approximate to those of a single sheet of foolscap ; the length and breadth are in the ratio that is obtained if a line is divided in what is known as " golden section," the longer part being in the same proportion to the shorter part as the whole line is to the longer part (3 to 5 is the usual workshop approximation).

Proportion is important not only in construction but also in decoration. The position and the " weight " of surface decoration, the balance between plain and decorated areas— these are matters that help to determine whether or not an object is a satisfactory whole.

2. Is there enough variety within the unity to make it interesting and to avoid monotony ?

A strictly symmetrical arrangement of ornaments and furniture can often be improved upon. It is the factor of diversity within the whole that makes hand-produced pattern and decoration more pleasing than similar work produced by drawing instruments or machines. Ruled lines lack beauty because they are monotonous ; the " character " type of person would say that they lacked life. A drawn line, on the other hand, is, in the words of Roger Fry, " a record of a gesture."

B. Relating to personal feelings.

3. Do I like or dislike the object because of irrelevant associations ?

We have already quoted some examples to show that our æsthetic judgment can be warped by associations, some of the most dangerous being those connected with names; all cottages tend to be called beautiful and all bungalows ugly. Another insidious type of association is that connected with wealth; an expensive but ugly vase tends to be preferred to an inexpensive but beautiful jam-pot.

4. Are my feelings the result of æsthetic appreciation or are they more superficial, the result of the arousal of simple instincts?

The instinct of self-assertion tends to make us accept the familiar and reject the unfamiliar, and this is one of the chief obstacles to appreciation of non-representational art. We tend to reject a child's picture of a room because the mat is " out of perspective," while we are blind to the fact that the picture is an artistic whole. On the other hand, there is the opposite danger of liking things merely because they are quaint and unusual.

5. Are my feelings due to some peculiarities of my own temperament? Do I make enough allowance for the large temperamental differences among the members of my class?

The Influence of the Environment

The arranging of environment is a matter in which all teachers should take an active interest. The design of buildings and the decoration of schools may be outside the direct control of teachers, but the possible influence of a teaching profession imbued with a sense of the importance of æsthetic training should not be underestimated. There are already signs that education authorities and architects are giving more adequate attention to æsthetic considerations when new schools are being built, but it will be many years before we have made up the enormous leeway created by years of indifference to the value of beautiful school buildings. In the meantime we must do all we can to improve the appearance of schools as they exist. We can begin in quite simple ways—by removing ugly litter from the tops of cupboards, by printing notices decently, by putting under cover most of the ugly untidy things that are needlessly displayed, by arranging tidily the hundred and one things that we must display in school, by keeping cupboards reasonably tidy, by removing ugly pictures and paying careful attention to the hanging of the few good ones that remain, and so on. From such obvious externals we should proceed to examine critically such things as the design and lettering on the covers of exercise and text-books, the print and format of books generally, the shapes of vases, the arrangement of flowers, the design of utensils used in domestic-subject rooms.

The environment does not consist only of things that can be seen. Much can be done to improve taste in other ways. Ugly and unnecessary noise can be eliminated ; many incidental opportunities can be provided for children to listen to good music and to good literature well read. Charm of manner and speech can be cultivated by all adults who have a place in our schools.

We cannot all be expert judges of beauty in all its forms but in creating environment we can, as we have already explained, begin in simple ways about which there can be little difference of opinion. When we come to more difficult matters, such as choice of colours and pictures for wall decoration, we can seek the advice of experts. This does not mean that we laymen must renounce altogether the privilege of exercising our choice according to our own taste, but that we should choose from among those things that æsthetically sensitive people judge to be worthy. This is particularly important for all of us whose experience of artistic matters is limited, for it is very striking how rapidly we tire of things that have a superficial attractiveness but lack the essential qualities of beauty.

Although direct instruction in the more advanced matters of taste may be dangerous, there are many small questions that can safely be approached by means of tactful suggestion and discussion. A hint now and then as to good taste in regard to personal conduct is not out of place ; the hanging of a new picture might well form the subject of a class discussion.

But even in this type of instruction great care is necessary. It is not easy for any grown-ups, however well-intentioned and tolerant, to exercise that degree of patience which is necessary if children's taste (especially in social matters) is to develop naturally, so that it is a reflection of a healthy personality and not merely an insincere pose or a morbid obsession. It is very important that we should not confuse good taste with unhealthy fastidiousness. It is possible for example to become absurdly fussy even about such a desirable thing as tidiness, and to allow ourselves in this way to become blind to matters of more fundamental importance.[1]

We should remember that disgust is an emotion that is often fanned by unwise suggestion, and that the first step in the production of good taste is to allow children to express themselves with as little direct adult interference as possible. Children must live through the stages when they take infantile delight in banging, drum-beating, making mud-pies and experimenting in crude ways with colour; later they must read their " comics " and freely express their crude fantasies in speech, drawing, writing, acting and construction. In a word, they must lead a full play-life, for any premature attempts to short-circuit these experinces in the supposed interests of good taste will do more harm than good.

Teachers cannot help conveying suggestions by their attitude to questions of taste, and, so long as the suggestion is the general one that such matters are worthy of individual attention and enthusiasm, the influence is good. Hayward tells us that " pictures hanging silently in the classroom have not much influence of any kind upon taste

---

[1] Tidiness must always be considered in relation to function. Places of reference, like libraries and cupboards, where things must be found quickly from among a large number, should always be kept scrupulously tidy; every thing should be in its appointed place. Places of work, like sculleries and workshops, where activity is intense, cannot be kept tidy in the same way; tools and materials must be apparently lying about. Beneath this superficial disorder, however, there should be some system; places of work should be " tidy " to the worker, although they may not appear to be so to a casual onlooker.

or character."[1] This may perhaps be true if the teacher is indifferent. But teachers should not be indifferent in matters of taste. As Delisle Burns says, " In order to discover whether anyone is civilised, it would be as reasonable to notice his taste in the choice of his material surroundings as to enquire what books he has read."[2] It is as important that teachers should be enthusiastic lovers of beauty as that they should be persons of good intelligence, high attainments and lofty moral character. A teacher does not hide his interest in knowledge or sport ; he should not hide his æsthetic enthusiasms. So long as our pupils are not made to feel that they must pretend to like what we like, it is good for them to see us enthusiastic about a favourite picture, poem or sonata. So long as we emphasize that we are merely giving personal views, it is good for them occasionally to hear us talk enthusiastically on such subjects. We do not try to teach mathematics by suggestion, but we do try by this means to communicate enthusiasm for mathematics. The same is true in matters of taste ; we should try to communicate enthusiasm for beauty of various kinds but not necessarily for particular examples of beauty that happen to appeal to us. The type of suggestion we should certainly avoid is that which gives children ready-made opinions that they cannot appreciate. Such suggestion develops insincerity rather than taste. Taste should be an

[1] *The Lesson in Appreciation*, F. H. Hayward, p. 195 (Macmillan, 1915). It should be noted, however, as Hayward himself points out, that there is " a fundamental principle which the philosophy of æsthetics has never adequately recognised—namely, that familiarity, habituation and custom are prime factors in determining our likes and dislikes." It is a principle that was, however, clearly appreciated by Plato. " Our guardians," said Socrates in the *Republic*, " must not be bred among symbols of evil, as in a pasturage of poisonous herbs lest by grazing freely they little by little and all unawares build up a huge mass of evil in their souls. But we must look for those craftsmen who are naturally able to follow the trail of beauty and grace, so that our young men, dwelling as in a salubrious region, may benefit from all things round them, whence the influence that emanates from works of beauty may waft itself to eye or ear like a breeze bringing health from wholesome places, and so from earliest childhood lead them insensibly to likeness and friendship and harmony with beautiful reason."

[2] C. Delisle Burns, " Examinations and the Social Needs of the Modern World " in a book entitled *Essays on Examinations* (Macmillan, 1936).

expression of personality and not merely a veneer put on for the sake of respectability. For this reason, free discussion is always better than authoritative teaching. An incidental discussion as to the excellence or the badness of design should often arise in craft lessons, and in fact in any lessons where everyday things are in use. For this purpose the method of paired comparison (see footnote, p. 219) will be found very useful.

As children grow older, the wider environment of street and landscape should play its part in the development of taste, and many opportunities for contemplating the contrast between beauty and ugliness will occur on educational visits and school journeys.[1]

CREATIVE WORK

It is now generally acknowledged that the best artistic work is to a large extent a product of the " unconscious " mind. It is true that such work generally needs deliberate thoughtful revision, but this is a subsequent and separate process from the act of creation, which is guided more by emotion than by conscious thought. The two types of activity are well described by A. E. Housman and Robert Bridges respectively in the following quotations :

" Having drunk a pint of beer at luncheon—beer is a sedative to the brain, and my afternoons are the least intellectual portion of my life—I would go out for a walk. As I went along, thinking of nothing in particular, there would flow into my mind, with sudden and unaccountable emotion, sometimes a line or two of verse, sometimes a whole stanza at once, accompanied, not preceded, by a vague notion of the poem as a whole. Then there would be a lull, and perhaps the spring would bubble up again. I say bubble up, because the source of the suggestions thus

[1] The *National Trust*, 7 Buckingham Palace Gardens, London, S.W. 1, was founded in 1895 " to promote the permanent preservation for the benefit of the nation of lands and buildings of beauty or historic interest."
See also literature issued by the *Council for Education in Appreciation of Physical Environment*, 13 Suffolk St., Pall Mall, London, S.W. 1.

proffered to the brain was an abyss." *The Name and Nature of Poetry*, A. E. Housman.

" It (the natural impulse) may come to perfection only after long conscious toil and difficulty—and the sort of toil is different in the different arts. In all of them the Reason is a most active helpmate, but always the servant of the emotion." *The Necessity of Poetry*, Robert Bridges.

Applying the principle of " unconscious " production in school, we see that, if beauty is to appear in children's creative work, we must provide conditions that will allow spontaneous expression as free as possible from all types of hindrance. Children can never produce beauty in a classroom ruled over by a martinet. To give an example, when we set young children to write a " composition " the subject should be one about which they want to write, and when they make their first draft they should be unhampered by fears lest their handwriting, punctuation, grammar and spelling should meet with severe adult disapproval. The pursuance of this policy of encouraging artistic quality instead of denouncing technical inaccuracies has already revolutionized the teaching of drawing in infant and junior schools.

The gradual development of technical skill must, of course, be looked for, but it is surprising how much progress most children make in this direction, even without specific instruction, when their work is inspired by intense interest and when they themselves are free from petty fears. There are doubtless times when some direct teaching of technique is necessary, but it is certainly true to say that in the past we have erred in attempting to force the pace and to teach technique too soon. The general principle appears to be that before such instruction is given children should discover the need for it as a result of their own joyous attempts to create for themselves.[1]

---

[1] There is a type of technical skill in drawing that is of great importance in the learning of scientific subjects and in many industrial occupations. The skill in drawing that children acquire incidentally when they are drawing pictures and patterns makes a valuable contribution, but it is necessary, in
[*Continuation of footnote on page* 236.

As children grow older, individual differences will become more marked and it may be that some, as a result of natural inaptitude, will show a distaste for certain forms of creative work and a special interest in other forms. With these children, the best policy in the interests of the all-round development of taste is to allow specialization, for no good can come from so-called creative work in which no joy is taken ; it ceases, in fact, to be creative in any real sense of the word.[1]

CONCLUSION

All æsthetic learning must be accompanied by joy. In this connexion it is interesting to note the close relation between artistic and play activities, a relation recognized in our use of the word " play " both in music and the drama. The affiliation of art to play proceeds, as Nunn says, from the sound observation that " the soul of art, like that of play, is the joyous exercise of spontaneity."[2] Whether æsthetic lessons be given by the silent influence of the environment, or by the more obvious influence of creative work, or by direct instruction in appreciation lessons and school celebrations, the eloquent words of Hayward apply with equal force :

" As the minds of the pupils play in retrospect around the lesson, there should not come, if we can prevent it, a single harsh or discordant association—no memory of a rasping voice, an unsympathetic face, a gloomy day, a

---

Continued from page 235]
addition, to cultivate technical drawing skill directly in subjects such as mathematics and science. The direct conscious learning of skill is apt however, to hinder creative expression by children, and there is much to be said for practising the two types of drawing—artistic and scientific—as distinct and separate activities. Among older pupils, there may be exceptiona individuals who ought to specialize in one type of drawing only.

Similar considerations apply to the teaching of technique in English See also discussion on teaching technique, pp. 203–5.

[1] See *The Effect of Creative Work on Aesthetic Appreciation*, K. B. Leopold Brit. Jnl. Educ. Psych., III, pp. 42–64 (1933).

[2] *Education : Its Data and First Principles*, Sir T. Percy Nunn, p. 90.

crowded or an ugly classroom, or a morning hour broken by a dozen interruptions from the outside."[1]

The development of taste has in the past suffered from neglect in schools. In some quarters the neglect has been deliberate on the ground that art is useless if not definitely harmful ; in others, the neglect has been due to indifference or preoccupation with matters (such as technical skill in drawing) supposed to be more important. We are now beginning to recognize that the search after beauty is one of the noble expressions of the human spirit equally with the search for truth and the pursuit of goodness. As Burt says, " It is not a fad or fancy of an erratic genius, but a special instance of a gift which lies within the reach of all, a gift, indeed, which, far better than logical argument, will enable the young, the dull, the uneducated (and in the face of the universe we are all uneducated and very dull and young) to grasp a fundamental value."[2]

OBSERVATIONS

1. Examine an ordinary classroom. What would you do to improve its appearance (*a*) without expenditure of money, (*b*) if unlimited money were available ?

2. Collect examples of common things found in schools. Discuss them in the light of the principles enunciated in this chapter. E.g., (*a*) school text-books, (*b*) exercise books, (*c*) handwork models, (*d*) handwriting specimens.

3. Observe a lesson in one of the arts with which you are familiar— literature, composition, drawing, music. Discuss it from the point of view of the development of æsthetic appreciation.

REFERENCES FOR READING

Handbook of Suggestions, New edition, 1937. (See *Index* : Appreciation.)
Modern Psychology and Education, Sturt and Oakden, chapter VI.
Educational Psychology, C. Fox, chapter X.
Experimental Education, R. R. Rusk, chapter X.

ADDITIONAL REFERENCES

The Psychology of Beauty, C. W. Valentine (Jack, 1919).
The Lesson in Appreciation, F. H. Hayward (Macmillan, 1915).
How the Mind Works, ed. C. Burt (Allen & Unwin, 1933).
Art and Counterfeit, M. H. Bulley (Methuen, 1925).

[1] *The Lesson in Appreciation*, F. H. Hayward, p. 8 (Macmillan, 1915).
[2] *How the Mind Works*, C. Burt, p. 308.

Have You Good Taste ?, M. H. Bulley (Methuen, 1933).
Education for Citizenship in Secondary Schools, chapter XIV, Art by J. E. Barton (Ox. Univ. Press, 1936).
Picture-making by Children, R. R. Tomlinson (The Studio, 1934).
Crafts for Children, R. R. Tomlinson (The Studio, 1935).
How to Look at Buildings, Darcy Braddell (Methuen, 1932).

ESSAYS AND DISCUSSIONS

1. The uses and dangers of " appreciation " lessons.
2. The value of educational visits for developing taste.
3. The inculcation of good manners.
4. Tact as an example of good taste.

CHAPTER XIV

THE DEVELOPMENT OF SOCIABILITY

WE learned in chapter II that children show their gregarious nature as early as the first week of life. Human beings, like sheep and cattle, inherit a " herd instinct "; they are gregarious animals. Hermits are abnormal individuals ; to a normal human being solitary confinement is a severe punishment. The " herd instinct " is probably a survival of a tendency that was stamped into human nature when men had to band together for defence and hunting. But whatever its origin, it is a natural endowment that is of great importance in learning and teaching.

The feeling of loneliness that is experienced when for any reason a child is separated from his " herd " may, like fear, be an intense emotion. For that reason, it should be used sparingly and with discretion. Montessori has recognized its force, and in cases of anti-social behaviour she isolates the offender from the group. Isolation is a form of punishment used by many teachers in various ways, but it has two dangers. First, the separation may be incomplete, and so far from the offender feeling isolated he may feel he is in the limelight. For that reason it is usually better to send a delinquent to the back of the class rather than bring him to the front ; " standing in a corner " was the solution of the problem used in years gone by. Second, the separation may be so complete that the offender suffers severely. This is the reason why it is usually unwise to emphasize isolation by making the delinquent wear some special garb ; anything that savours of ridicule should always be avoided.

It is not necessary for a child to be separated in space from his fellows in order to feel lonely. Any kind of difference may separate him—a difference in dress, in speech, in manners, in ability, in physical strength. The converse is also true. Members of a society find satisfaction in having some sign by which they can recognize one another. This is the reason for wearing house colours, school uniforms and old school ties. It is also the fundamental reason why a cultured English speech should be taught in all schools ; a common standard of speech would do much to break down barriers between social classes.

A feeling of loneliness, like a feeling of fear or disgust, has an inhibiting effect on a child's mental activity. It tends to make him introspective, and although in isolated cases he may seek relief by intense study he is more likely to become lazy and apathetic. A lonely, completely self-centred child is abnormal, and one of the chief functions of a teacher is to help children to grow up naturally, delighting in the company of their fellows. This is the subject of the present chapter—the development of the art of living together in good fellowship. It overlaps what we have already said about the development of character, but the subject is so important that it warrants a separate chapter. This separate treatment is particularly necessary, because, with the modern emphasis on individuals, the importance of helping children to become sociable tends sometimes to be overlooked. It must be emphasized at once that social development is not opposed to individual development, for no human being is fully developed as an individual unless he has learnt to adapt himself to his fellows, to take pleasure in their company and to find joy in social service. There are, of course, large individual differences in aptitude for this kind of learning, as for all other kinds, but some degree of sociability is a necessary ingredient in the character of every one who is really human.

A great deal of philosophic argument has raged round the question whether the individual or the community is ultimately of greater worth.[1] In the light of recent experience in democratic and totalitarian states there can be no doubt

[1] See *Education: Its Data and First Principles*, Sir T. Percy Nunn, chapter I.

about the answer. We now see, perhaps more clearly than ever before, that the only hope of reform and progress in any society lies in the free activities of its individual members. This principle applies equally to the small societies of classroom and school as to the larger societies of nations, and to the supra-national world society which we hope will in time emerge. Our present society has many defects. We have to admit, for example, that in it many of the individual characteristics most valuable for the progress of man—co-operativeness, altruism, social and æsthetic sensitivity—do not make for personal success. School society cannot therefore be a mere imitation of the imperfect society of the world outside. It must rather be, as Branford says, " an *idealized* epitome or model of the world, not merely the world of ordinary affairs, but the whole of humanity, body and soul, past, present and future."[1] In such a school there is no need to take sides as to whether the individual or society should dominate, for they are mutually dependent.

THE DEVELOPMENT OF SOCIABILITY IN SCHOOL

We have already sketched the early development of sociability in pre-school years (pp. 29–30). We have further shown (pp. 176–8) how the early family sentiments should be gradually widened by school life until finally they are caught up in a self-regarding sentiment—" I am a member of the human family ; I enjoy the company of my fellows and I am happy to serve them."

We must now retrace our steps and consider in more detail how school life can help children to develop this particular character-trait, sociability. Before we do so

---

[1] *Janus and Vesta*, B. Branford, p. 145 (Chatto & Windus, 1916). Cf. Nunn, *op. cit.*, p. 202 : " A nation's schools are an organ of its life, whose special function is to consolidate its spiritual strength, to maintain its historic continuity, to secure its past achievements, to guarantee its future. Through its schools a nation should become conscious of the abiding sources from which the best movements in its life have always drawn their inspiration, should come to share the dreams of its nobler sons, should constantly submit itself to self-criticism, should prize its ideals, should re-inform and re-direct its impulses."

it is worth emphasizing how important are the social experiences of pre-school years. It is noticeable that first-born children are generally less sociable than their brothers and sisters, a fact that seems to indicate that they have missed valuable experience in the earliest months. " Only " children, as we should expect, are often very unsociable.

Sociability is more than gregariousness ; it is a human quality, and it marks us off from such merely gregarious creatures as sheep and wolves. But gregariousness, with its two close allies, subjection and self-assertion, is the root from which sociability develops. When children first come to school they have begun to develop sociability in the family circle ; in a school classroom, however, they are at first gregarious rather than sociable. This fact should be recognized and no attempts should be made to hurry the development of sociability. Young children are naturally suspicious of advances made by strangers, and though they will play happily in the presence of strangers they need time to get accustomed to the new " herd " before they begin to be sociable with its members. This beginning, as we have seen, takes the form of playing in small groups, and these groups are subject to many sudden disintegrations and redistributions. This is one reason why rooms for nursery classes should be large ; little children need the presence of other children, but they also need space so that they can pursue without interference their individual projects and their small-group activities.

The non-co-operative character of young children's play has often been noticed. Piaget[1] has gone a stage further and by recording the speech of young children playing together he has shown that each child tends to talk to himself rather than to his companion ; the speech of children under the age of seven tends to take the form of soliloquies rather than of conversations. Children, in their play and speech, tend to be egocentric rather than social. English observers of children playing under free conditions are of opinion, however, that Piaget has exaggerated the egocentric

[1] See *The Language and Thought of he Child*, J. Piaget (Kegan Paul, 1926).

character of children's speech. The truth appears to be that, as we have already suggested, the development of sociability begins very early, that it proceeds slowly and suffers many temporary set-backs. Above all, its development depends very much on the kind of " social atmosphere " in which the child is learning.

SOCIAL ATMOSPHERE

There are three main types of social atmosphere observable in schools and classrooms. First, there is the atmosphere created by domineering teachers of strong personality. This results in children being overtly submissive, but it tends to breed secret and undesirable forms of assertion such as bullying and persecution. From the point of view of learning and teaching, this atmosphere is favourable to dogmatic teaching and the results often appear to be good. In reality, however, the learning is generally superficial and it consequently lacks permanence ; very little direct interest is aroused in any subject. Furthermore, the pupils show little, if any, enterprise or initiative.

Second, there is the atmosphere created by submissive teachers of weak personality. This results in children being over-assertive and it tends to breed quarrelsomeness and disorder, a state of affairs that is obviously unfavourable to both learning and teaching.

Finally, there is the atmosphere created by teachers who, while tacitly admitted to be masters of the situation, are neither domineering nor submissive ; the atmosphere is neither one of subjection nor of assertion but of primitive comradeship.[1] In such an atmosphere there is a great deal of " give-and-take " between teacher and class, and between individual members of the class. That is to say, every one displays in some degree a spirit of sociability. Such an atmosphere, as Edgell[2] has pointed out, is favourable for

[1] See *Psychology and Primitive Culture*, F. C. Bartlett (Cambridge University Press, 1923).
[2] See *Mental Life*, B. Edgell, pp. 148–50 (Methuen, 1926).

learning. When family relations are good, children pick up instruction from brothers and sisters in an easy attitude of comradeship, and this is why in pre-school years children with brothers and sisters generally learn more quickly than " only " children. Teachers in school notice the same phenomenon. No method of teaching can ever take the place of the " give-and-take " of oral discussion, a fact that is very clearly demonstrated in the teaching of mathematics.

There are many occasions in school when the whole class is inconveniently large, and when " group work " should be organized. Thus, a class of thirty may be divided into three groups for practising dramatic work, into six groups for investigating mathematical problems, into ten groups for doing scientific experiments, into fifteen groups for learning facts by heart.

Individual work and private study are important, but it should be noted that this type of work also gains by being done in a social atmosphere. Even in imaginative drawing, a child never reaches the same heights when working by himself at home as he does when he belongs to a class all of whose members are engaged in similar work. The same is true of expressional work in English. Children write best when they feel they are writing for an audience. They welcome help and criticism when it is given in a spirit of comradeship and when they find that it is helping them to realize their social intentions. It will be seen that the term " self-expression " is apt to be very misleading unless it is clearly realized that no child can be truly and fully himself except in so far as he is in an attitude of responsiveness to others in his group. The blind worship of the crude expressional work of individual children is a serious psychological error. If children are to experience the satisfaction that comes with progress, they need help and criticism from older people ; they expect it and they get it in their " free " play with other children, and there is no reason why, on account of a false sentimentality, we should withhold it from them in school activities. The only necessary condition is that it must be given in an atmosphere of primitive comradeship. We will now consider some ways in which this atmosphere can be developed in the classroom.

PRIMITIVE COMRADESHIP

Leaders and followers.—In every animal herd there is an outstanding individual, generally a creature of exceptional physique and beauty, who gives a lead. A class, too, needs a leader and generally speaking it looks to its teacher. He has, in the eyes of young pupils, many of the qualities of a leader—superior physical size and strength, superior knowledge, intelligence and skill ; he is also, by virtue of his place in the hierarchy of educational officials, taken without question as a leader. But, as many young teachers soon discover, it is very easy to forfeit this position. This is not surprising when we reflect on the disparity in age, experience and interests between a teacher and his pupils. Though he may be the accepted leader of the class, he is not the natural leader in the same sense as a pupil-leader would be. The trouble usually begins when he shows some slight sign of hesitation, diffidence or embarrassment, for in every " herd " there are would-be leaders ready to take advantage of such signs and assume a rival leadership. Beginners are advised to take precautions. First, they must prepare themselves so well for all eventualities that no happening can take them unawares and cause embarrassment (see p. 182). Second, they must at an early stage secure the co-operation of the natural leaders in the class. Sometimes it may first be necessary to bring these prominent individuals into subjection. If a teacher decides that he can only create an atmosphere of comradeship by starting from one of subjection, he should begin by tackling the big, assertive, troublesome individuals. As soon as possible, however, he should begin to make a gradual retreat from his position of dominance ; he should abandon the role of tyrant and assume that of leader. This new relationship can be suggested to children in many subtle ways. A leader does not talk so much of " I " and " you " as of " we " ; he communicates his wishes by tactful suggestions rather than by irritating commands. Whereas a tyrant would say, " You must," a leader would say, " Let us try."

Some young teachers try to create a spirit of comradeship in a more direct way than that described above. They try to divest themselves of their adult characteristics and they pride themselves on behaving " as a boy among boys," hoping that they will be accepted as natural leaders and not as teacher-leaders. There is, however, something incongruous in such behaviour and children are not slow to perceive it. They may accept the boyish teacher as leader, but they do so in an attitude of amused tolerance. There are other objections to the practice. It involves a pose that is very difficult to maintain ; an adult cannot be as exuberant as a child without wasting energy that should be devoted to more worthy ends. The maintenance of such a pose tends to arrest the normal development of the teachers themselves and it thus tends to make them unacceptable in ordinary adult society. It also deprives children of normal adult companionship that is necessary for their social development. There are in every class plenty of natural pupil-leaders, and a teacher is behaving very unwisely if he tries to usurp their functions.

There are, in fact, few, if any, members of a class who do not at times crave to be leaders themselves, and a teacher-leader should give opportunities for leadership to as many pupils as possible. To do this, the life of a classroom or school must be many-sided ; while some pupils will be successful leaders of a football team, others will find outlets for leadership in societies of various kinds ; some will make admirable prefects, while others may be temperamentally better fitted to edit and manage a class magazine. Ideally all members of a class should have experience both of leading and following. This applies to the teacher and especially to the teacher of adolescents. Although he is generally giving a lead, there are times when he should subordinate himself and take his place as a humble member of the class. He should always be ready to receive suggestions and he should consider them as he would consider suggestions from equals in life outside school. The same rhythm of leading and following should punctuate his teaching. At times he should be the teacher giving his followers the benefit of his superior knowledge and judgment; at other times, the initiative should come from the class working either as groups or as individuals.

Although the natural leaders among pupils in a class usually stand out prominently, this is not always so. A quiet pupil, belonging more to the introvert than to the extravert type, will sometimes be found to exert a very strong influence on his fellows. This fact explains why the results of a prefect election are sometimes surprising to a teacher. The pupils seldom make a mistake, however, for they have better opportunities for judging quiet leadership than the teacher has.

The process of social welding.—There is a great difference between an unorganized collection of people and a community. Watch two hundred children in a school playground during a recreation period, and then consider the same children when they are marshalled under a leader to watch a school match or to take part in community singing. The individuals are then united by common interests; they have become a psychological unit. It is as if the individual units had coalesced to form a new whole. Between an unorganized collection of pupils in a playground and the community represented by an assembled class or school there are other degrees of group organization.[1] There is the crowd that assembles to watch a street fight; it comes together under the force of a special instinctive interest, but it soon dissolves and the same crowd will never exist again. Then there is the club composed of a few individual pupils bound together by some special acquired interest, as, for example, an interest in model railways. The community, as

[1] See *The Psychology of Education*, J. Drever, p. 214 (Arnold, 1922); *The Groundwork of Educational Psychology*, J. S. Ross, p. 257.

I

represented by a class, school or nation, differs from a crowd or a club in being relatively more permanent and in being welded together by broader and more varied interests, by traditions and memories of the past as well as by experiences of the present.

It has often been remarked that, as members of a crowd, individuals will behave very differently from the way they normally behave. Feeling seems to be intensified and inhibitions released. One reason is that we tend by nature to imitate the feelings of others ; a wave of primitive sympathy passes quickly through a crowd. This is further intensified by our tendency to imitate the actions of others ; we see the outward signs of emotion in our neighbours, we cannot help making the same signs and as a result we experience the emotion.[1] If, in addition, a leader suggests some suitable idea it is at once accepted without reflection. The direction of crowd behaviour by the suggestions of a responsible leader is very important. In its absence the behaviour tends to sink to a low primitive level. This is generally explained by means of the principle of fusion and arrest. Those primitive, instinctive tendencies that are common to all members of the crowd tend to fuse and reinforce one another while the more civilized, acquired tendencies that are possessed only be certain members of the crowd tend to be arrested. But, whatever the ethical nature of its behaviour, a crowd inspired by a common interest always behaves psychologically in the same way ; it behaves—feels, acts and thinks—as one man.

This is the fundamental method for welding individuals into a group ; they must be inspired by common interests.

[1] This is an example of the Lange-James theory of emotion which states that we perform the appropriate action and this action arouses the emotion. Thus we do not run away because we are afraid ; we run away and this makes us afraid. We perform the physical movements of laughing and this arouses the feeling of amusement ; we do not laugh because we feel amused. There are doubtless occasions when feeling is induced by making the appropriate physical movement, and this is a fact worth remembering in school. It is difficult, however, to believe that this is always the order of events. The truth seems to be that body and mind are so intimately related that either may take the lead according to the circumstances of each situation.

In school it is often necessary to begin by appealing to some strong primitive interest, such as the interest in games, sports and competitions. But a good school or class is not held together merely by an interest in athletics ; as our group becomes educated this interest becomes reinforced by others—by interests in craftmanship and art, by intellectual and social interests.

Dr. F. H. Hayward urges that educationists make insufficient use of group emotion and suggestion. He stresses the value of inspirational lessons given to large classes and particularly the value of special services attended by the whole school. These services, in which music, literature and lectures are incorporated, he calls *celebrations*. " The Celebration," Hayward says, " is an attempt to organise Inspiration. . . . High-temperature conditions exist and much is felt that is not fully understood."[1]

To these special celebrations should be added the more usual type of school ceremony—services for opening and closing school, meetings for instituting school prefects and for bidding farewell to leavers, services on Empire and Armistice Day, harvest festivals. The great importance of all these occasions should be recognized ; they should be carefully plannned as means of stirring worthy emotion, of inspiring high ideals and of strengthening corporate life.

Interest can only be kept alive, however, if it finds outlet in activity. Although in the process of social welding it is important to arouse mass emotion, care must be taken not to allow this emotion to evaporate ; opportunities for appropriate social service must be created for each member of the group. It follows that it is impossible to weld a class or a school into a community either by the mere preaching of high ideals or by the practice of a single interest of a narrow kind. A head teacher who relies exclusively on mass emotion without giving outlets for its individual expression will do very little to develop sociability

---

[1] For a summary statement of the celebration case, see *A Fourth Book of Celebrations*, F. H. Hayward, pp. 204–8 (Russell).

in his school. A teacher who places excessive emphasis on one narrow type of interest, for example on efficiency in one subject or on proficiency in games, is bound to make some children feel they are social outcasts. Emphasis should always be placed on the fact that every one is needed and that different members have different gifts. Even the dullest child can make some useful contribution to the life of a classroom if it is well organized ; from the point of view of social worth there are no backward children.

In this work of welding individuals into a group, a teacher is greatly helped by the good traditions of the school. It is easier to develop group spirit in a well-established school than in one that has just opened.

Sympathy.—Among the acquired interests that bind a class together none is more important than sympathy. At first sympathy is exclusively instinctive ; it is the primitive passive sympathy that flows from one individual to another, that sweeps through a crowd when emotion is aroused. This is the only type of sympathy manifested by very young children. Later, about the age of three, they appear to be consciously sympathetic as they ask questions about the feelings of other people and even things. This is an important stage in development, but it is not a sign of real sympathy. It is probably a projecting of their own personal feeling rather than any *feeling with* other people, for at this egocentric stage children are concerned almost exclusively with themselves. As they grow older and learn to distinguish themselves more clearly from their environment, the tendency to ask such questions disappears.

As children gain social experience, they gradually become conscious that they feel in the same way as other people ; they know, for example, that other members of the class are feeling afraid as they are. By degrees they learn to look upon some members of the herd not merely as companions but as friends ; they are then not content to share emotion in a primitive gregarious way, but they seek actively to share experiences. They see a friend in trouble ; in imagination they enter into *his* feelings ; they may feel sorry for him and angry with his assailant, and they will then seek to communicate these feelings to the sufferer. That is to say, a process of " give-and-take " is set up. The children are no longer merely sympathetic in a passive, primitive way ; they are sympathetic in an active, social way.

A teacher can do a great deal to help children to develop this attitude of active sympathy. As a first step, he should foster a responsive give-and-take relationship with each member of his class. He should enter into active sympathy with his pupils and show a sincere interest in their projects both in and out of school. He should carefully avoid " favouritism." Without in any way being sentimental, without sacrificing any of the dignity that appertains to his position as teacher-leader, he should treat every individual as he would treat a young personal friend. In time many real friendships will develop. There are many little acts of sympathy that ought on no account to be neglected in classrooms—a kindly enquiry about an elder member of the family who has left school, a sympathetic message to some one in distress. Whenever possible, the children themselves should co-operate in these and other social courtesies ; a class letter to a pupil in hospital is a good example. This spirit of active sympathy among members of a class or school should be definitely cultivated ; it is more important than many of the lessons that appear on the time-table. With the younger children it is largely a question of developing good habits, but with adolescents genuine social sympathy can be aroused.

The ordinary lessons of the curriculum provide many opportunities for extending the range of human sympathies. Rightly taught, there is no subject more valuable than literature for this purpose. In other subjects our work is not merely to teach facts of geography, mathematics and science, for example, but to help pupils to enter in imagination into the lives of other people—of foreigners, of research scientists, of workers of all kinds. In every subject, not only in history, we should help children to appreciate that they are indebted to those who lived before them.

Social experiences.—The development of sociability is no exception to the general rule—children learn most surely by experience. We have already mentioned various forms of desirable social experience ; group work, team games, " house " activities, meetings of school societies, elections of prefects, celebrations. Many others could be enumerated : projects of various kinds such as school concerts, dramatic work, compilation of school and class magazines, team competitions, reception of visitors, the taking of verbal messages, open days.

A very important type of social experience is participation in an argument. In a crude form argument begins in early childhood and at this age it generally ends in a quarrel. The same is true unfortunately of many adult arguments, for very few people have learnt how to argue without becoming angry. Debates are often organized in school, but, as Pear[1] has pointed out, they have serious limitations. They may tend to form the tiresome habit of speech-making for the sake of being controversial, and without any real desire to come to a useful conclusion or to arrive at truth. But the chief objection to the debate, Pear argues, is its fundamental dishonesty. " In debate, thinking tends to be based, not upon a strict and honest effort to find truth, but upon a desire to beat an opponent. Debate accentuates differences and gives them an antagonistic flavour where differences ought to be a source of interest, and their discussion ought to increase sympathy and knowledge." For developing sociability, informal discussion is more effective than formal debate. It arises naturally out of the life of the classroom and has a definite, useful object. It may, for example, aim at solving a problem that has emerged either in a lesson or in connexion with classroom administration. It is carried on in a co-operative rather than a competitive spirit, and there is more scope for give-and-take than is possible in a set debate.

[1] See *The Desirability of Teaching School Children the Technique of Discussion,* T. H. Pear, Brit, Jnl. Educ. Psych., Vol, VI, pp. 9–22 ; *The Psychology of Effective Speaking,* T. H. Pear (Kegan Paul, 1933).

Co-operation and competition.—In a classroom pervaded by an atmosphere of comradeship, co-operation must obviously take precedence over competition. Where competition is used, the ultimate aim will always be social. Thus individuals may usefully compete against their previous best performance, but, at least in secondary schools, they should do so in order to promote the welfare and prestige of their group. One group may compete against another group and in so doing weld together its individual members. Competition between individuals will be reduced to a minimum ; if marks are given, the team or class average rather than the individual performances will be emphasized.

One common form of group competition is between boys and girls in mixed schools. Used very occasionally in a friendly spirit, it may do little harm ; but co-operation between men and women is of such vital importance in everyday life that it seems unfortunate to suggest sex antagonism to school children.

Friendly rivalry is a necessary part of all social life, but it is necessary to take care that all rival groups are changed and enlarged from time to time. Thus teams in a class may compete daily, but they should occasionally be required to combine as a class and compete against another class ; classes should combine and feel that they are part of the school and so on. A group spirit of any kind in school is a means to an end—a realization of the duties and privileges of citizenship. And, as we suggested on page 177, man has not reached his fullest development until he becomes conscious of belonging not only to his town and country but to humanity as a whole. This is admittedly an ideal, but it is an ideal we ought to keep in mind, for without it we are always in danger, when promoting the lesser loyalties of team, class and school, of fixating social development at an unnecessarily low level and of sending our pupils out into the world with minds obscured by narrow, petty prejudices.

OBSERVATIONS AND EXPERIMENTS

1. Observe the way in which a new pupil settles down in his class. Consider his attitude to members of the class, and the attitude of the class towards him.

2. Observe from the point of view of sociability the free play activities of (a) infants, (b) juniors, (c) seniors.

3. Find by experiment which is the better method for learning a short poem by heart—(a) individual method, (b) pupils working in pairs.

4. Observe a class at work during a session. Consider and note :
    (a) Use of competition.
    (b) Use of co-operation.
    (c) Occasions when the teacher (i) leads, and (ii) follows.
    (d) Occasions when pupils act as leaders.
    (e) Percentage time given to (i) class work, (ii) group work, (iii) individual work.
    (f) Children who are very sociable or unsociable.

5. Make a list of children who are (a) exceptionally sociable, (b) exceptionally unsociable. Find the position of each child in its family, i.e. 1st, 3rd out of 4, and so on. What conclusion (if any) can you draw ?

6. Observe the speech of a small group of young children at play, noting the occasions when they converse, and when they merely soliloquize.

7. Observe the play of a small group of young children, noting the corrections and criticisms that they give one another, and the attitude of the children to these corrections.

8. Find by observation the natural leaders in a class. Make a list of the qualities that appear to make for leadership.

9. Investigate the extent to which secret societies exist among school children.

REFERENCES FOR READING

Education : Its Data and First Principles, Sir T. Percy Nunn, chapter I, and pp. 173 ff.
Modern Psychology and Education, Sturt and Oakden, chapters III and IV.
Groundwork of Educational Psychology, J. S. Ross, chapter XV.
Modern Education, T. Raymont, chapter XI.
The Process of Learning, C. Bloor, chapter XVI.

ADDITIONAL REFERENCES

Instincts of the Herd in Peace and War, W. Trotter (Benn, 1916).
The Crowd, G. Le Bon (Fisher Unwin).
Social Psychology, Wm. McDougall (Methuen, Twentieth Edit., 1926).
The Group Mind, Wm. McDougall (Camb. Univ. Press, 1920).
Education for Citizenship in Secondary Schools, Association for Education in Citizenship (Ox. Univ. Press, 1936).
Modern Developments in Educational Practice, Sir John Adams, chapters V, VI (Univ. Lond. Press, 1922).
Sane Schooling, J. H. Simpson (Faber, 1936).
Man and Society in an Age of Reconstruction, Karl Mannheim (Kegan Paul, 1940).

ESSAYS AND DISCUSSIONS

1. Loneliness in school.

(Consider : children who seem to prefer solitude ; ways of helping children to overcome shyness ; the effects on children of personal slights ; ways in which teachers may inadvertently slight individual pupils.)

2. Sociability in school.

(Consider how it can be developed (a) incidentally, (b) as a by-product of instruction in the usual subjects of the curriculum, (c) by extra-classroom activities.)

3. The qualities of a teacher-leader.

(Consider : natural and acquired qualities ; personal details that enhance a teacher's prestige.)

4. Practical advice for a teacher who has difficulty in keeping order. (See pp. 181–88.)

5. The ideal relationship that should exist between teacher and class.

6. The election of prefects.

(Consider : preparatory advice ; the actual election ; the investiture ceremony.)

7. Ways of widening human sympathy among school children.

8. An annual programme of social events for a school.

9. Social events in which boys and girls should co-operate.

(Consider : their importance, especially where boys and girls are in separate departments ; suitable occasions.)

10. The uses and limitations of debating societies.

11. Education should aim at developing " a sane mind in a sane society." (cf. Discussion No. 6, p. 216.)

1*

Chapter XV

THE CURRICULUM

THE modern curriculum is generally described as being over-crowded. Compared with curricula of schools in former times it certainly looks formidable. In ancient Greece, for example, the curriculum for children to the age of 14 consisted of three subjects—letters, music and gymnastic. It is true that these subjects had a fairly wide connotation : the Greek boy learned to read, write, and perform simple calculations; he was taught to play the lyre, to sing and recite, to dance and to engage in a varied programme of athletic exercises. But the fact remains that the Greek curriculum did not consist of a multiplicity of subjects.

If we turn to the history of education in England we find that most early curricula were equally simple. For example, at the beginning of the nineteenth century, most of our grammar schools had a curriculum that consisted almost exclusively of classics. In the elementary schools for children of the poor most curricula consisted of religious instruction and " the three rudimentary subjects "—the three R's as they came to be called—together with needle-work for girls.

There were some notable exceptions and the elementary curriculum had widened considerably when, in 1862, the famous Lowe Code came into operation. By this code, grants to schools and consequently teachers' salaries were made largely dependent on pupils' successes in examinations in the three R's.[1] The regulation was defended on the

[1] Capitation grants were paid to school managers who then bargained with their teachers. " The grant was limited to 12s. a head, 4s. to be paid on average attendance, and 8s. on the results of examination, one-third of the latter sum being withheld for failure in each of the three R's." See *History of Elementary Education*, C. Birchenough, p. 116 (Univ. Tut. Press, 1925) ; *The Education of the Adolescent*, chapter I (H.M.S.O., 1926) ; *The Primary School*, chapter I (H.M.S.O., 1931).

ground that it would discourage teachers from neglecting the younger and less brilliant pupils. Its effect, of course, was to make the minimum curriculum a maximum one, and it was soon recognized that this was a meagre diet even for children who left school at the early age of 12. Schools were then encouraged by special grants to teach additional subjects. Curricula were widened, not in accordance with any well-considered philosophy, but according to the interests or qualifications of individual teachers. Thus we read of a school in the Midlands earning a grant by teaching nautical science, though probably no pupil had ever been on the sea.

The curricula of schools in England have developed partly under the influence of official regulation, partly as a result of the influence of inspectors, but largely as a result of the freedom that has gradually been conferred on head teachers.[1] The result of this freedom is that, in spite of continual complaints that the curriculum is becoming over-crowded, it has continued to expand. The reason is that our conception of the aim of education has widened, and our curricula are, after all, reflections of our views on this fundamental question. In the early nineteenth century, the chief aim in elementary schools was to teach children to

[1] The *Code of Regulations for Public Elementary Schools* issued by the Board of Education (1926) was a ten-page pamphlet, and the following extract, which was the only regulation governing the curriculum, indicates the degree of freedom that elementary schools enjoyed under it :
" The secular instruction in a School or Centre must be in accordance with a suitable curriculum and syllabus framed with due regard to the organisation and circumstances of the School or Schools concerned."
The Board of Education gave general guidance in its *Handbook of Suggestions for the Consideration of Teachers and others concerned in the Work of Public Elementary Schools* (1937). This Handbook contained chapters on English Language and Literature, History, Geography, Mathematics, Nature Study and Science, Music, Art and Craft, Needlework, Housecraft, Gardening and other Rural Activities, Health and Physical Training. It stated, however, that " it is not possible to lay down any rule as to the exact number of the subjects which should be taken in an individual school " and suggests that " the curriculum must vary to some extent with the qualifications of the teaching staff."
Local Education Authorities sometimes make special rules governing certain aspects of the curriculum, but it is probably true to say that such rules are never made to-day without prior consultation with teachers.

read the Bible, and a very simple curriculum sufficed. What is the aim of education to-day ? Much has been written on the subject in recent times and, although the aim is expressed in many different ways by different writers, there appears to be a fairly well-defined concensus of opinion, at least in this country. This opinion we may express by saying that education should aim at enabling each individual to lead the fullest life of which he is capable. Remembering what we have learnt about individual differences we must face the fact at once that the content of a full life is something that varies from one individual to another. But let us first consider whether there is not in all these varied lives something that might be termed their greatest common measure. There are two ways of approaching this problem. We can consider the life of man either as reflected in the development of the race, or as reflected in the development of modern children. Whichever approach we adopt, we reach the same conclusion—there are a number of interests that appear to be characteristic of human life, and these interests all spring from man's universal instinctive endowment. Thus, as we learned in chapter II, children are interested in bodily activity, in making things, in exploring and understanding their environment, and in extending their social circle. As a result of these interests, they develop a number of interdependent activities, each gradually becoming more or less well defined. They run races and play games ; they build and fashion things ; they compose jingles and stories and write them down ; they ask questions and frame hypotheses ; they count and measure ; they talk and sing ; they quarrel and make friends. These, it will be noticed, are the same activities that man has always pursued. Each generation, however, learned from its forefathers : games became more organized ; tools were gradually improved ; methods of expression, both spoken and written, became more precise ; constructions, whether of wood or metal, or in the form of scientific hypotheses, of mathematical generalizations, or of stories and music, were handed on. In this way, on the basis of a few fundamental forms of spontaneous human activity, our great human traditions—physical culture, art, craft, language, literature, science, mathematics, religion, history, geography and music—have been built up. They are the inevitable result of the natural reactions of man to his environment, and without any one of them life would be immeasurably poorer. This is why they must form the curriculum of our schools, and this is why, despite all the clamours about an over-crowded curriculum, no body of educationists can ever agree to exclude one or more of them as a solution of the difficulty. They are all necessary ingredients of a full human life. Healthy children in pre-school years indulge spontaneously in all these activities and it would be " going against nature " if we in school deprived pupils of the opportunity of continuing to pursue them. On the contrary, education should intensify natural interests in all these directions, and by introducing children to their full social heritage it should make their lives fuller and more joyful than they could ever have been if the children had been left to their own devices. This, it should be noted, is the root meaning of the word " education." It is the process of nourishing (Latin, *educare*, to nourish), and the diet that will nourish children is the same varied programme of activities that has nourished the race during the progress of its development.

If we look at the curriculum in this way, it will be seen that its various component parts appear not as subjects but as activities.[1] It is easy to appreciate that art, craft, and music are activities, but the same ought to be true of all branches of the curriculum. It does not merely mean that all subjects should be taught by so-called " practical " methods (valuable as these may be), but that they should be learnt as the result of eager activity, both mental and physical, on the part of interested pupils. Mathematics, for example, is not a body of knowledge to be laboriously learnt by heart, or a collection of tricks to be mastered by

[1] We are indebted to Professor Sir Percy T. Nunn for this important suggestion. See his book, *Education : Its Data and First Principles*, pp. 242 ff.

imitation ; it is an activity to be pursued, and the successful teacher of mathematics makes his pupils feel that they are following in the footsteps of excited pioneers, actively measuring and calculating in response to some practical need, and in the higher stages actively entering into the generalizations of mathematicians. Composition is not an exercise to be done grudgingly at the behest of a teacher, but an adventure in expression, a letter with a purpose, an article for a class magazine, or a record for a personal note-book. " In short," as Nunn says, " all subjects should be taught in the ' play-way,' care being taken that the ' way ' leads continuously from the irresponsible frolic of childhood to the disciplined labours of manhood."[1]

We must now return to the problem of the over-crowded curriculum. Over-crowding is clearly undesirable, for it is impossible to pursue subjects as activities if teachers and pupils are continually in a state of hurry and bustle. Such a state inevitably leads to the short-circuiting of real creative work—notes are dictated instead of being composed, important truths are told and forgotten, when they might be dis-covered and remembered, practical work is omitted because it consumes too much precious time, the classroom work becomes formal and joyless, and confidence is undermined. There is something seriously wrong with a school in which life is a mad race against time.

It is not claimed that the suggestions that follow pro-vide a complete solution to the problem, but they are given as promising lines along which a solution may be sought, and as worthy of consideration before we admit defeat and seek a solution by a return to a restricted and less worthy curriculum than the one that we are now attempting.

Unifying the Curriculum

Correlation.—Our first suggestion is that we ought to experiment with schemes that aim at producing a greater

[1] *Op. cit.*, p. 247.

degree of unification among the various parts of the school curriculum. One method that aimed at doing this had a vogue in school some years ago under the label of correlation. The subjects were still taught as separate subjects, but an attempt was made to make one subject impinge on another, to correlate them. The effort led to much foolish formalism. Thus we read, for example, of work being centred round a daffodil. Children read about daffodils, they learnt poetry about daffodils, they had nature lessons about them, they sang about them, they painted them. Such a scheme could have only one result; the pupils were exasperated.

Correlation was also practised in forms less obviously futile. Science and handicraft, for example, were taught as one subject. Such a scheme has some merits; the science is realistic, and the handicraft is purposeful. But, pressed to extremes, it results in a serious limitation of both subjects. Handicraft should not be confined to the making of scientific models nor should science be confined to those aspects that can be demonstrated by working models. The idea of correlation is valuable, but unless it is sensibly applied it leads to an unnatural warping rather than to any real unification of the curriculum.

The project method.—A more promising attempt at unification has recently been made, and is now labelled the project method. It is a method of educating in which children learn by working out projects. As we noted in chapter III, this is the way in which children learn in pre-school years, and it is very successful. Now children of school age are still full of plans and schemes, but unfortunately these are too often competitors with the plans and schemes that we teachers arrange for them : teachers and pupils are, as we say, at cross purposes. Under the project method an attempt is made to bring these purposes into line, and the work of teachers is not so much to teach school subjects as to guide and organize children's projects.

As an illustration, let us consider the learning of the rule for calculating the areas of rectangular surfaces. A

" subject " teacher might ask his pupils which is the largest of three rectangular pieces of paper. After discussion, the rectangles might be drawn to scale and divided into square inches. Thus the problem is solved and a hint of the necessary rule is obtained. A " project " teacher would scorn the use of pieces of paper. He does not believe that his pupils want to know which piece is the largest, and it is their wishes, not his own, that are his guide. He therefore looks about for some project from real life in which pupils may be interested. Perhaps some new houses are being erected in the neighbourhood, and the occupant will soon be busy covering the floors. How much will it cost? What is the best floor covering? Catalogues are written for; the suitability of linoleums, carpets and parquet is discussed; prices are compared and the term square yard is encountered; finally, armed with square yards cut out of paper, the young furnishers set off to one of the houses (by kind permission of the builder). As the project is worked out the necessary arithmetical rule is discovered, but the learning is not confined to arithmetic. Questions of good taste, of sound economy, of letter writing, of how to ask a favour—all are taken in the stride of a single project. The working of a project is very different from the giving of a lesson in which care must be taken " not to lose the thread." The " project " teacher believes that in education we are not dealing with single threads so much as with woven pieces. A child sees that there are certain problems in his life to be unravelled. He starts with the real-life problem, and he soon finds that he must know something about the threads. Each thread, however, instead of being isolated and comparatively meaningless, is now seen to fit in as warp or woof to form a whole which, though complex, is yet simple to the child. It is familiar and it has formed part of his vital experience. There is no longer any danger of a single thread getting lost, or of it being developed so long that it gets into a tangle.

Some successful experiments have been reported in which a whole curriculum has been devised on the basis of projects, and the tendency in infant schools is certainly in the direction of projects and away from subjects. It is not suggested that drill in fundamentals becomes unnecessary, but as a result of the keen interest aroused in the projects, the necessary drill is undertaken with zest, and the learning is done more rapidly and more joyfully than when it is undertaken as a piece of technique isolated from activity. As children grow older the subject approach becomes more justifiable and perhaps more necessary, though in all schools there is always a place for projects that will correlate subjects in a natural way and bring subject-specialists into schemes of real co-operation. School plays and concerts, educational visits, school journeys, are examples. Some schools organize special weeks in which attention is concentrated on some project; we hear, for example, of " Better-English Weeks," " Music and Anti-noise Weeks." Other schools set aside one afternoon each week for the pursuit of projects.

A scheme of particular interest to junior schools is the Winnetka Plan in which " tool " subjects—reading, writing and arithmetic—are taught on graded systematic lines, while the other subjects are approached through projects. Much of the work in a school for senior girls might well be done with housecraft as the central feature. Similarly in a rural school for senior boys gardening is a valuable centre of interest.

Ideally, the project method[1] brings school work into close contact with life, and it correlates subjects so naturally that the dividing lines practically disappear. Another important feature of the method is that much school work must be done outside the confines of school desks. If listening to a lesson, or even a lecture, is necessary to the

[1] Like all " new " methods, the " project method " is not really new. William Cobbett, for example, educated his family on project lines. As we read in *The Primary School*, p. 101 (H.M.S.O., 1931).
" His method was to engage the interest of his children in the work and occupations of his rural holiday, and to let them discover that these could not be carried on successfully without ' book learning ' . . . ' calculations about the farming affairs forced arithmetic upon us : the *use*, the *necessity* of the thing led us to the study '." See Cobbett, *Advice to Young Men* (1830).

working out of a project the pupils will listen, but such lessons will be only incidents in the working out of a larger scheme which it is the united purpose of teacher and pupils to carry to completion.

The reader will probably feel that the project method is a doubtful solution of the problem of an over-crowded curriculum. Although it unifies subjects, it leads into many by-paths and it clearly consumes a great deal of time. There are two answers to this criticism. First, the increased interest aroused compensates to some extent for the time involved. Second, it must be admitted that the acquisition of conventional facts may suffer. But if care be taken that pupils acquire the minimum of necessary knowledge (by drill, if necessary), may not the pupils be better educated through their active experiences, even though their store of conventional facts is less than it would be under formal methods ? How many of the unwanted facts painfully acquired by uninterested pupils remain after school days are over ? And what educative influence did they have ? The curriculum is over-crowded, not because it deals with too many aspects of human activity, but because it is conceived in terms of too many isolated facts. A hall containing three hundred children, each moving independently, would be over-crowded, but if we arrange the children in ten orderly classes, the over-crowding disappears ; the hall is now full but not crowded. The same is true of the curriculum ; it may be over-crowded with unrelated facts, but it is not over-full with vital experiences.

If we had the courage to break away from the conventional view of the curriculum we should probably find that our pupils would in the long run acquire more facts than they do now. They might not be the same facts as we ourselves learned at school, but having been acquired with interest and related to some real experience they would be a permanent possession of the pupil and not a mere temporary decoration. They would be the interrelated facts that compose assimilated knowledge and not the unrelated facts that compose memorized information.

Simplifying the curriculum.—It will probably be a long time before a many-subject curriculum crowded with facts gives place to a few-project curriculum full of experience. Meanwhile much can be done involving less revolutionary changes. Not only can the traditional curriculum be enlivened with projects, but the subjects themselves can also be unified, and conceived in broader terms with less pedantic insistence on the memorizing of petty details. That is to say, our subjects can be simplified. As Kenneth Richmond points out, this does not mean " that we must practise talking about small details in words of one syllable, but that we must teach principles, and be watchful never to present a detail except in relation to a principle."[1] Much has been done in this direction in recent years. For example, geography, which once meant the memorizing of lists of names, is now the study of human life in regions of the world, and it is based on first-hand study of the local environment. The study of a number of isolated branches of science is giving way to the study of general science with human life as its central feature.[2] Attempts are also being made to make history a more living subject, to study great movements in the life of mankind, and to use as starting-points the history of the everyday things we see around us.

Another important movement in the direction of a simpler curriculum is beginning in junior schools. In mathematics, for example, instead of pressing pupils to perform feats of complicated computation divorced from reality, we are beginning to appreciate that it is more profitable to lay a broad foundation of mathematical experience. We are beginning to discover that the curriculum must be adapted to the child, and that one of the most serious errors we can make is to impose adult standards prematurely on young children. Perhaps one of the greatest benefits to be derived from any raising of the school-leaving age is the

---

[1] See *Education for Liberty*, Kenneth Richmond, chapter XII (Collins, 1918).

[2] See *Elementary General Science, A Book for Teachers*, A. G. Hughes (Blackie, 1933).

removal of pressure designed to achieve abnormal " results " in infant and junior schools.

When considering the curriculum in terms of subjects, it is useful to think of these subjects as belonging to a small number of groups, e.g. :

Social studies : history, geography, literature.
Arts and crafts : music, drawing, handicraft, housecraft.
Scientific studies : mathematics, general science.
Physical education : hygiene, physical training, games.

And, most important of all, we should in all our discussions of the curriculum remember that in the last resort the curriculum consists of one subject only—*living*.

SPECIALIZATION

Specialization by pupils.—Children come to school to be introduced to those lines of human activity that have enriched human life. An important question now arises : Is it reasonable to expect all children to pursue all these activities ? It is difficult to give a simple answer to this question. It is probably true to say that all children are by nature interested in all these activities, but it is equally true that by virtue of differences in intelligence, temperament and special aptitudes, and as a result of differences in their upbringing and education, individual children do show marked preferences. They tend as a rule to prefer those activities that they can do best. This fact reminds us that each activity has two aspects—the executive and the appreciative. It will be generally agreed that the appreciation of literature, art, music and craft should form part of the education of all children at all stages ; this is one way in which the natural many-sided interest of children can be kept alive. It is not generally recognized that many lessons in history, geography and science are, as a matter of fact, given more with the object of increasing children's interest than of increasing their understanding. The same should be true of mathematics, a subject in which the executive aspect is at present in many schools the only one that receives recognition ; lessons on the history of mathematics, lessons designed to show the beauty of mathematical truths, and the fascinating properties of numbers—all these have an important place in school, and pupils do not require high executive mathematical ability in order to appreciate them. Speaking generally, both aspects of all subjects should be developed together, for they are mutually helpful. When, however, specialization begins, appreciation lessons in the " dropped " subjects should continue.

Specialization by pupils is commoner in grammar than in other kinds of secondary schools, but it is too often determined by the exigencies of examinations without adequate regard to the interests of the pupils. Ideally, specialization should be determined by pupils' interests. In early stages these interests are wide and diffuse ; so the curriculum should not be narrowed. It is true that junior children show preferences, but they are not usually permanent, and often they are preferences for certain teachers rather than for certain subjects. Perhaps the chief factor that leads to a definite focusing of interest is the prospect of leaving school and earning a living. Thus the age for specialization depends rather on the school-leaving age than on the pupil's age. Secondary-school pupils who are leaving at 15 should be allowed to specialize at 13 or 14, if they show strong interests. In any case, the time-table should contain some optional periods for all, so that attention is called to the desirability of cultivating some special interest while still at school. The specialization advocated does not mean that the last year of school life should be narrowly vocational ; it means that the interest in vocation and the interest in independent leisure hours should be harnessed with other interests in the service of a liberal education. At all stages education should be realistic, and when pupils are looking forward to a vocation and to " grown-up " methods of spending leisure time, they will not be satisfied if school life proceeds as if these important prospects did not exist. Teachers should show a human interest in the latest films, they should know something of the literature which their pupils choose to read and of the careers to which they look forward, they should use newspapers in the classroom, they should be prepared to sacrifice the symmetry and efficiency of pre-arranged schemes so that each individual has a chance to develop some white-hot interest before he leaves school. If these principles are to be put into practice, the organization of the last year at school must be much more elastic than is now common. We suggest a programme of appreciation lessons in the main lines of human activity with a limited number of drill lessons on fundamental skills ; the rest of the time, and it may be as much as 50 per cent. of the total school hours, should be filled in by individual programmes arranged by pupils in consultation with their teachers.

Specialization by teachers.—Generally speaking, there ought to be more specializing among teachers in secondary schools than among teachers in infant and junior schools. Looking at the question from the standpoint of subjects, there should be most specializing in those subjects for which the teacher needs some special technical ability, e.g. in music and craft, where the teacher needs executive ability, and in art where the teacher should possess a high degree of æsthetic sensitivity. We have argued that, particularly for young children, the curriculum should be unified as far as possible, and for this purpose it is clearly desirable to avoid having many specialist teachers. Teaching the technique of reading and writing should go hand in hand with the study of history, geography, literature and nature, and there are obvious advantages in having all this work done by general practitioners. With older children, where the subject (or the grouped-subject) approach is less inappropriate, some degree of specialization is desirable. A teacher should know far more of a subject than he is ever required to teach, and it is impossible for one person to be really well informed on all or most of the subjects of a secondary-school curriculum. In small schools it is not always possible to organize the teaching on a specialist basis ; in these circumstances it is, however, desirable for different members of the staff to take a special interest in a related group of subjects and to act as specialist advisers for their colleagues. The day is gone when schemes of work in all subjects were drawn up by an omniscient dictatorial head teacher.

The dangers of specialization should be clearly apprehended. Chief among them is the danger that instead of being nurtured in a unified curriculum with one fundamental theme—the art of living—pupils may be bombarded with isolated subjects all competing for a share of their time and attention. Specialist teachers are always in danger of forgetting that they are teaching not only subjects but children also. To guard against this, they should, like specialist pupils in their last year at school, keep up at least an " appreciation " interest in other subjects, and they should let their pupils become aware that they have these other interests. A broad-minded specialist teacher will not expect every pupil to develop a specialist interest in his own subject ; if he is a science teacher, for example, he will expect to foster the natural scientific interests of all his pupils, but he will not expect every pupil to choose science as his intellectual hobby.

An Experiment in Curriculum Reconstruction

Dissatisfaction with the conventional curricula of schools is gaining ground and some interesting experiments are now being tried. As an illustration we will describe an important pioneer experiment now in progress at Bishop Wordsworth's School, Salisbury. The headmaster is convinced that far-reaching changes are necessary for three reasons :

(a) The growing discontent with the pressure imposed by the present examination system in secondary schools.

(b) The over-crowding of the curriculum due to the " addition in isolation " of new subjects.

(c) The fact that, although children are fundamentally the same as they always were, they are growing up to take their place in a changed, difficult world.

He suggests that the curriculum should consist of the following three parts, the first two being common to all, the third to be determined by individual choice :

(1) The two essential skills, viz. the ability to speak and write one's own language, and the ability to carry out those simple mathematical processes required in ordinary life.

(2) A body of basic culture, conceived without reference to the present artificial subject divisions, but including some study of the pupil's heritage and environment ; an elementary introduction to scientific ideas and processes, particularly biological processes ; a training of the emotional and æsthetic side through poetry, music and drama ; some work of a manual character ; the thorough study of one foreign language.

(3) A superstructure of studies carried to a higher standard, but varying for different types of pupil. Thus some pupils but not all would pursue the study of mathematics proper ; some but not all would make a specialist study of history ; and so on.

The above programme is designed for a grammar school. It will be seen that, if the over-crowding of the traditional curriculum for secondary-school children who leave school at the age of 15 is to be relieved, drastic changes will be necessary in our conception of what constitutes a desirable body of basic culture. This problem has been tackled in the experiment. The normal subject-divisions between English, history and geography have to a large extent been abandoned at all stages below that of the School Certificate, a course called Social Studies being substituted. It is found that through this course the schools can give " an excellent form of intellectual training, involving much practice in speaking and writing, in the collection and arrangement of material, in the use of books and in logical and careful thinking." On the knowledge side, the course includes " a general survey of combined world history and geography with a reading of some of the world's great stories, a closer study of the development of the English people in relation to their physical and economic environment, combined with such English literature as will illuminate this theme, reduced to reasonable proportion by the elimination of much of the English history at present taught through concentration on significant eras, and a survey of the modern world in relation to its origins, in which the study of the recent history, types of government, geographical conditions, economic organization, and such manifestations of modern life as the Press, the cinema, the radio, and town and regional planning are linked up to give the boy an insight into modern social, political, and economic problems." The general conclusion is that the course results " in a saving of time and energy, in the elimination of overlapping of function and content, and in a clearer picture in the minds of boys of what modern civilization is like and how it has originated."[1]

REFERENCES FOR READING

Handbook of Suggestions, New edition, 1937.
Education, Sir T. Percy Nunn, pp. 233–249.
Modern Education, T. Raymont, chapters VI, VII.

ADDITIONAL REFERENCES

The Organisation and Curricula of Schools, W. G. Sleight (Arnold, 1920).
The Curriculum, Kenneth Richmond (Constable, 1919).

ESSAYS AND DISCUSSIONS

1. Principles of curriculum building.

(Consider these criteria : usefulness ; mental training ; a full life.)

2. The distinction between knowledge and information.

3. Discursiveness in teaching.

4. Remedies for an over-crowded curriculum.

5. Specialization.
(Consider : pupils ; teachers.)

6. Housecraft as the central feature of a curriculum for the last year in a girls' school. (Gardening for boys.)

7. Choose the subject in which you are most interested and suggest some ways in which it can be presented in school as an " activity."

[1] F. C. Happold, *Curriculum Reconstruction with Special Reference to Social Studies*, The Preparatory Schools Review, March, 1936. See also *Citizens in the Making*, F. C. Happold (Christophers, 1935).

8. Suitable projects to be worked out on one afternoon each week for a term.

(Consider : 7-year-olds ; 11-year-olds.)

9. The organization of a special week in school during which attention will be concentrated on some important project.

10. The place of (a) educational visits and (b) school journeys in a school curriculum.

11. Do boys and girls need different curricula ?

(Read : *Differentiation of the Curriculum for Boys and Girls respectively in Secondary Schools*, H.M.S.O.)

CHAPTER XVI

DIFFICULT CHILDREN

IN one sense every child is a difficult child. As we have
learnt in previous chapters, it is by no means easy to
understand all the intricate workings of the mind of a single
individual. Fortunately it is not necessary. For the great
majority it is enough if we treat them humanely and sensibly as normal human beings. They do not all learn at the
same rate nor do they all react to our teaching in the same
way. But, broadly speaking, they make a satisfactory response to the school environment. Their unpleasant moods
soon pass, their fits of temper or laziness are neither serious
nor permanent. In most classes, however, there are at least
one or two pupils who cause teachers special anxiety.
They are children who in one direction or another make
unsatisfactory progress in learning. They may be slow in
acquiring knowledge, awkward in developing skill, or
prone to anti-social behaviour. There are at least these
three types of specially difficult children—backward, clumsy,
and troublesome.[1] The types are, of course, not mutually
exclusive ; in fact, it often happens that a difficult child is
difficult all round. This is almost sure to be the case when
the root of the trouble is some emotional disturbance.

Many of our difficult school children are manufactured
in pre-school days. As we described in chapter III (pp. 34–
35), strong instinctive interests are often denied suitable
forms of expression, with the result that they seek devious
routes or alternatively they burst out in violent ways. It is

[1] The reader will notice that the three types of difficult children are
the result of unsatisfactory development of (a) intellect, (b) muscular skill,
and (c) character and sociability. The fact that a fourth type of difficult
child—the insensitive—is not recognized is an indication that the development of taste has not yet been given the important place in school that
it deserves.

probably true to say that most children who are lazy or clumsy or badly behaved are suffering from some emotional trouble that was caused by unwise repressive treatment in early childhood. A continuation in school of the same type of treatment merely aggravates the trouble. Such children need, even more than those whose behaviour is satisfactory, opportunities for the free expression of their emotional urges. Creative work of all kinds—drawing, painting, dancing, talking—in a free, friendly atmosphere will do much to help such children to readjust themselves. As a means of curing and preventing backwardness, clumsiness and naughtiness, there is nothing to equal the training given in modern nursery and infant schools, where children lead a happy, active life, free from premature pressure towards adult types of behaviour and adult standards of skill, and free from premature forcing along the paths of formal learning. There is no doubt that in the past we have erred, as over-zealous parents have erred, in expecting young children to conform too soon to an adult pattern. We have created many difficult children by being over-anxious to get rid of the " difficulties " that all normal children present to grown-up people. Tolerance, even a happy-go-lucky spirit in bringing up children during the first five years, would do much to help them to grow up free from those internal emotional tensions that make them difficult in later years. Those teachers in junior schools who insist that *all* children should achieve high standards in formal work by the age of 7, may be making their own work far more difficult than it need be. If at the age of 7 children's natural curiosity has been kept fully alive, if their lives have been full of purposeful experience, if they are still capable of facing new problems without fear, if their muscles have been exercised by free, joyous activity—much that is now taught with labour and difficulty in infant schools could be taught in junior schools with a great saving of time and energy. And most important of all, the children would be mentally healthier ; there would be fewer difficult children.

Some of our difficult children are manufactured by the

system of teaching that treats a class as a unit and not as a collection of individuals. Any attempt to make all children in a class advance at the same rate along the same route is bound to create difficulties. Many a slow child becomes discouraged by being continually compared, to his disadvantage, with other children in the class, until finally a hopeless position is reached ; the child, either consciously or unconsciously, resists all efforts to teach him and the harder the teacher tries the less progress the difficult pupil makes. The system of class-teaching as opposed to individual-teaching, it must be remembered, is a legacy of the days of monster classes. Teachers have therefore two kinds of responsibility in regard to the problem of difficult children ; they should modify their methods to keep pace with the improved conditions in the size of class, and they should also press for still smaller classes to enable them to adopt individual methods still more whole-heartedly.

But when everything possible has been done in school, some difficulties will still remain. We shall still have to contend with many evil effects of bad social conditions and unwise parental treatment, and with defects that are the result of heredity. This is clearly exemplified by recent investigations into the problems of backwardness.

BACKWARD CHILDREN

" Backward " is an epithet frequently applied by teachers to individual pupils. It is noteworthy, however, that it is seldom used in reference to practical subjects; children below average in these subjects are called " clumsy," or " tone-deaf," or " inartistic," but not " backward." There seems to be a tendency to accept complacently the fact that some children are inferior in craftwork, music or drawing ; these types of inferiority, so long as a pupil is good at book-learning, are not considered serious and the pupil is not thought of as being " backward." But if he is below average in bookish subjects he is dubbed " backward," and no talents of other kinds that he may possess are enough to lift him out of that category. This attitude is largely a reflection of our one-sided view of education, and when considering backwardness it is important to bear this fact in mind.

There is, however, some justification for reckoning backwardness in terms of book-learning. Reading, writing and the art of computing are, in descending order of importance, necessary accomplishments for every one in modern life. A craftsman who lives for his work should be able at least to read his trade journal, to write a simple letter and to compute costs. And, in addition to being a craftsman, he will have other functions carrying with them responsibilities that necessitate some further amount of book-learning; he will, for example, probably be the father of a family and he will certainly be a citizen. The same argument applies with equal force to housewives. And if we consider men and women who must earn their living by repetitive work in factories, some interest in book-learning is necessary if they are to lead satisfying lives in their leisure time and satisfactory lives as citizens in a democratic community. School learning must therefore always be to a large extent book-learning, and, by the time a pupil is 10 years old,[1] it is not unreasonable to measure backwardness in terms of his attainments in the so-called " three R's."

A further justification for paying serious attention to achievements in book-learning lies in the fact that as a general rule they furnish some indication of the degree of general intelligence that a pupil possesses. As we learned in chapter IV (pp. 66–67), intelligence pervades in varying degrees all types of human activity; most children who are inferior in intelligence will not only be inferior in book-learning but also in practical subjects. There are, nevertheless, many complicating factors in individual cases, and though attainment in reading, composition and arithmetic may form a convenient criterion of backwardness when

---

[1] This qualification is very important. Reading ability is not a safe criterion of backwardness at age 7, for at this age children may be educationally advanced and yet be unable to read. Conversely they may, as a result of intensive mechanical drill, be able to read well and yet be educationally backward.

considering children in the mass, it cannot be too strongly emphasized that each backward child is a special problem; and he should be studied as such, regard being paid not only to his attainments in the "three R's," but also to his general intelligence and to his special abilities and interests.

But even if we agree to use the term "backward" in reference to a small number of fundamental subjects, it still has a vague, arbitrary meaning. How far must a pupil's attainments fall below average before we call him backward? It is clearly a matter of administrative convenience. When schools were organized in "standards" a pupil aged 10 would normally be in standard IV; if he were fit only for standard III the situation was not serious, for he could, without serious detriment, work with pupils about one year younger; if, however, he were fit only for standard II, a difficult situation was created, for the pupil really needed some special provision. He was definitely backward, but not so backward as to be certified as mentally defective. Thus Burt defines as "backward" all those pupils who, without being mentally defective, would, in the middle of their school career, be unable to do the work even of the class below that which is normal for their age. Translated into terms of educational ratios, backward children are those whose average educational ratios are between 70 and 85.

Two systematic surveys of backwardness have been made in this country—in London[1] and in Birmingham.[2] Additional information is given in reports by school medical officers, but, as it is not based on the results of standardized tests, it is of little value for comparative purposes. A third source of information is the survey of an entire age group

[1] See L.C.C. Report on *Distribution of Educational Abilities* (1917).

A summary account of the London investigation and its findings is given by Burt in his book, *The Subnormal Mind*, pp. 113–153 (Ox. Univ. Press, 1935).

For a detailed account see *The Backward Child*, C. Burt (Univ. Lond. Press, 1937).

[2] See Report of an *Investigation of Backward Children in Birmingham* (1920).

undertaken in Scotland in 1932.[1] In London and Birmingham it was found that about 10 per cent of the school population was backward. After reviewing all the available evidence, Burt concludes that " in most large areas the proportion of backward children will vary between 10 and 20 per cent. of the school population." The incidence of backwardness varies in different districts ; it is higher in most rural areas than in most towns, and it is higher in slum areas than in well-to-do areas.

When a child is backward, the condition is, as a rule, the result of a number of causes. The commonest and most potent cause is lack of native general intelligence. In his own researches, Burt found that three out of every five backward children were dull (I.Q. 70 to 85) ; these pupils " were suffering from a marked inferiority, apparently congenital and presumably permanent, in sheer intellectual ability." We should expect these dull children to be educationally backward, and attempts to force them up to normal standards of attainments in reading and elementary arithmetic are to be deprecated. As Burt says, " Certainly by means of regular, intensive drill, it is possible to speed up the mechanical achievements of the dullest dunce ; but the advance is made at the cost of any real intellectual interests the child might have, and often to the detriment of his physical and nervous health."[2] When dealing with backward children, the first essential is to get a measure of their intelligence by means of standardized intelligence tests, for this will help to indicate what our aim ought to be in individual cases. An intelligence test will help us to divide a group of backward children into two categories :

(a) Those whose backwardness is to a large extent natural and inevitable ; they are usually called *dull* children.

(b) Those whose backwardness is due to some defect in their upbringing or education ; such backwardness is in theory remediable, at least partially. Children

---

[1] See *The Intelligence of Scottish Children* (Univ. Lond. Press, 1933).
[2] *The Subnormal Mind*, C. Burt, p. 126 (Ox. Univ. Press, 1935).

in this category are not dull ; they are *under-developed*.[1]

Backwardness should be looked upon as a symptom, and in each case an attempt should be made to diagnose its causes so that suitable forms of treatment may be devised. A dull child who is naturally backward is not mentally under-developed, any more than a healthy man, 5 feet in height, is physically under-developed, and in neither instance is there any cause for reproach or remedial treatment. A child who is backward because of adverse extraneous conditions is, however, suffering from under-development. This distinction between *natural backwardness* and *conditioned backwardness* is an important one for teachers. The following questions, based on the results of Burt's investigations, will prove useful for diagnostic purposes :

(i) What is the child's I.Q. ?

(ii) Is the backwardness all-round or specific ?

Compare, for example, by means of standardized tests, ability in reading and arithmetic ; ability in oral and written arithmetic.

(iii) (*For backward readers*) Is the child predominantly eye-minded or ear-minded ?

The nature of spelling errors and reading difficulties gives some guidance in this matter. For example, an eye-minded child relies mostly on visual memory and he may be satisfied with a word that looks approximately correct ; the fact that the word he writes has a very different sound from the word he intends to write does not worry him at all. Thus, he writes " bead " or " beard " for " bread." When reading, he is more likely to know long words that

---

[1] It should be noted in passing that children are often under-developed without being backward. In school many exceptionally bright children do not work up to the limit of their capacity ; their under-development does not create any special difficulty and consequently it often escapes notice. Intelligent children who are educationally under-developed do, however, often prove difficult to manage ; they find insufficient scope for their energies in school work, they are vaguely dissatisfied with their achievements, and the result is that they indulge in petty delinquencies. A special programme of individual work, providing scope for effort and for the exercise of initiative and responsibility, is generally the best form of treatment for this type of difficult child.

K

for him have a distinctive pattern than short words that have no very special shape. In a similar way, an ear-minded child relies mostly on auditory memory. He can read long words if they are composed of syllables that he can " build up " from sounds. His spelling may look very wrong but phonetically it is often quite a good attempt; thus, he writes "plesent" for "pleasant," "pickshure" for "picture."

(iv) Has the child difficulty in remembering (a) immediately, (b) after an interval?

(v) Are home conditions bad?

E.g., insufficient food, improper food, inadequate sleep, fatigue from excessive home duties, friction between parents, over-indulgence, undue severity.

(vi) Are physical conditions unsatisfactory?

E.g., signs of under-nourishment, eye defects, deafness.

Backwardness is often caused by deafness that has not been detected. Burt calls attention to the further point that some children are deaf to high notes, with the result that their hearing is blurred. He suggests that the speech they hear may be no clearer than that emitted by an ill-adjusted loud-speaker which intensifies the bass and cuts out the treble.

(vii) Are there signs of abnormal emotional tension?

E.g., stammering, left-handedness, twitching, excessive fears, lack of concentration, laziness, inability to play, proneness to tears.

(viii) Are there any unsatisfactory school conditions? Have such conditions operated in the past?

E.g., frequent casual absences, long absences at such critical times as the ages of 6 or 7, when the first formal lessons in reading and number would normally have been received, frequent changes of teacher, unwise promotions (too rapid or too slow), unsuitable work (too difficult or too abstract), repressive treatment.

The urgency of the problem of backwardness was revealed when senior schools were instituted. In London, for example, where 30 per cent. of the children went at age 11 to central and secondary schools, from 15 to 30 per cent.

of senior school pupils were backward according to Burt's definition. At age 11 the dullest of these pupils must be expected to do work in the three R's that the majority of pupils can do at the age of 7.7 ; at age 15, they will only have reached the level of most children aged 10.5. That is to say, at the beginning of the secondary-school course we should expect to find some pupils who in reading, composition and arithmetic have barely reached the standard that the average pupils reach at the end of the infant-school course. At the end of the course, we should expect to find some pupils who have only reached the old standard IV level. It is not always realized that we must always have differences in standard of attainment among school children. By improving social conditions and educational methods, it may be possible to advance the attainments of those children who are now termed " backward." Such improvements, however, will enable the other children to move forward, so that some will still be backward compared with their fellows. From a practical point of view there is much to be said for reckoning backwardness, not from the average, but from a suitable minimum standard. Backwardness would then be a state of affairs that could be remedied, and we could concentrate our attention on " forwardness," with special attention to the problem of under-development.

Space does not permit an extended discussion of the problem of educating backward children, but the above questions will suggest most of the important principles. These principles, it must be emphasized, are not different from those that have been enunciated in other chapters dealing with the education of normal children. The point is that, since backward children have experienced difficulty in learning, the recognition and observance of sound psychological principles of eduation are matters of urgent necessity for those who teach them.

Much of the difficulty experienced in teaching backward children comes from the fact that, instead of finding what interests them, we continue to bore them by extra doses of the kind of work which has already proved futile. Instead

of finding what they can learn, we start by making wrong
assumptions about what they ought to learn ; having ourselves been more or less successful in book-learning, we
are tempted to assume that this is the one road to culture
that all must follow. We become over-anxious about
their lack of progress towards this impossible goal, and we
suggest to them, perhaps unwittingly, that they cannot
learn. In this way we may inflict on pupils, already suffering from serious handicaps, still another handicap—a form
of stupidity that comes from emotional stress. It should
now be clear that a programme consisting exclusively of
dull mechanical work is fundamentally wrong. The first
essential in any satisfactory solution of the problem of
teaching backward children is to find interesting work in
which it is possible for the pupils to reach a high standard
This may mean the complete abandonment for a time of
ordinary routine work in the " three R's," and probably the
project method (see pp. 261–265) offers the most promising
alternative.

It is a truism to say vaguely that the instruction of backward children must be practical ; it is a problem to discover
precisely what this really means.[1] In general terms, it means
that the pupils must get a *working* knowledge of the great
human traditions that are their heritage, in contradistinction
to a *wordy* knowledge. By performing a series of graded
experiments and by " playing " with a model, even a dull
boy can understand how a common pump works. With
the model in his hand, he can then with the aid of appropriate actions tell others how it works ; deprive him of the
model and his explanation will be unintelligible. He has
a working but not a wordy knowledge. By taking part
in dramatic work, a dull girl will get a working knowledge
of widely different characters, though she will never acquire
the wordy knowledge of the psychologist or the literary
critic. By studying pictures and films, by making school
journeys, by making regional surveys, and by carrying out

[1] cf. E. Thring, " A dull boy's mind is a wise man's problem." *Theory
and Practice of Teaching* (Camb. Univ. Press).

other projects of various kinds, dull children will get a working knowledge of geography and history. Dull children are relatively less handicapped in practical activities than in theoretical activities; in ability to do woodwork, for example, they are not so inferior to bright children as they are in ability to do algebra. The same is probably true of such æsthetic activities as music and dancing. Dull children find it easier to acquire skill than to acquire ideas, to work with concrete materials and movements than to work with abstract signs and symbols.

We must beware, however, of underestimating the importance of reading for backward children. It is an art which practically all children can be taught by the age of 11, and so much depends upon reading in modern life and in school that most teachers now agree that special efforts should be made to help children to overcome reading difficulties. The first step is to arouse in backward children an interest in reading and then to give them confidence. Frequent short periods of practice will be necessary, but it should not be taken from infant primers; a motive for reading should be sought in a programme of activities such as we have described, and until more simple books are made available some of the reading material will have to be specially prepared by teachers of backward children; it should relate to the activities in which the pupils are already interested.

The need for individual diagnosis and treatment, and the need for a special programme of work indicate that backward children should be taught in small classes, and it is now generally agreed that special classes should be formed. There are obvious objections to this plan of segregation, but they are probably outweighed by the advantages.[1] A backward child, like other human beings, needs

---

[1] An investigation into this question of classifying children according to ability has recently been made in America. It was found that a reaction against the practice had set in. In terms of scholastic improvement, however, the evidence was slightly in favour of ability grouping. No experimental evidence was available to support the contention that such grouping produces

[Continuation of footnote on page 284

the stimulus of success. If he is in an ordinary class, so far from being stimulated, he is likely to be depressed by an exaggerated sense of inferiority. Every care should be taken to refrain from referring to special classes or backward children in a derogatory or contemptuous way, and no opportunities should be lost of mixing backward children with other children of their own age for the pursuit of activities in which their backwardness is not an obvious handicap. They should, for example, co-operate on terms of equality with other classes in games and social functions.

Backward children should, in fact, be treated as far as possible as if they were normal members of the school community. The dullest children are not a separate species nor are they suffering from an obnoxious disease. It is true they need individual attention, variety of approach and great patience ; they need a great deal of repetition, and their syllabuses should therefore be arranged on a concentric plan and not necessarily on strictly logical lines ; they are more likely to be successful in practical activities than in abstract reasoning ; they need practical instruction rather than verbal teaching, physical activity rather than immobility ; they need work that is simple, but it must be presented so that it makes an appeal to their natural interests. Dull children make little response to urgent and repeated exhortations to do better ; they are more likely to appreciate beauty than to follow abstract thought ; they may never be good " scholars," but they find great satisfaction in rendering social service and they respond eagerly to any human person who can create a confident, cheerful atmosphere free from petty restrictions ; they will not be intellectual leaders, but there is a great deal of necessary routine work in the world that they can perform cheerfully and well, and there are

Continued from page 283]
undesirable attitudes. In the absence of experimental evidence, the present divergence of views on this question is probably a reflection of individual differences in temperament and personal philosophy. See *Ability Grouping*, H. S. Wyndham (Melbourne Univ. Press).

For a statement of the case against " ability grouping," see *Full Stature*, H. G. Stead, p. 98 (Nisbet, 1936).

many excellent ways in which they can spend their leisure time. In short, there is no reason why so-called backward children should not receive an education full of experiences that will enable them to become useful citizens and happy individuals.

And all this applies in varying degrees and with very little modification to 90 per cent. of our population. It is not a mere chance that advances in education methods have often begun in schools containing pupils who are difficult to teach. The difficulties that young and defective children experience have forced teachers to reflect both on the content of education and on methods of teaching. Methods of educating defectives have proved useful for educating infants, and infant-school methods are beginning to influence the education of older children. Similarly, when we have discovered how to educate backward children we shall have learnt a great deal that should help us to reform the education we are now giving to both normal and bright children.

CLUMSY CHILDREN

Under this heading we propose to include a wide variety of difficult children : those who are clumsy in physical training lessons and inept at games ; those who find it impossible to walk across a room in an easy, controlled manner; those whose handwriting is bad, and whose books are always marred by blots and smudges ; those who are prone to accidents and breakages in craft and science rooms ; those who find it difficult to speak out clearly, and finally those who stammer and those who are left-handed.

Our knowledge of the causes of clumsiness is not yet extensive or precise, but as with backwardness, there are probably two kinds, natural and conditioned. Just as athleticism seems to run in some families, so may clumsiness. But it is probable that the commonest cause is emotional disorder, and that the ultimate sources of the disorder lie in the forgotten experiences of early childhood.

Clumsiness in early childhood and adolescence.—All who have to deal with very young children should remember that for them clumsiness is a natural phase out of which they will grow if they have the right kind of experience and help. As with other forms of childish difficulty, any attempt to hurry the process of learning merely aggravates the trouble. Many modern developments in educational practice recognize this fact. Early physical training lessons, for example, are informal; the handwork and handwriting of young children employ groups of large muscles; thick pencils with soft lead are used in preference to thin pens and ink; much speech drill is done by children in chorus and not by timid individuals in isolation.

Another form of clumsiness that will disappear naturally is the clumsiness often exhibited by adolescents. It is due to a temporary loss of bodily control, and the chief cause is probably the rapid bodily growth at this period, though mental causes may also be operative. This type of clumsiness should, as far as possible, be ignored by teachers.

Emotional clumsiness.—We have suggested that extreme cases, in which the clumsiness is both permanent and widespread, are usually suffering from some emotional disorder. They are the so-called " nervous " children. They are not merely clumsy in one or two special ways, but they manifest clumsiness on practically all occasions, and as it were, with their whole bodies. In addition, they often manifest other symptoms of emotional disorder, such as thumb-sucking, nail-biting, enuresis, extreme shyness, inability to speak out, stammering, lack of concentration, perpetual tiredness. Such cases are very difficult to treat successfully in school. The psychological principles of teaching apply with particular force: methods that rely on an appeal to fear are obviously bad; the children need encouragement and the stimulus of success; they need a friendly atmosphere as free as possible from criticism and correction; above all, they need to be treated with great patience. We must always remember that, though their clumsiness may be extremely irritating to us, it may also be extremely painful to them, and moreover it is something that they cannot overcome by sheer will-power. It is a symptom of some forgotten trouble—fear of parents, jealousy of a younger brother or sister, or even disgust connected with experiences in early childhood. Under the influence of a happy school many of these troubles do in time clear up ; if they do not, they are outside the teacher's province and they must receive expert psychological treatment. This applies, for example, to all bad cases of stammering.

Left-handedness.—This is a type of clumsiness that often causes teachers some anxiety. We live in a world arranged for right-handed people ; we write from left to right ; many machines (e.g. sewing machines) can be worked more conveniently by right-handed than by left-handed people. There is no doubt that in some commercial and industrial occupations left-handedness is a handicap. The question then arises whether children who show a tendency to use their left hands ought not to be taught to use their right hands. If left-handedness were merely a habit acquired by continual practice in early childhood (as it may be in some cases), there could be only one answer, and we could refer readers to chapter V on habit-forming for advice as to procedure. The problem is, however, far more compli-cated. Some left-handedness is probably hereditary ; it runs in families and appears to be natural. In such cases a great deal of effort may be wasted in trying to make the change. There is also a second type of left-handedness that is very resistant to change ; it is a symptom of emotional disorder and might therefore be classified as a form of emotional clumsiness. Owing to unwise repressive treat-ment the child has become a rebel, and in using his left hand he is asserting his independence, though he himself is unaware of this fact. If efforts are made to change his customary mode of behaviour, he resists them ; if pressure is brought to bear, the emotional trouble may be aggravated. It has been observed, for example, that a left-handed child may under pressure develop a squint or a stammer ; that is, he finds new ways of asserting his rebellious spirit. Many psychologists believe that a great deal of left-

K *

handedness is the result of unconscious motives of the kind described.

It is difficult to discover in any particular case what is the origin of left-handedness, and for this reason teachers and parents should exercise caution when they are trying to induce right-handedness. But since left-handedness may be a serious handicap, it is generally agreed that we ought in school to try, especially with young children, to encourage them to use their right hands. If this is done tactfully and without pressure, habitual left-handedness and the less serious cases of emotional left-handedness may be overcome without harm being done. It is a matter of common knowledge that many children have been successfully treated in this way. On the other hand, if any signs of increased emotional disturbance are noticed, teachers would be well advised to discontinue their treatment, for in such cases left-handedness may be the lesser of two evils.

Incidental clumsiness.—It must not be lightly assumed that all clumsiness in school is emotional clumsiness of the types described above. Before we diagnose it as such, we must be careful to consider whether it may not be due, at least partially, to more superficial causes that can be more easily dealt with. The following questions may prove helpful to teachers when they are considering whether clumsiness among their pupils is the result of deep-rooted personal troubles or whether it is of a more incidental nature :

1. Is the clumsiness manifested by a large number of pupils in the class ?

If so, there must be some special causes close at hand.

2. Are the pupils suffering from boredom or bodily fatigue ?

Long lessons for practical subjects are generally desirable, but if tedious or heavy work is being done, arrangements should be made for short breaks or changes of occupation.

3. Are the pupils specially excited ?

An impending match, sports meeting or school election may cause a temporary wave of clumsiness. Some teachers can calm an excited class ; others may be well advised not to expect first-class work at these special times.

4. Is the work suitable for children of their age ?

There is always a temptation in practical work, as in academic work, to press on prematurely to work that needs powers that have still to develop as a result of natural growth.

5. Is anything wrong with the tools ?

Are they too heavy, too large, too small, too blunt ?

6. Is anything wrong with other equipment ?

Are chairs, tables, sinks, taps, too high or too low ?

7. Have the pupils been taught the best way to hold and use their tools ? Are they handicapped by bad habits that they have been allowed to develop ?

8. Is anything wrong with the conditions of work ?

For example, is the room adequately lighted ? Are the pupils too crowded ?

9. Is anything wrong with the relations between teacher and class ?

Although the pupils are not aware of it, they may be making blots or breaking apparatus as a protest against unjust or harsh treatment. Some may be clumsy because they fear the teacher.

10. (*In relation to individual pupils.*) Are there any physical conditions likely to cause clumsiness ?

For example, are the child's muscles under-developed ? Does he suffer from rheumatism ? Has he had chorea ?

TROUBLESOME CHILDREN

It is a commonplace to say that a child may be troublesome with some teachers but well-behaved with others ; he may be uncontrollable at home but quite amenable at school. Such variableness is more noticeable among the delinquent type of difficult child than among the other types we have discussed. Dull children do not suddenly appear bright with certain teachers, for their dullness is an inevitable reflection of their inherent mental capacity. Even if a child's backwardness is remediable, it does not suddenly disappear with the advent of favourable circumstances. Similarly, most clumsy children tend to appear clumsy in all circumstances, for their clumsiness is, as a rule, the result of mental states that are outside their conscious control. Delinquency, on the other hand, is not an inevitable manifestation of the delinquent's personality ; it is rather the resultant of the interaction of the personality and a particular circumstance. It follows therefore that delinquency is more susceptible to the influence of the school environment than either backwardness or clumsiness. The first step towards the prevention of delinquency in school is a realization of the type of circumstance that is likely to provoke it.

Broadly speaking, it may be said that all acts of delinquency in school are examples of instinctive behaviour. That is to say, they are forms of behaviour that have survived because of their biological value. In prehistoric times they might have been valuable and even worthy, but in our modern civilized life they are rightly denounced as indecent or immoral. The first essential in the prevention of delinquency is therefore the provision of adequate outlets of a socially desirable kind for instinctive behaviour. Wood-carving may take the place of desk-cutting ; debates, discussions and mutual help may take the place of furtive " talking " ; and so on. The more natural activity there is in a school programme, the less likelihood there is of children being difficult to manage. On the other hand, a school that suppresses natural activity is bound to create troublesome children.

Such children are found, however, in the best schools and in the classes even of the most gifted teachers. This is not because some children are naughty by nature ; there is, in fact, little or no evidence that any child inherits a definite tendency to delinquency as such. Some do appear to be specially prone to crime ; they are abnormally aggressive, or precociously interested in sexual matters. So far as this is due to inheritance, it is probably the result of certain instinctive tendencies being abnormally strong, but under favourable circumstances this inheritance might possibly have been turned to good account. A naturally aggressive person need not necessarily develop into a bully or a tyrant; he might become an ardent social reformer. Our discussion leads us once again to the importance of environment in early childhood. Many of the causes of conditioned backwardness and emotional clumsiness are also the causes of delinquency. Emotional disorder may manifest itself in different ways. In some it may result in laziness and lack of concentration and so produce backwardness; in others it may manifest itself in lack of bodily control and so produce clumsiness; in others it may show itself in acts of an anti-social character and so produce delinquency.

Treatment of delinquents.—The general principles that should guide us in dealing with troublesome children are the same as those we have described when discussing the other types of difficult children. They are: (i) Find the causes, (ii) Remove the causes as far as possible, (iii) Apply positive educational treatment. The following questions and notes are given as suggestions to teachers who have to deal with a troublesome child:

1. Has the child been punished frequently in the past?
It is often found that the same few names recur year after year in a school punishment book. The conclusion is that punishment has proved futile and that some positive remedial treatment ought to be tried instead. Punishment is not always futile (see pp. 185–188). As regards delinquents, the matter is well summed up by Burt: " Punishment, as a rule, proves far more effective with mild impulses than with strong: as a mode of deterrence, it is like a blast of the wind, which will extinguish the flickering taper, but may only fan the burning coal to hotter flame."[1]

2. What is the child's mental age?
There is no doubt that lack of general intelligence is often a contributory cause to delinquency. Burt found in his investigations that most delinquents were below average in intelligence; about 8 per cent. were mentally defective,

[1] *The Young Delinquent*, C. Burt, p. 535 (Univ. Lond. Press, 1925).

28 per cent. were dull. Mentally deficient and dull children may lack the intelligence to foresee the consequences of their actions ; they tend to act on the spur of the moment, to give way to instinctive impulses without reflection. This is very likely to be a cause of delinquency with young children. Another reason why children of low intelligence break rules is that they find it difficult to acquire moral ideas. Such ideas are the result of generalizing from concrete experiences, and the Binet tests show that they are not formed by most children until the age of 12 ; it is therefore a stage that some children in secondary schools will hardly reach before they leave.

At the other extreme is the very intelligent delinquent who exercises his ingenuity in perverse ways for want of adequate outlets of legitimate kinds for his superior abilities. This suggests a very important question, viz.,

3. Has the child scope in school for any strong interests he may possess ?

In this connexion it is interesting to note that not only are disciplinary difficulties less during practical lessons, but that the average attendance tends to be higher on those sessions when practical work predominates. Many beginners in teaching have welcomed the respite that a dictation lesson brings, but this is only one of many forms of individual practical work that can be provided in a modern school. With troublesome adolescents it is often a good plan to find out their dominant interests and then to arrange a personal time-table for them so that they can, at least for a time, concentrate on work in which they find absorbing interest.

Many delinquents have a strong interest in achieving power, and though it would not be politic to make them prefects, a wise teacher will find many minor positions of responsibility that can be safely and profitably entrusted to them.

4. Has the child any physical abnormality ?

A child who is abnormally small and weak, or who suffers from some other inferiority such as defective speech, is very apt to become troublesome. By emphasizing and encouraging any accomplishments in which he is not inferior, it may be possible to sow some useful seeds from which a healthy self-respect may develop. A troublesome boy who is weak and undersized, clumsy at handwork, inept at games and untidy in his written work, may possibly prove an ideal character in some classroom play or he may prove a very efficient property-man for a school concert. If the life of a school is many-sided and if no undue emphasis is placed on any one of its aspects, it should be possible to help even the most " hopeless " individual to find some niche where he feels he is a useful and even indispensable member of the community. Furthermore, every teacher should aim at developing such a spirit of tolerance and goodwill in his class that children who suffer from physical abnormalities may at least not suffer the additional penalty of public ridicule.

5. Is the child goaded to delinquency by causes outside school ?

It is necessary to exercise great tact in obtaining information about a child's home life. Such information is, however, essential if effective remedial treatment is to be devised. A child may be generally unhappy as a result of harsh treatment ; he may be denied the companionship of other children of his age ; he may have undesirable friends. In such cases part of the treatment consists in giving advice to parents. If the relations between parents and school are close and cordial, such advice can be given without arousing resentment. Much can be done in a general way by means of parents' meetings, for it is always less embarrassing to address a meeting on the subject of bringing up children than to tackle an individual parent about his own child. The individual approach is, however, often necessary, and it should not be avoided. It is natural for parents to adopt a defensive attitude if a teacher complains of the behaviour of their child ; if, however, a teacher adopts a sympathetic human approach, and suggests to parents that they and he together must co-operate to help the child to overcome his difficulties, there is generally a reasonable chance of success. Without the co-operation of parents a school has little chance of successfully re-educating many of its most troublesome pupils.

6. Is it possible to give the child a change of surroundings ?

In extreme cases it is necessary to remove a delinquent to a special school or home. The same principle can be applied to the milder cases that remain in ordinary schools. A temporary change, such as is provided by a period in an open-air or camp school, by a school journey or a country holiday, may help to give a delinquent a new start. Inside the school it may be possible to try a change of class.

It is not possible to give any detailed directions of universal validity in the treatment of delinquents, for each troublesome child is a unique problem. Two children may, for example, be addicted to lying, but it does not follow that they will respond to identical forms of treatment. As Burt says : " Lying takes countless shapes and has a thousand different motives. It may be employed to compensate for almost any form of intellectual weakness. It may be inspired by almost any emotion—by fear more than any other, but also by greed, anger, self-display, submissiveness, and even by mistaken loyalty and affection."[1] It may be helpful, however, to consider in more detail the treatment of one class of delinquents, and we will take " stealers " as our example.

Stealers.—Stealing is a symptom of excessive acquisitiveness. Its causes, both the immediate superficial causes and those that are deeper and more ultimate, generally lie outside the school, so that the co-operation of parents must be enlisted. The deeper causes are probably connected with emotional disorder of some kind, so that, accompanying all the detailed measures aimed directly at the superficial causes, there should be a coherent policy designed to improve the child's social and emotional reactions. Excessive repression should be removed and plenty of opportunities

[1] *The Young Delinquent*, C. Burt, p. 381.

for joyous creative work should be provided. Among the direct measures, two are obviously necessary. First, the chances of undetected stealing should be removed as far as possible : cloakrooms should be locked ; stock should be unobtrusively checked ; money should not be left about. Second, the child's reasonable needs in regard to pocket money should be satisfied as far as possible, and he should be left free from petty interference when spending it. Next, a programme of graded moral training, designed to build up the child's self-respect, may begin. The child should be entrusted with money to buy things of known cost ; later he should be allowed to go on more elaborate shopping excursions entailing the keeping of simple accounts ; in school he could be trusted to count small sums of " milk " money, and perhaps finally he might be promoted to some such proud position as " milk accountant " or " stock monitor."

It is important, however, in all our dealings with delinquents to guard against sentimentality. There is no doubt that in the past we erred on the side of harshness, but there is a real danger that to-day we may err on the side of leniency and apparently condone delinquent behaviour, just because we understand more about its causes. We must beware lest we become more interested in the psychology of delinquents than in their reformation. Any suggestion to them that they are to be pitied, as victims of circumstances unable to help themselves, will hinder the development of character in which their hope of reform lies.

CONCLUSION

Our discussion of difficult children has shown from yet another angle how closely interrelated are the various forms of child-development—physical, intellectual, emotional and social—and in particular, what an important part emotional factors play. The children we have been discussing are difficult to teach, but a more helpful attitude to the problem is implied in the statement that they are children who find it difficult to learn. A modern psychologist does not emphasize that these are children who present difficulties to teachers ; he rather takes the view that they are children who are suffering from individual personal difficulties themselves. Herein lies the answer to those who object that psychologists are to-day magnifying the problem of " difficult " children, and that in the good old days large numbers of difficult children did not exist. It may be granted that many school children who to-day are called " difficult " would not have been recognized as such forty years ago. They did not present great difficulties to teachers ; the backward children were left in the lower classes doing simple work or no work at all ; the clumsy children were perhaps bad writers, but they did not present the difficulties they do in a modern school with its physical training, dancing, practical science and craftwork ; and there was always the fear of corporal punishment to keep the trouble-some children from too much mischief. There can be no doubt, however, that these children experienced many personal difficulties both during and after their schooldays, and that many of them were extremely " difficult " members of society when schooldays were over. By reducing the size of classes and by developing individual methods we are doing much to educate individual children, but in the process we have discovered a problem—the problem of individual personal difficulties. The solution of the problem depends on expert psychological diagnosis and treatment, and it seems clear that in addition to a school medical service we need a school psychological service.

The criminals of to-day were school children a few years ago, and many of them doubtless belonged to one or more of the types of difficult children described in this chapter. Is it too much to hope that, when we have learnt to under-stand the real nature of the personal difficulties of each potential criminal, we shall be able during their schooldays to start many of them on a life so satisfying that no sub-sequent difficulties will be strong enough to divert them to a life of crime ?

REFERENCES FOR READING

Handbook of Suggestions, New edition, 1937. (See *Index :* Backward Children.)
Modern Psychology and Education, Sturt and Oakden, chapters XVIII, XX.
Your Mind and Mine, R. B. Cattell, chapter XIII.
Psychology and Practical Life, Collins and Drever, chapter XI.

ADDITIONAL REFERENCES

The Nervous Child, H. C. Cameron (Ox. Univ. Press, 1924).
The Subnormal Mind, C. Burt (Ox. Univ. Press, 1935).
The Young Delinquent, C. Burt (Univ. Lond. Press, 1925).
The Backward Child, C. Burt (Univ. Lond. Press, 1937).
The Education of the Backward Child, D. Kennedy-Fraser (Univ. Lond. Press, 1923).
The Psychology of the Criminal, M. Hamblin Smith (Methuen, 1922).
The Education of Backward Children, Foreword by Sir Percy T. Nunn (Evans, 1936).
Difficulties in Child Development, M. Chadwick (Allen & Unwin, 1928).

ESSAYS AND DISCUSSIONS

1. The prevention of " difficult " children.
(Consider : parental treatment in early childhood ; activities in modern infant schools ; methods in junior and secondary schools.)

2. School organization problems in relation to the teaching of backward children.
(Consider : advantages and disadvantages of the following plans : special classes ; cross-classification for arithmetic and English ; special coaching of small groups drawn for short periods from ordinary classes ; individual and group teaching within an ordinary class containing children of widely varying intelligence and attainments.)

3. The ideal curriculum for backward children.

4. Methods of teaching children to read.

5. The influence of the cinema on juvenile delinquency.

6. The treatment of different classes of delinquents, for example, " liars of various types, bullies, cheats, thieves, children who upset order in petty ways, tale-bearers.

7. " Talking " in the classroom.

8. The modern treatment of criminals and potential criminals.
(Consider : Children and Young Persons Act, 1933 ; Borstal Institutions and Juvenile Colonies. See *The Young Delinquent,* C. Burt, pp. 233–239.)

9. The treatment of different classes of clumsy children, for example, bad writers, untidy workers, awkward pupils.

10. The place of punishment in the treatment of difficult children.

11. Child Guidance Clinics.

(The following quotation is from a pamphlet entitled *The Establishment of a Child Guidance Clinic*, issued by the Child Guidance Council, Woburn House, Upper Woburn Place, London, W.C.1 :

" A clinic is an attempt to bring together the various resources of the community on behalf of children who are in distress because of unsatisfied inner needs or who are at war with their surroundings. Such children often show peculiar character traits, undesirable behaviour and a general inability to fulfil the demands made upon them either at home or at school."

The work of a clinic is done by a team of three persons—a psychiatrist, an educational psychologist, and a social worker.)

12. How does a good modern school satisfy the fundamental " wishes " of children ?

(Consider the following " wishes " suggested by W. I. Thomas in his book, *The Unadjusted Girl* (Boston, Little, Brown, 1923) : recognition ; response or affection ; security ; new experience or adventure.)

13. How does a good modern school meet the psychological needs of children ?

(Consider the following " needs " suggested by H. E. Field in his essay, " Psychological Aspects of Juvenile Delinquency " in *The Education of Backward Children* (Evans, 1936) : learning how to work ; social adjustment ; development of sense of responsibility ; achievement of a constructive attitude towards personal handicaps ; understanding of and respect for moral values and ideals.)

CHAPTER XVII

STAGES OF DEVELOPMENT

THE difference between a grown-up person and an infant is so striking that it is not surprising that many attempts have been made to describe the process of growing up. A favourite plan is to try to describe successive stages by naming them after qualities that are supposed to be characteristic of each stage. It has been suggested, for example, that childhood can be divided into seven overlapping stages called respectively the Dependent Age, the Dramatic Age, the Angular Age, the Paradoxical Age, the Age of the Gang, the Age of Romance, the Age of Problems.[1] Another plan is to distinguish stages according to the type of learning that is supposed to be predominant at each stage. Thus it is often suggested that children pass successively through stages of sense-perception, muscular activity, memory and reasoning. There is no doubt some element of truth in many of these classifications, but they are too facile. Modern psychologists emphasize the unity of all mental processes, and recent researches in child psychology tend to show that children do not develop in layers, one " faculty " emerging after another. All types of mental process are in operation from infancy onwards ; with very few exceptions, all kinds of mental quality are displayed at every age. The chief danger of the kind of classification given above is that it tends to be interpreted rigidly and to blind us to the real facts of children's development. A great deal of harm has been done by popularizing the notion that the period of 7 to 11 is the age of memory, and the age of 11 onwards is the age of reason. It is true that junior children generally like memorizing and that senior children begin for the first time to take an interest in reasoning for its own sake. But it is

[1] *The Seven Ages of Childhood*, E. L. Cabot (Routledge, 1921).

quite wrong to suggest that children's power of memorizing is at its maximum in the junior school or that young children cannot reason. The more we learn about the mental development of children, the more certain it appears that they develop not by the successive emergence of " faculties " but by the more or less steady all-round growth of inter-correlated abilities. The various methods of describing stages of development by giving picturesque labels to certain ages seem to be more plausible than valid ; like the " culture-epoch " and the " recapitulation " theories of development,[1] they need to be accepted and applied with great caution.

We therefore fall back on the less spectacular method used by Shakespeare and generally adopted by modern psychologists :

> " At first the infant,
> Mewling and puking in the nurse's arms,
> And then the whining schoolboy, with his satchel,
> And shining morning face, creeping like snail
> Unwillingly to school. And then the lover,
> Sighing like furnace, with a woeful ballad
> Made to his mistress' eyebrow."

This picture may be untrue to-day in some details, but it suggests that it is convenient to consider development in three stages, infancy, childhood, and adolescence. These stages are usually subdivided as follows :[2]

Stage.	Age-limits.
I. *Infancy.*	
1. Babyhood	0–4
2. Infant-school stage	4–7
II. *Childhood.*	
3. Junior-school stage	7–11
4. Lower secondary-school or pre-pubertal stage	11–14
III. *Adolescence.*	
5. Early adolescent stage	14–18
6. Late adolescent stage	18–21

It will be noticed that the age divisions coincide with those associated with our school system. It should not be concluded, however, that our system is based on a scientific

[1] See p. 20.   [2] See *The Primary School*, p. 255 (H.M.S.O., 1931).

knowledge of child development; it is probably truer to say that the age-limits for schools have been chiefly determined by administrative convenience. Children can recognize and write simple word- and number-symbols by the age of 7, and they have made a start in the "three R's"; they are therefore ready to leave the infant school. By the age of 11 most of them have mastered the essential tools of learning, and the differences in their mental abilities have caused an inconveniently wide diversity in their attainments; they must therefore be drafted to various types of secondary education. The transfer at this age is also necessary administratively because many of these pupils will, under present conditions, leave school at 15. In this connexion it is significant that, in the older public-school system that developed for children leaving school at 17 or 18, the transfer from preparatory to public school is not made until the age of 13 or 14.

The present age-limits are conventional rather than scientific, and it is unlikely that they will always remain as at present. The stages seem to be governed ultimately by the ages at which children enter and leave school rather than by any natural phases of child development. Consequently many educationists would prefer to see a scheme similar to the following:

Stage.	Age-limits.
1. Babyhood	0–2 or 3
2. Nursery-school or infancy stage . .	2 or 3–6 or 7
3. Primary-school or childhood stage .	6 or 7–12 or 13
4. Secondary-school or adolescent stage .	12 or 13–16 or 17

For some practical purposes it may be useful to try to distinguish in general terms the differences between infants and juniors, and between juniors and seniors. But, in order to avoid false generalizations, we must bear in mind that mental growth is continuous and that its rate varies from one individual to another.

The continuity of mental growth.—The mental growth of children is more or less continuous; it should be compared with fairly steady progress up an inclined plane rather than with jerky progress up a series of steps.

It is more important for teachers to get some picture of this gradual progress from year to year, or even from term to term, than to memorize general statements of the differences between infants, juniors and seniors. Beginners are often sadly at a loss to know what should be expected from children at different ages, for the formation of suitable standards is largely a matter of careful observation based on experience. This is, however, a slow and uncertain method, and it should be supplemented by more scientific procedures. It is a good plan, for example, to collect typical samples of average work done by children of different ages and to keep them as a basis for reference. It is helpful to keep notes of the character development of individual pupils, and to read them over from time to time—for this is a matter in which progress is so very gradual that without such records we should fail to observe it. In addition to gaining knowledge by first-hand systematic observation, we should also take advantage of the facts discovered by standardized mental tests and by careful observations made by trained psychologists. We tend to rely far too much on our vague impressions of what children of different ages ought to do, and we make far too little use of psychologists' discoveries of what they actually can do. We ought frequently to refresh our memories with the answers to such questions as the following :

(i) What type of reasoning problem is appropriate for children of different ages ? (See pp. 161–2.)

(ii) What length of sentence can children of different ages remember immediately after hearing it ? (See p. 151.)

(iii) What is the average speed of handwriting for boys and girls of different ages ?

(iv) What is the kind of composition they can write ?

(v) What quality of handwriting should we expect ?

(vi) What is the average standard in mechanical and problem arithmetic at various ages ?

(vii) What kind of definition can children give at various ages ?

Careful observation shows that even the striking changes that take place at puberty are not as sudden as they are popularly believed to be. They are rather the culmination of a process of gradual and continuous growth than the sudden emergence of new qualities. It has been observed, for example, that important mental changes take place by imperceptible degrees in what is physiologically the pre-pubertal period.

Individual differences in the rate of mental growth.—Detailed information about the development of children of various ages can only be obtained by considering the stage reached by the majority. Standards of attainment and norms of development can only be given in terms of averages or of medians, for, as we have emphasized in this book, there are large individual differences of many kinds among children of the same age. It follows therefore that if we accept the broad stages of development enumerated on page 300, the dividing lines will always be blurred by these differences between individuals. For example, puberty is the most significant change that takes place in the process of growing up, but if the " age of puberty " were taken as the age for beginning secondary-school education, girls would, on an average, go to secondary schools two years earlier than boys, and within one sex there would be considerable variations in the age of entry.

In addition to the individual differences caused by differences in innate endowment there are others that appear to be created by the social environment. This is still another factor that complicates any scheme of developmental stages. Thus a child is relatively submissive and dependent each time he is transferred to a new type of school. It is remarkable how the independent, resourceful monitor of an infant school becomes the dependent " baby " of the junior school, and how a similar process is repeated four years later. Not less remarkable was the way in which 10-year-olds rose to the occasion when all-standard schools were reorganized and the older children were transferred to separate senior schools. Another striking example is afforded by the boys and girls of 16 who have been earning wages for a year; in many ways they are more grown-up than young people several years older in secondary schools or even in universities.

It will now be clear that when we speak of infancy, childhood and adolescence, or of infants, juniors and seniors, we are comparing and contrasting children in general as most of them appear about the middle of each of the periods. We are not suggesting that at some definite age all children undergo some sudden, magical change, nor are we suggesting that all children show the special characteristics of a given stage of development at the same age.

GROWING UP

Speaking generally, children seem to grow up in two main stages. They begin as infants endowed with instinctive impulses, which they gradually learn, more or less successfully, to control. This first stage lasts until the ages of about 11 to 14, when our pupils seem to begin a very similar process all over again; they become adolescents and, as we shall see, they once more exhibit many of the characteristics of early childhood. Again they have to learn to control strong instinctive impulses, and so they arrive for the second time at a stage of stability—the stage of adulthood that lasts until senility sets in. Then they enter upon what is popularly called " second childhood," a stage that, according to modern views, would be more correctly called " third childhood."

The first developmental phase covers the period during which children are attending nursery, infant and junior schools. A steady increase of stability is noticeable, especially in junior schools; and during this period children become more and more at home in their world, both in and out of school. Thus gradually they have less and less need of fantasy as they adjust themselves to the conditions of reality. As Nunn says, " The boy of twelve is, in the main, a realist who has learnt to comport himself in his world (especially in his social world) as its nature requires."[1] By the time children reach the top of the junior school, they resemble in many ways staid, grown-up adults ; they have achieved what has been described as a " pseudo-maturity." How far this state is the result of natural and inevitable development, and how far it is the result of the cramping influence of a wrong type of junior-school education is still a matter of controversy. " The years from seven to eleven or twelve," says Burt, " might almost be termed the Dark Ages of childhood . . . no psychologist has hitherto concentrated specifically on the characteristics of the growing boy or girl from the age of 7 to the onset of puberty . . . it still remains an urgent problem for the future investigator to inquire what, if anything, distinguishes the mental life of the child at that stage."[2] But, under present conditions, it is doubtful whether junior schools contain children in a sufficiently natural state for psychologists' tests and observations to have any validity. It seems probable that many junior children are, like many adults, far less alive than they should be ; their stability is often the result of repressed rather than of disciplined impulses. We cannot know the natural characteristics of children until freer methods of education can be employed, and to make these possible junior schools must be relieved from examination pressure, they must be given smaller classes, more space and more sensible furniture. Meanwhile we know enough from observations of children at play to be sure that the junior stage is not merely " a colourless transitional stage," and that children need, in this stage, much more than a thorough drill in essentials. We must beware lest the relative stability of children compared with infants and adolescents should lead us to exploit the characteristic in undesirable ways. Children like memorizing, but this is no excuse for neglecting to provide them with opportunities

[1] *Education*, p. 173.
[2] *The Primary School*, p. 254 (H.M.S.O., 1931).

for adventurous thinking; they are willing to submit to authority, but this is no reason for staffing junior schools with dictators.

Wrong treatment in the early stages almost certainly aggravates the difficulties of the adolescent stage. Adolescence is generally described as a period of "stress and strain," and for many this is certainly true. But it is by no means certain that it need be. When we know more of the science and art of living, we shall doubtless be able to eliminate many of the troubles of adolescence just as we have eliminated much of the "mewling and puking" of infancy.

Puberty is marked by physiological changes in the sex organs, but it is a mistake to think that these affect the sexual life only; they affect the whole personality. Adolescence is not a time when one new instinctive impulse appears; it is rather a time when the sex instinct comes to its full maturity and when most, if not all, other instincts receive new accessions of energy. This is what we should expect on the "whole" view of human nature that we have tried to maintain in this book. Thus an adolescent is not merely "troubled" by sex feelings, but he is also at times excessively assertive, at other times shy and submissive; he is by turns courageous and fearful, solitary and gregarious; he often has strong impulses to wander and explore. For the time being the stability achieved in childhood has been upset and the child on the threshold of adulthood, the adolescent, must learn once more to control strong emotional impulses.

In some ways this learning is more difficult than the similar learning that takes place between infancy and childhood, and the teacher's function is correspondingly more delicate. The difficulties of adolescence are due to a number of different causes which we will now consider briefly.

The intensity of emotion in adolescence.—The emotions of an adolescent are intensified and complicated by the ripening of the sex instinct, and the difficult personal problems connected with sex must now be faced. It is a mistake, however, to think that sex problems arise in adolescence for the first time. There is a period during infancy when children are very curious about problems closely connected with sex; unless they are repressed they ask many questions about bodily excretions, the origin of babies, and about differences in physical form between the sexes. Their subsequent attitude to sex is to some extent formed by the way in which such questions are treated. If, for example, the questions are answered in the same matter-of-fact way that other questions are answered, something will have been done to lay the foundations for a healthy attitude to sex in adolescence and adulthood. Another type of preparatory training should be given by the study of Nature in school. Beginning with a study of natural phenomena, animals and plants in infant and junior schools, it should develop in the secondary school into a course of general science with a definite biological bias. Thus children learn a body of scientific knowledge that should have a steadying influence when personal sex problems become insistent, and they receive a training that should help them to approach many personal problems in a relatively impersonal way free from unhealthy emotional reactions. It should not be concluded that this preparatory training in the home and science-room will provide all that is necessary. It will help to form a good attitude to sex, but its effects remain largely in the " unconscious " mind. Before the age of puberty a child has " forgotten " the questions he asked and the answers he received in infancy, but when similar questions again become insistent his feelings about such questions are coloured by his previous experience. A child studying reproduction in flowers and insects does not necessarily connect the process with himself and his parents, but his mind is being made ready to receive personal sex instruction; when it comes, it will not come as a shock.

Another important kind of preparatory training is the social training given in home and school throughout infancy and childhood. The attitude of adolescents towards sex depends very largely on their attitude towards parents, brothers and sisters. If they have been starved of parental affection, their relations with the opposite sex will tend to be warped by cravings for compensatory affection ; if they have been subjected to excessive parental love, they may be abnormally late in adjusting themselves to persons of the opposite sex, and if they marry they are likely to choose a parent-substitute rather than a mate ; girls who have brothers, and boys who have sisters generally develop more normally than those who lack this kind of company in family life. We live in a bisexual social world and we all need some amount of co-education. This does not necessarily mean that all schools should be mixed. Mixed schools have their advocates,[1] but in this country such schools (apart from infant schools) are more often formed on grounds of expediency than of principle ; they are generally formed because the number of available pupils is too small for two single-sex departments to be organized satisfactorily, or in order to prevent children having long or dangerous journeys. There are, moreover, some good practical reasons for preferring single-sex schools, at least for adolescents, and these may be summarized as follows :

(a) *The difficulty of staffing mixed schools.*—There are many excellent teachers who are not temperamentally suited for teaching mixed classes or for organizing mixed schools. The appointment of head teachers to mixed schools presents a further difficulty, for the fact must be faced that schools which have a woman head teacher are often unattractive to men assistant teachers. We are then on the horns of a dilemma, for it is as manifestly unfair to reserve all headships for men as it is undesirable for mixed schools to be staffed predominantly by women.

(b) *The difficulty of organizing mixed schools.*—We have already seen (pp. 68–70) that the mental differences between the sexes are less than was formerly believed, and in the world at large we see that the traditional differentiation of function between the sexes is being rapidly modified. There still

[1] See, for example, *The Mixed School*, B. A. Howard (Univ. Lond. Press, 1928) ; *Advance in Co-education*, edit. A. Woods (Sidgwick & Jackson, 1919).

remain, however, fundamental differences, particularly in interests and in physique, that will always differentiate men from women and that must always be reflected in the school curriculum. It is probable, for example, that girls will always spend more time at domestic subjects than boys, and boys more time at wood- and metal-work than girls ; pure and applied mathematics will probably always have a higher educative value for boys than for girls ; most of the instruction in subjects such as physical training, games and personal hygiene must always be given to boys and girls separately ; and so on. Some differentiation of curriculum will always be necessary and this is much easier to arrange in single-sex than in mixed schools.

(*c*) *The disturbing influence of one sex upon the other.*— Although the intellectual development of boys and girls is more or less parallel, this is not true of their emotional development. The age of puberty is earlier for girls than for boys and their relationships are further complicated by the fact that their social development proceeds on rather different lines as indicated in the following table which shows the normal social attachments at various ages :[1]

Girls.	*Boys.*
0–10 Mother	0–8 Mother
10–15 Girl friends	8–12 Father
15–18 Father	12–18 Boy friends
18+ Mate	18+ Mate

During early adolescence boys and girls appear to be drawn towards members of their own sex, and it is not until later that they begin to develop what is ultimately a normal heterosexual attitude. Furthermore, both boy and girl adolescents pass through a phase of strong interest in themselves, an interest that shows itself in many different ways. A young adolescent is, for example, much interested in his dress and personal appearance, in his own physical fitness, in his future career ; at times he may exhibit a conceit and cocksureness that tries the patience even of his adult friends.

[1] See *The New Psychology and the Teacher*, H. Crichton Miller (Jarrolds, 1921).

It will be seen therefore that there are three factors complicating the behaviour of adolescent boys and girls :

(i) Girls are sexually more developed than boys of the same age.

(ii) Boys and girls tend to be strongly interested in themselves.

(iii) Boys and girls tend to attach themselves to members of their own sex for companionship.

It is not surprising therefore that in school-days the behaviour of adolescent boys and girls in the presence of one another is tentative, uncertain and in some ways unnatural. In reality they are learning to adjust themselves to persons of the opposite sex, but they show the awkwardness and self-consciousness of most inexpert learners in any field. The result is that the sexes tend to band together, and to compete against each other where, as in many school subjects, competition is possible. It is therefore by no means certain that in early adolescence the atmosphere of mixed classes is the best for general development.

It is not suggested that the above arguments against mixed schools are conclusive or that they need always be as cogent as they are to-day. Some of the difficulties of organizing mixed schools could be overcome by a more generous basis for staffing ; others will become less serious when classes become smaller and it becomes possible to organize teaching on a group and individual basis rather than on a class basis. It may further be argued that some of the difficulties of staffing mixed schools arise from the fact that men and women of to-day have received imperfect or insufficient co-education. One fact is certain : there is scope for a great improvement in the relations between the sexes and much could be done by more adequate co-education during adolescence. While, therefore, it may be desirable for various reasons to organize separate-sex departments, it is certain that these departments should co-operate to a far greater extent than is usual, especially for social functions. It may be desirable for boys and girls to receive much of their school instruction in single-sex classes, but it is equally desirable for them to receive much of their social education in mixed groups. Boys and girls should have opportunities, under the controlled conditions possible in school, for getting to know and to understand one another and, in particular, they should have practice in co-operative activities that need the special but different abilities of each sex. This is particularly important in these days of small families, and it applies with special force to boarding schools.

Sex education is obviously a far wider subject than the term usually connotes. It is an education that should enable boys and girls to grow up in such a way that they will be able to enjoy full lives as men and women, each developing his or her own personality and each making his or her own contribution to a harmonious social life. Sex education is both personal and social; it begins in infancy and should be continued throughout childhood and adolescence. At each stage it should be furthered both by social experiences in family and school life and by the study of Nature. But, in addition to this valuable preparatory training, adolescents need some direct personal instruction to prepare them for the onset of puberty and for the sexual problems of adult life. Without such instruction, they are apt to acquire inaccurate information in undesirable ways and in some cases to become seriously worried. It is far better that adolescents should receive sex instruction frankly from qualified adults than surreptitiously from unreliable sources. Some experiments in giving such instruction to classes of adolescents in school have been tried. Given suitable instructors, it is claimed that this method is satisfactory and that it gains the approval of a majority of parents. Most authorities, however, agree that individuals differ so much in temperament and in rate of sexual development that personal sex instruction should be given to individuals rather than to classes. It should, if possible, be given by parents. It would be idle to pretend that it can be given in an unemotional, impersonal way or that adolescents can receive it in the same matter-of-fact way in which they receive instruction in science. The important point is not to over-emphasize the emotional

L

aspect of the subject and particularly not to associate sex instruction with unworthy emotions such as false sentimentality, fear, disgust, or with feelings of embarrassment and guilt. Most people would agree that some degree of reserve on these personal matters is right and proper, and if adults responsible for giving sex instructions feel any difficulties about broaching the subject the best course is probably to introduce it by giving the adolescent a good written account to read.[1] The instruction cannot, however, be considered complete without a frank personal talk.

In school, while it is important for teachers to be aware of the difficulties caused by the ripening of the sex instinct, matters directly connected with sex need have very little place. It is a mistake, for example, to imagine, as many people do, that biology is primarily a means of giving sex instruction. The fundamental reason for teaching biology is the same as that for teaching any other subject of the curriculum, viz. to increase our pupils' general intellectual interest in life ; reproduction is an important biological topic, but not more important than other topics such as respiration and nutrition. Sex naturally plays a large part in the thoughts and interests of adolescents, but emotional energy at this stage must not be absorbed by sexual interests. The difficulties caused by the natural intensity of emotion during adolescence may be alleviated by adequate sex education conceived on broad lines as described above, but they can also be alleviated by draining off interest into non-sexual channels such as those provided by physical training, games, hobbies, and, above all, creative work. It cannot be too strongly emphasized that adolescent interests are not confined to physical matters such as sex and games ; they overflow into matters of the mind and spirit. The intensity of emotional life shows itself in a heightening of interests of many kinds. The danger is that adolescents are liable to find a spurious satisfaction for these interests ; they tend to allow their emotions to evaporate in mere

[1] See, for example, the pamphlets published by *The Alliance of Honour*, 112–114 City Road, London, E.C.1.

fantasy instead of harnessing them to some form of practical activity. The consequence is that although they grow older they fail to grow up. It is, for example, very easy for adolescents to drop into a habit of getting a cheap satisfaction of their interests by the frequent uncritical watching of cinema pictures. The result is that, instead of the cinema being an aid to the process of growing up, it becomes a means of fixating interest at a childish level. It is therefore most important that teachers should keep themselves acquainted with the films their adolescent pupils see so that they can help them to follow up visits to the cinema by some form of activity. Films should be the subject of informal discussions in school ; they should be used as a stimulus to reading and study, and they should often be referred to in ordinary lessons. For example, practical work in domestic subjects can, in the hands of a wise, sympathetic teacher, be made an excellent corrective to the fantasy life that is stimulated by many popular films. There is little harm in girls losing themselves in dreams of beautiful homes and clothes as seen in cinema pictures so long as they are helped to correct their fantasies by lessons learned in attempts at making their dreams come true. Similarly, schools should take care to provide practical outlets for adolescent interests in subjects such as art, religion, construction, adventure, and social service. It cannot be doubted that, from the point of view of emotions and interests, many adults remain at the adolescent stage of development, a state of affairs that constitutes a very serious criticism of our present system and methods of adolescent education. It is of first importance therefore that schools for adolescents should provide opportunities for a variety of creative work and give their pupils some freedom of choice, so that every individual can pursue a type of creative work in which he can find absorbing interest and literally lose himself. In addition, adolescents can be greatly helped by the general character-training that should be given at every stage and in the teaching of every subject. The foundations of an ideal of self-control can, for example, be laid if all teachers in a school maintain a resolute attitude towards such details as the need for pertinacity in tackling pieces of ordinary school work that are distasteful but nevertheless necessary. Modern methods rightly attach great importance to interest, but we must be careful lest an indiscriminating adherence to the doctrine of interest should lead us to give children wrong ideas about the need for personal effort and endurance in resisting temptation.

Physical growth during adolescence.—Adolescence is often a period of rapid physical growth and there is consequently some loss of physical poise. This need not, however, cause serious trouble any more than the special psychological growth we have been considering. A wise teacher will turn a blind eye to hobbledehoy clumsiness, trusting to natural growth for a remedy and avoiding any suggestions that may increase the adolescent's self-consciousness. Teachers of adolescent girls particularly must remember that girls are liable to be physically over-tired, especially as this is the age when they are very useful at home ; they must guard against encouraging over-exertion, and be watchful lest their pupils develop bad postural habits.

Attitude to authority during adolescence.—The adolescent's sphere of action is wider than that of the infant and he does not submit so readily to adult control. This difficulty is, for many adolescents, accentuated by the fact that they have, as a result of unwise training in earlier years, developed a wrong attitude towards parents and teachers, and finally towards adults and authority in general. The attitude may be one of suspicion, the result of parents refusing to answer urgent personal questions in early childhood, or the result of parents giving answers that children discover later to be untrue. It may be an attitude of rebellion, the result of parents and teachers prematurely forcing children into an adult mould. It may be an attitude of disrespect for adults caused by a lack of proper control in earlier stages. It may be an attitude of dependence upon adults, the result of excessive care and affection. Adolescence is the time when we reap the harvest of what has been sown in early education.

Another possible cause of difficulty is a feeling of jealousy that may develop in an insidious way between adults and adolescents. Unless we ourselves have grown up satisfactorily we are very apt to resent (perhaps without being fully aware of it) the promise of happy adulthood that we see in the healthy adolescents in our classes. An adolescent, on his part, finds it difficult to accept us as superiors and yet, without sympathetic help and encouragement, he also finds it difficult to accept us as equals ; he is hobbledehoy, neither man nor boy. This is doubtless one reason why adolescents show the gang spirit so strongly, and it explains why they are often influenced much more strongly by companions of their own sex and age than by well-meaning adults. It suggests that in schools and clubs for adolescents we should provide opportunities for team work and play and adequate outlets for leadership.

Another reason tending to make it difficult for us to enter into active sympathy with adolescents is the fact that we have forgotten many of our own adolescent experiences. According to psycho-analytic interpretation we are very prone to forget these experiences because they are humiliating and unpleasant ; the forgetting is an example of active forgetting due to repression. If this is so, it follows that, as Ross suggests, " The student looking forward to work among young people will do well to recall now, before they are forgotten, the events and mental attitudes of his own adolescent years."[1] Furthermore, it is important for all of us to be on our guard lest unwittingly we behave in a cruel way towards adolescents, justifying our actions to ourselves by saying that we are teaching them the hard lessons of real life, when we are really seeking compensation for forgotten humiliations and disappointments that we have suffered in our own lives. It should now be clear that teachers of infants and of adolescents should have a particularly lively appreciation of the far-reaching influence that

[1] *Groundwork of Educational Psychology*, p. 146.

their attitude and teaching may have on the emotional development of their pupils. It is probably not an exaggeration to say that the peace of mind of individuals and of communities depends in large measure on the kind of treatment that individuals receive in these two crucial stages of their lives. Teachers of difficult adolescents have a special responsibility, for unless the opportunities of remedial work presented in this second period of intense emotional life are seized, it is unlikely that equally favourable opportunities will ever recur. Adolescence has been likened to a tide that rises in the veins of youth ; if, in the words of the Hadow Report, this tide " be taken at the flood, and a new voyage begun in the strength and along the flow of its current, we think that it will ' move on to fortune.' "[1]

Another type of difficulty arises from the fact that the intelligence of an adolescent has almost reached its maximum development. In sheer reasoning ability there is little difference between an adult and an adolescent ; in fact, some exceptional adolescents may even be more intelligent than their parents. They lack, of course, the advantage of an adult's years of experience and in school they are handicapped by their relative lack of knowledge. But the fact remains that in solving personal problems that are intensely interesting and the data of which are familiar, an adolescent has a shrewd idea that he himself is no less capable than the adults who are in authority over him.

The foregoing considerations suggest that a teacher of adolescents needs to have a very sympathetic understanding of the minds of his pupils. He must, however, be a real grown-up person himself, contented to be grown up and to be growing older, and not for ever pining for the days gone by. He must avoid petty-minded jealousy ; he must be tolerant of the excesses of youthful enthusiasms ; he must be prepared to give his pupils scope for initiative while giving them tactfully the benefit of his larger experience and knowledge. In a word, a teacher must treat adolescents more as equals than as inferiors if he is to be successful in

[1] *The Education of the Adolescent*, p. xix (H.M.S.O., 1926).

giving them the guidance and help they need ; a pompous authoritarian attitude, dangerous at any stage, is likely to lead to disaster at this stage.

OBSERVATIONS AND EXPERIMENTS

1. Make lists of the books in the school library which prove most popular among children of various ages.

2. Get children (boys and girls) of various ages to write down in order of preference the six cinema films they like best. What light do these lists throw on the facts of psychological development ?

3. Observe the standing and sitting posture of adolescent children in the needlework room and the practical workroom.

(Consider how bad postures can be tactfully corrected, and whether any of them are caused by unsuitable equipment.)

4. Visit a club for adolescents. Try to find out (a) the most popular occupations, (b) how authority is divided between adult organizers and adolescent members.

(Consider in what ways school classes might be run as clubs.)

5. Visit a modern secondary school. Make a list of the varieties of creative work catered for, and consider their relative values.

REFERENCES FOR READING

Handbook of Suggestions, New edition, 1937, Part II.
Education, Sir T. Percy Nunn, pp. 177–84.
Modern Psychology and Education, Sturt and Oakden, chapter V.
Groundwork of Educational Psychology, J. S. Ross, chapter VIII.
Psychology and Practical Life, Collins and Drever, chapter III.

ADDITIONAL REFERENCES

Hygiene and Health Education, M. B. Davies, chapter XXIV (Longmans, 1933).
Adolescence, G. S. Hall (Appleton, 1904).
The Adolescent, J. W. Slaughter (Geo. Allen, 1911).
Youth, O. A. Wheeler (Univ. Lond. Press, 1929).
The Growing Girl, E. Saywell (Methuen, 1928).
Infant and Nursery Schools, 1933 ; *The Primary School*, 1931 ; *The Education of the Adolescent*, 1926 ; *Sex Education*, 1943 (H.M.S.O.).

ESSAYS AND DISCUSSIONS

1. Discuss the special difficulties of teaching adolescents in evening classes.

2. The importance of housing conditions as a factor in the process of growing up.

3. Discuss the reasons why many girls prefer factory work to domestic service. Consider what (*a*) mistresses in homes and (*b*) teachers in schools can do to increase the popularity of domestic service.

4. The importance of creative work in the education of adolescents.

(Consider: leisure occupations; self-respect; emotional stability; standards of craftsmanship; varieties of creative work; arrangements to enable pupils to exercise choice.)

5. Opportunities for co-operation between boys' and girls' schools.

(Consider: open days; concerts; school journeys; leavers' parties; old pupils' associations; combined lessons; interchange of staff; practical work done by girls for boys' school and *vice versa*.)

6. Ways and means of training adolescents to take responsibility.

Chapter XVIII

THE ART OF TEACHING

It has been well said that "teaching" means "causing to learn." Nothing has been given until it has been taken; nothing has been taught until it has been learnt. Teaching is more than the efficient delivery of thoroughly prepared lectures, and a clear realization of this simple fact will save many beginners in the art of teaching from much disappointment.

A knowledge of how children learn is the first essential for success in teaching, and that is why the emphasis in this book has been placed on learning rather than on teaching. It may now be helpful, however, to consider, in the light of our knowledge of children, some of the general principles of teaching.

The Teacher's Function

We expect children in school to develop intellect, character, skill, taste, and sociability. We say we teach them knowledge, habits, ideals, skills, manners. We mean by this statement that we help them to adjust themselves to their environment, both the material and the social environment. This view of education as adjustment puts us, as teachers, in our proper position. We are *subsidiary* to the process of learning, for in this process there are two main factors—a child on the one hand and its world on the other hand. The teacher's function is to bring the two into contact, to help to put them *en rapport*. In some respects teaching is like lighting a fire. We bring heat to paper to enable it to start combining with the oxygen in its environment. In the classroom our function is similar; we bring to bear various teaching devices with a view to producing a "flash" between each child and some part of its environment. The essential activity is not the adjustment of child to teacher but the adjustment of child to world. This view of the teacher's function is fundamental and is nowhere so clearly expressed as in the following statement by Adamson :[1]

" The whole business is between the individual and his worlds, and the teacher is outside it, external to it. He may facilitate it, turning his attention to one or other member of the wedded pair. He may approach the individual, and his avenues of approach will be one or other of the instincts or emotional dispositions which are the prime movers of mental life. He may try fear, pugnacity, curiosity, or sympathy, or a combination of them, to quicken the current which seems to him sluggish. Or he may approach the fact or truth, whichever of the three worlds it belongs to, and see whether anything can be done by lighting it up, or lining in main features and blotting out detail, to facilitate adjustment. But whether he tries subject or object or both together he remains outside the process, a spectator, a manipulator, perhaps a disturber ; he is never in it and of it. Within that mysterious synthetic activity through which the individual is at once appropriating and contributing to his environment, forming and being formed by it . . . the teacher has neither place nor part."

This view of teaching accords perfectly with what was said in chapter XV (pp. 259–260) of subjects being treated as activities. When we really teach children the geometry of the circle, or, in other words, when we enable children to learn it, we do not merely instil into them a fraction of our own knowledge ; we put them *en rapport* with geometrical facts about circles. We arrange and present certain data ; we do this in ways that excite the children's interests ; their minds then play with these data and as they do so flashes of illumination, or at least glows of dim understanding, are produced. If this does not happen, no real learning has been done and no real teaching has been given.

[1] *The Individual and the Environment*, J. E. Adamson, pp. 26–7 (Longmans, 1921). This book treats education as the process of adjustment of the individual to three worlds,—nature, society and morality.

A growing appreciation of the subsidiary nature of the teacher's function has led many reformers to belittle the value of teaching. Children, we are told, must be left free to express themselves ; they must discover knowledge for themselves ; the only true education is self-education. Teachers, we are told, must stand aside ; they must talk less, explain less, direct less, correct less. All this is a very natural and a very necessary reaction against much traditional classroom practice. It must be emphasized, however, that teachers are not as superfluous as some enthusiasts suggest ; teaching is not the baneful evil it is sometimes represented to be. It is true that children are by nature curious, assertive and creative, but they are also submissive, imitative and ready to appeal for help. It follows, therefore, that we are not necessarily working contrary to child nature when we teach. We must, however, know when to teach and when to stand aside, when to explain and when to leave children to make discoveries, when to demonstrate and when to leave children free to experiment, when to require children to listen and when to give them scope for free expression. No simple rule can be formulated on this matter ; teaching is an art and correct procedure in given circumstances depends upon the whole situation. Clever, experienced teachers know intuitively what to do ; they have developed a particular sensitivity to the needs of a situation, a result partly of their experience in similar circumstances and partly of their acquired knowledge of children. A statement of some general considerations may, nevertheless, be helpful, especially to beginners.

Most children in school are over-taught.—The truth of this statement is nowhere so clearly shown as in the results of recent developments in the teaching of drawing. Formerly, children were carefully taught the technique of model-drawing as a preliminary to any attempts at drawing scenes of everyday life. Now, they are encouraged to draw pictures from their earliest years, and the teaching of technique is made subordinate to the needs that the children feel as they work. Far less teaching is given than formerly, but incomparably better results are obtained. The reason is that the teaching comes when the children want it. This is the second important fact for teachers.

The best time to teach children is when they feel the need for it. —This may sound a counsel of perfection and it must be added at once that an important part of the art of teaching consists in making children feel the need for instruction.

One method is by arranging that children learn through practical activities that are intrinsically interesting. Thus children learn to draw by making patterns and pictures, and they are taught technique incidentally, as the need arises ; they learn to write English by writing stories, invitations and articles, and again the teaching arises out of these activities. The project method (see pp. 261–264) is an attempt to organize school life so that children will want to learn and to be taught. It cannot be too strongly emphasized that, however interested children are in their work, some teaching is necessary. Some very skilful teachers apparently give very little direct teaching ; they themselves may be hardly aware that they teach at all. The fact is, however, that they are continually teaching in many subtle ways of which they are not fully conscious. Beginners should not allow themselves to be deluded into thinking that children will, without skilled help and guidance, make adequate progress in any subject. It is true that, when a child is engaged in creative work, any teaching of technique must be done with a very light touch so as not to tamper with the sincerity and freshness of the child's creation ; it is equally true that technique must be taught with a very sure touch so that the child makes the technical progress that he earnestly desires. It should be further recognized that, important as it is to encourage artistic creative work among children, it is equally necessary to train them in many ordinary workaday activities. In many composition lessons, for example, our aim is not to inspire children to create literature so much as to teach them to express a few plain facts clearly, concisely and accurately.

Another method of inciting children to want to learn

and to be taught is by giving them a problem to solve, by presenting them with a challenge. Much good teaching begins by propounding a question.

A third method of producing conditions in which children want to be taught is by selecting subject-matter that appeals to their natural interests. It is probably in this direction that we have most yet to learn. In the early days of universal education, the curriculum was very narrow, and in training teachers emphasis was placed on " method " rather than on " matter." Old-time teachers used to boast that they could teach 90 per cent. of what they knew, so completely had they mastered " the method " of teaching. The tutor in education in a training college was called the " master " or " mistress of method." Three developments in education have contributed to a change of attitude. First, the increased facilities for secondary education that followed the Education Act of 1902 produced young teachers with increased interest in knowledge and learning. Second, the widening of the elementary-school curriculum created a demand for teachers well equipped academically. Third, the diminution in the size of classes made some of the problems of the technique of teaching less urgent than they had been formerly. A great change took place in the training of teachers. " Matter " became as important as " method " ; in both academic and practical subjects courses of advanced study were introduced into training colleges ; many teachers began to take courses leading to university degrees and diplomas. Each system of training was appropriate in its day, but modern developments in education have produced a need for further modifications. The old " method " courses have been replaced by courses in principles of education ; instead of memorizing mechanical rules designed to make class teaching possible teachers are now beginning to study the scientific principles of how children learn. Equipped also with academic knowledge and practical skill, they then apply these principles to help them to pass on this knowledge and skill to children in school. It is at this point that reform is necessary. We know a good deal about how children learn, but we know comparatively little about what children of various ages ought to be learning. We are all too prone to assume that children ought to learn what we have learnt, and the sooner the better. We tend to ignore and forget the difficulties we ourselves experienced in acquiring our present knowledge, and we sometimes teach as if all our pupils were preparing to become purveyors of knowledge in their turn. It is probable that we are all too anxious to systematize the knowledge of young children and to make them conform to adult standards of technique and behaviour. Premature teaching is, in our opinion, one of the greatest hindrances at present to educational progress, for more than any other single factor it makes teaching difficult. It wastes energy and causes unnecessary irritation, and it makes children want to avoid learning. This is not an argument for merely simplifying what we now try to teach ; children do not want to learn what seems to them easy and childish. It is an argument for a reconsideration of the content of the subjects we teach. To carry out the reform we envisage, teachers will need more rather than less academic knowledge, but they will also need more psychological knowledge of children than psychologists can at present give them— knowledge of what subject-matter is appropriate for children at various ages. The type of history, geography and science that is obtained by diluting degree syllabuses in these subjects is not suitable for children. The whole field of knowledge needs to be reconsidered from the point of view of children and this is a task in which psychologists, teachers and academic specialists should collaborate.[1] When we have solved this problem, we shall have made a great advance in the art of teaching, for we shall be teaching what children want to learn and many of our present problems of teaching technique will have disappeared.

Children who are well taught are very active.—Teachers who

[1] See pp. 269–71. Some promising pioneer work in this direction is also being done in connexion with broadcast lessons. Another promising line of progress is in connexion with the manufacture of educational films.

enjoy teaching are always in danger of judging their work by the exhilarating effect that it produces on themselves. Teaching ought, of course, to be exhilarating, but its effects ought to be spread to the pupils. A good teacher always asks himself : What will this piece of teaching inspire my pupils *to do* ? A lesson period should seldom be devoted wholly to teaching, and the younger the children the more frequently do they need scope for activity. It should be noted that the activity need not always be physical activity ; the brighter children particularly will enjoy the activity of thinking and a great deal of teaching should be designed to stimulate children to think.

ORDERLY PROCEDURE IN TEACHING

The modern attitude to teaching has led educationists to place less emphasis on single lessons than they used to do. Carefully prepared lessons are, of course, still necessary, but they should be recognized as being only one element in the very complex process of educating children. Furthermore, a lesson does not always fit exactly into a time-table lesson period. Sometimes two or three 5-minute lessons will be given during a half-hour period ; sometimes a lesson will need several whole periods before it is completed.

Provided we keep the above warnings in mind, it may be useful to consider the problem of orderly procedure in the giving of lessons. Various attempts have been made to state general rules for the conduct of lessons, the most famous being those associated with Herbart[1] and his followers. According to this school of pedagogy, lessons should proceed by orderly steps. Various names for these steps have been suggested, but the following are the most usual : Preparation, Presentation, Association, Generalization, Application. These steps are generally known as the

[1] J. F. Herbart (1776–1841). His chief educational work was done at the University of Königsberg, where he conducted courses of study in pedagogy, supplemented by observation in a practice school attached. See *The Secret of Herbart*, F. H. Hayward (Watts, 1907) ; *The Student's Herbart*, F. H. Hayward (Allen, 1907) ; *Herbartian Psychology*, J. Adams (Heath).

Herbartian Formal Steps—"formal" because they are concerned with the form as distinct from the content of lessons. The ideas underlying these five steps are very useful, but, as we shall see, any attempt to make every lesson proceed step by step in this way is bound to lead to much futility.

Preparation.—The preparation step is probably the only one that applies to every lesson, for it is always necessary to prepare the minds of pupils for what is coming. Insistence on the need for preparation is another way of stating that the interest of the pupils must be aroused before any teaching is possible. Beginners are warned, however, against allowing the value of this first step to tempt them to begin lessons in unnatural and foolish ways. Long catechisms designed to "elicit" the subject of the lesson are a waste of time. The minds of children are as a rule best prepared by a short, direct introduction. A puzzling question expressed in a few words, an arresting title written on the blackboard, a short reference to the last lesson and a brief statement that we intend to continue the subject, a plain invitation to consider the work done last week—these are some legitimate methods of opening a lesson. The general principle is that children's interest must be aroused by a clear appreciation of the purpose or aim of the lesson, and the more quickly and emphatically this is done, the better.

Another danger in using preparation as a formal step is that, having taken the step, we are then apt to conclude that all is well and that the remainder of the lesson consists in advancing steadily along the remaining steps. This is not true, for in many lessons it is necessary to remind pupils during the lesson of its aim and purpose. It is a good plan to write the subject of the lesson on the blackboard at the beginning so that it can be kept in the pupils' minds without fuss.

The preparation step is of even greater importance at the beginning of a course of lessons than it is at the beginning of a single lesson. We have seen (p. 25) that pre-school children learn by analysing wholes ; the same is true of all subsequent learning. The best introduction to a course of lessons is a broad survey of the whole field, for such a survey gives a pattern into which all subsequent lessons fit. For example, when beginning the study of a fresh period in history, a time-line sets the period in its proper place and an introductory survey lesson reveals the main problems to be studied. An excellent introduction to a secondary-school course in bookbinding is to show the prospective pupils an exhibition of work arranged in its stages. Many teachers of nature study survey the whole course in one or two lessons, the pupils writing appropriate headings on pages throughout their note-books ; they are thus prepared not only to receive lessons but also to make relevant observations on their own initiative. The work of preparing a survey lesson is an excellent discipline for teachers, for it forces us to look at our proposed course as a whole and to make up our minds what are its main objectives. After having given a survey lesson, we shall tend to give a course of coherent instruction rather than a series of isolated lessons.

Presentation.—The presentation step is specially relevant to lessons in which new facts are to be taught. There are two ways of presenting new knowledge—it can be told or it can be revealed. From the children's point of view, it can be received or it can be discovered. Both methods of presentation are useful and necessary.

A great deal of historical, geographical and even scientific knowledge must be told, either by spoken or by printed words. Nothing is more tiresome than to attempt to " elicit " information that children cannot possibly deduce from their previous knowledge. When school days are over, the chief source of new knowledge will be books, newspapers and magazines. It is therefore important to train children in school to acquire new knowledge in this way, and private study should accordingly play an increasingly large part in the presentation of lessons as children grow older. Most children find it more difficult to study than to listen, and for this reason private study needs a more elaborate preparation step than an oral lesson does. It is often desirable, for example, to provide children beforehand with an outline of the subject-matter or with a series of questions to be answered.

Intermediate between the methods of private study and oral teaching is the method of reading aloud to a class. Vivid descriptions and well-told stories are often more effective if read than if told. Teachers cannot, however, rely on private study and reading aloud, and they should therefore practise the arts of narrating and describing. It is easier to tell a story than to describe a scene, partly because the time sequence in a story determines the order in which it must unfold, and partly because the action of a story tends to attract and hold the attention of children. At the beginning of a teaching career it is therefore a good plan to gain confidence by practising story-telling[1] first, and then to practise short descriptions, preferably those that can be woven into a story. There is a tendency in school to underestimate the value of good, clear narration as a method of teaching. We do not suggest that lessons should be lectures; many lessons, however, would be greatly improved if teachers developed the art of continuous, interesting narration and were not afraid of using it for short periods during oral lessons.

The second method of presenting knowledge is by revealing it, that is to say, by helping children to discover it. The essence of this method is to arouse intense interest and then to present the necessary facts arranged in such an order that children see the relations between them. For example, let us suppose we want to teach the relation between the diameter and the circumference of circles. Having collected circles of all sizes, from a three-penny piece to a bicycle wheel, we propound the problem and invite guesses which are recorded in a prominent place. A secondary

[1] For advice see books on the art of story-telling, e.g., *A Guide to Story-telling*, A. Burrell (Pitman, 1926); *Children's Stories and How to Tell Them*, W. A. Bone (Christophers, 1923); *How to Tell Stories to Children*, S. C. Bryant (Harrap, 1910).

problem soon arises—Will the answer be different for circles of different diameters ? More opinions are collected and recorded. Then follows a discussion of methods of finding the facts. The necessary practical work is done and the results are arranged in some definite order, preferably on the suggestion of the pupils. They can, for example, be arranged in ascending or descending order of diameters. All that is now necessary is a discussion guided by the teacher ; the new knowledge flashes on some pupils and dawns on others.[1] Some perhaps cannot " see " it. From this point a number of methods of procedure are possible, e.g.,

(a) All who " see " it can write out a statement of their discovery while the others receive further help, or

(b) The class is dismissed with the suggestion that every-one will know the correct answer next lesson, or

(c) Those who " see " it are allowed to tell the others in the hope that the statement will now produce the necessary " flash."

The first method can often be employed with excellent results, the procedure developing into an enjoyable game as one pupil after another experiences the " flash " and retires from the group that is being taught.

The second method ought to be used frequently, for, as we learned in chapter X (pp. 158–159), the process of unconscious assimilation is a valuable mode of learning. Lessons should not always be completely " rounded off " at the end of a period ; it is often a much better plan to leave them to be continued next time. In many instances it will be found that pupils have actually progressed during the interval, even though they may not have given any further conscious thought to the problem. There is always the additional possibility that some will continue to ponder on the unsolved mystery.

The exigencies of time will often necessitate the adoption of the third method, but it should not be assumed that the

[1] In the example given, it is important to note that the " flash " does not complete the thinking process required. Measuring cannot do more than suggest the probable answer. The story of π still remains to be told.

attempt to reveal the new knowledge has failed. A child who has followed an argument even imperfectly is in a better position to grasp the conclusion than he would have been if he had been told without any preparatory striving. We now see that the distinction between " telling " and " revealing " is not always clear-cut. A child may just fail to get the revelation spontaneously, but it comes with the telling. Sometimes the revelation may still elude him after he has been told and he has to accept the knowledge on trust ; but even then, if interest is keen, the revelation may come after quite a long interval. To tell a child a conclusion after an attempt at revealing it has failed may be a second-best method of teaching, but it is better than the third-rate method of merely telling and re-telling the fact until it has been memorized.

A very common form of teaching is *explaining*. We usually speak of this process as one that is performed by teachers but, as with all forms of teaching, the ultimate process is one that takes place in the minds of our pupils. The surest form of explanation is one that presents and arranges the necessary facts in such a way that pupils draw their own conclusions ; they themselves complete the explaining process. If we rely on telling our explanations, that is, if we tell not only the relevant facts but also the conclusions, we are always in danger of giving an explanation that consists of mere words with little or no meaning. There are, of course, many occasions when we must tell explanations because we have not the necessary time to help children to discover them. When we do this, we must not assume that our explanation has been successful, however convincing it may seem to us. The facial expression of our pupils may give us some indication how far we have succeeded, but we need to know our pupils well before we can draw reliable conclusions from such a clue, for most children can look very wise when they want to. The only sure test comes when children use the new knowledge, but we will reserve discussion of this point until we consider the fifth step—application.

Another way of teaching is by *suggestion*, that is, by conveying ideas so that they are accepted even though the grounds for doing so are inadequate. It is analogous to the method of teaching practical subjects by imitation ; in fact, the accepting of suggestions is often referred to as the imitating of ideas. Teaching by suggestion is one example of the method of teaching by telling.

Children are by nature extremely suggestible. In the classroom this suggestibility is enhanced in several ways. The teacher, by virtue of his age, position and superior knowledge, enjoys a high degree of prestige ; most pupils are consequently ready to accept his suggestions uncritically, and the others find it difficult to resist following the example of the group. The suggestibility of children gives teachers great power, and the use of suggestion in the classroom entails a great responsibility, comparable to the responsibility appertaining to the use of such powerful influences as the cinema and wireless in the social life of the world at large. It is therefore necessary to consider the use of suggestion very carefully.

In the first place, it is useless to recoil from the responsibility and pretend not to influence children by suggestion. We cannot remain in our classrooms without conveying suggestions either directly by our words and attitudes, or indirectly by our choice of text-books. Furthermore, we must realize clearly that learning by suggestion is a necessary method ; progress would be impossible if children were required to learn everything by discovery and reason. " Without question," as Nunn says, " man's ultimate aim should be to order all his affairs, from the lowest to the highest, in the cold, clear light of reason. But life cannot be suspended until that ideal has been realized ; and by suggestion the people obtain meanwhile at least the partial vision without which in literal truth they would perish."[1] If this applies to adults, it applies *a fortiori* to children. In fact, there is a place in school for

[1] *Education*, p. 149.

learning, not merely by suggestion but also by memorizing. As Newbolt says in *Clifton Chapel* :

> " This is the Chapel : here, my son,
> Your father thought the thoughts of youth,
> And heard the words that one by one
> The touch of Life has turned to truth."

This quotation reveals the first principle that should guide us in using suggestion—it should be used for conveying what is universal, for conveying only those ideas that the " touch of Life " may later turn to truth. We should not use suggestion to inculcate the ideas of one political party, but we should use it to inspire children with a desire to seek truth and avoid prejudice (see also p. 162–3). Used in this way, suggestion, so far from being the enemy of reason, is its ally. It helps us to send children into the world not merely waiting passively for the touch of Life to convert knowledge into Truth, but with a desire actively to pursue Truth. An important corollary follows. In addition to using suggestion, we must use the method of discovery so that children will learn the " rules of the game " for pursuing Truth and experience some of the joys of its chase. Most learning is, in fact, an amalgam of learning by reasoning, by accepting suggestions and by memorizing. We must adapt our teaching procedure to this fact.

There are several practical considerations that beginners in teaching should remember when using suggestion. A suggestion is much more likely to work positively than negatively. " Don't make a noise " suggests the idea of being noisy rather than that of being quiet. As far as possible, therefore, suggestions should be given in a positive form.

It is very easy to arouse a contrariant attitude when making suggestions. A direct suggestion conveyed in a bullying tone will tend to produce rebels. An indirect suggestion that allows pupils to feel that the idea was originally their own is much more likely to be accepted. " Have you ever thought of trying . . . ? " is a much more potent suggestion than " I should try. . . ." With adolescents particularly it is better to give suggestions incidentally during the course of a discussion than dogmatically during a lecture.

When using the method of discovery, it is very necessary to avoid suggesting the desired conclusion. In fact, it is often justifiable to suggest the opposite. For example, when magnesium is burnt in air, children always expect it will lose in weight. A wise teacher will at least not suggest that this is doubtful. He may by his suggestions even encourage children in their wrong belief. The result, when it comes, is then very impressive.

As we learned in chapter IX (pp. 131–133), the more meaningful a fact is, the more easily it is remembered. This principle reminds us that " telling " as a method of teaching is not as simple as we have so far suggested. When children repeatedly forget facts that we tell them we are apt to put all the blame on them, but some blame probably attaches to us ; we may be guilty of taking too naïve and simple a view of the process of " telling." We tell so that children can hear, but we do not always tell so that they can understand ; the children hear us, but they do not listen to us. For example, the effectiveness of narration and description depends very largely on a child's previous knowledge and on the way in which the new knowledge is connected with it. The same is true also of the explanations and the suggestions we give. A child who is listening, and not merely hearing, is actively relating what he hears to what he knows ; he is not merely receiving new facts, but he is educing relations between these facts and others. That is to say, the method of " telling " involves the method we have called " revealing." The only fundamental difference between the two methods is a difference in emphasis. When a teacher is telling, he is emphasizing the new facts and he is leaving his pupils to make their own connexions with previous knowledge as he proceeds. We might therefore say that " telling " is effective in proportion as a child experiences " flashes of revelation." An experienced teacher is sensitive to the reactions of his class ; he knows whether they are listening or merely hearing and whether they are hearing or not hearing. As he proceeds he continually modifies his lesson, first to convert individual non-hearers into hearers, and second to transform his class of hearers into a class of listeners. The necessary modifications may take many forms—a question to recall an inattentive pupil, a gesture to emphasize some important statement, an explanation interpolated on the spur of the moment in response to looks of puzzledom. If we speak naturally, as we ought to do when teaching, we are bound at times to use some word or phrase that we recognize at once to be outside our pupil's vocabulary. For example, when describing the action of sweat glands we may say, " All this happens automatically." We immediately feel that this sentence has made no impression, so we continue. " Like an automatic machine ; you put in a penny and the machine works by itself, automatically. You get hot, and the sweat glands work by themselves, automatically. You can't stop them, out comes the sweat." This example reminds us that if we use many new words in one lesson, progress will be tedious. The art of talking to children of various ages in appropriate language, neither talking down to them nor talking over their heads, can only be cultivated by long practice. Observation of the language used by skilled teachers and the study of the language used in well-written children's books[1] may help, but the art of

[1] See, for example, books by Beatrix Potter, Arthur Ransome, and Hugh Lofting.

In books like these a large vocabulary is used. Hard words are not avoided if they are needed ; they are skilfully introduced in contexts where their meaning can be grasped. Similarly in teaching, hard words and technical terms should be used where they are necessary. (See p. 205.)

The essential truth about the use of technical terms in teaching is vividly expressed in the following passage from a novel, *The Wainwrights*, Edgar Meredith : " Mart got as far as looking into botany college books. Flop right down into the disgustment-pool. All names and names. Slicing up live things into vulgar fractions, and finding wicked crack-jaw names for the broken bits. Not just two, like ' numerator ' and ' denominator.' Maddening words, like things made up to call each separate spark in a firework by."

talking, like all complex arts, must be learnt by experience.

The reference to the automatic machine in the above example illustrates how new information can be linked to old knowledge ; this linking is the third Herbartian step—association. We have said enough to indicate that it is not a separate step but rather a process that is interwoven with the process called presentation. In fact, in many accounts of the formal steps association is not mentioned. It may be helpful, however, if we consider it separately, for the neglect of this step is a very common fault in teaching, especially with beginners.

Association.—In considering association, the linking of new facts with old knowledge, it is important to remember that children gain their first knowledge through experience. This initial stock of knowledge grows in three ways—(*a*) as a result of futher experience, (*b*) by the association of new facts, and (*c*) by the eduction of new relations between facts. The idea that knowledge grows like a tree and is not built up like a heap of stones is of fundamental importance to teachers. The essence of the art of teaching consists in presenting new facts so that they will grow into and form part of the child's previous knowledge ; it is not enough merely to pile up facts as a stone-breaker piles up stones or even to try to cement one stone to another. The ultimate process is a process of growth and it takes part in the minds of our pupils ; in this process, as Adamson says, " the teacher has neither place nor part." The teacher's part is in the preliminaries ; he must arouse interest, give pupils opportunities for gaining experiences, stimulate them to think, help them to associate new facts with old knowledge. This process of association makes children feel at home with the new facts and teachers can effect it in several ways.[1]

---

[1] It is interesting and instructive to compare the teacher's function with that of the makers of literature.

    cf. Quiller-Couch, who quotes Emerson's fine remark that all good writers " do not anywhere make us feel that we intrude, that this is for our betters. Rather it is true that, in their greatest strokes, there we feel most at home."

[*Continuation of footnote on page* 336.

Indirectly all that we have said in this chapter about preparation applies to this problem. A teacher when presenting new facts will try to revive in his pupils' minds memories of previous relevant experiences and knowledge. When, for example, he is giving lessons on types of climate he will make continual reference to children's experience of varying weather conditions ; when teaching about the work of Parliament he will give it reality by comparing it with the children's own experience of law-making in the classroom community. Sometimes new knowledge can be made vivid, not by comparison but by contrast with the children's experience. Teachers of history must continually contrast conditions of life to-day with those of bygone times.

In all teaching we must ask ourselves whether pupils have had the necessary previous experience to make our proposed lessons meaningful. In many instances we shall find they lack this experience and, furthermore, that we cannot provide it ; the solution is to be found in reforming the curriculum. In some instances we shall find that the lacking experience can be provided ; the solution is to be found in reforming our methods of teaching. In the early stages of teaching any topic it is often more important to concentrate on giving children experiences rather than on presenting them with facts. In infant schools it may be better to spend time giving number experiences than on premature training in the manipulation of number symbols ; in junior schools children must be given experience in making plans and maps of the immediate environment and in using maps of their neighbourhood before they can understand maps of other countries ; in secondary schools

---

Continued from page 335]
He then summarizes the matter thus : " As we dwell here between two mysteries, of a soul within and an ordered Universe without, so among us are granted to dwell certain men of more delicate intellectual fibre than their fellows—men whose minds have, as it were, filaments to intercept, apprehend, conduct, translate home to us stray messages between these two mysteries, as modern telegraphy has learnt to search out, snatch, gather home human messages astray over waste waters of the Ocean." (On the Art Of Writing, p. 10.)

children must be given experience of freedom and self-government before they can assimilate history lessons on the growth of democratic government.

Valuable experience is given by practical activities of all kinds—experiments, dramatic work, model-making, educational visits, school journeys, team games. A very useful means of providing a substitute for first-hand experience is the cinematograph film. We cannot take our children backward in time or far out in space, but by means of historical, geographical and industrial films we can do something to compensate for this handicap. By means of films children can also be shown scientific experiments that cannot be performed in school. Other forms of experience that cannot be obtained directly, but which can be given by films are various forms of observation : skilled movements that are too rapid to be observed in detail can be shown in slow motion ; the movements of microscopic things can be shown in magnified pictures. With the advent of sound and colour films[1] the range of realistic experience that can be brought into the classroom is still further enlarged.[2]

[1] It should be noted that sound on films can be used for three different purposes : (a) for reproducing the natural sound accompaniments of the picture, (b) for giving a running commentary on the picture, and (c) for giving a musical accompaniment designed to arouse appropriate emotions.

[2] cf. *Documentary Film*, Paul Rotha (Faber, 1936). " It (a film, *Drifters*) humbly brought to the screen the labour of the North Sea herring catch from such an approach that the ordinary person was made to realize, probably for the first time, that a herring on his plate was no mere accepted thing but the result of other men's physical toil and possibly courage. It ' brought alive ' . . . not just the routine of the catch but the whole drama of emotional values that underlay the task, interpreting in its stride the unconscious beauty of physical labour in the face of work done for a livelihood. Moreover, there was brought to the conception all the poetic qualities of ship, sea and weather."

A very valuable use of films is the widening and deepening of human sympathies. We tend to accept as commonplace the familiar things of daily life, and we make our pupils memorize colourless phrases about such topics as " the fishing industry," " the colonization of Africa," " bacteriological infection." It is not until our pupils see films like *Drifters*, *Rhodes of Africa*, and *The Story of Louis Pasteur* that the men and women to whom we are indebted really come alive.

The use of films in school will doubtless be very greatly developed in the future. There are two main kinds of film (a) the *foreground* film for

[*Continuation of footnote on page* 338.

The technique of wireless lessons is being developed i
a similar direction. In dramatic interludes, for example
pupils are enabled to experience, at least through the ear
incidents of the past. They listen to a conversation takin
place in the Middle Ages in a notary's office as a boy i
apprenticed to learn the art and mystery of baking ; the
listen to a crowd jeering at a dishonest baker in the pillory
The development of television will open up many furthe
possibilities for the realistic presentation of knowledge
Modern teachers cannot afford to neglect these mechanica
aids to teaching, for, as Rotha says, " Radio and cinema
jointly or separately, represent the biggest revolution i
instructional methods since the introduction of the printin
press."[1]

There are many other methods of helping to ensure tha
the information we present is meaningful. We can throv
light on it by means of illustrations of various kinds—models
pictures, drawings, diagrams, examples, stories and analo

Continuation from page 337]
direct teaching in the classroom, and (b) the *background* film which can be
shown at mass demonstrations and used for broadening children's experience
in a general way. As Lauwerys suggests, background films can be furthe
classified into those that are mainly informative and those that are usec
mainly for training taste. The British Film Institute (4 Great Russell Street
London, W.C. 1) has recently been formed to promote the use of educationa
films and to act as a clearing-house for ideas. Under its auspices, thre
important parties are enabled to meet, (a) the academic specialist, (b) the
practising teacher, and (c) the film-producer. The Governors of the Institute
have come to the conclusion that 16 mm. is the most convenient size fo
school films, that projectors should be capable of showing both sound film
and silent film at their appropriate speeds, and that sound films should be o
the sound-on-film type.

A number of experiments on the use of films in school have been reported
Generally speaking, it is agreed that information conveyed by films is
retained better than information conveyed by other methods. Many of the
beneficial effects of educational films are, however, of a subtle kind tha
cannot be easily measured. As suggested in this chapter, films should be
used chiefly, not for presenting mere facts, but for giving experience that wil
enable children to convert information into knowledge. See *The Film in the
School*, edited by J. A. Lauwerys (Christophers, 1935). This book contains
a list of the principal film libraries and a bibliography. *The Cinema in School*
W. H. George (Pitman, 1935) ; *Sight and Sound*, Quarterly Journal of the
British Film Institute ; *The Educational Film Review*, a Monthly Journal.

[1] *Documentary Film*, p. 39.

gies. All these methods, it should be noted, have this in common—they are all directed towards helping children to relate new facts to previous experience, towards helping them to convert information into knowledge.

The younger the children, the less likely they are to comprehend the full meaning of our words, and therefore the more important it is to use concrete illustrations. All teachers should, from the beginning of their careers, make collections of useful illustrations for the subjects they teach, and in these days of cheap illustrated papers the help of the pupils should also be enlisted. In some areas the local librarian makes a classified collection of pictures for loan to schools.[1] Every school should possess an epidiascope; if, then, collections of pictures were organized and catalogued to facilitate quick reference, lessons on all subjects of the curriculum could be well illustrated.

The value of verbal illustration should not be overlooked. In the course of our general reading of books, magazines and newspapers we all find much valuable illustrative material that is worth collecting in a systematic way. To give one example, no fewer than five hundred items of scientific news appeared in a daily newspaper during a recent year.[2]

In all these ways—by giving children experience, by relating lessons to previous experience and knowledge, by the use of films, pictures and illustrations of all kinds—we can help to ensure that the new facts we present are meaningful. If we are successful, the facts will not remain as isolated facts; the children will assimilate them into the body of knowledge they already possess. The facts will not remain as dead, useless information; the children will convert them into living, useful knowledge.

Generalization.—In scientific subjects like mathematics, science and grammar, lessons sometimes have as their aim

[1] Attention should also be called to the use of lantern slides. The London County Council has a collection of slides for the use of schools.
[2] See *Elementary General Science : A Book for Teachers*, A. G. Hughes, pp. 94–8 (Blackie, 1933).

the formulation of a general rule or definition. We have already given one example and made some suggestions for procedure (see pp. 329-330). We may summarize these suggestions by saying that children should always approach general rules and definitions by a consideration of particular examples. The teacher's function is to help his pupils to appreciate the problem, to help them to collect relevant data and to arrange these data in a suitable way, and then to help them to discover the generalization for themselves. This latter stage is often very difficult and it demands the exercise of a high degree of technical skill in teaching. No precise rules can be given ; the teacher must respond to the needs of the situation as it develops and, if the pupils are taking their proper share in the work, the same lesson will never develop in exactly the same way on two successive occasions. In general terms, the teacher can help by keeping the aim of the enquiry clearly in the children's minds, by encouraging his pupils and sustaining their interest, by dealing tactfully and sympathetically with wrong conclusions, by giving wise suggestions and asking helpful questions. The use of suggestion and questioning needs great skill when children are wrestling with a problem, for it is very easy by unwise suggestions or leading questions to give away the conclusion and save children the trouble of thinking.

When helping children to generalize, there comes a time when, for some children in the class, further teaching would do more harm than good. A decision then has to be made whether to postpone the generalization or to tell it.

When a generalization has been made, further discussion is usually necessary in order to express it in a convenient and concise form of words. In mathematics this process is then often carried a stage further and the generalization is finally expressed as a formula. Formulations of important general rules, whether in words or in mathematical symbols, are often worth memorizing. It is of equal importance, however, to revise from time to time the method by which the formulation was made.

It is necessary for teachers to realize how complicated the process of generalization is. When a child makes a generalization he must abstract the common elements from the given data, become conscious of the exact nature of the underlying identity, and then express it clearly in words. Generalization, in this mature form, is obviously beyond the scope of infant and most junior children. But even young children show a tendency to generalize. At a very early age all men are greeted as " Da-da," all puddles are called " bath."[1] This rash generalizing is not the result of logical reasoning ; it might even be looked upon as an example of faulty discrimination. The examples quoted show, however, that children have a strong tendency to notice similarities. It is a tendency that should be exploited in many ways among young children, in preparation for its more formal use in secondary schools. Junior children, for example, can be led to discover that words have different uses and that some words are names. If then they are told that these words are called nouns, they are able to recognize nouns in use and they enjoy the game of finding nouns. They have not tried, however, to formulate a grammarian's definition of a noun. At this stage it is neither necessary nor desirable to do so. The important point is to gain experience of nouns, so that the definition, when formulated at a later stage, will possess real meaning.

The concise clear-cut nature of generalizations makes a strong appeal to many teachers and for that reason we are often tempted to present mere forms of words or even formulæ before our pupils have had the necessary experience that alone can make them meaningful. It is worth emphasizing, therefore, that generalizations are of very little value to children unless they are the results of their own thinking, of careful reflection on knowledge gained from actual experience. This warning is important for teachers of scientific subjects, but it is even more important for teachers of art and literature. As Quiller-Couch suggests,

[1] Other examples we have observed are the following : elm tree called large parsley ; irises called big aubretia ; macaroni called rhubarb.

it is desirable to aim constantly " at the concrete, at the study of such definite beauties as we can see presented . . . under our eyes; always seeking the author's intention, but eschewing . . . all general definitions and theories, through the sieve of which the particular achievement of genius is so apt to slip."[1]

Application.—One important use of this fifth step in the Herbartian scheme has already been mentioned (p. 330); it reveals how far our teaching has been successful. In the presentation part of our lesson, we narrate, describe, explain and illustrate ; we call in the aid of other teachers through the medium of books ; perhaps we use such modern aids as films and wireless lessons ; we and our pupils enjoy ourselves. During and after the lesson we call upon pupils to reproduce parts of the information we have been teaching. But until our lesson has been applied we cannot be sure that it has been fully successful. Reproduction tests whether pupils have acquired facts, but application is necessary to test whether these facts have been converted into faculties. In practical subjects and in arithmetic, the application step is hardly ever omitted. We are never satisfied that we have taught long division until all our pupils have shown that they can apply their new knowledge by getting long division sums right, and by solving problems that necessitate the process. A similar practice should often be followed when teaching history, geography and science ; children should be given opportunities to apply their knowledge to the solution of simple problems.

It would be very wrong, however, to look upon application as a formal step to be specifically arranged at the end of every lesson. While it may be true to say that all teaching should lead not merely to increased information but to increased power, the application of new powers cannot always be arranged as classroom exercises to be done with pen or ink or even with tools of any kind. Literature lessons, for example, cannot be applied in this way. A fitting conclusion to many literature lessons is a quiet

[1] *On the Art of Writing*, pp. 12–13 (Camb. Univ. Press, 1917).

dignified dismissal; the application must be left to the children. Most probably neither they nor anyone else will be conscious of any " application step," but it may be none the less real. An increased sensitivity to beauty, a more civilized way of life, a deeper interest in reading—these are some of the subtle, imperceptible ways in which literature lessons are applied.

If we try to find a classroom application step for all our teaching we shall be guilty either of confining our pupils to relatively trivial exercises or of restricting the scope of our teaching to relatively trivial subject-matter. Some teaching in all subjects, mathematics included, should be given with faith that it will find application in the lives of our pupils; it may not be useful to them in the ordinary sense of the word, but it will make them more alive.

So far, we have considered " application " as a means of testing the success of teaching, but this is not its only function. It is often desirable to give children application exercises during the course of a lesson even though we know that the new knowledge has not yet been fully grasped. Children often learn best by trying to apply what they are learning. Many a half-understood process or fact becomes clear when pupils are striving to use it. Application, like each of the other four steps, is sometimes not a step but an aspect of the whole process of teaching.[1] Lessons in which efforts are made to complete the presentation steps before allowing pupils to attempt the application steps are often boring to the pupils and irritating to the teacher. When explaining a new rule in arithmetic, it is a good plan to give children a chance to use it as soon as possible; this applica-

---

[1] As a matter of historical accuracy, the steps ought not to be attributed to Herbart, for, as Adams points out, Herbart does not speak of steps but of " modes of teaching."

It was apparently Ziller, Professor of Education at Leipzig from 1864 to 1882, who tried to apply Herbart's doctrine to every lesson or to all groups of lessons, and in this way invented the " formal steps." " Herbart," say Green and Birchenough, " was much too great a master ever to have approved of the formal rigidity of Ziller." See *A Primer of Teaching Practice*, Green and Birchenough, pp. 239–40; *Exposition and Illustration*, J. Adams, pp. 143–5 (Macmillan, 1910).

tion will help some pupils to complete the learning, while for others it will serve as an excellent preparation for further teaching.

In some subjects, in drawing for example, the best plan may be to start with work of the " application " type even though the children's technical knowledge and skill be very imperfect. The teaching is given incidentally—a hint to one individual, a short lesson to two or three others, and so on until the whole class has learnt the lesson that the teacher set out to teach.

In many subjects, in composition for example, it is desirable to use both the " application " method of approach and the more straightforward " presentation " method. Thus children should sometimes be given scope for free creative work, lessons in technique arising incidentally from the errors, they make. Side by side with this mode of teaching, formal lessons should be presented in the usual way, the steps leading systematically to technical exercises in which the pupils apply the new knowledge that has been taught.

Speaking generally, the modern tendency in teaching is to use the " application " approach more, and the " presentation " approach less. That is to say, we are discovering that children learn best in school by the methods they used in pre-school days. They learn by doing, by plunging into a partially-understood activity, by working out projects. The series of formal lessons, each lesson logically arranged in five steps, beginning with preparation and ending with application, is giving way to the more informal type of procedure. As we succeed in this mode of teaching, we shall find that it is unnecessary to make our lessons interesting ; they are interesting because· they appeal to the children's interests.

Recapitulation.—If teaching is given in the spirit of the Herbartian scheme, the question of recapitulation will not be overlooked. The more successful the " association " and " application steps," the less need there will be for formal recapitulation. In the first place, interest helps children to learn with relatively little repetition. In the second place, the processes of associating new facts with the old knowledge and of applying new knowledge in various situations ensure repetition of facts in the best possible way ; they are not repeated mechanically but they are repeated from various points of view. It is generally necessary, however, to arrange at convenient points during a lesson for some definite summing up and revision of the main facts taught ; this may be termed sectional revision. Sometimes it may also be useful to have a general revision towards the end of a lesson ; this may be termed final recapitulation. Revision and recapitulation should not always be done by the teacher ; it is often a good plan to call upon individual pupils. Children who are systematically trained to " tell back " what they have learnt not only learn thoroughly, but also develop a remarkable facility in expressing themselves in speech.[1] Our ultimate aim may be " original " expression, but as a basis we should not overlook the very great value of humble reproduction.

In order to give all children in a large class adequate practice in reproduction some work on paper is essential. This is one of the reasons why pupils should keep note-books. For young children drawing is often more suitable than writing as a means of " telling back," and at all ages the written reproduction is made more interesting if the children are encouraged to collect pictures with which to illustrate their work. Care should be taken not to allow the keeping of note-books to become a fetish. The fetish may take one of two forms—a fetish for perfection or for originality. An unnaturally neat and accurate compilation can be obtained by dictating notes or by having them transcribed ; there is little virtue in this type of work, although it is occasionally justifiable. At the other extreme, little good purpose is served by allowing children to write long

[1] See *An Essay Towards a Philosophy of Education*, Charlotte M. Mason (Kegan Paul, 1925). Charlotte Mason was the author of the method used by the Parents' National Educational Union. " Telling back " is an important feature of this method, which is now generally known as the " Mason method " or the " P.N.E.U. method." (See pp. 382–5.)

rambling accounts full of inaccuracies. Children need systematic and graduated training in writing notes. They can begin by drawing pictures and writing titles ; later they can write sentences instead of titles ; sometimes they may be guided by questions or headings ; at other times the " completion " method may be used ; often, an oral discussion may prepare for the writing of a paragraph. The aim in all this work is not so much the making of a note book for exhibition as the development of an ability that will remain long after the note-book has been burnt.

TEACHERS' NOTES

It is difficult to give detailed guidance on the compilation of teaching notes. First, as we have seen, teaching procedure is largely determined by the actual happenings during a time-table period, and it is not easy to foresee what course events will take. Second, teaching notes should be personal documents and no outsider can prescribe for any teacher the exact form of notes that he will find most useful for his own purposes. These objections apply, however, more to the notes of experienced teachers than to those of beginners and we propose therefore to make a distinction between the detailed, formal notes of a teacher in training and the more informal notes of the experienced teacher.

In the early stages of learning to teach it is desirable to plan the procedure in some detail and it is also helpful to have some form for the notes themselves, and to use this form until personal experience suggests useful modifications. Even though the pre-arranged plan is not followed in all its details, the thought that has been given to its construction gives a teacher a sense of mastery that makes him feel free when he is confronted with his class. An experienced teacher has this freedom that is born of mastery because he has actually followed similar procedures on previous occasions, but a beginner must gain it by conducting his classes in imagination as he prepares his notes. The writing of notes is for most persons a valuable aid to this process of imaginative thinking, but it must always be remembered that the essential process in preparing lessons is thinking out plans, not writing down notes.

Teaching notes—(a) Teachers-in-training.—Formerly, the teaching notes of training-college students were notes of lessons. Note-books contained daily programmes set out as a collection of lessons—on dictation, history, arithmetic, composition, reading. To-day the notes are not so much notes of separate lessons as notes of proposed procedures for conducting courses—in English, arithmetic, history. The basis of the note-book arrangement is therefore courses rather than lessons. This change in emphasis is important ; the preparation of lessons has given way to the preparation of courses. These courses must be divided into sections according to the time-table periods available, but it does not follow that a set lesson will be given in every period.

Forty years ago notes of lessons were arranged in two columns, one headed Matter, the other Method. This practice has to a large extent disappeared. As the subject-matter of lessons increased in range and complexity, the choice of matter became an important aspect of method ; it became difficult to decide where to draw the line between matter and method. Although the columns have disappeared, the underlying idea is still important. When preparing courses, it is still necessary to bear in mind that there are two aspects to consider—the subject and the children, what to teach and how to teach it, matter and method. Neither is independent of the other, but each needs special and separate consideration.

The other feature of teaching notes that has largely disappeared is the use of Herbartian headings. As we have shown, the so-called steps are aspects of one indivisble whole rather than steps, and it is therefore unwise to try to force all teaching notes into the five-step plan. But again, the underlying ideas are important and beginners are advised when preparing courses to keep the five steps in mind—preparation, presentation, association, generalization, application. When giving a course of lessons, all these modes of teaching must be used sooner or later, and they will probably all be used many times in a month; on some occasions they may all be used more than once during a single time-table period.

The following questions and notes may prove helpful to teachers in the preparation of courses and the writing of teaching notes :

Procedure for the course as a whole.

1. What are the main outlines of the subject-matter to be taught ?

It is a useful plan first to scribble an outline without reference to books. This exercise will reveal where knowledge is hazy and it will suggest the exact points on which attention should be focused when books are consulted. It will help teachers to cultivate the necessary art of skimming books to get the special information they need.

Whenever information is extracted from a book, a note should be made of the exact reference, for it is often necessary to refer again to the same page. These references should be incorporated in the teaching notes. The same systematic procedure should be followed for all passages that are to be read as part of the instruction.

2. Can I give a rapid bird's-eye view of the whole course during the first time-table period ?

This is an excellent procedure, for it forces teachers to master the subject-matter as a whole and it prepares the pupils for subsequent work (see p. 327).

3. Allowing adequate time for revision and testing, how many time-table periods are available and what is a reasonable way of sub-dividing the course ?

This form of preparation will help to prevent an over-leisurely procedure being adopted at the beginning, followed by a hurried scamper at the end of the course. The consideration of this question is also important because it helps teachers to judge whether the course is reasonable for the time allowed, whether its scope should be curtailed, or, if not, which parts should be treated lightly.

Procedure for single time-table periods.

4. Consider the beginning.

We have discussed this problem in general terms in connexion with the preparation step (p. 326). When preparing teaching notes, it is, however, necessary to have in mind the particular class you are going to teach. Imagine yourself to be in the classroom and try some alternative beginnings. Choose the most direct, the beginning that will most quickly launch you and the class into the work for the period.

5. Consider the development of the work.

The development will depend on a large number of factors, and the work during any particular time-table period may take one or both of the following forms :

(*a*) Exposition and demonstration by the teacher. If a story is to be told, a description given, or a passage read, it should be practised beforehand. This preparation will, as a rule, be done silently, a few notes of outstanding points being jotted down. If an explanation is to be given, it is no preparation to write " Explain . . ." The steps in the explanation must be thought out, and the teaching notes will then always take the form " Explain . . . as follows : . . ." The essential steps in a demonstration should be thought out and if it is an unfamiliar operation it should be rehearsed. The teaching notes should indicate the main points needing special attention, just as in an exposition lesson they indicate the main headings of the subject-matter to be taught. Questioning is an important aid in developing a lesson, and it is sometimes useful to think out a few of the important questions by which the main arguments can be begun and developed (see chapter XIX). Illustration is another important aid, and the teaching notes should indicate what illustrations are to be used and when they are to be introduced.

(*b*) Individual work by pupils. This may take many forms, written work in exercise books, private study from text-books or practical work involving the use of tools. The teacher's preparation consists in thinking out how the work can be best organized. Arrangements must be made to distribute and collect material without wasting time. Care must be taken that every pupil has a definite task that he can begin without delay. In craftwork, pupils are often able to continue their work without special instructions; written work should also be organized in " wholes " so that pupils know what to do without having to be told on each occasion. The programme of work in arithmetic, for example, can be given in advance for the following month; if each pupil writes down the numbers of the examples to be worked he need never have to wait for orders. Private study must be organized so that pupils know what to do; a few headings or questions to guide their investigations should be prepared. Finally, it is necessary for the teacher to decide what his own function should be during these periods of pupil-activity. In preparing practical lessons, he should think out the points to watch for to avoid accidents and to promote skill; the making of lists of such points is one of the best ways of becoming observant in practical workrooms (see chapter VII).

It will be seen that teaching notes should refer to three aspects—(a) to the pupils' activities, (b) to the subject-matter, and (c) to the teacher's function in putting pupils and subject-matter into active relationship.

6. Consider the conclusion.

It is important, especially if a school is organized for specialist training, that the work of each period should finish punctually. Time must be allowed not only for clearing away apparatus but also for bringing together the threads of the learning and teaching done during the period. Sometimes the last few minutes can be spent on a critical examination of work done, sometimes on recapitulating the incidental teaching that has been given, sometimes on propounding a question preparatory for the next lesson, sometimes on a final impressive reading of a poem that has been studied. The various ways of concluding a period of instruction are too numerous to mention. The general principle is, however, simple; the end of a period is, psychologically, important and the last few minutes should always be spent in a worthy manner. Lessons should not end in a mad rush against time nor should they be allowed merely to "peter out." The end of a lesson needs the same careful preparation as the beginning.

7. Review the plans for the period in the light of the following questions :

(*a*) Have I made adequate provision for activity by the pupils ?

(*b*) Am I clear about the particular aim of the work to be done in this period ?

(*c*) Have I made adequate provision for repetition and revision ?

8. What apparatus is required during the period ?

At the end of the notes it is helpful to make a list of the things required—maps, books, tools. At the beginning of the period these things should be checked so that once work has begun it is not interrupted or delayed.

Teaching notes—(*b*) *Experienced teachers.*—Many local education authorities have regulations requiring teachers to keep notes of lessons. Notes that are kept merely to comply with regulations are, however, of little value. A teacher's note-book should be a reflection of his interest in his work, and should contain much more than the chapter headings of the pupils' text-book with a summary of its contents. Many of the detailed notes relating to methodical procedure, which are valuable in the note-books of training-college students, are unnecessary at this later stage. A working note-book of an experienced teacher should, however, contain copious notes of subject-matter, indications of the order in which this is to be presented, references to suitable illustrations, both pictorial and verbal, and references to supplementary information. In addition, it should contain records of important and noteworthy reactions of the pupils, for example, unusual questions and common errors.

The compilation of such a book need not be in any sense a burden. The first time a course is given the notes will be a mere skeleton with many spaces and perhaps blank pages. Gradually the gaps will be filled in until some pages become overcrowded ; after a time the book may be unintelligible in parts to every one except its author. But to its author it is a valuable possession that grows in interest from year to year, an endless source of ideas that keep his teaching alive and fresh.

OBSERVATIONS AND EXPERIMENTS

No specific suggestions need be given, for the daily work of teaching and school practice will provide many opportunities for observations and experiments relating to the subject-matter of this chapter.

The student of education will find it interesting to note how much there is to observe in a classroom as his knowledge of the principles of learning and teaching increases. Beginners ought to observe skilled teachers at work ; when doing this, it is a good plan not to observe in a general diffuse way, but to select a limited number of points on which to concentrate. For example, in one lesson, consider the way in which new facts are associated ; in another lesson, note particularly the use made of illustrations ; and so on. Watch how skilled teachers begin their lessons, how much they tell and how much they reveal, how they end their lessons. As you observe put yourself in imagination in the teacher's place and consider how you yourself would proceed at each point.

REFERENCES FOR READING

A Primer of Teaching Practice, Green and Birchenough, chapters III, IV, V, XV.
Modern Education, T. Raymont, chapter VIII.

ADDITIONAL REFERENCES

Exposition and Illustration, J. Adams (Macmillan, 1910).
The Approach to Teaching, H. Ward and F. Roscoe, chapters II, VI, VII.
Teaching : Its Nature and Varieties, B. Dumville (Univ. Tut. Press, 3rd edit., 1933).
The Use of Diagrams in the Teaching of English, M. M. Lewis (Ginn, 1936).
The Teacher in Training, J. C. Hill (Allen & Unwin, 1935).

ESSAYS AND DISCUSSIONS

1. Choose an example of " explanation " such as you might need to give in school, e.g.,
Why is the eastern side of England relatively dry ?
Why did William the Conqueror come to England ?
Why is a barometer used as a weather-glass ?
Explain vitamins.
State the age of the pupils and set out the stages of your explanation. Indicate clearly how the pupils are to acquire each necessary item of knowledge.

2. Choose an example of " description " such as you might need to give in school, e.g.,

An oasis, Niagara Falls, A street in a mediæval town.

State the age of the pupils and write a suitable description. Indicate clearly what material illustrations you would use, and how you would use them.

3. The dangers of illustration.
(Read : *Exposition and Illustration,* J. Adams, chapter XVI.)

4. Collect examples of children's errors, e.g.,
" Vitamins are little things in greens that do you good."
Discuss what these errors reveal about the teaching given.

5. Discuss the following introduction to a lesson :
What would you like to have for breakfast ?
(Consider : (i) Lesson on " The way to make coffee." (ii) Lesson on diet.)

6. Collect examples of the beginnings and endings of lessons. Discuss them.

7. The use of suggestion in teaching.
(Consider : its meaning ; conditions favourable to suggestibility ; examples of its desirable use and of its undesirable use in the classroom ; auto-suggestion.)

8. The use of pictures in teaching.

9. The value and limitations of wireless lessons.

10. The cinema as an aid to teaching.

11. Discuss the function of (*a*) association and (*b*) application in a lesson on some definite topic, e.g., decimal fractions.

Chapter XIX

QUESTIONING

In chapter II we learned that children are endowed with an instinct of curiosity. One way in which this instinct obtains expression is by means of questions. Children in pre-school years are persistent questioners, but in school the position is generally reversed, and most of the questions are asked by the teachers. Much has been written in educational text-books on the art of questioning but very little on the art of answering questions.

Children's Questions

There are several possible reasons why pre-school children should ask more questions than school children. In the first place, children are inevitably confronted with a large number of novel situations when they are very young for the obvious reason that their experience has been relatively limited. When they feel puzzled, they satisfy their natural impulse by asking questions, for, unlike older children, they have not learnt to control this impulse and to think for themselves. Another type of question that is closely connected with the impulsive question is one that seems to be prompted not so much by curiosity as by a desire to be sociable; questioning is one of the methods used by young children for making conversation. Finally, we must remember that in early childhood many questions are prompted by irrational childish fears, some of which are operating below the level of consciousness. But when allowance has been made for these facts, we are still left with the feeling that the average school pupil displays far less curiosity than he ought. Large classes and examination pressure are two of the causes. Conditions, however, are improving, and one result will doubtless be a large increase in the number of questions that pupils in school will propound to their teachers. An important test of the educational atmosphere of a classroom is whether its pupils feel free to ask questions ; an important test of the educational efficiency of a teacher is afforded by the way in which he treats the questions that his pupils ask.

A wise teacher will not merely welcome questions ; he will encourage them by positive action. He will pause occasionally during oral lessons and invite questions ; so far from showing annoyance, he will show pleasure, if his oral exposition is interrupted by a sincere questioner ; he will make a collection of specially interesting questions for his own edification ; he will institute a question book in which pupils can write down questions that they have been unable to ask orally.

No hard-and-fast rule can be laid down as to how children's questions should be dealt with. Some questions may be impertinent and the questioner must be rebuked. Some questions may be trivial and thoughtless, and the best treatment may be to turn the question back to its author for answer. Some questions may reveal a misconception and may necessitate a re-statement of part of a lesson. Some questions may reveal a difficulty that can best be cleared up by putting one or two questions to the questioner. Some questions may be due to intelligent anticipation of what is coming in a later part of a lesson ; such questions may merit a word of commendation, but the answer must be postponed. Some questions may be of interest to so few members of a class that they are best answered in private. Generally speaking, however, a sincere question deserves a sincere answer, and the answer should be given directly and promptly. Pupils soon learn not to ask questions when they find that their questions always provoke a tedious retaliatory inquisition. It may not always be possible to give a complete answer orally, in which case a book reference may be given. Teachers who encourage questions are bound to be asked some to which they do not know the answer. In such a situation they should say frankly and without shame that they do not know, but that they will find out. The fundamental principle in dealing with serious questions asked by children is to show a sincere interest in them. Many answers are bound to be partial because the children are not sufficiently advanced to understand a more complete answer ; in such cases it is well to point out that there is more to be said on the matter. Some teachers keep a record of questions that are unanswered or only partially answered, and they use them as starting-points for subsequent teaching.

TEACHERS' QUESTIONS

Although under modern conditions and with modern methods there is less need than formerly for teachers to be continually asking questions, the art of questioning remains an important part of teaching technique, and many of the rules laid down in method books of last century are still useful. It is, for example, better to ask direct questions than elliptical ones. The form—What is the capital of England ?—is preferable to—The capital of England is ?— if only because it sets children's minds working in the desired direction as soon as the first word is uttered. Unless something happens to make a question inaudible, it should be asked once only, for pupils can in this way be trained to listen. There is a great temptation when questioning to recast a question immediately it has been put or even before the first version has been completely expressed. Such a procedure tends to produce muddled thinking. If it is realized that a question has been badly constructed, it should be cancelled by a definite statement before a second version is attempted. This practice ensures that the class is confronted with a single clear-cut issue. The same consideration rules out as unsatisfactory the asking of more than a single question at a time. As a rule, questions should provoke thought or require the giving of some definite information ; there is little virtue in formally asking questions that merely require the answer Yes or No. Such questions can be used with good effect occasionally, but they are not really questions ; as in everyday conversation, they are used to give emphasis to a point, to recall wandering attention, or merely to make the discourse more sociable. When asking questions it is worth while practising economy of language. Short questions that go straight to the point provoke thought ; wordy questions often merely bewilder. Good teachers can sometimes ask a question by a mere lifting of the eyebrows, and it is possible when demonstrating practical subjects to use this silent method of questioning to very good effect. In arithmetic lessons, when a point is being driven home by a number of small problems of one type it is often unnecessary to repeat all the words of the question every time.

Questions may serve a variety of purposes in oral teaching. They provide a ready method of testing the results of teaching, of finding whether explanations have been understood, of determining whether it is safe to proceed to the next step. Sometimes questions are used to start a line of thought, to puzzle children and provoke their curiosity. Sometimes questions are used to develop a line of argument. Care must be taken that questions used for this purpose are searching questions, for it is easy to break up the argument into such small pieces that, although the correct conclusion is reached successfully, all the essential thinking has been done by the teacher. In fact, when an argument has been developed by questioning, it is never safe to assume that the teaching has been successful until we have tested whether our pupils can restate it in full. At other times questions are used to recall relevant knowledge on which it is intended to build the lesson. In this connexion beginners are warned to avoid vague questions that merely encourage random answers ; it is, for example, futile to begin a lesson on " Milk " by asking children what they had for breakfast. Unless questions definitely focus attention, it is better to begin by a straightforward statement of the subject. Some teachers have a tendency to ask too many questions, just as some have a tendency to lecture too much. All schools have not yet outlived the tradition of the days when it was a sin to tell anything, and when everything had to be " elicited," even the subject of the lesson.

As a rule, questions are addressed to a class and those who can answer are expected " to put up their hands." This is probably a necessary procedure when teaching large classes, but it is an artificial way of conducting a conversation, and some teachers now find it possible to dispense with it. Ideally, the relations between teacher and class should be so friendly and intimate that no special method of indicating readiness to answer is necessary. Some teachers prefer to call on one pupil, and then put the question to him alone. Though there are objections to this plan it is useful on occasion. A better plan, and one which might well be adopted whenever the questions constitute a straightforward test, is to require each pupil to jot down an answer on scrap paper. This procedure is often used in " mental arithmetic " lessons, and it is worth trying in many other types of lesson. The plan of testing a class by oral questions and oral answers may be very deceptive ; bright children give good answers and we delude ourselves that all is well. It is always necessary in oral teaching to be on our guard lest the answering is monopolized by a few eager members of the class.

Many teachers develop a habit of repeating every answer given by a pupil. Sometimes this repetition serves a useful purpose, as, for example, when it is desired to give an answer special emphasis, or when a chance noise has made the answer inaudible to the rest of the class. The repetition of all answers is, however, unnecessary and undesirable. It tends to encourage slovenly, mumbled answering and it slows down the pace of the lesson for no good reason ; a correct answer can be accepted with a nod, a very meritorious answer with one word of commendation and the lesson should proceed without delay. Answers that are clearly correct in intention although badly expressed are very common, and there is a great temptation for teachers to accept them and to make the necessary amendment themselves. In the long run it is more economical to throw the onus of amending the answer on to the pupil, care being taken to avoid tedium. Children who give wrong answers should never be left in any doubt that their answers are wrong. Sometimes it is possible, without taking up undue time, to help a pupil to see where his answer is wrong. For example :

Pupil : A magnet is something that attracts other substances.
Teacher (rubbing a fountain pen, and picking up specks of dust with it) : So this is a magnet.
Pupil : No, a magnet is made of iron or steel.

And so the dialogue proceeds until the correct answer is given. This was the method of teaching used by Socrates, and it is often referred to as the *Socratic method*. Socrates, however, made considerable use of irony when dealing with wrong answers. It will be generally agreed that irony is out of place in school ; in fact, when the Socratic method is used, it is important to adopt a kindly helpful attitude, and not to pursue the method for a long time. " Hunting " a bewildered pupil with a long series of questions is not a helpful method of teaching him, and it is often a sheer waste of time for the other members of the class.

As far as possible, question and answer in class teaching should follow the lines of a natural everyday conversation. The observation of this principle will help beginners to avoid the commoner faults of technique, and it will prevent them from acquiescing in pedantic rules ; it is, for example, sheer pedantry to require every answer to be a complete sentence.

EXAMINATIONS

It is generally assumed in the classroom that written questions can be satisfactorily framed on the spur of the moment. Recent research into examinations reveals, however, that it is by no means easy to frame questions that have only one meaning for a large number of children. It is a good plan, therefore, to make up written questions as a course proceeds so that, when the time comes for an examination paper to be set, there is a reservoir of questions to draw from, questions, moreover, to which some thought has been given over a period of time. But if it is difficult to set perfect questions it is still more difficult to find a perfect method of assessing the answers. If one essay written by a child is marked independently by ten teachers, the marks may vary from 30 to 70 per cent. If the same set of essays is marked on two occasions by one teacher, the discrepancies are still very disquieting. A solution of the difficulty has been sought in two directions. Some reformers have boldly recommended that the essay should be abandoned as an examining instrument. Instead of setting six questions, each requiring a short essay, they would set, say, a hundred questions each requiring an answer of one or two words. The same principle is used in mathematics, a large number of " mental " questions being set instead of a small number of more involved problems. This atomized type of examination is similar in form to that used by psychologists in their intelligence tests, and it has a number of advantages over the older type. The marking depends less on personal whim ; it is objective and therefore reliable : the examination can be made to cover a very wide field ; it is therefore a better test and less dependent on chance : the marks given are earned by ability in the subject being tested ; they are not given for facility in verbal expression.

While admitting the advantages of the " many-little-questions " type of examination, particularly for young children, many educationists doubt the advisability of dispensing with essay-answers altogether. They argue that in history, for example, the extent to which the subject is really grasped can only be tested by a connected answer. The ability to express thought clearly in a continuous narrative is so important that it would be unwise to rely exclusively on one-word answers. The best plan is probably a compromise, and examination papers might well contain a variety of questions, some requiring answers of one word, others calling for a sentence or a short paragraph, together with one or two questions to be answered at greater length. Opinion differs as to the most reliable method of marking essay-answers. Some prefer to analyse an ideal answer and allocate marks for definite points of information; that is to say, they atomize the answer. Others prefer to mark by general impression obtained by reading the answer as rapidly as possible. Whatever method be chosen, teachers should be aware of the extreme unreliability of essay-marking, and not delude themselves into thinking that they can fairly make fine distinctions. The most that can be done is to put essay-answers into a small number of categories, say five, and it is very doubtful whether every number in a large range of marks ought to be used.[1]

Written questions for children, we have suggested, should be clear and unambiguous, and they should call for answers varying in length from one word to a complete

---

[1] The same general principles apply to the marking of literary essays. Instead, however, of atomizing the essay into "points of information," the markers atomize it into "sets of qualities." The essay may, for example, be marked in respect of the following five qualities :

      (i) Range of ideas.
      (ii) Quality of ideas.
      (iii) Style.
      (iv) Technical accuracy.
      (v) General form.

A maximum of 10 marks may be given for each set of qualities. For a scheme of essay marking with seven sets of qualities, see *The Technique of Examining Children*, p. 77, B. C. Wallis (Macmillan, 1927). The experience of the present writers suggests that it is inadvisable to have so large a number of sub-divisions, for they tend to prevent the marker from getting a view of the essay as a whole. There is, indeed, much to be said for marking essays as wholes by general impression as a result of rapid reading, the above sets of qualities being kept in mind. If this method be used, the best plan is to put the essays into five categories—poor, fair, average or fairly good, good, very good—on a first reading. Marks can then be awarded on a second reading—1 or 2 marks for poor essays, 3 or 4 marks for fair essays, and so on up to a maximum of 10 marks for an excellent essay. If it is desired to give a maximum of 50, the marks so awarded should then be multiplied by 5. To mark out of 50 by general impression, giving three essays, say 33, 35 and 37 marks, is a very doubtful practice.

The question of the relative reliability of various methods of marking essays needs to be subjected to scientific investigation.

essay.[1] The following are some additional details of examining technique with which teachers should be conversant :

(a) The questions should be graded to meet the needs of pupils of varying ability. Thus all pupils will meet with some success and all pupils will find some questions hard enough to test their powers. The most economical plan is to arrange the questions in order of increasing difficulty in one paper, though where a class is taught in sections separate examination papers may sometimes be desirable. The easy questions should always appear at the beginning of a paper, for they help to create confidence, especially among " nervous " children.

(b) The paper should be long enough to keep the best pupils busy all the time. If this is not done, the examination must fail to reveal the true differences between the best pupils and the others. It is sometimes objected that long papers tend to produce a harassed feeling, but this is largely a question of training. It ought to be generally recognized among teachers and pupils that in examinations all the questions can never be answered by all the pupils.

(c) After an examination the distribution of the marks obtained should always be considered, for it reveals, as nothing else can, whether the paper was of a reasonable degree of difficulty. A good examination will " spread " the candidates over a wide range, and if the number of candidates is large, the distribution should correspond approximately with the curve of normal distribution (see p. 61).

Examinations are an ancient human institution, and despite widespread criticism and some violent denunciation they continue to flourish. The reason is that they are indispensable, and moreover not wholly bad. Children as a rule like examinations, and many schools find that the average attendance rises during examination week. They

---

[1] *Mutatis mutandis*, this remark applies to examinations in mathematics. It should be noted that some solutions to problems in arithmetic ought to be set out in such a way that they can be read as a piece of continuous prose.

act as a stimulus, and enable many pupils to put forward that extra effort which is necessary to convert superficial " woolly " knowledge into knowledge that is clearly apprehended and thoroughly learnt. At their best, they may be considered as a not unwholesome disciplinary influence in school life. They are useful, too, from the teacher's point of view. Few business men can afford to dispense with an annual stocktaking, and examinations are one form of educational stocktaking. Their results give us information about individual children that may have escaped observation, and they also reveal strong and weak points in our teaching. It is true that many of the most important results of education are not susceptible of measurement by examination ; it is often said, for example, that the real test of education lies in the depth, breadth and permanence of interests that our pupils acquire rather than in the facts they learn ; one cynic has remarked that education consists in what is left when our pupils have forgotten all the facts they learned at school. This is no more than a half-truth, for it must never be forgotten that there is no antithesis between interest and knowledge. And even if we take character as the supreme test of education, the fact remains that intellectual achievement is both an aid to character-formation and also one of its by-products. The truth is that the highest aims of education are not incompatible with good examination results. No one can raise any serious objection to the plan of terminal examinations, interspersed with a reasonable number of informal tests. The determination of what is reasonable must be left to individual discretion ; it may be said, however, that the common practice of setting aside one mathematics lesson for a weekly test should be unnecessary. Informal tests should arise naturally from the work in hand, and should not be regulated by mechanical rules. They are particularly valuable as a stimulus to the memorizing of essential facts such as historical dates, arithmetical tables and geographical names.

External examinations.—So far we have been discussing school examinations set and marked by teachers. Such examinations, if properly conducted, do not deflect a school from its highest aims ; on the contrary, they can be very helpful to the general work of the school. The same cannot always be said of external examinations, where syllabuses are prescribed and examination questions are set by authorities outside the school. No matter how much care be taken to frame syllabuses and questions to meet the current practice of schools, there is always a tendency for examination requirements to lag behind the progress of the most advanced educational thought. External examinations thus tend to hamper progress. Again, there is always a greater element of chance in external examinations than in school examinations, where weight can be given to the results of the term's work ; as a result, teachers not unnaturally tend to prepare very carefully for the examination, and there is a tendency for the curriculum to become unduly narrow. Subjects outside the scope of the examination tend to be neglected, and in the teaching of examination subjects there is a reluctance to stray from the bare requirements of the examination syllabus. Instead of concentrating on the all-round education of individual pupils, attention tends to be concentrated on methods of outwitting examiners. There is then a danger of setting up a vicious circle ; the more successful schools are in their preparation, the more ingenious and complicated the examination questions become. The result is that children are pressed and crammed ; their natural healthy interests in learning are destroyed ; both they and their teachers are engaged in a soul-destroying grind when they ought to be living joyous and interesting lives. It should be emphasized that the above description refers to tendencies ; it is not intended as a realistic picture of all schools and all external examinations. Many schools take these examinations in their stride, and apart from a little special preparation shortly before the actual examination, they concentrate on the real educational needs of individuals. The development among teachers of a healthy professional conscience in regard to examination results will probably do more to reform examinations than any other single factor. Much is already being done to reduce the evils of external examinations, chiefly in the direction of making them more internal in character. Examining authorities keep in touch with schools ; teachers are represented on boards of examiners ; schools are allowed to submit alternative syllabuses for their own use. The result is that on the whole examinations are improving ; syllabuses are being revised to accord with changes in school curricula ; examination questions are becoming more reasonable. Behind the scenes, a great deal is also being done to make the marking as reliable as possible.[1] There is still, however, a great deal of dissatisfaction with our examination system, and we should look forward in the future to many drastic alterations to the current practice, both in the examinations held near the end of the junior- and preparatory-school stage, and in the certificate and scholarship examinations held near the end of the grammar-school stage. At both stages the argument for an external examination has rested upon the necessity for some impartial and absolute standard of reference by means of which the abilities of pupils from different schools could be directly compared.

As secondary education is now a universal right and not a privilege reserved for a selected few, a competitive examination at age 10 to 11 for entrance to grammar schools is now unnecessary. The problem is no longer that of selecting a small percentage of pupils for a superior type of education, but of allocating all pupils to that type of education for which they are best fitted. For this purpose school records carefully compiled during the whole junior-school stage will be far more useful than the results of a " snap " examination in English and arithmetic. In compiling these records the position in class from term to term and the results of routine internal examinations and of standardized tests (see p. 367) in all examinable subjects will be invaluable. These results should however be supple-

---

[1] For an interesting account of the machinery of a modern external examination, see *Secondary School Examination Statistics*, J. M. Crofts and D. C. Jones (Longmans, 1928).

mented by recorded observations of character and temperamental qualities and of special interests as they emerge. In many cases important light will be shed on all these records by the results of intelligence tests and of tests of special aptitudes. Intelligence tests will, for example, reveal pupils who for various reasons—adverse home circumstances, ill-health, irregular attendance, ineffective teaching—are not progressing as rapidly as they should in their school studies. Conversely such tests will reveal relatively unintelligent pupils who, perhaps as a result of parental pressure, are abnormally advanced in basic skills, but who are unlikely in the long run to profit by an academic type of education. It is also to be hoped that further progress will be made by psychologists in devising tests of special aptitudes which will help to reveal at an early age pupils of various degree of general intelligence who are likely to profit from courses with a practical as distinct from a purely bookish bias. In this way it may be possible to guide a number of highly intelligent pupils into courses which will tend ultimately to advanced technical work and to careers in industry, and so correct the present tendency which deprives industry of the services of its just and necessary quota of highly intelligent recruits.

It is clear that a great deal of experiment is necessary in order to devise suitable forms of school record cards. But such records, no matter how complete and reliable they may be made, cannot of themselves provide a final answer at age 10 or 11 to the question of the most appropriate type of secondary education for each individual. For example, the reasonable wishes of parents must be given full consideration. And when all this has been done, mistakes will still be made. It is of the utmost importance therefore that transfers from one type of secondary course to another should be made as easy as possible at any age. Administratively the best method of doing this is to organize secondary education in large multilateral schools where transfers can be made from one course to another within the one institution.

It will be interesting to watch how, under the new conditions of secondary education for all, the pupils become distributed among the various types of course that will be devised. A relatively small number, perhaps smaller than at present, will be suited by traditional grammar-school courses of an academic type; others, a much greater number than at present, will best be educated by courses of a predominantly practical nature such as have hitherto been given in junior-technical and home-training schools; some pupils, particularly girls, will be suited by courses similar to those hitherto provided in central schools with a commercial bias. There will remain many pupils, including those ordinarily classed as dull and backward, for whom practical courses will have to be devised, and in this sphere there will be scope for radical experiment by teachers not one whit less able and imaginative than those engaged in other forms of secondary education. Some teachers will continue to specialize, for example in advanced academic or technical work, or in work with dull and backward pupils, but it is to be hoped that the organization of secondary education will enable many teachers to divide their time among pupils of all grades of ability.

The case for an external examination at age 16 is not strong. It may be true that some absolute standard is necessary to decide fitness to enter upon a university course, but since only about six per cent. of grammar-school pupils go to universities, there is no need to inflict a rigid external examination with its attendant evils upon all the pupils.[1]

Standardized examinations.—A great deal of work has been

---

[1] Space does not permit a detailed discussion of possible reforms. The question is one of fundamental importance for the development of secondary education, and in so far as it concerns grammar schools it has recently been investigated by a committee under the chairmanship of Sir Cyril Norwood. This committee recommends drastic changes and suggests that after an experimental period of seven years the question of making the examination completely internal should be decided. (See the Norwood Report, *Secondary School Examinations*, H.M.S.O., 1943.) Since the Norwood Committee was appointed, however, the whole conception of secondary education has been revolutionized by the Education Act, 1944, and it seems desirable that a further investigation in the light of the new conditions should now be made.

done in recent years to determine what level of performance or knowledge the majority of children reach at various ages. A series of addition sums, for example, is given to large numbers of children and the average number of items done correctly in five minutes calculated for each age. That is to say, the test is standardized in exactly the same way as a group test of intelligence. By giving the same test under exactly the same conditions to a class of children we can quickly determine their proficiency in adding. If a boy aged 10 can score the marks which on an average are scored by boys aged 12, we may say that his mental age for arithmetical addition is 12. Using the same convention as in intelligence testing, we can calculate a mental ratio (M.R.) :

$$\frac{\text{Mental age}}{\text{Chronological age}} \times 100,$$ in this case 120. Tests in many

of the common school subjects have been standardized so that it is now possible for teachers to measure the attainments of their pupils on an absolute scale. But, as we have seen, scholastic attainment is largely dependent on inborn general ability. If, therefore, we wish to know whether an individual is up to standard, we require to measure not only his mental ratios for basic school subjects, but also his mental ratio for intelligence. A child whose I.Q. is 120 should have mental ratios of the same order for school subjects. His real achievement can only be estimated in the light of his natural ability. This achievement can be measured as an achievement ratio (A.R.) :

$$\text{A.R.} = \frac{\text{M.R. (attainments)}}{\text{M.R. (intelligence)}} \times 100.$$

Normally the achievement ratios of a child or the average achievement ratios of a class should be 100. This method of measurement gives a teacher a very useful method of determining the standard of an individual or of a class. It does not give him an absolute measure of the extent to which his pupils have been educated, for standardized tests cannot be devised to test all the results of education. There are no satisfactory tests, for example, of literary appreciation, permanence of interests and so on. Subjects like history, geography and science, which should be definitely related to the school environment and in which it is desirable to have syllabuses that reflect the special interests of the teacher, are also unsuitable for standardized testing. Perhaps the most valuable tests for practising teachers are those that relate to the more basic parts of the curriculum—arithmetic (mechanical and problematic), reading (recognition of words and comprehension), and spelling.[1] Some critics have objected that the use of such tests will tend to focus undue interest on the more mechanical aspects of education. The answer is that their use should have the opposite effect, for having found by standardized tests that the level of attainment in basic arithmetic and reading is up to average, teachers should be freed from the temptation to give undue attention to mere drill. This is particularly important at the infant and junior stages, where it is possible by intensive coaching to force young children to an unnatural standard in mechanical learning to the detriment of their subsequent education.

Diagnostic tests.—When discussing examinations we suggested that their results should be helpful to teachers as a basis for subsequent improvements in teaching. This diagnostic value of examinations has been studied particularly in America, where many tests have been published having as their express purpose the diagnosis of defects and difficulties in children's learning. The idea is one that experienced teachers are using daily. Errors in composition, difficulties in arithmetic, defects in speech—all these are noted and made the basis of specific teaching in subsequent lessons. A diagnostic test, however, is framed in such a way as to make a systematic survey of children's ability in some direction. It is of little value, for example, for a teacher

[1] Standardized tests for composition, handwriting and drawing have been prepared. As before, the test is applied to large numbers of children and median samples for each age are selected. In order to measure the attainment of a pupil, the test is given to him and a mental age is found by comparing his work with the standard samples. See *Mental and Scholastic Tests*, C. Burt (King, 1921).

to know vaguely that arithmetic in his class is weak. He therefore makes a test in which all the fundamental operations are tested in turn, and by a careful statistical scrutiny of the results he is able to determine the roots of the difficulty. He is then in a position to devise appropriate remedies. It is, however, easy to become too coldly scientific and to spend much time in detailed testing that would be better spent in vitalizing our teaching. We ought to take as far as possible a positive view of our work, to spend our energies in stimulating interest rather than in diagnosing defects. In proportion as we are successful, we shall find ourselves busy praising merit rather than detecting error, and we shall spend more time answering the questions of our pipils than in forcing our unwanted questions upon them.

OBSERVATIONS AND EXPERIMENTS

1. Observe an oral lesson and write down (a) the pupils' questions and (b) the teacher's questions.
Discuss them in the light of the principles enunciated in this chapter.

2. Set an essay to a class of children. Mark the essays according to some definite scheme. Then pass them on to a number of teachers, asking them to mark the essays independently. Discuss the results.

3. Set a class two examination papers covering as far as possible the same ground and having the same time-limit. Compose the first paper of, say, five questions requiring long answers but make the second paper a " many-little-questions " test. Compare the results. (The method of correlation (pp. 53–5) would be useful.)

4. Towards the end of a period of school practice set your class a test on some definite piece of work you have taught. Consider the results from the point of view of (a) your teaching, (b) the technique of examining.

REFERENCES FOR READING

Handbook of Suggestions, New edition, 1937. (See *Index :* Examinations.)
A Primer of Teaching Practice, Green and Birchenough, chapters XIII, XIV.
Modern Education, T. Raymont, chapter IX.
The Process of Learning, C. Bloor, chapter XII.

ADDITIONAL REFERENCES

The Approach to Teaching, H. Ward and F. Roscoe, chapter XIII (Bell, 1928).
The New Examiner, P. B. Ballard (Hodder & Stoughton, 1923).
Examinations and their Relation to Culture and Efficiency, P. J. Hartog (1918).
The Science of Marking, T. Thomas (Murray, 1930).

The Art of Interrogation, E. R. Hamilton (Kegan Paul, 1929).
The Reliability of Examinations, C. W. Valentine (Univ. Lond. Press, 1932).
The Technique of Examining Children, B. C. Wallis (Macmillan, 1927).
An English Bibliography of Examinations, 1900–32, M. C. Champneys (Macmillan, 1934).
The Selection of Children for Secondary Education, Davies and Jones (Harrap, 1936).

ESSAYS AND DISCUSSIONS

1. Discuss the following main types of classroom questions :
Questions that (*a*) pupils ask of their teachers, (*b*) teachers ask of their pupils, (*c*) teachers ask themselves, (*d*) pupils ask themselves.

2. Collect some examination papers that have been set to children. Discuss their merits and demerits.

3. Methods of selecting pupils for different types of secondary education.

4. Methods of provoking children in school to ask sensible questions.

5. Internal school examinations.
(Consider : their frequency ; oral or written according to age ; by whom should the questions be set and the answers marked ? suitable types of question for different ages ; informal tests.)

Chapter XX

PRINCIPLES, PLANS AND METHODS

A PRINCIPLE is defined in the dictionary as " a fundamental truth as basis of reasoning," " a general law as guide to action." These definitions suggest the reasons why principles have been so often referred to in previous chapters. We have been trying to give readers a basis of fundamental truth about learning and teaching that will enable them to think rationally about education. We have been trying to set forth general laws of learning and teaching that will serve as a guide to action in schools and classrooms.

Each teacher, it should be noted, must determine his own detailed plan of action by personal reflection on the principles so far as these are at present understood. There are relatively few general principles, but there are innumerable ways of putting them into practice. Principles are general and universal, but methods are particular and personal. Some study of the methods of other people is, however, useful, for it helps to elucidate the meaning of fundamental principles and it often suggests plans of action which, when suitably modified, prove to be very valuable in many different circumstances. Thus we have in this book always tried to illustrate general principles by concrete examples of classroom method, and we propose in this chapter to describe some of the more notable plans and methods that have been devised in recent years by gifted pioneer teachers.

Before doing so, it may be helpful to summarize some of the more important principles that underlie most modern developments in educational practice. A principle of education, it should be noted, is always double-edged. It refers to the children who are learning and to the teacher who is teaching. Thus, in our enunciations below, each principle has been stated in a two-fold way, first as a principle of learning and then as a correlative principle of teaching.

Some Important Principles of Education

1. Children learn through activities that derive their motive power from instinctive tendencies. Teachers should therefore teach by giving children scope for activities that appeal to their instinctive tendencies.

2. Children learn by vaguely grasping complex wholes which they subsequently analyse. Teachers should therefore teach, not by building up single isolated elements, but by presenting wholes and helping children to discover the elements in their natural settings.

3. The method and rate of learning depend upon the mental qualities of each individual. Some mental qualities are more or less common to all children, and consequently it is possible to devise some general methods of teaching that can be used for children organized in classes. In detail, however, children differ one from another—physically, temperamentally and intellectually ; it is therefore necessary to devise methods of teaching which cater for the special needs of each individual.

4. Children learn to develop their full powers only in a social atmosphere. Methods of teaching must therefore provide for some work to be done by children co-operating in groups.

Playways of Learning and Teaching

Many examples of teaching method based on these principles can be seen in every modern school to-day. Much school work appeals to instinctive interests. For example, we appeal to children's curiosity by presenting puzzles and problems, by asking arresting questions ; we appeal to their self-assertion by competitions of various kinds ; their interest in construction finds outlets in creative work of many kinds ; and so on.[1]

---

[1] A good exercise is to make a list of the instinctive tendencies of children (see Table on pp. 22–3), and then to write opposite each one as many examples as possible of ways in which they can be wisely used in connexion with school and classroom work.

Many modern methods—the project method, the sentence method of teaching reading, the topic method of teaching science, history and geography—are examples of how our second principle of starting with " wholes " is now being put into practice. The needs of individuals are being catered for in many schemes of individual work and private study. Illustrations of our fourth principle in action can be seen in many of the activities of modern schools—team games, school societies, group work.

Speaking generally, the tendency in modern schools is to devise methods that will enable children to learn with the same enthusiasm that characterizes their spontaneous play. Such methods are often called " play-ways."[1] This does not mean that they are methods that pander to children's desire to be amused or that they allow children merely to " play about." Play-way methods make use of the play-impulse, and the resulting activities are in no sense trivial ; they are serious, intense, spontaneous. They are analogous to play activities at their highest level ; they constitute work of the highest type. When learning by the play-way, children are like artists ; the distinction between play and work has disappeared. The reader will recognize that all the plans and methods described in this chapter are in reality different ways of bringing the play impulse into the service of school education.

Laughter.—Another example of the way in which instinctive tendencies are to-day used in the classroom is seen in the use made of laughter. In bygone days many efficient teachers would have been shocked to hear children laughing in school. Children learn by working, and laughter was therefore considered to be a waste of time. We now realize that laughter is one of nature's ways of removing handicaps to learning. As Lowenfeld says, " A good laugh, a piece of good-humoured horseplay at the right moment . . . dis-

[1] See *Education : Its Data and First Principles*, Sir T. Percy Nunn, chapters VII and VIII, Play and The " Play-Way " in Education.
For an example of the application of " play-way " methods to the teaching of English, see *The Play-Way*, H. Caldwell-Cook (Heinemann, 1917).

charges an overplus of energy which otherwise can only too easily hamper serious intellectual work."[1] Children who live in the company and under the direction of adults feel the need occasionally to laugh at them; such laughter " eases the strain of the child's perpetual subordination to authority and redresses the balance of superiority."[2] That is why in modern homes children have their little good-humoured jokes at the expense of their parents. It may sound alarming to say that pupils ought to feel free to laugh at their teachers, but where this is possible without children becoming conceited and without teachers feeling embarrassed, an excellent atmosphere for learning and teaching has been created. Children need some outlet to relieve their pent-up feelings, and a playful outlet such as laughter will prevent much anti-social behaviour. After a good laugh children will work with renewed zest and increased efficiency.

It would, of course, be unwise for beginners deliberately to give children excuses for laughing at them. The reading of humorous literature, the telling of a funny story, the making of a good-natured joke—these are safer means of accustoming children to laughter in the classroom, for they provoke laughter in which all can join on equal terms.

As we learned in chapter II (p. 15), children enjoy as humorous, experiences in which things go wrong. Adult sense of humour is different from that of children, but it is desirable for teachers at least to preserve some sympathy with childish humour. To be able to enjoy the irrational, instead of being irritated by it, is a passport to life[3] and we ought to be careful not to lose it. It is not easy to avoid being irritated in school and there are some occasions when irritation should be shown (see p. 186). It is very important, however, for teachers to be on their guard against developing a habit of being irritable. A sense of humour is a great help; " children and grown-ups who have laughed together

---

[1] *Play in Childhood*, p. 259 (Gollancz, 1935).
[2] *Op. cit.*, p. 261.   [3] *Op. cit.*, p. 260.

N

do not easily fall out." "Laughter is the great healer, as it is the peacemaker among peoples, and when it is not malicious it is both the creator and the outer evidence of sanity."[1]

THE MONTESSORI METHOD

The founder of this method, Dr. Maria Montessori, was an assistant doctor at the Psychiatric Clinic of the University of Rome when, about 1900, she became interested in the education of idiot children. She studied the methods of Itard and Seguin, two French doctors who were engaged in this type of work in the nineteenth century, and during the course of her work and study she became convinced that the special methods used for subnormal children were more rational than those used for normal children. In 1906 she received an invitation to organize infant schools for some model tenements in Rome. The suggestion was to gather together in a large room all the children between the ages of 3 and 7 belonging to the families in one tenement; this room was to be a " school within the house." The first of these new schools was opened in 1907 and was called " The Children's House." Thus Montessori was enabled to apply her educational principles and methods to normal children.

The idea that inspired her work was that a child " is a body which grows, and a soul which develops,—these two forms, physical and psychic, have one eternal font, life itself." It followed then that " we must neither mar nor stifle the mysterious powers which lie within these two forms of growth, but we must await from them the manifestations which we know will succeed one another."

Montessori began, therefore, by creating an environment in which children could have physical freedom. She furnished her schoolroom with portable chairs and tables, not with desks, " instruments of slavery " as she called them. Her school had a playground with space for a garden to which there was direct access from the schoolroom.

[1] *Op. cit.*, p. 280.

Next, she set to work to give the pupils spiritual freedom. She refused to admit material prizes and punishments,
for these degrade the spirit. " The prize and the punishment," she writes, " are incentives toward unnatural or
forced effort. . . . The jockey offers a piece of sugar to his
horse before jumping into the saddle, the coachman beats
his horse that he may respond to the signs given by the
reins ; and, yet, neither of these runs so superbly as the free
horse of the plains."[1] In her school the children were to
work for the joy of working. To make this possible,
Montessori provided the children with sets of didactic
materials. This material was chosen and graded after observing the types of activity that children perform spontaneously, and it was so arranged that any errors made when
using it were controlled and corrected by the material itself.
Thus the children educated themselves and the teacher was,
to a large extent, left free to observe ; she became more
of a psychologist than a teacher. " The educator," says
Montessori, " must be as one inspired by a deep *worship
of life*, and must, through this reverence, *respect*, while
he observes with human interest, the development of the
child-life."[2]

In the early stages the didactic material is designed
chiefly for the education of the senses, to which Montessori
attaches great importance. Later, graded material is provided to enable children to teach themselves reading,
writing and numeration.[3] It is not, of course, suggested
that the teacher never intervenes. It is necessary for her to
give the pupils the language they need while they are working
with the material, and to help them to acquire ideas. But
the general principle is observed—active intervention by the

[1] *The Montessori Method*, Maria Montessori, p. 21 (Heinemann, 1912).
This book contains a description of the method for children from 3 to 7
years of age. For an extension of the method for children from 7 to 11
years, see *The Advanced Montessori Method*, Vols. I and II (Heinemann, 1917).
See also *The Secret of Childhood*, Maria Montessori (Longmans, 1936).

[2] *Op. cit.*, p. 104.

[3] For a description of the didactic material and of the methods of using
it, see *The Montessori Method*, chapters XII–XIV.

teacher is limited as far as possible. When lessons are given, they are generally given unobtrusively to individuals. Such lessons are always brief and simple, and they are presented objectively, that is, in such a way that the personality of the teacher does not obtrude itself. If for any reason a lesson is unsuccessful, the teacher does not persist by repeating it, and she is careful to avoid making the child feel he has made a mistake. The teacher is confident that at the right time the child will accept the lesson; meanwhile she must be careful not to undermine his confidence.

Compared with the orthodox methods of education in vogue at the beginning of this century, the Montessori method was revolutionary, especially in its emphasis on the need for individual freedom. Consequently, its aims and methods were often misunderstood and even to this day it is popularly believed that in Montessori schools children do as they like. Nothing could be further from the truth. Social training is a cardinal feature of the method, and one of the most delightful features of a Montessori school is the consideration that its young pupils, of their own free will, give to the needs of others. As a matter of fact, the day begins with " exercises of practical life " designed to promote cleanliness, order and poise, and to encourage social conversation.

Another feature that is often overlooked is the importance that Montessori attaches to the study of nature. In discussing this question, she refers to the education of the savage of Aveyron. Abandoned in a forest, this idiot boy grew up in the natural state more like a wild animal than a man. Then he was captured by hunters and entered the civilized life of Paris. His education was undertaken by Itard, a physician interested particularly in deaf-mutes. In the forest the child " had found one happiness; he had immersed himself in, and unified himself with, nature." But socially he was a savage, and one of Itard's tasks was to teach him the restraints of social life. For example, he always ran and he had to be taught to walk. At first, Itard ran with him in the streets of Paris rather than violently check the boy's natural running gait.[1] There is a strong contrast between the life of nature and the life of society, but children must pass from one to the other. Montessori looks upon the study of nature as one means of softening the transition. Thus the garden is an important part of the educative environment in the Montessori method. Here children learn to observe the phenomena of life ; they receive practical lessons in the need for foresight and patience ; gradually they acquire " a peaceful equilibrium of conscience, and absorb the first germs of that wisdom which so characterized the tillers of the soil in the time when they still kept their primitive simplicity."[2] Closely allied to these gardening activities are the manual activities of moulding clay into vases and bricks. " Thus the age of childhood epitomizes the principal primitive labours of humanity, when the human race, changing from the nomadic to the stable condition, demanded of the earth its fruit, built itself shelter, and devised vases to cook the foods yielded by the fertile earth.'[3]

It is, of course, impossible in this short note to give any adequate idea of the Montessori method, but it will have served its purpose if it reveals some of the inspiring principles that underlie it and if it corrects some of the popular misconceptions about it. To sum up in the words of its originator, the method aims at substituting " for the critical and sermonizing teacher a rational organization of work and of liberty for the child. It involves a conception of life more usual in religious fields than in those of academic pedagogy, inasmuch as it has recourse to the spiritual energies of mankind, but it is founded on work and on liberty, which are the two paths to all civic progress."[4]

---

[1] As Montessori says : " The gradual and gentle leading of the savage through all the manifestations of social life, the early adaptation of the teacher to the pupil rather than of the pupil to the teacher, the successive attraction to a new life which was to win over the child by its charms, and not be imposed upon him violently, so that the pupil should feel it as a burden and a torture, are as many precious educative expressions which may be generalized and applied to the education of children." (*Op. cit.*, p. 153.)

[2] *Op. cit.*, p. 160.   [3] *Op. cit.*, p. 167.   [4] *Op. cit.*, p. 372.

THE DECROLY METHOD

Like Montessori, Decroly first became interested in education through teaching defectives. He was a physician in Brussels, where in 1901 he founded a school for defectives. In 1907 he established a school for normal children so that he could apply to their education the principles he had formulated as a result of his experience in his special school. The Decroly School is co-educational; boys and girls begin at the age of 4 and remain until they leave school about 15. The Decroly Method, as practised in this school, has proved so successful that it has since been adopted in many classes of the elementary schools of Brussels.

The fundamental idea of the Decroly Method is that children " learn through living." To make this possible, Decroly recommends that schools should be located in natural surroundings where children can observe the phenomena of nature and the manifestations of life in plants, animals and man himself. The classrooms should be equipped and furnished as laboratories or studios and not as auditoriums. The classes should not exceed 20, or at the most 25 pupils.

In a Decroly class the first part of the morning is devoted to work in the techniques of language and number, such work largely taking the form of competitive games. Then follow lessons in observation, comparison and association, together with such practical subjects as handwork, singing, drawing and physical games. The afternoons are devoted to manual work and to foreign languages. On certain mornings, visits are made to various places of educational interest.

A special feature of the scheme is the organization of the subject-matter of the curriculum as a " programme of associated ideas." The curriculum has two main branches —(a) a study of living creatures including man, and (b) a study of the surrounding universe including society. These studies are pursued, not by studying a number of isolated academic subjects, but by exploring a number of important " centres of interest." For example, the pupils study the following primary needs that have always exerted the widest influence on society :

(a) Food.
(b) Protection against the elements.
(c) Defence against dangers and enemies.
(d) Activities such as work and recreation.

The centre of this course of study is the child himself, so that the work begins by direct observation. Work in number is classified as observation. This method tends to prevent too much emphasis being placed on those branches of the curriculum that can be taught verbally. Verbal instruction is, of course, necessary in order to extend the children's knowledge to facts not directly accessible to them in time and space. These facts are, however, made meaningful by being compared and associated with the facts learnt by direct observation. In this way the chief danger of verbal instruction is avoided. Finally the study is completed by some form of expression of which Decroly recognizes two kinds :

(a) Concrete expression, such as model making and drawing.
(b) Abstract expression, such as reading, speaking and writing.

The techniques of reading, writing and spelling are not considered to be the most important part of education in early years ; they are taught as part of the general experience provided by the centres of interest. The results of observation are summarized in short sentences. It is then necessary for the children to read and record these sentences ; they attempt to do so and in this way they are introduced to the techniques of reading, writing and spelling. Thus they learn to write by writing sentences in which they are interested ; they do not begin by laboriously copying isolated elements or even letters. They learn to read in a similar way by tackling a meaningful whole. The analysis into words, syllables and letters comes later. Special lessons are necessary to give children adequate practice and to assist the analytic process ; these, as we have seen, are given each morning and take the form of games.

Much importance is attached in the Decroly School to social training. Good and bad marks are not used, and " comparisons are never made between a child and his fellows. He is compared only with himself, with his own record, which he is constantly trying to improve."[1] The school is organized as a miniature community and the children are left as free as possible, for " it is by learning to act on their own initiative, not by quiescence, that children prepare themselves for the demands of life." " Recognizing this," says Hamäide, one of Decroly's collaborators, " we do not check their spontaneous activity, nor do we impose on them action in accordance with our own desires. Discipline for our children is the outcome of their activities, of their work, of their own necessities. It is not associated with immobility, passivity, and obedience."[2]

THE MASON METHOD

This method is named after its author, Miss Charlotte Mason, the founder of the Parents' National Educational Union. This union exists for the benefit of parents and teachers of all classes ; it supervises a school, the House of Education in Ambleside, and by means of correspondence it enables schools elsewhere to use the curriculum, methods and examinations which it arranges. The method is therefore often called the P.N.E.U. method. The following is a summary of its underlying principles :[3]

Children are born persons, neither good nor bad, but with possibilities for good and for evil. Authority and obedience are necessary, but the personalities of the children

[1] *The Decroly Class*, A. Hamäide, p. 98 (Dent, 1925).
[2] *Op. cit.*, pp. 96–7.
[3] See *An Essay Towards a Philosophy of Education*, Charlotte M. Mason (Kegan Paul, 1925).

must not be encroached upon " by the direct use of fear or love, suggestion or influence, or by undue play upon any one natural desire." The three legitimate instruments of education are : (a) the atmosphere of environment, (b) the discipline of habit, and (c) the presentation of living ideas. A child's mind is not a receptacle for holding isolated facts but a " spiritual organism, with an appetite for all knowledge." Knowledge should be presented so that children can grasp the relations between facts ; if this is done and if the knowledge is various, so that monotony is avoided, children need and welcome a great deal. Their minds, no less than their bodies, need sustenance. We provide children with a varied diet ; they eat and drink and their bodies assimilate what is necessary. Similarly, we should provide children with a broad and generous curriculum ; they will then study and learn, and their minds will assimilate knowledge according to their needs.

On the practical side the method has several very interesting features. Much importance is attached to learning from books written in good literary style, for it is believed that children attend naturally to what is conveyed in literary form. In fact, it is claimed that a *single* reading or hearing should be insisted on. If children are trained in this way, they attend naturally with great concentration. If, on the other hand, passages are re-read, paraphrased, summarized, and made the subject of questions, the natural ability of children to concentrate is dissipated. The method obviously puts the responsibility of learning on the pupils, who are expected to do the work by self-effort. The teacher does not, of course, always stand aside ; in addition to giving sympathy, it is occasionally necessary for him to elucidate, sum up or enlarge. Generally speaking, however, " the teacher who allows his scholars the freedom of the city of books is at liberty to be their guide, philosopher and friend ; and is no longer the mere instrument of forcible intellectual feeding."[1] Furthermore, " marks, prizes, places, rewards, punishments, praise, blame, or other inducements are not

[1] *Op. cit.*, p. 32.

N*

necessary to secure attention, which is voluntary, immediate and surprisingly perfect."[1] The method of a single reading or telling is not applicable to what are called " disciplinary subjects, such as Mathematics and Grammar " ; in these, it is considered that success depends largely on the power of the teacher, though it is obviously a great advantage to be teaching children who have developed a habit of attending closely. In order to help children to assimilate what they have heard or read, they are required, after the single presentation, to tell it back or to write on some prescribed part. The children read so much that there is no time for revision, but this is found to be unnecessary, for " what the children have read they know, and write on any part of it with ease and fluency, in vigorous English."[2] Acting on these principles and methods, Mason says they find that " the educability of children is enormously greater than has hitherto been supposed, and is but little dependent on such circumstances as heredity and environment."

Another important feature of the method is the direct training that the children receive in the arts of " moral and intellectual self-management." On the moral side they are taught to use their wills. The first step is to distinguish between " I want " and " I will." If these are in conflict, the children are told that the best way of helping the will to prevail is to divert their minds temporarily from the struggle by doing something quite different, something that they find entertaining or interesting. Then they can return to the conflict with will-power invigorated. Children are thus trained, as they become mature enough to understand such teaching, to accept responsibility for determining their own conduct. Of course, they sometimes experience failure, but this is a necessary part of the training and teachers should not try to shield children from such experience by using extraneous aids. The use of suggestion, for example, as an aid to the will is deprecated, " as tending to stultify and stereotype character." On the intellectual side, children are warned not to trust too confidently to

[1] *Op. cit.*, p. 7.　　　　[2] *Op. cit.*, p. 6.

their own understanding. While reason may be an infallible guide in solving a mathematical problem, it may be a very unsafe guide when deciding an ethical problem. Whether a line of conduct be right or wrong, we tend to confirm our own wishes by irrefragable proofs. Mason considers that children should be made conscious of the dangers of prejudice, and in order to help them further she recommends that they should be given principles of conduct. " These principles," she says, " should save children from some of the loose thinking and heedless action which cause most of us to live at a lower level than we need."[1]

THE DALTON LABORATORY PLAN

The Dalton Laboratory Plan is named after Dalton, a town in Massachusetts, where in the High School it was first tried on a large scale. Its author, Miss Helen Parkhurst, was a teacher who began work in a rural school with forty pupils organized in eight classes. She was thus forced at the beginning of her career to abandon class teaching and to consider how school work could be organized to keep every pupil busy.

After experience in various types of school and in a training college, Parkhurst was profoundly influenced, in 1908, by reading Swift's book, *Mind in the Making*. " The didactic method," wrote Swift, " belongs to the Middle Ages. It still dominates our schools, though the conditions that · made it serviceable have long since passed. Mental expansion of the teachers themselves is the first step towards removing this mediæval debris. They will then investigate their pupils, the schoolroom will become an educational laboratory, and activity will not be limited to the manual training department. . . .

" . . . Economy of energy is quite as truly a problem for education as for mechanics. Efficiency—the ratio of useful work to the energy spent in accomplishing it—may be increased by lessening the resistance, or by applying more

[1] *Op. cit.*, p. xxxi.

power, and teachers have occupied themselves too exclusively with producing power."

In 1911 Parkhurst drafted a plan of work for children from 8 to 12 years of age to be carried out, not in a conventional classroom, but in an educational laboratory. Gradually the time-table was abolished and the children were organized in groups with a free choice of work in a number of laboratories. In 1914 Parkhurst visited Italy, where she studied the Montessori Method, and for several years she was interested in promoting this method in America. In 1919 she had the opportunity of resuming her experiments with the " laboratory " plan in a school for crippled boys, and in 1920 she began to apply it in Dalton High School. Parkhurst attaches importance to the use of the word " laboratory." " I cling to it," she writes, " in the hope that it may gradually shift the educational point of view away from the atmosphere of prejudice and moribund theories which the word ' school ' calls up in our minds. Let us think of school rather as a sociological laboratory where the pupils themselves are the experimenters, not the victims of an intricate and crystallized system in the evolution of which they have neither part nor lot. Let us think of it as a place where community conditions prevail as they prevail in life itself."[1]

The main principles underlying the Dalton Plan are freedom and co-operation. The pupils are free to continue without interruption the work in which they are absorbed unhampered by time-tables. The conditions of school life encourage the pupils to behave as members of a social community ; their lives are not ruled by arbitrary authority.

In practice the essence of the plan consists in giving each pupil a written statement of the work to be done and leaving him free to do it in his own way and at his own rate. The year's work in each subject is divided into monthly " contracts " or " assignments," and each contract is subdivided into daily units of work. Each classroom becomes a " laboratory " for a special subject and it is presided over

[1] *Education on the Dalton Plan*, Helen Parkhurst, pp. 13–14 (Bell, 1922).

by the specialist teacher. In small schools one room is used for two or more subjects. Each pupil is then free, subject to certain inevitable restrictions, to tackle his contract in his own way. At any particular time he is free to choose his subject for study so long as the subject-room in which he desires to work is not already full. He may elect to begin his month's work by concentrating on one subject, say mathematics, to the neglect of other subjects. When he has completed the mathematics contract for the month he is not allowed, however, to proceed to the second month's work in mathematics until he has completed the first month's work in all the other subjects. Thus with the advice of teachers if necessary, each pupil is trained to apportion his time suitably. He spends more time on his weak subjects than his strong ones ; he works according to an individual time-table arranged to suit his own particular needs. A graphical record of progress is kept so that each pupil can see at a glance those aspects of his total programme that need special effort. Group work is encouraged if a number of pupils in one room happen to be working at the same stage. Much of the teaching is given to individuals and arises out of the pupil's efforts to complete his assignment. Some group lessons, called " conferences," are, however, given in order to elucidate general difficulties or to give a general survey of a new topic.

" In this manner a pupil advances steadily, job by job, through the curriculum. If in a school year of nine or ten months he only finishes eight jobs on account of absence or illness, he begins the ninth job in the following year. The clever child may, on the contrary, accomplish in one year the work mapped out to cover eighteen months. Often the slow, apparently less intelligent, child gains in rapidity, and in any case he builds well and soundly at his own natural rate."[1]

[1] *Op. cit.*, p. 36. For information on the Dalton Plan, see also : *The Dalton Laboratory Plan*, Evelyn Dewey (Dent, 1922) ; *Individual Work and The Dalton Plan*, A. J. Lynch (Philip, 1924) ; *The Triumph of the Dalton Plan*, C. W. Kimmins and Belle Rennie (Ivor Nicholson & Watson Ltd., 1932). The address of the Dalton Association is 35 Cromwell Gardens, London, S.W.7

The Winnetka Plan

This plan, originated by Dr. Carleton Washburne, Superintendent of Schools in Winnetka, U.S.A., is based on the following principles :

(*a*) Every child should master those facts and skills that he will probably need to use in life.

(*b*) Every child should live naturally, happily, and fully as a child.

(*c*) Human progress depends on the development of each individual to his full capacity.

(*d*) The welfare of human society requires the development of a strong social consciousness in each individual.[1]

The curriculum is accordingly divided into two parts, the first part common to all, the second part based on individual interests. The time of each school session is divided equally between the two types of work. The essential facts and skills have been determined by investigations, and research is also being done to discover at what stage of a child's development each item can be most effectively learnt. All children are required to master the first part of the curriculum, but they are not expected to do so at the same rate. The work is carefully graded in well-defined steps so that each child can work individually, proceeding from step to step by means of self-instructive, self-corrective teaching materials. The text-books, for example, are arranged in steps, and answers to examples are provided so that children can mark their own work. For each main section of the course a special diagnostic test has been prepared. The results of this test are marked by the teacher, and a child is required to obtain 100 per cent. in it before he begins the next section. If he makes an error of any kind he is given special practice on that particular point.

The first part of the curriculum includes arithmetic,

---

[1] See *Towards a New Education*, edited by Wm. Boyd, p. 173 (Knopf, 1930). *Adjusting the School to the Child*, C. W. Washburne (Harrap, 1932).

language, reading, spelling, general science and social studies. The essential facts connected with the social studies (history and geography) are learnt individually, but each new topic is introduced by a class discussion. The social studies also overflow into the second part of the curriculum, which consists of group and creative activities, in which children are not expected to be alike, and on which they are not tested or marked.

A special technique has been developed in order to prepare children for creative activities. Expression is not obtained by merely leaving children free " to express themselves." Thorough preparation is necessary, for expression in the Winnetka schools is considered to be " the overflow of rich experiences "; it springs from " a background of information, imagery and feeling," and this background is given by the intensive study of one topic for several weeks. Not until the children are full to overflowing with a feeling for the topic are they considered to be ready to choose some creative activity. The types of activity chosen are various ; children may choose, for example, to make a model, to transform the classroom into a Viking banqueting hall, or to write and produce a play. In addition to these activities, which are stimulated by teaching, provision is made for hobby-activities ; for children of 12 to 13 there may be " twenty or thirty different electives, such as art metal craft, pottery, woodworking, printing, journalism, dramatics, orchestra, as well as academic electives in advanced arithmetic or perhaps Esperanto."[1] The group work in this second part of the curriculum includes such activities as team games and the appreciation of music and literature.

The schools in Winnetka are run on self-governing lines. Committees of pupils are set up to take charge of such departments as the school museum, the library, athletic events, the distribution of school supplies. Every pupil serves on some committee.

An important feature of this plan is the attention that is paid to research. There is a department of educational

[1] *Op. cit.*, p. 178.

counsel that corresponds to what is generally called a child-guidance clinic. Each school building has the services of a psychiatric social worker, and the part-time services of a psychiatrist, a psychologist, and a physician. This department deals with difficult children, and it not only gives advice on the treatment of individuals, but it also influences the general policy of schools with a view to preventing children from becoming so difficult as to need special treatment.

The department of research co-operates with teachers in their investigations into school administration, curriculum content and methods of teaching; it also assists teachers in their efforts to evaluate the results of the plan. Thus the Winnetka Plan is not in any sense a finished product but is being continually modified in the light of research and experience.[1]

THE WORK OF SANDERSON OF OUNDLE

It must not be thought that all experimental work designed to apply modern principles of education results in some plan or method to which a specific label can be attached. There are many pioneer schools and classes which are not following any single "method," but which are making valuable contributions to the improvement of educational practice. This fact is clearly illustrated by the work of Sanderson, who was headmaster of Oundle School from 1892 until his death in 1922.

Sanderson began his professional career as a "student teacher" in a village school. Later, he studied theology and mathematics at Durham University, mathematics and science at Cambridge, and then he became senior physics master at Dulwich. At the age of 35 he was appointed headmaster of Oundle, where he found a school of less than a hundred boys. H. G. Wells, in a graphic description of the school at that time, sums up the state of affairs thus: "From the sunshine and reality of the swimming-pool,

[1] *Op. cit.*, pp. 173–80.

the boats, the cricket or football field, the boys came back into the ill-ventilated classrooms to pretend, or not even to pretend, an interest in languages not merely dead, but now, through a process of derivation and imitation from one generation to another, excessively decayed. The memory of school taken into after life from these establishments was a memory of going from games and sunshine and living interest into classrooms of twilight, bad air, and sham enthusiasm for exhausted things."[1]

Sanderson first instituted reforms in the teaching of mathematics and science. Very soon " the work ceased to have the form of a line of boys all racing to acquire an identical parcel of knowledge, and took on the form more and more of clusters of boys surrounding an attractive problem. There grew up out of the school Science a periodic display, the Science Conversazione, in which groups of youngsters displayed experiments and collections they had co-operated to produce."[2]

The group system of work next spread to other departments of school life. Plays were no longer studied by bored classes from annotated editions ; they were acted, and questions of language and interpretation were dealt with in relation to the production. In order to give all boys a share, groups of boys were cast for each part. Similar changes were introduced into the study of literary and historical work. After a preliminary survey of a new section under the direction of a master, the class was divided into groups, each with a problem to study. The school library became for these subjects what the laboratories and workshops were for science and mathematics.

Sanderson did not introduce group work merely because it increased interest in study, but also because he believed in the importance of creative and co-operative work as a preparation for real life. He wanted his boys to go out

---

[1] *The Story of a Great Schoolmaster*, H. G. Wells, pp. 27–8 (Chatto & Windus, 1924). For a fuller account of Sanderson's work, see the Official Life : *Sanderson of Oundle* (Chatto & Windus, 1923).

[2] *Op. cit.*, pp. 40–1.

"into the factory, or mine, or business, or profession, imbued with the spirit of the active love of humanity."[1] In his view schools should be copies in miniature of the world as we would love it to be. "We should, in fact, direct school life so that the spirit of it may be the spirit which will teach to alleviate social and industrial conditions."[2]

Sanderson attached great importance to science, but again he looked beyond the mere acquisition of an interesting store of knowledge. "It is not sufficient to say that Science should be taught in schools. . . . We claim that scientific thought should be the inspiring spirit in school life. Science is essentially creative and co-operative, its outlook is onward towards change, it means searching for the truth, it demands research and experiment, and does not rest on authority. Under this new spirit all history, literature, art and even languages, should be re-written."[3]

Education, as Sanderson conceived it, would need a new type of school building and equipment. Spacious workshops would to a large extent take the place of classrooms, and in the category of workshops he included well-stocked libraries, art rooms, music rooms and theatres. "This is not a Utopian scheme," he declared, "but one within possibility in town and country. To each large central high school should be associated groups of elementary schools, and there should be free highways between them, neither barred by examinations nor barred by expense."

Finally, Sanderson conceived the idea of a House of Vision, a beautiful building in which all the activities of this ideal school were to be represented. It was to contain records of man's great deeds and of man's progress, and the record of his needs, but it was to be something more than a museum. "In it the individual boy was to realize the aim of the school and of schooling and living. It was to be the eye of the school, its soul, its headlight."[4] This idea was never successfully realized, for it was still growing in his mind when he died. But, says H. G. Wells, "I know

[1] *Op. cit.*, p. 119.
[2] *Op. cit.*, p. 60.
[3] *Op. cit.*, p. 100.
[4] *Op. cit.*, pp. 116–17.

surely that neither Sanderson nor his House of Vision are in any real sense dead at all. A day will certainly come when his name will be honoured above all other contemporary schoolmasters as the precursor of a new age in education and human affairs. In that age of realization every village will be dominated by its school, with its library and theatre, its laboratories and gymnasium, every town will converge upon its cluster of schools and colleges, its research buildings and the like, and it will have its Great Chapel, its House of Vision, as its crown and symbol, even as the cathedral was the crown and symbol of the being and devotion of the medieval city. And therein Sanderson's stout hopefulness and pioneer thrustings will be kept in remembrance by generations that have come up to the pitch of understanding him."[1]

CONCLUSION

We have tried in this chapter, within the limits of a few pages, to give a fair description of some recent plans and methods that are influencing current practice in schools. It is necessary, in conclusion, to give a few warnings.

First, the reader is warned that the descriptions he has read are inadequate to give a complete conception of any of the plans. They are intended to arouse interest, to provoke further study from the books to which reference has been made, and to encourage readers to visit, if possible, schools where the plans are in operation.[2]

Our second warning is against over-emphasizing the modernity of "new" plans and methods. The educational movements we have reviewed all belong to the twentieth century, but it is helpful to realize that they all have their roots in the past, and that they all owe something to the work of pioneer educators who lived and worked in times gone by. The idea of learning in a play-way is, for example,

---

[1] *Op. cit.*, pp. 125–6.
[2] For descriptions of experimental schools, see *Schools of To-morrow*, J. and E. Dewey (Dent, 1915); *The Modern Schools Handbook*, edited T. Blewitt (Gollancz, 1934).

found in the writings of many educationists. Plato (420–348 B.C.), in the *Republic*, tells us that " knowledge which is acquired under compulsion obtains no hold on the mind." " Then do not use compulsion," he says, " but let early education be a sort of amusement ; you will then be better able to find out the natural bent." (Quintilian (A.D.35–95), in his educational classic, *Institutes of the Orator*, calls attention to the value of physical play as a mode of relaxation and also as a means of revealing children's temper and moral character. He suggests that ardour in play is some indication of a child's disposition for study, which in his opinion should be pursued without any need for corporal punishment. The whipping of children he describes as " mean, servile, and a gross affront," and he gives it as his opinion that the scholar's punishment is most commonly caused by the master's neglect. Locke (1632–1704) emphasizes the need for developing bodies and minds able to endure hardships. This is not, however, to be achieved by harsh methods. For example, in his *Essay on Human Understanding* he writes, " He that has found a way how to keep up a child's spirit, easy, active and free, and yet at the same time to restrain him from many things he has a mind to, and to draw him to things that are uneasy to him ; he, I say, that knows how to reconcile these seeming contradictions, has, in my opinion, got the true secret of education." In his *Thoughts Concerning Education* he suggests that reading should be taught in play, and French should be taught by what we now call the Direct Method, " by talking it into children in constant conversation, and not by grammatical rules." Thus the way is prepared for modern views and we come to Froebel (1782–1852), who, in his *Education of Man*, sets forth the philosophic significance of play and also suggests methods by which the spirit of play can be brought into the classroom. " Play," he writes, " is the highest phase of child-development—of human development at this period ; for it is self-active representation of the inner—representation of the inner from inner necessity and impulse. Play is the purest, most spiritual activity of man at this stage, and, at the same time, typical of human life as a whole—of the inner hidden natural life in man and all things. It gives, therefore, joy, freedom, contentment, inner and outer rest, peace with the world. It holds the source of all that is good."

It is both salutary and refreshing for students of education (and this term should include all practising teachers) to turn aside occasionally from modern plans and methods, and to read some of the educational classics ;[1] or alternatively to study books that deal with the evolution of educational ideas.[2]

Our third warning is that the descriptions of the modern plans and methods given in this chapter are uncritical. This does not mean that they are all unreservedly recommended in every detail. Such a recommendation would, in fact, be absurd, for in some respects the methods tend to cancel out. It cannot be too strongly emphasized that every teacher, when confronted with an enthusiast's description of a modern method, should approach the method critically, seeking to discover both its merits and its defects. He should beware of being unduly biased by the professional prestige that the enthusiast may possess, but he should also beware of reacting too violently in the opposite direction. It is true, on the other hand, that schools have in the past suffered from " stunts " (often purveyed by inspectors, as many would say) ; such " stunts " have been accepted too readily and uncritically by earnest teachers. But it is equally true, on the other hand, that many schools are suffering because they are clinging stubbornly to methods that now have little to recommend them. There are teachers who are continually running after something novel, but there are others who are equally ready to denounce any idea that they have not heard of before. To the first type of teacher we would say that current educational practice is the result

[1] For a short list of educational classics, see Appendix B, p. 438.
[2] For example, see *The Evolution of Educational Theory*, J. Adams (Macmillan, 1912) ; *The Growth of Freedom in Education*, W. J. McCallister (Constable, 1931).

of the experience of many thoughtful teachers over a long period of years and that it cannot all be wrong. But we would remind the second type of teacher that traditional practice tends to outlive its usefulness ; methods that were necessary for classes of eighty may be neither necessary nor desirable for classes of thirty ; the average school is now very different from what it was even thirty years ago, and it is most unlikely that schools thirty years hence will be as they are to-day.

A sane, balanced attitude of mind, tolerant and receptive on the one hand, cautious and critical on the other hand, would help to solve many problems in school, particularly the problem that sometimes arises from a conflict of views between a young teacher and an experienced head teacher. There are, of course, many honourable exceptions, but on the whole we tend to be enthusiastic for change and reform and to undervalue tradition when we are young, and we tend to become hidebound as we grow old. This is a fact of which we ought all, young and old alike, to keep re-minding ourselves. Every young teacher should begin his career ready to learn from experienced craftsmen ; every head teacher should be equally ready to learn something even from his youngest recruit.

In conclusion, we should remember that

> " It takes the ideal to blow a hair's breadth off
> The dust of the actual."

It is therefore necessary for some teachers to be " mad " pioneers, for some schools to be " crank " schools ; and none of us can afford to disdain or neglect these modern movements. At the same time we must not allow ourselves to be stampeded by them. Most of us must, perhaps, pursue a relatively unspectacular path in school and class-room, but we should all nevertheless be alive to the educational movements going on around us,

> " Not clinging to some ancient saw,
> Not mastered by some modern term,
> Not swift nor slow to change, but firm."

OBSERVATIONS AND EXPERIMENTS

All teachers, whether experienced or in training, should occasionally pay visits of observation to schools where experimental methods are being tried. Some Local Educational Authorities make special provision to enable their teachers to do this.

The field of educational research is one that deserves the attention of practising teachers. Post-graduate courses in educational research are now arranged by the education departments of most universities. From time to time, the Ministry of Education and L.E.A.'s make special inquiries and surveys. The Education Act 1944, provides that " there shall be two Central Advisory Councils for Education, one for England and the other for Wales and Monmouthshire, and it shall be the duty of these Councils to advise the Minister upon such matters connected with educational theory and practice as they think fit, and upon any questions referred to them by him." In addition, research is fostered by the following associations :

Educational Research Foundation. Secretary, A. Lea Perkins, University of London Institute of Education, London, W.C. 1.

Scottish Council for Research in Education, 47 Moray Place, Edinburgh.

The British Psychological Society (Education Section), 55 Russell Square, London, W.C. 1.

Reports of educational experiments in this country are published in most educational journals, and particularly in *The British Journal of Educational Psychology*, published jointly by the British Psychological Society and the Training College Association (Editor, Professor C. W. Valentine, The University, Birmingham).

REFERENCES FOR READING

Education, Sir T. Percy Nunn, chapter VIII.
Experimental Education, R. R. Rusk.

ADDITIONAL REFERENCES

Modern Developments in Educational Practice, J. Adams (Univ. Lond. Press, 1922).
Research in Education, R. R. Rusk (Univ. Lond. Press, 1932).
See also the books referred to in footnotes to this chapter.

ESSAYS AND DISCUSSIONS

Discussions of new methods are generally most fruitful if they are opened by individuals who have special knowledge gained either by the study of books or by first-hand observations and experience.

The suggestions that follow are suggestive rather than exhaustive :

1. Note and discuss some of the arresting declarations made by pioneer educators, e.g. :

(*a*) " I soon perceived that children were well equipped to deal with ideas, and that explanations, questioning, amplifications are unnecessary and wearisome. Children have a natural appetite for knowledge which is informed with thought . . . the whole intellectual apparatus of the teacher, his power of vivid presentation, apt illustration, able summing up, subtle questioning, all these were hindrances." (*An Essay Towards a Philosophy of Education,* C. Mason, pp. 10–11.)

(b) " The school should be a place where a boy comes not to learn but to create." (*Sanderson of Oundle*, p. 325.)

(c) " The main purpose of a school is not to teach but to open the vision of the boys to the condition and needs of man ; that they may know something of the evolution of man's soul and spirit, and the drift of his thoughts and ideals." (*Sanderson of Oundle*, pp. 325–6.)

(d) " To-day we hold the pupils in school, restricted by those instruments so degrading to body and spirit,—the desk and material prizes and punishments. Our aim is to reduce them to the discipline of immobility and silence,—to lead them,—where ? Far too often towards no definite end." (*The Montessori Method*, pp. 26–7.)

2. The bearing of new plans and methods on the education of dull and backward children.

3. Compare and contrast the Montessori and the Decroly methods of teaching reading and writing.

4. A teacher has full charge of a class in an orthodox, conventional school. What innovations, based on the plans and methods described in this chapter, can he introduce ?

5. Sanderson's House of Vision.
(Consider whether such a building is (a) practicable, (b) desirable.)

6. Schools in A.D. 2000.
(Consider : school buildings and environment ; curriculum ; methods.)

Chapter XXI

WORK AND FATIGUE

We have had occasion several times in this book to call attention to the intimate relation that exists between mind and body. It is now universally recognized that not only has general bodily health a direct influence on mental activity but that mental activity also reacts on bodily health. The word "disease" itself, "*dis-ease*," in fact carries with it some suggestion of this kind, and medical science has probably a great deal yet to learn about the part that the mind plays in causing bodily disease. A child, we must reiterate, is a whole person, a body-mind or a mind-body according to the emphasis of the moment. When mind and body are in perfect harmony the child is in a state of health, i.e. of "wholth" or "wholeness"; he is not suffering from any "dis-ease."

As practical teachers, we are particularly interested in health from the point of view of output of work. We want to know under what conditions body and mind function most efficiently. Some of these conditions are mainly subjective, such as the pupil's happiness and readiness to work; others are mainly objective, such as good ventilation and lighting. All these conditions, whether subjective or objective, affect the worker in mind and body. The importance of subjective conditions is borne out by the results of research into the causes of mental breakdown. Only a small percentage are found to be due to overwork. In the majority of cases the cause is some personal unhappiness or emotional conflict. In fact, where the whole personality is in harmony there is little danger of overwork. Throughout this book we have been dealing for the most part with the subjective conditions favourable to effective work. In this chapter we shall consider especially the more objective conditions. This aspect of the subject can best be approached by means of a simple experiment :

Provide each subject with some columns of newspaper containing solid blocks of printed material. At the word " Go " the subjects cross out certain letters, say, all the a's and e's as fast as they can. This work is continued for ten minutes, a line being drawn on the paper to mark each minute's work. For this purpose the time must be called out at the expiration of each minute : " one minute ; two minutes ; . . . nine minutes, one more to go." A rest of,

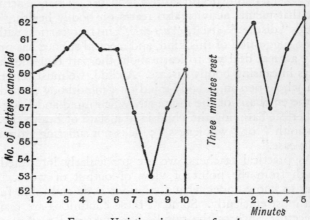

FIG. 4.—Variations in output of work.

say, three minutes follows. Then a five-minute work period of the same nature is given as before. It will be noticed that the subjects are definitely told when they have only one more minute to go.

When the results for a number of subjects are averaged and plotted on squared paper, it will be found that the work curve is similar in form to that shown in Fig. 4.

This graph, obtained by averaging the performances of ten subjects, shows the usual variations. Owing to individual differences (temperamental and other) the graphs for individual subjects are not always of this form. Some individuals, for example, start with a spurt and show the effects of fatigue very soon. Others improve steadily and do not show the effects of fatigue in such a short period as ten minutes. There will also be large individual differences in the amount of " work " done by different subjects.

Experiments under laboratory and industrial conditions with many varied kinds of " work " have shown that work curves, as a rule, exhibit the characteristics revealed in our simple experiment, viz.,

1. At first the rate of work is relatively slow, but it gradually increases to a maximum. This is due partly to practice. It cannot be wholly explained as a practice effect, however, for a similar initial increase in efficiency is generally found even when the work is of a very familiar nature. It is seen in our work curves, for example, when the subject starts afresh after a rest. The usual explanation is that, when work is started, human beings, like engines, need an initial " warming up " period before maximum efficiency is attained. Another factor is the need for time to settle down to the work in hand, to become oblivious of external distractions.

2. After a time the rate of work decreases ; a result, as we say, of fatigue.

3. When the end of the task is in sight, the rate increases as a result of a final spurt.

4. After a rest the worker starts off again at a higher rate, and the same cycle of events is repeated. Generally speaking, however, the short rest does not wholly obliterate the fatigue effect of the first work period.

Similar variations in the output of work occur in school, and it will now be helpful to consider separately each of the four facts mentioned above,—warming-up periods, fatigue, spurts and rests.

WARMING UP AND SETTLING DOWN

The phenomenon of " warming up " has several points of application to school work. It is part explanation of the slowness of children on Mondays and on the first few days after a long holiday. It is also a factor in determining which are the most effective work periods in a school day. Children's efficiency is probably at its maximum each session shortly after the opening of school when they have had time to settle down. The need for " warming up " and " settling down " further shows itself in individual lesson periods, and though one important function of teachers is to train children in the habit of getting quickly " off the mark," it is also necessary for us to be aware that most children, as also we ourselves, need a little time to get under way.

FATIGUE

Fatigue is a term used to cover a number of factors which have this in common—they all produce some abnormality in the output of work. This abnormality consists in an increased variability in output usually accompanied by a decrease in amount, but sometimes with certain kinds of work and with neurotic people for example, the variability may actually be accompanied by an increase in output. The first type of disturbance may be called *physiological fatigue*, for it is due to the presence of toxic products in the blood and muscles. One result of strenuous physical activity is to increase the production of lactic acid so quickly that the normal rate of oxidation is insufficient to remove it, and the worker is forced to slow down his rate of work, both physical and mental. This is probably the chief objective cause of decreased work capacity. It used to be thought that fatigue was due, partly at least, to some kind of exhaustion of nerve tissue, but recent experiment has shown that so long as a nerve is, by suitable washing, kept free from the poisonous products of its activity, there is no observable diminution in its capacity to respond to a stimulus. That is to say, nerves are not directly subject to fatigue. The crux of the problem of physiological fatigue is the removal of excess of lactic acid by an increase in the rate of oxidation. Thus it is important to ensure an adequate supply of oxygen for children engaged in classroom work. There are two methods—good ventilation and suitable physical exercise. The importance of physical exercise in helping children to withstand the onset of fatigue is not always appreciated. Its effect is described as follows by one investigator : " It increases lung capacity, induces a slow pulse rate, increases the stroke volume of the heart, reduces systemic blood pressure during work, and probably greatly increases the capillary diffusion area in the muscles as it does in the lungs."[1] The effect of increasing the time given to physical exercises, at the expense of time usually given to academic subjects, has recently been investigated in a boys' secondary school. Two forms, equal in ability and attainments, were arranged.[2] One form, called the control form, spent the normal time on physical exercises, viz. a weekly period of 45 minutes plus a games period. The other form received six weekly periods of 45 minutes plus an afternoon for games. The results at the end of two terms were very striking. The boys in the experimental class not only increased in height, weight and chest capacity more than the boys in the control class but they also more than held their own in academic subjects, while as judged by group intelligence tests they actually appeared to have become brighter. The daily lesson in physical training now advocated appears to be sound policy not only in the interests of physical development but also in the interests of mental hygiene. The old-fashioned device of an occasional minute of brisk physical exercise in the classroom was probably also not without value. It should be noted that the value of physical exercise is to help children to resist the onset of fatigue rather than to help them to recuperate when once they are fatigued. Physiological fatigue seems to be general in character so that once a state of fatigue has been produced, rest is the only cure. If, for example,

[1] *Dynamical Changes Occurring in Men at Work,* A. V. Bock, Jnl. of Physiology, LXVI, p. 159.

[2] This very useful method of conducting experiments in educational method is called " the method of equal groups." It was first used by Mr. W. H. Winch.

children are fatigued by a long walk or a strenuous game they cannot be expected to do hard mental work successfully. Similarly, strenuous physical exercise is unsuitable for children tired out after a long, trying examination.

In previous chapters we have learnt that habits enable both children and teachers to economize energy. This economy, as we saw in chapter XII, is particularly noticeable as skill is acquired. The development of skill in physical movements is clearly an additional method of preventing fatigue. The modern emphasis on posture, carriage and rhythm not only in physical training lessons but in all lessons where movements are taught should react favourably on the whole of school work. Fatigue can also be lessened in practical workrooms by eliminating the need for useless stooping and lifting ; tools and saucepans should be kept as far as possible on the level where they will be used.[1] Standing is itself fatiguing, and much unnecessary "standing still" can be eliminated in school by a thoughtful teacher.

So far as can be ascertained by experiment, children in school seldom suffer from severe fatigue as a result of mental work. Their efficiency, as is well known, decreases towards the end of a school day, but this is probably due to a variety of other causes. It may be partly the result of adverse physical conditions—bad ventilation, insufficient food or sleep, over-heated classrooms. It is to some extent the result of unavoidable variations in human efficiency, for it has been found that such variations occur even when short periods of work are separated by long periods of rest. The cause is probably more psychological than physiological.

We have considered various methods of reducing fatigue because fatigue reduces efficiency in work. It must not be supposed, however, that a moderate amount of fatigue is any cause for alarm. We should look upon it as an indication that energy has been used, not that energy has been exhausted. In fact, it probably acts as a safety device to

[1] See *Posture in Housework* (National Society's Depository, 1935).

minimize the risk of such exhaustion. The device, however, does not work mechanically and inevitably, for we can all, on occasion, ignore the warning and continue working. This fact reminds us that the problem of fatigue is psychological as well as physiological.

SPURTS

The inadequacy of purely physiological theories to explain fatigue is clearly shown in the " spurt " phenomenon. The knowledge that a task is nearing completion enables a student as well as an athlete to put forth an extra effort to counteract the effect of physiological fatigue. For this reason, long tasks can often with advantage be subdivided into sections. The spurt is, of course, simply another example of the principle that all activity is regulated by interest. There are two types of interest—positive stimulating interests such as those that spring from the aggressive instincts of curiosity, self-assertion and anger, negative inhibiting interests like those arising from fear and repulsion. The " spurt " phenomenon appears to be the result of the arousal of the aggressive instincts, and in view of its comparative universality may be considered normal. If, however, fear is aroused an abnormal result may ensue ; the child is likely to be extremely variable and his output may be either abnormally high or low.[1] A more common situation with ordinary children is the arousal of the instinct of disgust. They express it by saying they are " fed up " or " sick of the work " ; they are suffering from the state of mind we call boredom. Since its results are often indistinguishable from those of physiological fatigue, boredom is often referred to as subjective fatigue. There is, however, a fundamental difference between the two states. A child who is really fatigued is relatively deficient in energy, whereas a child who is bored may have plenty of potential energy, but it is untapped because his dominant interest is in avoiding

---

[1] Cf. the behaviour of a frightened child. He may run away in a state of excitement or remain immobile, paralysed with terror.

work. The fatigued child is unable to work, but the bored child is unwilling. The general diminution in output in our experiment was almost certainly due in part to boredom.

Another important psychological influence is that of suggestion. Its remarkable effect has been demonstrated by a simple experiment with an ergograph, an instrument for recording muscular contractions. The subject raises and lowers a weight by moving his finger until he can do so no longer. He is then given another weight, exactly the same as the first one but with the suggestion that it is lighter. He is then able to continue the lifting. This laboratory experiment is not one that we should try to copy in school, for a very inspiring teacher could by this method induce an undesirable degree of fatigue in his pupils. Used with discretion, however, suggestion is a legitimate device, and the suggestions of a cheerful encouraging teacher can do much to increase output both in physical and mental work. Similarly, suggestions of an opposite nature can easily reduce the efficiency of a pupil to a very low ebb.

The commonest cause of boredom is monotony. It is very difficult, however, to determine what particular tasks are monotonous. Investigations in factories have shown that repetitive work, which to an intelligent observer appears extremely monotonous, is actually enjoyed by some workers. Their level of intelligence may be such that the task presents sufficient problems to keep interest alive, or the task may be so mechanical that it leaves the mind free for pleasant day-dreaming. Monotony is not a simple attribute of a task; it depends on the whole situation—the temperament and intelligence of the worker and the general conditions of work, including such material factors as lighting[1] and heating, and such personal factors as the attitude of super-

---

[1] It has been found that when factory work has to be done in artificial light the output is adversely affected. Another observation that emphasizes the importance of sunlight is that young children often show bursts of exceptional activity on bright, sunny days.

visors. As teachers, we should therefore beware of judging monotony of work from our own personal, adult point of view. In an effort to reduce monotony for young or dull children it is very easy to err in the opposite direction and give them tasks that are so complicated as to be worrying. Another consideration is that the general atmosphere of a classroom, for the creation of which we are largely responsible, is an important factor in determining children's attitude to work. Finally, we may suggest that children in school, like adults in the world, must sometimes face the fact that monotonous work has to be done. Instead of allowing the primitive instinct of disgust to dominate the situation, children should be trained to bring into action their self-regarding sentiment—" I am a person who can tackle distasteful work." In other words, they should be taught to use their will power and to persist in face of monotony. This is not an argument for introducing monotonous work into school in order to develop " moral athleticism," still less in order to habituate children to monotony. The general principle is that school work should appeal as far as possible to children's positive interests. But when everything possible has been done by choosing suitable work, by presenting it attractively, by introducing variety into the day's work, by showing children the need for monotonous work as part of a larger, more interesting job, there will always be a residue of boring work and it is this residue that must be faced with determination. It is very doubtful whether children ought to be allowed to give up work in response to their own feelings, for they may thereby merely form bad habits unnecessarily. They may even be depriving themselves of an immunity to the quick onset of feelings of fatigue.

It is, however, necessary to be watchful for occasional special cases where pressure of any kind is undesirable. Children (especially adolescent girls) do sometimes suffer from overstrain, particularly before examinations ; they become unusually restless, unaccountably irritable ; they may show a tendency to nervous laughter. In such cases it is

o

advisable to consult the parents particularly in regard to the question of sleep, for any abnormality in sleep is a sure sign that something is wrong. Children who are always tired, even at the beginning of a day, should be brought to the notice of the school medical officer.

It will now be appreciated that abnormalities in output of work may be due to a variety of causes, and that the measurement of fatigue is a very difficult matter. Attempts have been made to establish fatigue coefficients for the various subjects of the curriculum, but in view of the many fluctuating personal factors—enthusiasm and excitement on the one hand, boredom and disgust on the other—the actual figures cannot be accepted as very reliable. The most fatiguing subjects are believed to be mathematics and physical exercises, and if these are taken as the standard of reference other subjects appear to come in the following order :

Language study (English or foreign) .	0.90
History	0.85
Geography. Nature study .	0.80
Drawing	0.60
Singing	0.40

This order agrees with the general opinion of teachers, and it is one of the factors that must be taken into account when school time-tables are being arranged. Among adults there are wide individual differences as to the best time of day for tackling difficult work, but with children there is little doubt that, after a short warming-up period, the early hours of the school day are the best. This question of fatigue has an important bearing on the topics of home-work and continued education. It is obviously very difficult for young adolescents to pursue serious academic study in the evening after a strenuous day's work either at school or in the factory.

RESTS

During the First European War the need for understanding the laws governing human efficiency became very urgent, and an investigating committee was formed, the Health of Munition Workers Committee. Its success led to the formation of a permanent research board, called at first the Industrial Fatigue Research Board, but from 1930 onwards the Industrial Health Research Board. This change of name reflects the growing appreciation of the complex nature of the many factors commonly grouped together under the term "fatigue." The interest in industrial psychology was further shown by the formation in 1921 of an independent institute under the direction of Dr. C. S. Myers, the National Institute of Industrial Psychology.[1]

Perhaps the most remarkable discovery made in munition factories was that under certain conditions a shortening of the hours of work actually increased production. In one factory a reduction of a 58-hour week by about 7½ hours was accompanied by a 21 per cent. increase in the weekly output. In another factory a similar reduction in working hours halved the time lost by irregular attendance. The value of systematic rests was also studied scientifically with good results; in one factory, for example, a 10 per cent. increase in output was produced by introducing a five-minute rest into each working hour.

There is, of course, a limit to the extent to which working hours can be usefully shortened and to the number of rests which can be introduced. It cannot be seriously maintained that the ordinary school day is too long, but experiments are needed to determine whether we are using it most economically. All specialist teachers tend to assume that results in a subject will improve in direct proportion to the extra time they can persuade the head teacher to allot to it. Some are reluctant to give up the time required in modern education for physical exercises, games, educational visits and school journeys. In view of the results obtained in industry, it should not, however, be lightly assumed that these time-consuming innovations will adversely affect even those results of education that can be measured by examina-

[1] Address: Aldwych House, Aldwych, London, W.C. 2.

tions. Some experiments have been done in school to find the effect of postponing written work in arithmetic until children are 9, and to determine the effect of reducing the time ordinarily given to this subject with older children. Such experiments proved conclusively that efficiency in arithmetic is not a function of the time devoted to it, and the results suggest that further experiments of the same kind ought to be tried.[1]

The increase in output that often occurs when hours of work are shortened is probably due in part to the fact that the workers unwittingly adjust their effort to the time they know they have at their disposal. The large output during the first minute after the rest in our experiment (p. 400) was due not only to the recuperative effect of the rest but also to the knowledge that the second period was to be five minutes only. It is surprising how quickly children work when they know, for example in mental arithmetic, that the time is definitely limited to a few minutes. The same is true of writing, and an excellent device for giving practice in expression is to give children a title and require them to write in pencil as much as they can in five minutes.

The beneficial effect of pauses between periods of work is already recognized by the usual arrangements in school for recreation periods, and the results of psychological research suggest that any deprivation of these short rests is false economy. The short breaks between lessons necessitated by a specialist system may also have a definite value, and general practitioners in continuous charge of a class may be well advised to allow some short breaks during spells of strenuous work. The physical freedom allowed in a modern classroom is, from the point of view of sheer mental efficiency, to be encouraged. Where mental work is concerned, the short pause not only gives an opportunity for recuperation from fatigue but it also facilitates unconscious mental assimilation (see p. 329).

There is no doubt that the efficiency of many school

[1] See also the experiment described on p. 409.

children is seriously affected by insufficient sleep. This fact is clearly illustrated by an experiment conducted by Burt with two " equal groups " of children who were very backward in arithmetic. One group was given an extra arithmetic lesson each afternoon while the other group slept in deck chairs. At the end of the term it was found that the " sleepers " had improved in arithmetic more than those who had been specially coached.[1] No more convincing proof could be given of the need for a scientific study of " rest " as part of the subject of mental hygiene.

CONCLUSION

Following the lead of industrial psychologists, we have approached our subject from the point of view of sheer efficiency. We have emphasized that if school conditions, both material environment and psychological atmosphere, were arranged in conformity with scientific principles, output of work could be increased while weariness and fatigue could be diminished. We have adopted this approach in order to make the lessons of mental hygiene impressive ; every one can at once appreciate an improvement if it is measured in terms of information acquired, facts remembered and correct answers obtained. But even in industry, psychologists were not long content merely to help factories to increase output ; they quickly realized that their function was to minister to the general mental and physical welfare of each individual worker. Similarly in school, the principles of mental hygiene must be put into practice, not merely to increase efficiency that can be measured, but in order to provide conditions under which the whole personality of each individual teacher and pupil can develop freely. Increased efficiency and greater output will then be viewed in their proper perspective as symptoms of a state of all-round healthiness.

[1] See *The Subnormal Mind*, C. Burt, p. 123 (Ox. Univ. Press, 1935).

OBSERVATIONS AND EXPERIMENTS

1. For an experiment on variations in output of work see page 400.

2. Watch a teacher at work. Observe what he does (*a*) to stimulate the pupils to work, (*b*) to repel them from work.

(Consider : (i) instincts appealed to, (ii) suggestions conveyed.)

3. Watch a class at work during a school session.
Make lists of :
(*a*) Signs of " settling down " and " warming up."
(*b*) Occasions for resting (i) authorized, (ii) unauthorized.
(*c*) Occasions when specially intense effort was shown.
(*d*) Signs of (i) boredom, (ii) fatigue.

4. Observe three pupils in a class. Choose different types—(*a*) industrious, (*b*) average, (*c*) lazy.
Find the percentage time not occupied in " work."
Analyse the " slack " time under such headings as (i) gossiping, (ii) daydreaming, (iii) walking about, (iv) aimless playing.

5. By experiment find which produces the better results—a half-hour devoted to writing one composition or (*b*) to writing two compositions with a short rest at half-time.
Consider both quantity and quality.

6. Watch two teachers at work—(*a*) an inexperienced teacher, (*b*) a practised teacher.
Make a list of the ways in which each teacher (i) conserves, (ii) wastes his energy.

REFERENCES FOR READING

Modern Psychology and Education, Sturt and Oakden, chapters XIX, XX.
Educational Psychology, C. Fox, chapter XII.
Experimental Education, R. R. Rusk, chapter XIV.
Psychology and Practical Life, Collins and Drever, chapter VIII.

ADDITIONAL REFERENCES

Hygiene and Health Education, M. B. Davies, chapters VI, XVII (Longmans, 1933).
Industrial Psychology, ed. C. S. Myers (Cape, 1929).
Directing Mental Energy, F. Aveling (Univ. Lond. Press, 1927).

ESSAYS AND DISCUSSIONS

1. Examine some time-tables for different types of schools—(*a*) infant (*b*) junior, (*c*) secondary.
Discuss the main differences.

2. Discuss in detail a time-table for the type of school in which you are most interested.
(Consider : order of subjects during the day ; lengths of lessons ; rests ; variety of work.)

3. Monotony in school.
(Consider: Can it be abolished? Ought it to be abolished?)

4. Methods of reducing monotony in school work.
(Consider: variety in daily programme, in lessons; means for arousing interest in the dull parts of a job; suggestion.)

5. The mental hygiene of teachers.
(Consider: temperament and methods of teaching; outside interests; worry; attitude of those in authority; proper attitude of teachers towards authority.)

6. The difference between fatigue and boredom.

7. Homework.
(Consider: values; dangers; kind of work that is legitimate; amount for different ages.)

8. Ways of enlisting the help of parents in promoting mental hygiene.

Chapter XXII

GENERAL EFFECTS OF LEARNING AND TEACHING

In educational discussions it is usually taken for granted that education is in a general way beneficial. It is undoubtedly true that an educated man is able to lead a more satisfactory personal life than one who is uneducated. He has more interests in life. But apart from this personal, private enjoyment of life, it is generally believed that an educated man is a better citizen and a more efficient member of society than he would otherwise have been. Employers report that boys who have had extra years at school prove to be more useful ultimately than those who leave school early; where day continuation schools have been established similar results have been obtained. On all hands, we hear of the need for " trained " minds in industry and commerce; many firms now take university-trained men and women into business, not because of their specialized knowledge of the business, for that is nil, but because of the general training they have received during a long education. This education, it should be noted, is often confined to the study of academic subjects many of which have no practical bearing whatever on any kind of business. What is the nature of this general training that education is believed to give? Let us consider first some of the popular beliefs about it.

Some Alleged General Effects of Education

It is often asserted that education makes people more intelligent. There is one sense in which this is almost certainly not true. As we learned in chapter II, intelligence is inborn. The evidence from intelligence tests points to the probability that its rate of development and its ultimate limit is for each individual already fixed at birth. The growth of intelligence is largely, if not entirely, independent of education. But if this is accepted, it may still be argued that education enables an individual to make a more effective use of his native intelligence than an uneducated person could do. It is possible that education can at least awaken or liberate intelligence that would otherwise remain dormant or inhibited. This is probably what the business man means when he says that education increases intelligence.

A second popular view is that education makes people more efficient in certain special ways. If it includes the right kind of training, education is believed to improve a person's ability to memorize, to concentrate, to observe, to reason.

Some subjects, we are confidently told, are particularly valuable for these purposes because they train one special mental faculty. Thus complicated and unreal problems in arithmetic are defended on the ground that they train " the reasoning powers." Nature study, we are told, deserves a place in the curriculum because it trains " the powers of observation "; children should learn poetry by heart because the exercise trains " the memory." The whole doctrine rests on a fallacious view of the human mind. Children do not possess mental faculties—observation, attention, memory—that work in isolation; they possess minds that work as wholes and their mental efficiency in any given situation depends on a large number of factors of which interest is the most important. Thus a child might memorize poetry very readily, but find great difficulty in memorizing multiplication tables. The probability is that no amount of practice in memorizing poetry will help him to overcome his arithmetical difficulty, for it is a difficulty that springs from a lack of positive interest in tables ; it is not a difficulty that springs from an " untrained faculty of memory."[1]

---

[1] Similar considerations apply to all so-called mental faculties. Every person has widely varying abilities within one and the same " faculty." He may remember faces but forget names ; he may be keenly observant of aeroplanes and yet be blind to stars ; he may reason logically when solving a mathematical problem but be swayed by irrational prejudice when confronted with a problem in politics.

O*

The view that we do not possess isolated mental faculties has been confirmed by the results of many carefully devised experiments. It has, for example, been proved that specific exercises of one type do not, as a rule, effect a general improvement in the ability to memorize.[1] Similar results have been found in other experiments. For example, boys have been successfully trained to be neat in mathematical work, but such training produced no appreciable increase in neatness in other subjects. The psychologist says that in these and similar cases there is very little transfer of training ; if transfer occurs at all when children are specifically trained in one type of work, the amount is much smaller than was formerly believed. We ought therefore to abandon for ever our fond belief that any particular subject-matter deserves a place in the curriculum solely because of its general mental-training value.[2] It is absurd to make children spend time on dull, useless, complicated work in the hope that such mental gymnastics will train their faculties.

Few teachers to-day would go so far as to preach the pernicious old doctrine that it does not matter what a child is taught so long as he hates it enough ; the belief in *formal training*, however, dies hard and not a little classroom practice is still based on an implicit belief in the exploded theory we have been discussing.

There are two reasons for the persistence of a crude belief in the inevitability of transfer despite the fact that, according to scientific evidence, such transfer is by no means certain. The first reason is that false conclusions as to mental training are often drawn from general observations that are in themselves correct. It was, for example, a commonly observed fact forty years ago that most, if not all, successful statesmen and administrators had excelled in the study of Latin at school. It was then argued that the excellent mental qualities they displayed in their life's

---

[1] See e.g. *Educational Values and Methods*, W. G. Sleight (Clar. Press, 1915).
[2] The philosophy of curriculum-building is expounded in chapter XV, which should be re-read in connexion with the present argument.

work must be the result of the mental training afforded by this study. Latin was therefore " proved " to be a good subject for training the mind. Now this conclusion is obviously not warranted by the data, and in the light of modern work on intelligence a much more likely explanation is that these successful public servants were persons of exceptionally high intelligence ; it was most probably this intelligence that enabled them to excel both at Latin in school and at work in later life. The study of Latin was useful as an indicator, but not as a creator of ability.

Some of the evidence quoted at the beginning of this chapter in support of the general training value of education may, in a similar way, appear less convincing when the possible influence of special selection is taken into account. In considering the effects of advanced education we must, for example, always remember that it is the more intelligent boys and girls who have the best opportunities and the keenest inclinations to pursue courses of further education. It may still be argued, however, that some studies tend to make all pupils more able than they would have been without them. General observation of educated people seems to indicate that there is some transfer of training, some general beneficial effect of learning and teaching. Or, to put the matter negatively, we all meet men and women who, we feel, might have been made more generally efficient if they had had more and better education. Let us suppose that a number of boys all possessing an equally high degree of intelligence were divided into two groups, one group leaving school at the age of 14, the other group receiving a secondary and university education. Let us further assume that they all have equal opportunity in a large business from the age of 22. We should feel confident that the " university " group would contain the larger number of success- ful men and the larger number of men leading full and happy lives. To take another example, many women, after receiving an expensive secondary and university education, become housewives and make little or no further direct use of their educational attainments ; we do not, however, believe that their education has been wasted. This is the second reason why a crude belief in transfer of training persists ; there is something in it.

We have tried to purify popular beliefs on the subject by showing the kind of general training that cannot be given by education ; in the remainder of this chapter we shall attempt to refine beliefs by showing the kind of general training that can be given.

SOME GENERAL EFFECTS OF EDUCATION

Awakening and liberation of intelligence.—Some general effect must first be credited to the increased interest in life that education gives. A person who, in addition to earning a living, leads a full personal life—a life filled with intellectual interests, practical hobbies, æsthetic interests, social activities and healthy recreations—is likely to be more generally alive than one whose private life is bored and empty. This liveliness, we may surmise, will affect both body and mind and tend to make the person more generally efficient. It is sometimes said that the aim of education in school is to prepare a pupil for a full life such as we have described. This is true if it is recognized that at any stage the only preparation for life is a full and interesting life at that stage. Intelligence can be awakened in school by the arousal of positive interests like curiosity and assertion ; it can be liberated by the removal of negative interests like fear and disgust.

Common factors.—The training given in one lesson will obviously influence other work if there is some common element in the two activities. Thus we should expect drill in adding numbers to effect some improvement in multiplication, because addition is one necessary process in working a multiplication sum. For a similar reason, training in any useful form of computation will facilitate problem-solving, training in handwriting will help composition. Practice in expressing ideas in any lesson, history, geography, science, will develop a child's command of English ; every lesson, as we are often told, is a lesson in English. In fact no single lesson need be so specific that it does not directly overlap some other lessons. The same principle should be applied to wider questions such as training in citizenship. Life in school should train children for life in a larger community and there should be many elements in school life that have their counterparts in ordinary life outside. In a well-organized class or school the instruction and the curriculum are arranged so that there is a maximum of overlap ; one lesson reinforces another, and school life impinges on life in the world outside at many points.

It should be noted that, where subjects overlap, transfer is not necessarily complete. It is found, for example, that a child may learn to spell a word correctly from a column in a spelling book and yet mis-spell it in a composition. This is merely another illustration that the result of mental activity in a given situation does not depend only on specific training but upon the whole situation.

General habits, methods and principles.—We have already seen that a specific habit formed in one situation, e.g. neatness in mathematics, will not necessarily transfer to other situations. Much can be done, however, to make habits general by deciding upon a school policy and then practising desirable habits in as large a variety of situations as possible. A good school will train its pupils in habits of industry in so many different settings that after a time one general habit of industry is formed, and even when the pupil leaves school he will tend to work industriously by sheer force of habit. If we apply this principle to mathematics we see at once the limitations of its mental-training value. The habit of careful accurate work accompanied by checking of the results may be formed in mathematics lessons, but it is likely to remain a specific habit. To make it general, it must be practised in all other suitable subjects of the curriculum. Thus we see that in order to promote general training it is futile to rely on one or two alleged " disciplinary " subjects ; a broad curriculum and a full school life offer the only possible conditions for any real success.

The training of the so-called scientific mind provides another apt illustration. It cannot be done in science lessons only ; even men of science sometimes display very unscientific procedure when confronted with ordinary problems of life outside their laboratory. Science lessons certainly provide many opportunities for developing good methods of thinking—collecting of evidence, rejection of irrelevancies, careful consideration of hypotheses, checking of hypotheses—but so do many other subjects, and if these desirable methods are to be made general enough to carry over to ordinary life they must be practised in as many different connexions as possible. As Thomson says, " If each and every subject is taught as a page or chapter of the universal subject ' how to think,' and the principles of ' how to think ' are constantly and consciously appealed to, transfer appears to be much more probable."[1]

The importance of making the older and more intelligent children conscious of general principles cannot be overestimated and we ought to lose no opportunity of relating specific actions to the principles to which they belong. Thus the election of prefects should be related to the principle of democratic government, the washing of hands to the principle of avoiding bacteriological infection, the silence rule in certain lessons to the principle of consideration for others. When teaching arithmetic, we should not concentrate exclusively on the method of solving each particular problem as it arises, but we should try to show how each problem illustrates some general principle. Incidentally we can often, when teaching mathematics or science, call attention to the general principles that underlie all efficient problem-solving whether the data be mathematical, scientific or of any other kind. This kind of emphasis on general principles is one of the most fruitful ways of making certain that our training does not remain confined to the specific situations in which it is given. Its effectiveness obviously depends on the degree of intelligence brought to bear on the problem, and this fact suggests that some forms of transfer

[1] *Instinct, Intelligence, and Character*, p. 144.

are probably dependent on native intelligence to a greater extent than has been generally recognized in discussions on this controversial subject. It should be noted, however, that the degree of intelligence used in any situation varies not only according to native endowment but also according to the intensity of interest aroused. When minds are intensely active there is a tendency to perceive relations and not merely to confine attention to isolated elements in the given situation. Köhler, for example, has found that this is true even with such unintelligent creatures as hens.[1] Pavlov, by experimenting with dogs and mice, has proved that these animals after being trained to respond to a given stimulus will respond to other stimuli of the same type.

As Fox comments, " If dogs and mice can respond to a generalized situation it is preposterous to assert that this is impossible in the case of human beings."[2] The lesson for teachers is obvious. If we want the effects of our teaching to become general, we must arouse intense interest, avoid rule-of-thumb instruction and help children to see relations between all the single items we teach. In a word, we must teach intelligently rather than mechanically. But apart from helping children to get an intelligent insight into problems, apart from giving them an intellectual grasp of general principles, much can be done, even with dull children, to inspire them with desirable general attitudes ; emotion can be aroused and brought into service for the development of ideals.

Ideals.—As we saw in chapter XI, it is possible to carry the formation of general habits a stage further, and to help pupils to become conscious of the value of the general

---

[1] The experiment was done as follows : Equal quantities of food were placed on two adjacent grey papers, one brighter than the other. The hens were allowed to feed from the brighter paper, but they were driven away if they tried to feed from the darker paper. This kind of training was continued until the hens chose the brighter paper, no matter in what position it was placed. Then the darker paper was replaced by one brighter than the paper from which the hens had learnt to feed. It was now found that they more often chose this new paper than their original " feeding " paper. See *Educational Psychology*, C. Fox, pp. 182–6.

[2] *Ibid.*, p. 186.

habits they possess and of the general methods they use. Thus a boy may progress from the stage of several specific habits of being neat to the stage of a general habit of being neat, to a third stage when he appreciates the general principle that neatness makes for accuracy and beauty, until finally he forms a conscious ideal, a sentiment for neatness itself. He will then strive to be neat in every possible circumstance. The same is true on the more purely intellectual side. For example, in addition to varied experience of scientific method, pupils should be inspired by striking examples of its successful application to appreciate its value ; they should develop a respect for clear and valid thinking.

In other words, transfer of training is facilitated by the formation of ideals or sentiments. But, as we have learnt, it is by developing sentiments that character is formed. Thus we arrive at the common-sense view that the more successful a school is in developing character the more likely are the effects of its training to affect the general life of its pupils when schooldays are over.

It should be noted that sentiments facilitate transfer of training in two ways. First, the effects of the training are transferred to a variety of situations all of which come under the more or less direct influence of a particular sentiment ; a sentiment of kindness to an individual pet will help children to be kind to pets in general. Second, the effects of the training will tend to transfer to a number of other analogous situations ; the child who is kind to his pet will tend to be kind to animals in general, and he is unlikely to be a cruel tyrant to his fellow-beings if in later life he achieves a position of power over them. As teachers we should, however, do all we can to make such transfer certain by widening sentiments as much as possible while children are still at school.

CONCLUSION

We have argued that education ought to produce certain desirable general results apart from the specific knowledge, interests and skills that are directly cultivated. The tremendous importance of the general results of education is seen when we reflect how little experience of real life we can give children during their schooldays. The most important lesson of this chapter is that these general results must not be left to chance, for they are not an inevitable by-product of education, especially if it is given by specialists working in isolation and each engrossed in his own subject. They must be consciously striven after by all teachers in a school working as a team. This does not mean that a subject has a place in the curriculum because of its mental-training value, for every subject worthy of a place in a school curriculum is there in its own right. No subject, however, is devoid of general training value if it is well taught and enjoyed by the pupils. When teaching a subject it is necessary to consider not only the special knowledge or skill we want to impart but also the general training it can give—training that children can apply in a wider field. That is to say, when teaching a subject we must remember that we are not only teaching the subject but we are also teaching children.

Contrary to popular opinion, no one subject is by itself capable of giving general mental training in any effective way ; this can only be done by means of a full school life and a liberal curriculum. Given these conditions, the possibility of transfer of training depends largely on methods of teaching. First, these methods must make an appeal to positive instinctive interests so that a full measure of the child's native intelligence is awakened and liberated. Second, they must aim not only at developing specific habits and methods of work but they must also be directed towards helping children to make these habits and methods as general as possible. One important way of making methods of work general is by making children conscious of the methods they use when they are successful. Third, the methods of teaching used should make constant appeal to underlying general principles. Finally, they should inspire children with a lively sense of the general value of what they are learning so that their conduct is brought more and more under the regulative influence of worthy ideals.[1]

[1] Attention must be directed to the fact that a large number of experiments have been carried out with the object of measuring the general effects of learning and teaching, and that the conclusions reached from these statistical investigations are by no means concordant. This is not, however, surprising in view of the complexity of the problem ; as we have shown the general effects of education depend on a number of important variables that are difficult to control in a scientific experiment. Another limitation of the experimental approach is the fact that the general effects of education are, as we have argued, matters of slow growth ; it seems doubtful if they can be measured by experiments that last only a few weeks. A third limitation of many experiments is that they are relatively artificial and they do not reproduce the type of teaching that is ordinarily given in school. All teachers, even if they are not consciously striving (as they ought to be) to produce general effects, are continually passing remarks that tend to make the effects of their teaching spread to other situations than the task of the moment. A composition or a piece of craftwork is often commended, not as a" a good composition " or as " a well-bound book " but as " a good piece of work " or " a good job." Thus, the lessons children learn in one subject may become associated with " work " or " jobs " in general. For a critical review of relevant experimental work, see *Educational Psychology*, C. Fox, pp. 168–82.

REFERENCES FOR READING

Education, Sir T. Percy Nunn, pp. 240–2.
Educational Psychology, C. Fox, chapter VII.
Instinct, Intelligence and Character, Godfrey H. Thomson, chapter XIV.
Experimental Education, R. R. Rusk, pp. 224–9.

ADDITIONAL REFERENCES

Herbartian Psychology, Sir J. Adams, chapter V (Heath).
How Children Learn, F. N. Freeman, chapter XIII (Harrap, 1919).
Educational Values and Methods, W. G. Sleight, chapters II, III, IV (Clarendon, 1915).
Education for Citizenship in Secondary Schools, chapter II (Ox. Univ. Press, 1936).
Mental Training and Efficiency, F. H. Hayward, chapters V and XIII (Sidgwick & Jackson, 1921).

ESSAYS AND DISCUSSIONS

1. How far can school life train adolescents in citizenship ?
(Consider the following topics which are quoted from *Education for Citizenship in Secondary Schools*, p. 30 :
   (*a*) The value of individual human personality.
   (*b*) Freedom of speech, criticism and action.
   (*c*) An agreed body of law for the settlement of disputes.
   (*d*) Changes effected by criticism, persuasion, argument, and reason—not by violence and force.
   (*e*) The responsibility of citizens for good government.
   (*f*) Service for the community.)

2. Choose some desirable social virtue, e.g., tolerance, kindness, honesty, " playing the game."

Discuss how a school can train its pupils so that they will tend to practise the virtue in their general after-school life.

3. Choose a subject of the curriculum in which you are specially interested. Discuss :

(a) the general training it can give ;

(b) the methods by which this general training can be achieved.

CHAPTER XXIII

THE DEVELOPMENT OF PERSONALITY

WE began this book by going into a classroom to get a view
of individual children and we have tried in all our discussions
not to lose sight of these children. For example, we have
avoided, as far as possible, such abstractions as attention,
observation and memory, and we have sought rather to give
a picture of children attending, observing, remembering,
thinking and imagining—a picture of children learning and
being taught. We have, in imagination, watched these
children developing in intellect, character, muscular skill,
æsthetic taste and sociability. We have watched them
gradually changing year by year in many subtle ways,
partly as a result of natural growth, partly as a result of their
varied experiences.

The person who entered school at 3 years of age is a very
different person when he leaves school twelve years later.
He has grown more mature and he has become more experienced. In straight-forward, simple terms we may say
he has developed *as a person*. Nothing more need be said,
but the abstract term " personality " is so commonly used
that it would perhaps be pedantic to avoid using it. We
must then say of our school-leaver that his personality has
developed.

The term " personality " as used here simply refers to
the " kind of person " an individual is. When, therefore,
we say that our aim in school is to help children to develop
their personalities we are not using the term " personality "
in quite the same sense as we do when, for example, we
refer to the " personality " of a prominent politician or
when we think of the " personality " of a teacher impressing
a committee in a short interview. In these examples we
are thinking particularly of those characteristics that enable

persons to exert a strong, immediate and sometime dominating influence on other people. Now, clearly, we do not wish in school to develop in all our pupils a " personality " of that kind, even if it were possible. It is, fortunately, impossible, for many of our pupils are by nature quite unfitted for a life in the limelight, and no education could change them. But such quiet, shy, retiring pupils may be " persons " just as much as the vocal, bold, assertive ones ; they have personalities that will develop in their own way. Some writers on education seek to avoid the difficulty that is created by the associations of " personality " with " domination " by using, instead, the term " individuality." This term has the advantage of emphasizing those personal characteristics that appertain specially to the nature of the individual concerned, without suggesting by association that any one type of characteristic is preferable to another. Unfortunately, it is often used in such a way as to suggest that an individual's characteristics should be developed without any reference to the needs of social life ; in the minds of many people the cultivation of individuality is synonymous with the cultivation of individualism. On the whole, therefore, we prefer to use the term " personality," carrying, as it does, two types of association, those connected with an individual's personal, private life and also those connected with his equally personal but social life. A pupil whose personality is developing satisfactorily is leading a life that is satisfying all round, that is, both to himself and to his associates ; he is both " fit to live and fit to live with." Such a pupil has " individuality " or " personality " in the best sense ; he is a sincere, individual person, and is not afraid to be himself, even if he knows that he is a very different type from most of those with whom he lives. He likes to be in company, and others enjoy his company, but at times he likes to be alone, for he is capable of enjoying a private life free from boredom. Such a person cannot help influencing other people in the long run even though his personality may not be obviously and immediately impressive.

The individual and the social aspects of personality are complementary; if either is undeveloped, personality is incomplete. The derivation of the word "person" is interesting and may help readers to become more sensitive to the real, root meaning of the word. It comes from the Latin word, *persona*, a mask, and it refers to the masks worn in Greek and Roman theatres by actors to enable each actor to play several parts. In these open-air theatres it was difficult for actors to make themselves heard and so the mouth of the mask was shaped as a megaphone. The Latin word, *persona*, may, therefore, be derived from *per sonare*, the mask being the contrivance through which the actor spoke to his audience. It is perhaps not too fanciful to suggest that our word "person" therefore carries associations both of an individuality and of the impression made by that individual on an audience.[1]

For teachers the most important fact about the development of personality is that every experience leaves its trace, even those experiences that we have apparently forgotten. For example, in the words of George Eliot: "So much of our early gladness vanished utterly from our memory, we can never recall the joy with which we laid our hands on our mother's bosom or rode on our father's back in childhood; doubtless that joy is wrought up into our nature, as the sunlight of long-past mornings is wrought up in the soft mellowness of the apricot."[2] Similarly, many of the facts we teach will vanish; our pupils will forget many of the joyful and sad moments of school life. But doubtless all this experience is wrought up in their natures; their culture or education is that which is left when school lessons have been "forgotten." In the classroom we are not always conscious of this fact, nor is it desirable that we should be. It is, however, good to pause occasionally in the hurly-burly of school life and lessons and to reflect that we are influencing for good or ill the personalities of our

[1] See *Modern Developments in Educational Practice*, J. Adams, pp. 114-15 (Univ. Lond. Press, 1922).
[2] *Adam Bede*.

pupils. We are helping to determine what kind of a person each pupil will ultimately be—the kind of person he will be to himself and also to other people. When we are giving a science lesson we are engrossed for most of the time (and rightly so) in enlarging our pupils' knowledge and in deepening their appreciation of the wonders of science. That is our immediate aim, and it is changing from one lesson to another throughout the day. But behind all these changing, minor aims there should be one steady, master aim informing and unifying all we do—the ultimate aim of helping each pupil to develop his personality. The activity of a particular lesson period may be predominantly muscular, it may be largely devoted to increasing the pupils' knowledge, it may be particularly suitable for stirring emotion, it may entail hard, concentrated thinking, it may be private study or a group game, it may be mere mechanical memorizing or it may be work requiring the exercise of creative imagination—but whatever the predominant characteristic of the lesson may be, the experience it gives the pupils is making some contribution to their personalities, and all the varied types of experience enumerated above are necessary in order to promote the all-round development of any person.

We have insisted throughout this book that each pupil is an individual and that no two personalities can be exactly alike. There is no single, ideal type of personality to which all our pupils must be made to conform. We should all be particularly on our guard against trying to make our pupils mere reflections of ourselves.[1] Our work as teachers should rather be designed to help each pupil to grow in his own way, to fulfil his own potentialities. There are, however, two characteristics of personality that are common to all well-educated pupils. Personality should resemble a work of art in being harmonious " whole " (see pp. 225,

---

[1] This is a general principle that applies equally to all people, like head teachers, organizers, directors of education and inspectors, who have to " direct " the work of others. In a good school every teacher is free to be himself and to express his own personality in his work.

228), but it should differ from a work of art in the sense that it should be continually developing. Two of the best tests of the success of a school are therefore the extent to which it develops a many-sided interest in its pupils and the extent to which its ex-pupils show an interest in continued education, remembering that education can be continued not only by attending classes such as those held in evening institutes and in connexion with the adult education movement but also by making good use of such educative agencies as churches, libraries, art galleries, museums, travel, rambling, broadcasting, theatres, cinemas, concerts, magazines and newspapers, clubs and societies of various kinds.

The comparison of personality with a work of art is illuminating. As Smuts says, "A poem or a picture is praised because it is a 'whole,' because it is not a mere artificial construction, but an organic whole, in which all the parts appear in a subtle, indefinable way to subserve and contribute to and carry out the main purpose or idea."[1] There is obviously something unwholesome about the personality of a pupil whose interest in sport is so absorbing as to exclude any kind of intellectual interest, and the same is true of a pupil who has no interests outside his books. Many other types of defective personality can be seen on all sides, e.g.,

(a) The person who is passionately interested in science, but has no interest in any form of art, and *vice versa*.[2]

(b) The person who always shuns the company of his fellows, and, conversely, the person who is never happy unless he is in a crowd.

(c) The person who is afraid to think and act for himself, being always morbidly apprehensive of what other people are thinking of him; and, conversely, the egotistic person who has no regard for the wishes and convenience of other people.

(d) The person who in his leisure time is always bored

---

[1] *Holism and Evolution*, J. C. Smuts, p. 98 (Macmillan, 1926).

[2] See *Elementary General Science: A Book for Teachers*, A. G. Hughes, p. 131 (Blackie, 1933).

unless he is being amused or entertained ; and, conversely, the person who is so solemn and earnest that he can find no time for light-hearted relaxation.

(*e*) The person who worries until he is physically ill.[1]

If we were all brought up under an ideal system of education, none of these and similar lop-sided types of personality would exist. This statement reminds us that education is not confined to the process of learning and teaching carried on in schools. A person's education begins at birth (if not prenatally), and it continues in some form throughout his life. As we have seen, the experiences of the first five years have a profound influence on the subsequent development of personality. We are all continually being impressed by general educative influences—the houses in which we live, the food we eat, the advertisements and temptations to which we succumb, the advice and treatment we receive from medical men, and so on. Teachers who are interested in the development of their pupils' personalities, and not merely in giving lessons or coaching for examination, cannot help taking a keen interest in many aspects of social reform. In this book, however, we are dealing primarily with school education, and we can only note in passing that schools are doing a great deal to counteract the evil influences of bad social conditions. As these conditions improve, there is no doubt that much time and energy that must now be spent in remedial work, will be released for positive educational work.[2] Despite the handicaps under which schools work, much is already being done to help children to grow up with wholesome personalities. We are beginning to understand the importance of the

---

[1] cf. F. Matthias Alexander : " Human ills and shortcomings cannot be classified as ' mental ' or ' physical ' and dealt with specifically as such, but all training, whether its object be the prevention or elimination of defect, error or disease, must be based upon the indivisible unity of the human organism." (*The Use of the Self*, p. 5.)

[2] cf. L. P. Jacks : " Measured by the scale of history the work of education has only just begun. It has effected a landing on the coast ; it has pitched its camp and consolidated its base ; but its mission of peaceful penetration into the main continent of human life has yet to be accomplished." (*The Education of the Whole Man*, p. 78.)

" co-education of mind and body " ;[1] despite the cramping influence of examination requirements, experiments in curriculum reform are being made ; and, perhaps most important of all, our schools are beginning to be pervaded by an atmosphere of joyful freedom in which children can be natural individuals with full scope for their creative energies.

The reader will have noticed that there is a strong similarity between what we have said in this chapter about the development of personality and what we said in chapter XI about the development of character. When thinking of character we are thinking primarily of moral development, but when thinking of personality we are thinking of the all-round development of the whole person—his religious, social, moral, intellectual, æsthetic and physical development. The development of personality is the real process ; all other forms of development are merely aspects of this process separated for convenience of theoretical discussion but in actual practice inseparable.[2] All that we have said in separate chapters about discipline and character, about the development of intellect, muscular skill, æsthetic taste and sociability can now be applied to the more comprehensive topic of personality. We have already pointed out the close connexion between the root meaning of " discipline " and that of a " learner " or " disciple." Fundamentally, this book has dealt with a single topic— discipline ; the present chapter might have been called " The discipline of personality " for this phrase is, in fact, synony-

[1] See *The Education of the Whole Man*, L. P. Jacks (Univ. Lond. Press, 1931) ; *The English Tradition of Education*, Cyril Norwood (Murray, 1929) ; *Creative Education and the Future*, O. A. Wheeler (Univ. Lond. Press, 1936).

[2] We have, in previous chapters, given some indication of the essential unity of the various aspects of personality development. Religious development provides another excellent illustration. Thus, as Nunn says, " A man may reveal the religious spirit in devotion to truth or to art, or in the loving service of his fellows." (*Education*, p. 244.)

For Macmurray, religion is essentially bound up with social development : religion is " primarily to be discovered in the behaviour of men and women in relation to one another. So far as they treat one another as equals and enter into relations as fellows, they are religious." (*Reason and Emotion*, p. 211.)

mous with the phrase " The development of personality."
As Macmurray has said : " Discipline really involves not
subordination but integration. It aims at co-ordinating all
the elements in personality and creating a harmonious unity
in which they all co-operate freely and without hindrance.
. . . Its achievement is shown in the freedom and grace of
action ; in its rhythmic quality ; in the absence of jerkiness
and effort. These are the external signs of discipline. The
inner signs are the feelings of freedom and joy[1] and ease in
action which testify that all the necessary factors are co-
operating harmoniously in the production of the desired
effect." But since human activity is essentially a co-operation
between individuals, " the discipline which will produce a
human result must succeed not merely in integrating the
various capacities of the individual but in integrating
individuals themselves in a community of free co-operation.
. . . It is impossible to do the one except in and through
the other. . . . Personality is something that only exists
between people and which cannot exist in the individual
in isolation."[2]

Finally, it should be noted that this growth into wholeness, this discipline or development of personality, is not
contrary to nature. In the words of Nunn, " life constantly
strives after unity " and, when achieved, it is felt by an
individual " as a pulse of the energy which is the very
stuff of his life."[3] We have seen in previous chapters many

[1] cf. Bergson : " Philosophers who have speculated on the significance
of life and the destiny of man have not sufficiently remarked that Nature has
taken pains to give us notice every time this destiny is accomplished ; she
has set up a sign which apprises us every time our activity is in full expansion ;
this sign is joy. I say joy ; I do not say pleasure. . . . True joy is always an
emphatic signal of the *triumph* of life. . . . We find that wherever joy is,
creation has been, and that the richer the creation the deeper the joy." See
Bergson and Education, O. Wheeler (Longmans, 1922).

[2] *Reason and Emotion*, John Macmurray, pp. 83 ff. (Faber, 1935).

[3] *Education*, pp. 12-13. cf. also Smuts : " The creation of wholes and
ever more highly organized wholes, . . . is an inherent character of the
universe. There is not a mere vague indefinite creative energy or tendency
at work in the world. This energy or tendency has specific characters, the
most fundamental of which is whole-making."

" Holism, as the operative factor in the evolution of wholes, is the
ultimate principle of the universe." *Loc. cit.*

varied examples of this unifying character of life—the growth of general ideas (p. 93), the co-ordination of movements in an act of muscular skill (p. 197), the integration of impulses in the development of character (p. 194), the appreciation of the unity of a work of art (p. 224), the assimilation of information and its conversion into living knowledge[1] (p. 339). Thus, as Macmurray says : " There is a craving for it (discipline) in all human nature. The longing for discipline of this kind is simply the longing to fulfil one's own nature, the longing for skill and for joy in living. . . . Give this instinctive craving a chance, and human nature, especially when it is fresh and unspoiled, will respond to the call of discipline with a rush of spontaneous happiness. . . . Children must grow into wholeness and the business of early education is to provide carefully and fully for this natural growth in the integration of the natural capacities. The early discipline of personality has to lay the foundations for the development of interdependence and co-operation in joy among all the elements of personality and between children. It is a training in rhythmic co-operation, in doing things that it is a joy to do together, not in learning things that may possibly come in useful later on. It is a great task but not a difficult one ; provided that we are prepared to follow nature and subordinate ourselves to nature. The difficulties mostly arise through the attempt to frustrate and thwart the natural processes in order to realize some unnatural ideal."

As social conditions improve and as the cumulative effects of education produce better-educated parents, we shall admit into our schools more and more children " fresh and unspoiled." Meanwhile, it is clearly the duty of all who are engaged in the work of education to persevere in the attempts now being made to gain a more complete understanding of the psychology of child nature, and to

[1] cf. Macmurray : Information is " the raw material out of which you and I can pick and choose what we want for our purposes, to build up our own knowledge, which is real knowledge just because it is ours and nobody else's." *Op. cit.*, p. 151.

experiment boldly with those new curricula and methods that this better understanding of children will suggest. Above all, let us beware of taking limited and unworthy views of the nature of our work. We may have to teach subjects, to prepare children for examinations, to become engrossed in many details of school, classroom and office routine, but fundamentally our real work is to help children to develop and discipline their personalities, to help them to satisfy their natural longing for skill and joy in living. It is our high privilege to follow in the footsteps of the Great Teacher, and in reverence and humility to take His words as our guiding principle :

" *I am come that they might have life and that they might have it more abundantly.*"

APPENDIX A

A SHORT LIST OF REFERENCE BOOKS

The following list is given as a nucleus for supplementary reading. All the suggestions given at the ends of chapters under the title *References for Reading* refer to books in this list :

Handbook of Suggestions for the Consideration of Teachers, Board of Education (H.M.S.O., New edition, 1937).
Education : Its Data and First Principles, 2nd edition, Sir T. Percy Nunn (Arnold, 1930).
Modern Psychology and Education, M. Sturt and E. C. Oakden (Kegan Paul, 1926).
Groundwork of Educational Psychology, J. S. Ross (Harrap, 1931).
Educational Psychology, C. Fox (Kegan Paul, 1930).
Instinct, Intelligence and Character, Godfrey H. Thomson (Allen & Unwin, 1924).
Experimental Education, R. R. Rusk (Longmans, 1921).
A Primer of Teaching Practice, Green and Birchenough (Longmans, 1912).
Your Mind and Mine, R. B. Cattell (Harrap, 1934).
Modern Education, T. Raymont (Longmans, 1935).
The Process of Learning, C. Bloor (Kegan Paul, 1930).
Psychology and Practical Life, M. Collins and J. Drever (Univ. Lond. Press, 1936).

For further references see lists entitled *Additional References* at the ends of chapters, and also the titles mentioned in footnotes throughout the book.

APPENDIX B

A SHORT LIST OF EDUCATIONAL CLASSICS

Plato	(420–348 B.C.)	*The Republic.*
Quintilian	(A.D. 35–95),	*Institutes of the Orator.*
Ascham	(1515–1568)	*The Scholemaster,* or plain and perfect way of teaching children to understand, write, and speak in Latin tongue.
Mulcaster	(1531–1611),	*Positions* wherein those circumstances be examined, which are necessary for the training up of children either for skill in their booke, or health in their bodie.
Comenius	(1592–1670)	*The Great Didactic,* setting forth the whole art of Teaching all Things to all Men.
Milton	(1608–1674),	*Tractate on Education.*
Locke	(1632–1704),	*Essay on Human Understanding.*
		Thoughts Concerning Education.
Rousseau	(1712–1778)	*Emile.*
Pestalozzi	(1746–1827),	*How Gertrude Teaches Her Children.*
Herbart	(1776–1841),	*Outlines of Educational Doctrine.*
Froebel	(1782–1852)	*Education of Man.*

For short accounts of the ideas of educational reformers see :

Essays on Educational Reformers, R. H. Quick (Longmans, 1890).
The Doctrines of the Great Educators, R. R. Rusk (Macmillan, 1918).

INDEX

A

Abilities, 67, 69 (*see also* Aptitudes)
Accuracy, 116, 118
Achievement ratio, 368
Acquisitiveness, 14, 294
Activity, 8, 17 (*see also* Practical work)
Adamson, J. E., 320, 335
Adler, A., 33
Adolescence, 41, 163, 227, 285-6, 292, 300, 304-17, 407, 408
Alexander, F. M., 202, 203, 215, 431
Anger, 8-9
Answers, 358-9
Appeals, 14
Application, 342-4
Appreciation—
  lessons, 266-7
  nature of, 220-30
  of literature, 124-5
Aptitudes, 66-7
Assertion, 11-12, 28, 230, 242
Assimilation, unconscious, 329, 410
Association—
  and development of intellect, 87-8
  and recalling, 140
  and taste, 220
  and teaching, 335-9
  controlled and free, 145
Attainment—
  Standardized tests of, 368-70
  Standards of, 1-2, 281, 303
Attending, 99-120
  and interest, 99-102
  and knowledge, 86
  continuity of, 106-8
  distracting and attracting, 108-11
  division of, 104-6
  reasons for, 103-4

P

B

Backward children, 67, 143, 160, 250, 275-85
Ballard, P. B., 54, 138
Bartlett, F. C., 109, 243
Beauty, 200, 204, 215, 219-37
Behaviourism, 28
Bergson, H., 85, 139, 433
Betts, G. H., 125
Binet tests, 52-4, 137, 143, 161-2, 218
Birchenough, C., 2, 256, 343
Boredom, 210, 405-8
Boyd, W., 92
Branford, B., 241
Bridges, R., 235
Buildings, School, 393
Bulley, M. H., 219, 220, 224
Burns, Delisle, 233
Burt, C., 47-8, 53, 68, 69, 143, 145, 168, 169, 225, 226, 237, 277, 278, 279, 280, 291, 294, 305, 411

C

Capitation grants, 256
Cattell, R. B., 46, 48, 53, 54, 72
" Celebrations ", 194, 249
Cellini, B., 202
Character, 172-95, 422, 432
Child guidance, 298, 390
Childhood, 300, 304-6, 379
Class teaching, 275
Classes, size of, 62, 64, 188, 283
Clumsy children, 285-9
Cobbett, W., 263
Co-education, 308-11
Collecting, 14
Composition, 235, 260
Concepts, 94
Conditioned reflexes, 28

439